PREFACE

Any study of power, authority and constitutional freedoms necessarily focuses on the relationship between the individual and the state. Some of America's most important public policy questions involve tensions between conflicting, democratic values. Is freedom, one of the nation's most cherished values, more important than equality? Or is equality more important than freedom? When and how do the two values conflict? What influential power groups are involved in struggles to dominate government and use rewards, punishments and coercive authority in these areas?

In a series of four chapters, we will explore some of the political tensions in American society. These involve conflicts between those who would use state power and authority to achieve particular civil liberties and civil rights objectives and others who have quite different agendas.

Chapter I focuses on the First Freedoms. These great liberties of Religion, Speech, Press, Assembly and Association are the first ones mentioned in the Bill of Rights. Religious liberty in America involves two key clauses in the First Amendment. The Free Exercise Clause guarantees Americans the freedom to worship as they please, or not to worship at all. The Establishment Clause mandates separation of Church and State, although the extent of that separation is debatable. We shall examine, through a study of landmark cases, the dimensions of religious freedom in America.

How much Free Speech and Press do we really want? Do Americans truly value free expression, or do they simply want a nation of "cheerleaders" to express "politically correct" ideas? How much free expression are Americans willing to grant to those whose ideas are stupid (as they see them), illogical or downright prejudiced? What are the "tolerance limits" of U.S. society? Should courts permit "hate speech" and allow racists, sexists and others to air their views in the public forum? Are we confident that Truth eventually will win in the competitive, free marketplace of ideas? Or do Americans fear "different" views? Is being "politically correct" necessary to "get along" on today's campus and in the larger society? What are some of the consequences of denying free expression to those whose views are currently considered "unpopular?" Is it all a power contest?

Chapter II focuses on the rights of the accused. After tracing the roots of our criminal justice system, we view the evolution of the Bill of Rights in several areas. Amendments 4-6 and 8, which comprise 40% of the Bill of Rights, protect individuals against "unreasonable" searches and seizures, guarantee Due Process of Law and protect against self-incrimination. The right to legal counsel and the right to a "fair trial" are detailed through a study of judicial landmarks. The chapter also surveys the Eighth Amendment's ban on cruel and unusual punishment, focusing on the capital punishment debate. Recent death penalty decisions of the U.S. Supreme Court in areas such as lethal injection are considered.

Chapter III deals with perhaps the newest of America's liberties: the right to privacy. Is this a judicially-invented right, as some critics of the U.S. Supreme Court charge? Or is it simply an old right that has finally been recognized? The chapter surveys landmark cases in controversial areas of public morality: birth control, abortion, private possession of "obscene" films, homosexual sodomy, gay marriage and civil unions, the "right to die" and physician-assisted suicide.

Chapter IV deals not with provisions of the Bill of Rights, but rather the 14th Amendment. We trace the Amendment's history, motives of its framers and its development in the courts. We focus on the quest for racial equality from the "separate but equal" doctrine of *Plessy v. Ferguson* (1896), to the 1954 *Brown* case. This decision ended legally segregated public schools in America.

Battles to achieve integrated schools and places of p   ed. A history of the Civil Rights Revolution of the 1960s is an impo   ler the enactment of the landmark Civil Rights Act of 1964, Voting   Act of 1968.

We will profile the men and women who have struggled for racial justice. This involves a study of leadership by groups like the National Association for the Advancement of Colored People, the Urban League and the Southern Christian Leadership Conference of Dr. Martin Luther King. Dr. King's role in the Montgomery, Ala., bus boycott, various demonstrations in the South and the massive, peaceful 1963 March on Washington are detailed. We consider the problems of Black community leadership after the assassination of Dr. King in 1968.

The chapter concludes with an account of woman's struggle to achieve sexual equality in a society historically dominated by males. The suffrage movement is considered, as is the modern "Second Wave" of feminism. Some attention is given to the failure of the proposed Equal Rights Amendment. We consider alternative efforts by feminists to advance their cause by legal means. Considerable attention is given to several Burger and Rehnquist Court rulings which have helped women to do precisely that. Such topics as affirmative action, particularly the University of Michigan's admissions policies, challenged in two U.S. Supreme Court cases, comparable worth and sexual harassment are detailed. Some attention is given to the rights of Americans with Disabilities.

ACKNOWLEDGMENTS:

Any book is the result of considerable planning, thought and effort. The research and writing that went into this work were facilitated by several of my colleagues in the Center for Integrative Studies/Social Science. I am particularly grateful to former CIS directors Philip R. Smith and Assefa Mehretu for their encouragement, as well as current director Thomas Summerhill. Jean Robinson of the Psychology Department was most helpful with computer production of the manuscript.

Laura Middleton and Diane Perry of Pearson Publishing Company were most cooperative in development of the book.

Over the years, a number of faculty members have stimulated my interest in Civil Liberties. I am indebted to the late J.C. Heinlein, University of Cincinnati Department of Political Science professor emeritus; the late Virgil C. Blum, S.J., a political scientist at Marquette University, Milwaukee, and Professors Emeriti Albert E. Levak and Matt Epstein of MSU's former Social Science department.

Several journalists and journalism professors have, in extensive discussions over the years, helped me to enlarge my understanding of the role of the press in a free society. I am particularly grateful to S. Craig Klugman, former director of the Medill School of Journalism at Northwestern University. Mr. Klugman, now editor of the *Ft. Wayne Journal Gazette,* made it possible for me to teach and do research as Visiting Professor at Medill. I also am indebted to the late Dean I.W. (Bill) Cole, the late Ben Baldwin and Ray Nelson, all former Medill colleagues. Others who helped include Ralph Holsinger, former managing editor of The *Cincinnati Enquirer* and professor emeritus of journalism at Indiana University, and two late members of the MSU School of Journalism, Chairman Frank Senger and John Murray. I also am grateful to the last four directors of the MSU Journalism School, the late Elizabeth Yamashita, Stanley Soffin, Steve Lacy and Jane Briggs-Bunting, who gave me the opportunity to share some of my 15 years of newsroom experience with both graduate and undergraduate students.

Last, but certainly not least, I wish to thank my wife, Carol, for her help and encouragement during the preparation of this work.

– John D. Molloy

TABLE OF CONTENTS

CHAPTER I: THE FIRST FREEDOMS

Dedication: to Carol, Mary, Susan and Ray, Tom and Dan

CHAPTER I: THE FIRST FREEDOMS

The First Amendment to the U.S. Constitution guarantees some of the most fundamental of all liberties. For this reason, these cherished rights often are called the "First Freedoms." They are not only the first ones mentioned in the Bill of Rights, but also of paramount importance to those who value liberties of religion, speech, press, assembly and association.

The First Amendment stipulates that *"Congress shall make no law respecting an establishment of religion, or prohibiting the free exercise thereof; or abridging the freedom of speech or of the press; or the right of the people peacefully to assemble, and to petition the Government for a redress of grievances."*

FREEDOM OF RELIGION

The meaning of freedom of religion has been debated from the very beginning of American history, although the intent of the Founding Fathers, in some respects, was clear enough. Wise in their understanding of European experience, America's constitutional fathers tried to remove the divisive question of religion from politics. As the late John Courtney Murray, a widely respected Jesuit scholar and student of church-state relations once observed, the First Amendment is primarily an "article of peace," rather than an article of faith.[1]

Three distinct patterns of church-state relations evolved in early America. First, there was the tradition of an established church, supported by Puritan ministers like John Cotton. Many settlers came to the New World to escape persecution, primarily in Anglican-dominated England. There, in the late 17th Century, it was a crime not to attend the established Church of England. Clearly, it had a legal monopoly on religious power and authority.

This situation may have pleased Anglicans, but it motivated Puritans, Roman Catholics and others to seek relief from religious oppression. They came to the New World where, in turn, they oppressed others when they had the power and authority to do so. Rhode Island and Maryland, in fact, were founded by religious people seeking liberation from Puritanism.

Lord Baltimore founded Maryland as a place of sanctuary for persecuted Roman Catholics and William Penn founded Pennsylvania as a place where Quakers and others could enjoy freedom.

Establishment: Nine of the 13 colonies had established churches before the American Revolution. Religious minorities commonly suffered disabilities. Roman Catholics and Jews, as well as other non-Christians, were barred from voting and seeking public office.[2]

In Pennsylvania, public officials were required to swear, "I do acknowledge the Scriptures of the Old and New Testament to be given by Divine Inspiration...I believe in one God."

Delaware demanded a belief in "Jesus Christ and the Holy Ghost."

Maryland required its officials to attest to their belief in the doctrine of the Holy Trinity and the divinity of Jesus Christ.

Only Christians could hold public office in Massachusetts. Only Protestant Christians could be elected in Georgia. North Carolina barred Jews and Catholics from holding office.

Only Anglicans could hold office in Virginia.

But religious pluralism eventually would lead to disestablishment.

Disestablishment, separation: Advocated by those who believed in religious diversity, like Roger Williams of Rhode Island, disestablishment was a movement that continued until well

2

after the American Revolution. It did not finally occur in Massachusetts until 1833 or in New Hampshire until 1852.

The final pattern of church-state relations to evolve was separation of church and state. It was endorsed by Thomas Jefferson and James Madison, who supported not only freedom of religion for believers, but freedom from religion for non-believers.

Jefferson, who lived so long and wrote so much, often is quoted on both sides of many civil liberties issues. He was not entirely consistent in some areas. But many students of U.S. constitutional history credit him with coining the phrase a **"wall of separation"** between church and state.

Jefferson received a letter from the Danbury Baptists Association requesting that he proclaim a day of fasting. He refused, noting:[3]

> Believing with you that religion is a matter which lies solely between man and his God; that he owes account to none other for his faith or his worship; that the legislative powers of the Government reach actions only, and not opinions, I contemplate with sovereign reverence that act of the whole American people which declared that their legislature should 'make no law respecting an establishment of religion, or prohibiting the free exercise thereof,' thus building a wall of separation between Church and state.

Interest groups like the public school teachers' professional associations and the American Civil Liberties Union generally like to quote Jefferson's "wall" theory. But they generally do not recognize that he was not an absolutist in his approach to church-state relations.

Jefferson believed, for example, that the public school core curriculum should include religion. There should be, he said, "no religious reading, instruction or exercise...inconsistent with the tenets of any religious sect or denomination."[4]

One should note that the First Amendment is addressed specifically to the Congress. It was intended to limit the power of national government, rather than that of the individual states. However, all 50 states are also restrained from infringing upon First Amendment Freedoms, including religion. Restraining them are their own state Bill of Rights, as well as U.S. Supreme Court interpretations of the 14th Amendment.

That amendment provides in part that no State shall "deprive any person of life, liberty, or property without due process of law..." The word "liberty" in the 14th Amendment has come to embrace the "First Freedoms," according to the U.S. Supreme Court.[5]

Two Key Clauses: The First Amendment has two main provisions on religion, the **Establishment Clause** and the **Free Exercise Clause**. Like other parts of the Constitution, these guarantees are not absolute and must be defined by courts as specific cases and controversies arise.

The U.S. Supreme Court has made, over the years, a distinction between religious beliefs and religious actions. One has an absolute intellectual freedom of **"religious belief."** However, **"religious actions"** enjoy no such protection.

Free Exercise Cases: May Mormons Practice Polygamy? No group of believers may use freedom of religion as an excuse to violate law. No group may threaten the peace, health, safety or morality of the community. For example, in *Reynolds v. U.S.*, the Mormon polygamy case, Chief Justice Morrison R. Waite rejected the argument that one had a constitutional right to commit bigamy.[6]

The **doctrine of polygamy** was basic to male members of the Mormon Church. They had a duty to practice it. Failure to do so would result in "damnation in the life to come," according to an 1853 church mandate.

Congress, in 1874, banned polygamy from the Territory of Utah. George Reynolds, charged with bigamy, argued that, in taking a second wife, he simply was following the dictates of his conscience. This right, he argued, was protected by the First Amendment.

To accept such a view, Justice Waite reasoned, would "make the professed doctrines of religious belief superior to the law of the land, and, in effect, ...permit every citizen to become a law into himself."

Waite wrote:[7]

> Laws are made for the government of actions, and while they cannot interfere with mere religious belief and opinions, they may with practices. Suppose that one believed that human sacrifices were a necessary part of religious worship, would it be seriously contended that the civil government under which he lived could not interfere to prevent a sacrifice?

The Flag Salute Cases

In some cases, however, government has accommodated certain religious beliefs when they conflicted with the duties of citizenship. During World War II, for example, the Jehovah's Witnesses won the right to be excused from compulsory flag salute exercises in *West Virginia State Board of Education v. Barnette*.[8]

The Witnesses challenged the law because it required them to commit serious "sin." They maintained that a flag salute and pledge of allegiance violated one of the 10 Commandments. They quoted from the Book of Exodus:

> Thou shalt not make unto thee any graven image, or any likeness of anything that is in heaven above, or that is in the earth beneath, or that is in the water under the earth; thou shalt not bow down thyself to them, nor serve them.

Barnette was the second of two compulsory flag salute decisions reached during the 1940s. In *Minersville, Pa., School District v. Gobitis,* the Supreme Court had upheld, 8-1, a compulsory flag salute law. At that time Justice Felix Frankfurter wrote that "mere possession of religious convictions which contradict the relevant concerns of a political society does not relieve the citizens from the discharge of political responsibilities."

Frankfurter said:[9]

> The ultimate foundation of a free society is the binding tie of cohesive sentiment...The flag is the symbol of our national unity, transcending all internal differences...To stigmatize legislative judgment in providing for this universal gesture of respect for the symbol of our national life...would amount to no less than the pronouncement of pedagogical and psychological dogma in a field where courts possess...no controlling competence.

As a result of the ruling, Lillian and William Gobitis were expelled from public school. A number of states, including West Virginia, then were stimulated to enact compulsory flag salute laws. An inflamed public opinion showed remarkable hostility, if not hysteria, toward the Witnesses.

They were called "traitors." Some of their churches were burned. More than 2000 of their children were expelled from the nation's public schools. Extreme violence occurred as several witnesses were tarred and feathered. One Witness was castrated.

But the Witnesses did have some allies, like the American Civil Liberties Union. ACLU vigorously attacked the Gobitis decision.

Only three years later, the Supreme Court reversed itself. Justices Hugo Black, William O. Douglas and Frank Murphy changed their views. President Franklin D. Roosevelt named two new members to the court, Robert H. Jackson and Wiley B. Rutledge.

In *West Virginia State Board of Education v. Barnette*, a case nearly identical to *Gobitis*, the Court focused on the question of freedom of religious expression. Jackson, speaking for the majority, argued that government should not require a citizen to express any belief contrary to the dictates of his or her conscience. In a widely quoted passage, he wrote:[10]

> To believe that patriotism will not flourish if patriotic ceremonies are voluntary and spontaneous instead of a compulsory routine is to make an unflattering estimate of the appeal of our institutions to free minds. We can have intellectual individualism and the rich cultural diversities that we owe to exceptional minds only at the price of occasional eccentricity and abnormal attitudes. When they are so harmless to others or to the State as those we deal with here, the price is not too great. But freedom to differ is not limited to things that do not matter much. That would be a mere shadow of freedom. The test of its substance is the right to differ as to things that touch the heart of the existing order.
>
> If there is any fixed star in our constitutional constellation, it is that no official, high or petty, can prescribe what shall be orthodox in politics, nationalism, religion or other matters of opinion or force citizens to confess by word or act their faith therein. If there are any circumstances which permit an exception, they do not now occur to us...

Nearly 60 years after *Barnette,* a different kind of flag salute issue arose, one involving the wording of the Pledge of Allegiance. In *Newdow v. U.S. Congress et al.,* a panel of the U.S. Court of Appeals for the Ninth Circuit ruled, 2-1, that the phrase "one nation under God" violates the First Amendment's requirement of separation of church and state.

The decision, written by Nixon-appointee, 78-year-old semi-retired (senior status) Judge Alfred T. Goodwin, immediately caused a national storm of protest. Goodwin was joined in his opinion by Carter-appointee Stephen Reinhardt, a noted liberal who wrote an opinion in 1996 that people have a constitutional right to die.

Judge Ferdinand Fernandez, an appointee of President Bush's father in 1989, dissented, remarking: "We will soon find ourselves prohibited from using our album of patriotic songs in many public settings. *God Bless America* and *America the Beautiful* will be gone for sure, and while the first and second stanzas of the *Star Spangled Banner* will be permissible, we will be precluded from straying into the third."

President Bush commented, "It's ridiculous."

The U.S. Senate voted unanimously (99-0) to condemn the ruling. Senate Majority Leader Tom Daschle (D., S.D.) called it "just nuts." Sen. Joseph Lieberman (D., Conn.), the Democratic vice-presidential nominee in 2000, urged his colleagues to propose a constitutional amendment to protect the words "under God" in the Pledge.

Rep. J.C. Watts (R., Okla.), chairman of the House Republican Conference, accused the two-judge majority on the Ninth Circuit of "California dreaming." His House colleagues, led by Speaker Dennis Hastert, rushed to the steps of the Capitol to stage a Pledge of Allegiance ceremony. Congress had added the words "under God" in 1954 during the Eisenhower Administration.

The House, of course, seldom acts with such speed, and its symbolic act made great video for prime-time evening television news on June 26, 2002. The court ruling also was featured on page one in virtually every major newspaper the next day.

Attorney General John Ashcroft said: "This decision is directly contrary to two centuries of American tradition. The Justice Department believes in the right of Americans to pledge allegiance to their flag and is evaluating the appropriate response."

Not everyone, however, was unhappy with Judge Goodwin's opinion. He wrote that the two words, "under God," were just as objectionable as a statement that "we are a nation under Jesus, a nation under Vishnu, a nation under Zeus, or a nation under no God" because none of these professions can be neutral with respect to religion.

Ellen Johnson, president of American Atheists, said her group was 100% behind the decision.

Americans United for Separation of Church and State also supported the ruling, pointing out that the court did not strike down the Pledge of Allegiance, but only held that Congress had acted unconstitutionally when they added "under God" to the pledge.

Elk Grove Unified School District v. Newdow, 542 U.S. 1 (2004)

In 2004, after a highly heated and emotional debate of four years, the U.S. Supreme Court avoided ruling on the issue directly in *Elk Grove, California, School District v. Newdow.*[11] In an 8-0 opinion, written by Justice John Paul Stevens, the Court held that Michael Newdow lacked legal standing to bring a lawsuit on behalf of his daughter because he was not her custodial parent and the girl's mother objected to the suit.

Stevens noted that the high court frequently has declined to intervene in domestic relations matters and that Newdow was seeking to prevent his daughter's exposure to religious ideas that her (Roman Catholic) mother, who wields a form of veto power, endorses.

Chief Justice William Rehnquist and Associate Justices Sandra Day O'Connor and Clarence Thomas wrote, however, in concurring opinions, that they would have ruled on the First Amendment issue, and found that the pledge does not violate freedom of religion. Justice Antonin Scalia also shares this opinion. He removed himself from the case because he had publicly criticized the Ninth Circuit decision that the pledge's phrase, "one nation, under God," was an unconstitutional intermingling of church and state.

Newdow, an emergency room physician and non-practicing lawyer, considered by some to be America's most famous early 21st Century atheist, filed suit in U.S. District Court in 2000, arguing that his five-year-old daughter, a kindergarten student at Elk Grove Unified School District in Sacramento County, should not be "exposed" to daily references to God in the pledge. This, he contended, amounted to a daily "prayer." School officials countered that it was merely a "unifying, patriotic exercise."

Newdow asked Federal judge Edward Schwartz to declare Elk Grove school district policies unconstitutional and to invalidate the 1954 act of Congress which added the words "under God" to the pledge at the request of President Eisenhower. This, Newdow claimed, was done for purely religious reasons. The U.S. then was engaged in a Cold War struggle with the Soviet Union and wanted to contrast American values to those of "atheistic communism."

Judge Schwartz dismissed the case on July 21, 2000.

But Newdow appealed and became a national celebrity (Time magazine named him "Man of the Week") when the U.S. Court of Appeals for the Ninth Circuit overruled the District Court and held that the pledge violated the Establishment Clause.

The U.S. Supreme Court accepted review on October 14, 2003, and, as noted above, reversed the Ninth Circuit ruling.

Newdow has made news on a number of other fronts:

He has tried, and failed, to have the phrase "In God We Trust" removed from the nation's coins and paper currency.

He attempted to stop the invocation prayer at President Bush's second inaugural on January 20, 2005, arguing that having a minister invoke God in the ceremony would force him to listen to unwanted religious beliefs. Federal Judge John Bates rejected the challenge, noting that inaugural references to God date back to George Washington's inauguration in 1789, and was upheld by the Court of Appeals. The U.S. Supreme Court refused to grant a hearing.

Subsequently, Newdow re-filed the Pledge suit in Sacramento Federal District Court, naming eight other plaintiffs who are custodial parents of the children. In September, 2005, U.S. District Judge Lawrence Karlton, an appointee of President Carter, ruled that the pledge's reference to one nation "under God" violates school children's rights to be "free from a coercive requirement to affirm God." Judge Karlton said that he had to follow the precedent set by the 2002 Ninth Circuit ruling for Newdow.

One can expect that the pledge case will find its way back to the U.S. Supreme Court.

Hein v. Freedom from Religion Foundation

The U.S. Supreme Court, in 2007, considered a case brought by a group of atheists and agnostics who challenged spending by President George W. Bush's White House Office of Faith-Based and Community Initiatives. In fiscal 2005, several Federal agencies awarded grants of more than $2 billion to religious charities. These groups dealt with such problems as substance abuse, housing for homeless veterans, emergency food assistance, community re-entry of former prison inmates and housing for patients suffering from AIDS.

Freedom from Religion Foundation filed a taxpayers' lawsuit, arguing that the Bush Administration could not encourage religious-based charities to seek Federal grants without violating the Establishment Clause's wall of separation between church and state.

Technically, this was an Article III case, under which the Supreme Court was asked to decide whether taxpayers had standing to challenge acts of Executive Branch officials, acting to carry out a presidential order, rather than a challenge to an Act of Congress.

Justice Samuel Alito, a Bush appointee to the high tribunal, was not impressed by the taxpayers' arguments. He wrote:[12]

...They say a federal agency could use its discretionary funds to build a house of worship or to hire clergy of one denomination and send them out to spread their faith. Or an agency could use its funds to make bulk purchases of Stars of David, crucifixes or depictions of the star and crescent for use in its offices or for distributions to the employees or the general public. Of course none of these things happened...In the unlikely event that any of these executive actions did take place, Congress could quickly step in.

The Supreme Court was deeply divided, although its 5-4 ruling that the group lacked standing to sue was a narrow one. Ordinary taxpayers, the tribunal held, cannot challenge a White House initiative that helps these faith-based charities get a share of federal funds. President Bush has argued that religious charities and secular charities should compete for money on an equal basis.

The administration also argued that the taxpayers group should not be permitted to contest the government's actions because Congress neither earmarked funds for specific programs nor distributed money outside the government. Money spent on White House conferences came out of general appropriations.

A Bush administration spokesman characterized the Supreme Court ruling as "a substantial victory for efforts by Americans to more effectively aid our neighbors in need of help."

The four dissenters' views were reflected by David Souter, appointed to the high tribunal by President George Herbert Walker Bush. He wrote that the Court majority "closes the door on these taxpayers because the executive branch, and not the legislative branch, caused their injury…I see no basis for this distinction in either logic or precedent."[13]

Souter also wrote:

Here there is no dispute that taxpayer money in identifiable amounts is funding conferences, and these are alleged to have the purpose of promoting religion…When executive agencies spend identifiable sums of tax money for religious purposes, no less than when Congress authorizes the same thing, taxpayers suffer injury.[14]

Conscientious Objector Cases

As long ago as the Civil War, Congress exempted conscientious objectors from combat. During World War I, the government excused members of traditional, pacifist denominations, like the Quakers and Mennonites. Their doctrines specifically forbade participation in war.

On the eve of World War II, Congress again resorted to conscription. The law set forth specific standards for religious exemption from combat. One had to derive his beliefs from traditional, theistic religion. **He must be opposed to all wars "in any form," not just a particular war.**

In 1948, Congress amended the Selective Service Act. It refused to extend Conscientious Objector status to non-religious opponents of war. The law provided:

…religious training and belief…means an individual's belief in relation to a Supreme Being involving duties superior to those arising from any human relation, but does not include essentially political, sociological, or philosophical views or a merely personal moral code.

These standards were challenged during the Vietnam War, when many suits were filed. Generally, it was argued, the law was discriminatory. In 1965, the Court ruled in *U.S. v. Seeger* that a belief in God or a traditional religion was unnecessary.

The test of belief in relation to a Supreme Being, the Court said, "is whether a given belief that is sincere and meaningful occupies a place in the life of its possessor parallel to that filed by the orthodox belief in God of one who clearly qualifies for exemption."[15]

The Supreme Court issued another highly controversial ruling in 1970 in *Welsh v. U.S.* The Court, through Justice Black, accepted a deeply held humanistic conviction as equivalent to religion. Opposition to war must stem, Black wrote, "…from the registrant's moral, ethical, or religious beliefs about what is right and wrong and...these beliefs must be held with the strength of traditional religious convictions." Chief Justice Burger and Associate Justices Stewart and White dissented.[16]

In 1971, the Court ruled in *Gillette v. U.S.* that one must be opposed to all wars in order to qualify as a conscientious objector. Guy P. Gillette's opposition to a particular war (Vietnam) was inadequate, the Court held. Only Justice Douglas dissented. The Court decision, to some extent, was based on purely practical grounds. **Individual draft registrants could not be permitted to "pick and choose" which wars they would and would not fight.**

This would have raised havoc with the Selective Service system, precisely what some of the litigants may have intended. Congress, the Court made clear, can require compulsory military service during wartime. The policy decision to exempt a small number of conscientious objectors from service is an **act of grace on the part of Congress, not a constitutional right of conscientious objectors.**[17]

Sunday Closing Laws

What about Sunday closing laws, still on the statute books in some states? **Is Sunday the only Sabbath?**

Early in U.S. history, many states passed laws requiring stores to close on Sundays to observe the Christian Sabbath. Although they were clearly religious in origin, these statutes went unchallenged under the First Amendment until 1961. As previously noted, the Bill of Rights did not apply to the states early in U.S. constitutional history.

The Supreme Court, in 1961, considered this issue in four cases. Two of them involved businesses which wanted to be open seven days a week. Two others, including *Braunfeld v. Brown*, were brought by Orthodox Jews.

Braunfeld observed the Jewish Sabbath, closing his furniture store on Saturday. To make up for lost business revenue, he opened on Sunday, a violation of Pennsylvania's Sunday closing law. Braunfeld challenged the constitutionality of the law, arguing that it restricted him in the free exercise of his faith.

The law also had the practical effect of forcing him to close his business for two days. This, he argued, gave a legal preference to Christians.

The Court found that such laws are not unconstitutional. Sunday closing, the nation's highest tribunal ruled, was an **effective way to achieve a valid state objective of giving citizens a uniform day of rest.**

Although the law may have indirectly made certain religious practices more expensive, it did not make any religious practices illegal. States, the Court noted, could have chosen to exempt from Sunday closing laws those who observed a Saturday Sabbath. But they did not, and the First Amendment did not require them to do so.

The Court then established a standard for judging whether a state law unconstitutionally infringes on free exercise of religion.[18]

If the purpose or effect of a law is to impede the observance of one or all religions or is to discriminate invidiously between religions, that law is constitutionally invalid even though the burden may be characterized as being only indirect. But if the State regulates conduct by enacting a general law within its power, the purpose and effect of which is to advance the State's secular goals, the statute is valid despite its indirect burden on religious observance unless the State may accomplish its purposes by means which do not impose such a burden.

Whatever the original purpose of the laws, the Warren Court held, the present effect and purpose is "pre-eminently secular."

Unemployment Claims: In 1961, the Warren Court modified *Braunfeld*, ruling that only a compelling state interest could justify placing limits on religious liberty.

Adell Sherbert, a Seventh Day Adventist, was fired from her job in a South Carolina textile mill because she refused to work on Saturday. Her employer had switched from a five- to a six-day work week. After Sherbert refused available jobs, South Carolina denied her unemployment benefits claim.

The Court overruled South Carolina in an opinion written by Justice William Brennan. **The state's actions,** Brennan wrote, **forced Sherbert either to abandon her religious beliefs in order to work, or to give up jobless benefits by remaining true to her conscience.**

"Governmental imposition of such a choice puts the same kind of burden upon the free exercise of religion as would a fine imposed against appellant for her Saturday worship," the Court held.

The state, Brennan wrote, could limit the exercise of an individual's religion only for a compelling state interest. "Only the gravest abuse, endangering paramount interests, give occasion for permissible limitation," he said.

Prevention of fraudulent claims was the only reason the state gave for denying benefits to Sherbert. The state, Brennan ruled, would have to show that it could not prevent such fraud by means less restrictive of religious liberty.[19]

The Amish and Compulsory School Attendance: In a 1972 case, *Wisconsin v. Yoder*, the Supreme Court held that Amish children could be excused by the First Amendment from state compulsory school attendance laws after they had completed the eighth grade. Wisconsin law required children to attend school until they reached the age of 16. The Amish, a simple people, reject modern technology, believing that it is tainted with evil.

Religious salvation is of paramount importance to the Old Order Amish. One can best be "saved" by living in a rural, religious community, detached from modern society and its false, materialistic values.

Jonas Yoder and others in the Amish community did not want their children exposed to "worldly influences." Contemporary public school goals and values are contrary to their beliefs.

Older Amish children received considerable "advanced," vocational education at home.

The Supreme Court ruled unanimously that this **informal vocational schooling that Amish children receive in their communities substantially achieves state educational goals.** Chief Justice Warren Burger wrote:[20]

> ... a state's interest in universal education, however highly we rank it, is not totally free from a balancing process when it impinges on fundamental rights and interests, such as those specifically protected by the Free Exercise Clause of the First Amendment, and the traditional interest of parents with respect to the religious upbringing of their children so long as they...prepare them for additional obligations.

Establishment Clause Cases

Although some fascinating issues involving "free exercise" of religion reach America's highest court, many more involve the troublesome "Establishment Clause." Although lawyers agree that the First Amendment requires separation of church and state, they vehemently disagree on the nature of that separation.

One school of thought clings with fondness to the idea that there must be erected a high "wall of separation" between church and state. Another school of thought embraces, with equal fondness, the concept that the state should prefer no particular creed, but generally should "**accommodate**" religion.

America's Founding Fathers clearly intended that no one faith should be established as the nation's "official" religion. No citizen, they believed, ought to be required to support in any way a specific creed which was contrary to the dictates of his or her conscience.

However, the U.S. is a nation with a distinctive Western culture, rooted in the **Judaeo-Christian ethic.** Americans are a religious people. The nation's armed forces have thousands of chaplains. The currency affirms, "In God We Trust." Most state legislatures begin their sessions with prayers.

Even the U.S. Supreme Court itself opens public sessions with the words "God save the United States and this honorable court." Several Presidents have held religious services in the White House.

Churches and Taxes

Historically, considerable church-owned property has been tax-exempt. Those who oppose such exemptions from property and income taxes challenged them in *Walz v. Tax Commission of the City of New York* in 1970. They argued that, for all practical purposes, a tax exemption amounted to a government subsidy of religion. The Court, however, found only an incidental church-state connection in this and upheld the practice as compatible with the First Amendment.

New York's tax exemption was given not only to churches, but also to a variety of nonprofit organizations. Among these were schools, hospitals and libraries. In short, churches were among a broad class of beneficiaries.

Chief Justice Burger wrote that "we cannot read New York's statute as attempting to establish religion...it is simply sparing the exercise of religion from the burden of property taxation levied on private profit institutions." He also noted:[21]

There is no genuine nexus between tax exemption and establishment of religion...The exemption creates only a minimal and remote involvement between church and state and far less than taxation of churches. It restricts the fiscal relationship between church and state, and tends to complement and reinforce the desired separation insulating each from the other.

How much encouragement, however, can laws give to organized religion without running afoul of the First Amendment? The answer lies essentially with the courts, particularly the U.S. Supreme Court. At times it has held to the "no preference" or accommodation theory, upholding statutes which benefit religion in general but no creed in particular. At other times, however, it has held to the "wall of separation" doctrine.

Everson: The Child Benefit Theory: In a 1947 landmark case, *Everson v. Board of Education of Ewing Township, N.J.*, the Court held by a slim 5-4 majority that a public school district could provide bus transportation to children attending parochial schools. Writing for the majority, Justice Hugo Black held that such transportation should be considered in the same category as police and fire protection.

To cut off such facilities would make it more difficult for parochial schools to operate, he reasoned. Justice Black held that the power of the state, under the First and 14th Amendments, is no more to be used to handicap religion that it is to favor it. Here, he said, children were receiving no more than the benefits of public welfare legislation and the law, therefore, was constitutional.[22]

The reasoning behind the Everson decision has come to be known as the "**child benefit theory**." The law gives aid primarily to the school child, rather than to a particular religious denomination. The Warren Court, in effect, reaffirmed *Everson* during its 1967-68 term by refusing to hear a Pennsylvania case presenting the same basic issue.

Another question arousing some interest and considerable passion was that of releasing children from public school classes to receive religious instruction. Does this practice violate the Establishment Clause of the First Amendment, which requires separation of church and state? There have been two landmark cases on this point, resulting in two different conclusions.

Time Release Programs

After World War II, the U.S. experienced a brief religious revival. Many Americans wanted their children to receive some instruction in religion. They pressured legislators and school boards to adopt "time release" programs in public schools.

The American Civil Liberties Union, the American Jewish Congress, and Protestants and Others Americans United for Separation of Church and State (POAU) teamed to fight what they regarded as a threat to separation of church and state.

In 1948, in *McCollum v. Board of Education*, the Court considered a challenge to a Champaign, Ill., "**time release**" program of religious instruction in public schools. Classes in Champaign were taught during the school day, by outside religion teachers representing the major faiths. They received no salaries from public funds for offering classes one day a week. Religion classes were about 30 minutes for lower elementary grades and 45 minutes for junior high school students.

Non-participating students worked on their regular assignments.

Mrs. Vashti McCollum protested that her fifth grade child Terry was subjected to this program.

The fact that the classes were taught in the public school building and that the whole arrangement was aided to some extent by public school personnel caused the Supreme Court to reject the program, 8-1. Justice Black, writing for the Court, said:[23]

> Not only are the state's tax-supported public school buildings used for the dissemination of religious doctrines...the state also affords sectarian groups an invaluable aid in that it helps to provide pupils for their religious classes through use of the State's compulsory public school machinery. This is not separation of Church and State.

In a concurring opinion, Justice Frankfurter noted succinctly, "Separation means separation, not something less."

Only four years later in a strikingly similar case, *Zorach v. Clauson*, the Court upheld a New York "**dismissed time**" program. These religion classes were conducted off the public school premises at neighborhood churches and synagogues. As in the Illinois program, children were excused on written request of a parent. They left school about an hour early one day each week. Other students remained in their classrooms.

In this case, a six member majority of the court found that **no students were forced to attend classes in religion. Schedules were simply being rearranged to accommodate religious beliefs of students and their parents. Nor were the classes conducted on public school property.** Writing for the majority, Justice Douglas held:[24]

> We would have to press the concept of separation of church and state to extremes to condemn the present law on constitutional grounds...When the state encourages religious instruction or cooperates with religious authorities by adjusting the schedule of public events to sectarian needs, it follows the best of our traditions. For it then respects the religious nature of our people and accommodates the public service to their spiritual needs. To hold that it may not would be to find in the Constitution a requirement that the government show a callous indifference to religious groups. That would be preferring those who believe in no religion over those who do believe.

Douglas viewed the New York program as equivalent to permitting Roman Catholic students to be excused to attend Mass on Holy Days, or a Jewish student to attend synagogue on Yom Kippur. "In each case," he wrote, "the teacher requires parental consent in writing. In each case, the teacher, in order to make sure the student is not a truant, goes further and requires a report from the priest, the rabbi or the minister. The teacher, in other words, cooperates in a religious program to the extent of making it possible for her students to participate in it. Whether she does it occasionally for a few students, regularly for one, or pursuant to a systematized program designed to further the religious needs of all the students, does not alter the character of the act."

What differences did the Supreme Court majority find between *Zorach* and *McCollum*? Douglas wrote:[25]

> In the McCollum case...classrooms were used for religious instruction and the force of the public school was used to promote the instruction. Here, as we have said, the public schools do no more than accommodate their schedules to a program of outside religious instruction. We follow the McCollum case. But we cannot expand it to cover the present released time program unless separation of church and State means that public institutions can make no adjustments of their schedules to accommodate the religious needs of the people. We cannot read into the Bill of Rights such a philosophy of hostility to religion.

But some Americans, such as atheists and agnostics, are hostile to religion in general. Others are hostile to faiths that do not teach the specific creeds that they cherish. In a pluralistic society, this presents tremendous problems.

It should be noted that *Zorach* is a landmark in constitutional law because many communities base their time release programs on the New York model.

The School Prayer Cases

Some of the most heated debates in recent U.S. church-state history followed the Warren Court's school prayer decisions in 1962-63. What were the facts in these cases? Just what did the Court rule? Why has the Congress failed to propose a constitutional amendment to permit voluntary prayer in the public schools? Why did the Republican Party platform and President Ronald Reagan push for school prayers? Why did most Liberals oppose such an amendment?

In 1961, the Supreme Court decided the case of *Engel v. Vitale*, one of the most controversial cases in the annals of the Warren Court. Petitioners argued that a 22-word, non-denominational prayer composed by the New York Board of Regents was an unconstitutional infringement of the First Amendment's guarantee of religious freedom. The prayer read as follows:

> Almighty God, we humbly acknowledge our dependence upon Thee, and we beg Thy blessings upon us, our parents, our teachers and country.

The Regents prayer clearly was intended to express a belief in God, something that Protestants, Jews and Roman Catholics all could accept. However, not all major religious groups like non-denominational prayers. They tend, rather, to prefer those which reflect their own dogmas and beliefs.

Separationist groups, led by the New York Civil Liberties Union, argued that the **religious neutrality of the prayer did not matter. The basic issue was state authorship. New York had no business writing prayers.**

The Supreme Court ruled, 6-1, with only Justice Stewart dissenting, that the prayer violated the Establishment Clause of the First Amendment. Speaking through Justice Black, the Court said:[26]

> It is no part of the business of government to compose official prayers for any group of the American people to recite as a part of a religious program carried on by the government...Under the First Amendment's prohibition against government establishment of religion, as reinforced by provisions of the 14th Amendment, government in this country, be it state or Federal, is without power to prescribe by law any particular form of prayer which is to be used as an official prayer in carrying on any program of governmentally-sponsored religious activity.

Concluding that there could be no doubt that New York had established the religious beliefs embodied in the Regents' prayer, Justice Black rejected the non-denominational character of the prayer or the fact that pupils could remain silent or be excused from the room if they so requested. Black held:[27]

> The Establishment Clause...stands as an expression of principle on the part of the Founders of our Constitution that religion is too personal, too sacred, too holy to permit its unhallowed perversion by a civil magistrate.

The Engel decision caused a storm of protest in the halls of Congress, in many pulpits and in some segments of the press. The nation's governors, holding their annual meeting in Hershey, Pa., at the time of the decision, urged Congress to propose a **constitutional amendment to permit voluntary prayer** in public schools.

Few journalists, political leaders or ministers who opposed the ruling recognized that many clergymen did not think the Regents' prayer was a "proper" one. *Christian Century*, a Protestant weekly, said the prayer was likely to deteriorate quickly into an empty formality with little, if any, spiritual significance.

Some Lutheran church leaders, meeting in Peekskill, N.Y., charged that the name of Jesus Christ had "deliberately been omitted to mollify non-Christian elements," and that "therefore the prayer is a denial of Christ...an abomination and a blasphemy."

To many citizens, it seemed simple enough. The Court was saying simply that in a nation characterized by enormous religious diversity, no public body should prescribe a form of worship which would be regarded by some as "too religious," by others as "not religious enough," or in conformity with their own denominational norms.

If Engel infuriated the public, what followed a year later in two school prayer cases was much more explosive. In 1963, in two companion cases, *Abington, Pa., School District v. Schempp and Murray v. Curlett*, the Court heard arguments dealing with the constitutionality of Bible readings and recitation of the Lord's Prayer in public schools.[28]

The Schempps were Unitarians who objected to Pennsylvania's law, requiring "at least 10 verses from the Holy Bible shall be read, without comment, at the opening of each public school on each day." The law also provided that a child could be excused on written request of parent or legal guardian.

These state-prescribed Bible readings, the Schempps argued, violated the First Amendment's Establishment Clause as applied to the states by the 14th Amendment's Due Process Clause. They also contended that the state of Pennsylvania, in adopting a Trinitarian prayer, had entered into the field of theology, distinctly beyond its proper province.

In Maryland, an atheist mother, one Madelyn Murray, objected to a virtually identical law, although on entirely different grounds. A highly flamboyant type, Mrs. Murray was called by one magazine "America's most hated woman." Why?

She denounced the Bible as "nauseating, historically inaccurate, replete with the ravings of madness." She argued that Baltimore public schools should "prepare children to face the problems of Earth, not to prepare for Heaven, which is a delusional dream of the unsophisticated minds of the ill-educated clergy."

In an 8-1 opinion, with only Justice Stewart dissenting, the high Court struck down Maryland and Pennsylvania's required Bible readings and prayers. It held that:[29]

> In both cases the laws require religious exercises and such exercises are being conducted in direct violation of the rights of petitioners. Nor are these required exercises mitigated by the fact that students may absent themselves upon parental request, for that fact furnishes no defense to a claim of unconstitutionality under the Establishment Clause...Further, it is no defense to urge that the religious practices here may be relatively minor encroachments of the First Amendment. The breach of neutrality that is today a trickling stream may all too soon become a raging torrent and, in the words of Madison, "It is proper to take alarm at the first experiment on our liberties."

The prayer amendment debate: The Warren Court rulings in the school prayer cases unquestionably went against majority opinion and the highest tribunal was accused, among other things, of thwarting majority rule. Constitutional freedoms, however, are not simply a matter of arithmetic, and majority rights go hand in hand with minority freedoms.

Scores of members of Congress reacted to the prayer decision by introducing constitutional amendments to permit voluntary prayer in the nation's public schools.

Perhaps most widely publicized was the amendment proposed by Senate Republican leader, Everett M. Dirksen of Illinois. Although a Senate majority favored Senator Dirksen's proposal, the measure failed to win the two-thirds vote necessary.

The Senate voted again on the School Prayer Amendment in 1984, favoring it, 56-44. But this fell 11 votes short of the constitutionally-required majority.

Although the Republican Party platform endorsed voluntary school prayers during the Reagan-Bush presidential campaigns, it appears unlikely that Congress will pass and submit such an amendment to the states in the foreseeable future.

The *Murray-Schempp* school prayer verdict has been openly defied by many school districts, particularly in the "Bible Belt" of Southern and Border states. Since court rulings do not enforce themselves, a complaint or a lawsuit is required to stop the practice. In many communities, however, the majority of people agreed with Justice Potter Stewart's dissenting viewpoint: "I see nothing unconstitutional in letting those who want to say a prayer to say it."[30]

Silent meditation, kindergarten grace: The state of Alabama, among others, reacted to the school prayer decisions by passing a law authorizing a period of silent meditation or voluntary prayer. Legislators thought that this would pass court muster because students did not actually read prayers. However, Mobile attorney Ishmael Jaffree disagreed.

He was upset because Chioke, his five-year-old son, had a second year kindergarten teacher who led the class each day in reciting musical grace before lunch: "God is great. God is good. Let us thank Him for our food. Bow our heads, we all are fed. Give us, Lord, our daily bread. Amen."

Jaffree filed suit In Mobile's Federal District Court against his children's teachers, school administrators and the school board. He argued that Alabama law subjected his children to religious indoctrination.

In one of the most remarkable rulings in recent Federal District Court history, Judge William B. Hand, an ardent advocate of states rights, upheld the law, ruling that the state of Alabama was free to establish a religion if desired to do so. Predictably, this was overturned by the U.S. Court of Appeals. The U.S. Supreme Court granted review of Alabama's appeal. It found that the law had a clearly religious purpose, was not neutral, and was unconstitutional.[31]

The Texas High School Football Stadium Prayer Case: *Santa Fe Independent School District v. Doe,* 530 U.S. 290 (2000)

Before 1995, a youth chosen as the student council chaplain at Santa Fe High School in suburban Houston, Texas, delivered a prayer over the public address system before each home football game. In Texas, one might note, high school football is approached with a kind of religious zeal. During this "rite of passage," youngsters who refuse to participate are in danger of social isolation.

Originally two families, one Roman Catholic and the other Mormon, challenged the school district's long-established policy that student prayer before games promoted good sportsmanship and student safety. They argued that the policy violated the Establishment Clause of the First Amendment, made binding on Texas by virtue of the Due Process Clause of the 14th Amendment.

The district responded to the lawsuit by modifying its policy. Henceforth, students would vote in two elections. They would decide, first, if there should be a pre-game invocation or message, and, second, if so, which student should deliver it. The school system argued that any such message delivered by a student speaker would be private in nature and thus protected by the First Amendment.

The U.S. District Court for the Southern District of Texas, in response to the student elections, which authorized football stadium prayers and chose a spokesperson, entered an order permitting only non-sectarian, non-proselytizing prayer.

The Does (a name which allows families to litigate anonymously) appealed the decision to the U.S. Fifth Circuit. A panel of judges held in 1999 that the football prayer policy was unconstitutional, even as modified by the District Court. Santa Fe authorities asked the Supreme Court to review the case, setting the stage for another school prayer controversy.

On June 19, 2000, the nation's Highest Tribunal affirmed the Fifth Circuit ruling, holding (6-3) that the school district's policy violated the First Amendment's required separation of church and state. The election of a student did not change the fundamental fact, the Court said, that school officials were, in effect, sponsoring pre-game invocations.

Writing for the majority, Justice John Paul Stevens said:

…The religious liberty protected by the Constitution is abridged when the state affirmatively sponsors the particular practice of prayer. Delivery of such a message over the school's public address system, by a speaker representing the student body, under the supervision of school faculty, and pursuant to a school policy that explicitly and implicitly encourages public prayer—is not properly characterized as 'private speech.'…The simple enactment of this policy, with the purpose and perception of school endorsement of student prayer, is a constitutional violation…Government efforts to endorse religion cannot evade constitutional reproach based solely on the remote possibility that those attempts may fail…

Chief Justice William Rehnquist, joined by Associate Justices Clarence Thomas and Antonin Scalia, dissented, writing:

…The Court distorts existing precedent to conclude that the school district's student-message program is invalid on its face under the Establishment Clause. But even more disturbing than its holding is the tone of the Court's opinion; it bristles with hostility to all things religious in public life. Neither the holding nor the tone of the opinion is faithful to the meaning of the Establishment Clause, when it is recalled that George Washington himself, at the request of the very Congress which passed the Bill of Rights, proclaimed a day of 'public thanksgiving and prayer, to be observed by acknowledging with grateful hearts the many and signal favors of Almighty God.'

Chief Justice Rehnquist also accused the majority of "venturing into the realm of prophesy about the kind of messages that would be delivered under the policy," and said the majority ruling "essentially invalidates all student elections."

"Had the policy been put into practice, the students may have chosen a speaker according to wholly secular criteria—like good public speaking skills or social popularity—and the student speaker may have chosen, on his or her accord, to deliver a religious message," Rehnquist wrote. "Such an application of the policy would likely pass constitutional muster."

The ruling in the Santa Fe's stadium prayer case was handed down during a presidential election campaign. Then Texas Gov. George W. Bush strongly supported the school district's policy. He said that he was disappointed by the ruling and would continue to support the "right of all students to express their faith freely and participate in voluntary student-led prayer."

The ruling played a role in sparking considerable debate during the 2000 U.S. presidential campaign over the role of religion in American life.

Jay Alan Sekulow, chief counsel of the American Center for Law and Justice, who argued the case for the school district, said that students' free speech was "censored" by the ruling. But Steven Shapiro, legal director of the American Civil Liberties Union, argued that the Supreme Court had merely "closed a loophole" that many school districts had used to circumvent the ban on clergy-led prayer.

The Santa Fe decision leaves intact the freedom of students to pray on their own in school, say grace before meals or meet for worship on school grounds, as long as other student clubs are treated similarly.

The 10 Commandments Case: For years after the school prayer decisions, a number of state legislatures tried to permit majority religious beliefs to be freely expressed in public schools. In Kentucky, for example, the commonwealth required "the posting of a copy of the 10 Commandments, purchased with private contributions, on the wall of each public school classroom in the State."

A notation at the bottom of the Commandments noted that, "The secular application of the 10 Commandments is clearly seen in its adoption as the fundamental legal code of Western Civilization and the Common Law of the United States."

In *Stone v. Graham*, 449 U.S. 39 (1980), the Supreme Court declared the law unconstitutional.

Although *Stone v. Graham* was clear, a number of states and local communities have "revisited" the issues in recent years. Several governmental units, in what appears to some scholars to be open defiance of the Supreme Court ruling, have enacted laws authorizing posting of the 10 Commandments.

The motives of some of these legislators may be suspect. There always are more votes to be gained by appearing to be "on the side of the Lord," rather than on the other side. Recent events like violence, mayhem and murder at Columbine High School near Denver, and the September 11, 2001, terrorist attack on the United States also stimulated a desire to put more "moral teaching" into the nation's public schools.

While religious interest groups generally support these efforts, the American Civil Liberties Union and like-minded groups keep busy filing lawsuits to prevent what they see as the infringement of the wall of separation between church and state.

McCreary County, Ky., v. ACLU of Ky., 545 U.S. 844 (2005)

In recent years, the issue of displaying the 10 Commandments again has become a major issue. On June 27, 2005, the Supreme Court pleased neither proponents of the "high wall of separation" theory nor the accommodationists when they split on two cases involving the 10 Commandments. The cases are *McCreary County, Ky., v. ACLU of Kentucky* and *Van Orden v. Perry (Governor of Texas)*.

In *McCreary*, the court drew the line on displays inside courthouses, ruling that they violated separation of church and state, required by the First Amendment. The Court found that framed copies of the 10 Commandments in two Kentucky courthouses went too far in endorsing religion. Justice David Souter, writing for the majority, said:[32]

> The touchstone for our analysis is the principle that the First Amendment mandates government neutrality between religion and religion, and between religion and non-religion…When the government acts with the ostensible and predominant purpose of advancing religion, it violates the central Establishment clause value of official religious neutrality.

Souter, writing for the five-member majority, was joined in his opinion by Justices Stevens, Ginsburg, Breyer and O'Connor.

In a strong dissent, Justice Scalia expressed concern about "the dictatorship of a shifting Supreme Court majority" and contended that displays of the 10 Commandments are a legitimate tribute to the nation's religious and legal history. He wrote:[33]

> Government officials may have had a religious purpose when they originally posted the 10 Commandments display by itself in 1999. But their efforts to dilute the religious message since then by hanging other historical documents in the courthouses made it constitutionally adequate. In the court's view, the impermissible motive was apparent from the initial displays of the 10 Commandments all by themselves. What that occurs, the Court says, a religious object is unmistakable...Surely that cannot be...The Commandments have a proper place in our civil history.

He was joined in his opinion by Chief Justice Rehnquist, and Justices Kennedy and Thomas.

In *Van Orden v. Perry*,[34] the court upheld, 5-4, the constitutionality of a display of a six-foot granite monument of the 10 Commandments on the Texas Capitol grounds. It was, however, only one of 17 historical displays on the 22-acre lot and was found by the majority to be a legitimate tribute to America's legal and religious history.

Chief Justice Rehnquist, writing for the majority, said:[35]

> Of course, the 10 Commandments are religious—they were so viewed at their inception and so remain. The monument therefore has religious significance...Simply having religious content or promoting a message consistent with a religious doctrine does not run afoul of the Establishment clause.

Equal Access

Although it is settled law that state-supported prayer, Bible readings and devotional exercises are unconstitutional, a number of related questions have come up in recent years.

The use of public school buildings for religious activities was at issue in *Board of Education of the Westside Community Schools v. Mergens*, 496 U.S. 226 (1990). The case challenged the **Equal Access Act of 1984**. Congress had required public secondary schools receiving federal funds to permit student religious groups to meet on school property, if other extra-curricular groups are permitted to do so.

If even one student group is given access to facilities, the school becomes a "limited open forum" and all groups then must be given equal access, including religious groups.

Bridget Mergens sought access for a Christian Bible study group. Since some 30 student organizations used the school facilities, the equal access rule was in effect. Separationists argued that to give access to a Bible study group was equivalent to state endorsement of religion. The Supreme Court disagreed, 8-1, upholding the law.

Justice O'Connor noted that Congress wrote the Equal Access Act because it wanted to "prevent discrimination against religious and other types of speech." This, she concluded, "is undeniably secular."

The law also was neutral. It did not, she wrote, advance religion. There is, she observed, a "crucial difference between government speech endorsing religion... and private speech endorsing religion."

O'Connor also concluded that high school students were "mature enough and likely to understand that a school does not endorse religion or support student speech, that it merely permits on a nondiscriminatory basis."

In 1981, the Court had ruled, in *Widmar v. Vincent*, against college officials who denied use of campus facilities to a student religious group at University of Missouri, Kansas City. The group wanted to use university facilities for Bible study and prayer. Administrators viewed this as a violation of separation of church and state.

However, the Court held by an 8-1 vote, to the contrary. College students, it found, are unlikely to be influenced by these activities. **If the university permits other student organizations to use campus facilities, and allows outside speakers to address a variety of student concerns, it would be discriminatory to single out religious groups for exclusion, the Court ruled.**[36]

Good News Club et al. v. Milford Central School, 533 U.S. 98 (2001)

The U.S. Supreme Court considered another access case, granting *certiorari* to review a decision of the U.S. Court of Appeals for the Second Circuit. It handed down its decision on June 11, 2001.

Acting under state law, the Milford, N.Y., Central School adopted a policy authorizing district residents to use its building for a number of after-school activities. These included "instruction in education, learning, or the arts and social, civil, recreational, and entertainment uses relating to community welfare."

Rev. Stephen D. Fournier and his wife Darleen, district residents eligible to use the school facilities upon approval of their proposed use, were sponsors of the Good News Club. The group is a private, evangelical Christian organization for children between the ages of 6-12. It operates more than 4600 chapters around the country, and urges children to accept Jesus Christ as a personal savior.

After a September, 1996, decision was made to stop busing members of the Good News Club from their school to the church, about six miles south on Route 28, the Fourniers submitted a request to hold the club's weekly after-school meetings in the school building.

Milford, N.Y., is a farming community located in the foothills of the Catskills Mountain Range. Baseball fans, making a pilgrimage to Cooperstown, site of the game's Hall of Fame, come within 10 miles of the village of about 3000 residents.

Milford school officials denied the Good News Club request on grounds that the proposed use—to pray, sing songs, hear Bible stories and memorize scripture—was the equivalent of religious worship, forbidden by the community use policy. The club, School Superintendent Robert McGruder concluded, was not simply a discussion group that talked about morals from a religious viewpoint, but was engaged in a form of religious instruction.

In barring the club from meeting on school grounds, officials claimed that they were following state law designed to avert any appearance of official sponsorship of religious worship and to protect children from getting the impression that the school endorsed a particular religion.

In January, 1997, the Good News Club's attorney informed school officials that, in denying the club access to a public building while permitting other groups, such as the Boy Scouts, Girl Scouts and 4-H Club, to use it, they were violating the Good News Club's constitutional rights. School officials agreed to reconsider the request, but again denied it. In February, 1997, the Board of Education adopted a resolution denying the group access once and for all.

A month later the club sued, alleging, among other things, that the denial of their application violated free speech rights under the First and 14th Amendments, and Equal Protection of the Law under the 14th Amendment and the 1993 Religious Freedom Restoration Act.

Initially, U.S. District Court Judge Thomas McAvoy issued a preliminary injunction preventing the schools from keeping Good News Club members from meeting in its facilities. Later, however, Judge McAvoy vacated the injunction and dismissed the case on grounds that the school was a "limited public forum" and had never allowed religious groups to meet on campus in the past. He found that the club's goal was to teach religion, not morals and values in a religious context, like the Boy Scouts.

The Good News Cub appealed to the Second Circuit, which rejected the club's contention that Milford's restriction was unreasonable. It held (2-1) that, because the club's subject matter was religious and its activities fell outsides the bounds of pure moral character development, Milford's policy was constitutional subject discrimination, not unconstitutional viewpoint discrimination.

The U.S. Supreme Court disagreed. It held (6-3) that Milford had violated the club's free speech rights when it excluded the group from meeting after hours at the school. The High Court noted that both parties to the dispute agreed that Milford operates a limited public forum. While such forums are not required to allow persons to engage in every kind of speech, the Court said that power to restrict speech is not without limits. Restrictions must not discriminate against speech based on viewpoint, and must be reasonable in light of the forum's purpose.

In denying access to the school's limited public forum because the Good News Club was religious in nature, Milford discriminated against the group because of its viewpoint. This violated the Free Speech Clause, the High Tribunal held. It also noted that permitting the club to meet on the school's premises would not have violated the First Amendment's Establishment Clause.

Meetings were to be held after school hours, were not sponsored by the school, and were open to any student who obtained parental consent, not just club members. Milford made its forum available to other organizations.

Justice Clarence Thomas reasoned that allowing the club to speak on school grounds would not threaten neutrality toward religion. On the contrary, it would ensure it. He noted that, to the extent that "the community" would feel coercive pressure to engage in club activities, the relevant community is the parents who choose whether their children will attend club meetings, not the children themselves

The Court, he added, has never foreclosed private religious conduct during non-school hours merely because it takes place on school premises where elementary school children may be present.

Even if the Court were to consider the possible misperceptions by schoolchildren in deciding whether there is an Establishment Clause violation, the facts of this case simply do not support Milford's conclusion.

Justice Thomas wrote:[37]

We cannot say that the danger that children would misperceive the endorsement of religion is any greater than the danger that they would perceive a hostility toward the religious viewpoint if the club were excluded from the public forum.

Justice Thomas' opinion was joined by Chief Justice William Rehnquist and Associate Justices Sandra Day O'Connor, Antonin Scalia, Anthony Kennedy and Stephen G. Breyer. Justices John Paul Stevens, David Souter and Ruth Bader Ginsburg dissented.

The Parochiaid Issue

Possibly the school prayer issue aroused the deepest feelings among those concerned with church-state questions during the early 1960s. Later in that decade and well into the 1970s, another issue stimulated intense debate between "separationists" and "accommodationists," the question of "**parochiaid**." A major First Amendment issue is whether the state may provide aid to church-connected schools. The Court has tried to distinguish between **permissible aid to the child and impermissible aid to religion.** The Court has not always been entirely consistent on the matter. It seldom makes broad, sweeping and philosophical rulings.

In 1968, a six-member majority found that a New York law supplying free secular textbooks to both parochial and public school children did not violate the Establishment Clause. Justice Byron White, speaking for the Court in *Board of Education v. Allen,* drew a line between state aid extended primarily to benefit students, such as textbooks, and the kind of assistance that constitutes direct aid to religion. The law, he said, must have a valid secular purpose and its primary effect must neither advance nor inhibit religion.[38]

A deeply-divided Supreme Court ruled, 5-4, in *Tilton v. Richardson,* that a Federal aid program for construction of church-owned classrooms not used for religious purposes was constitutional. The case challenged the constitutionality of Title I of the Higher Education Facilities Act of 1963. The law provided building construction grants to colleges and universities as long as the facility would be "used exclusively for secular education purposes."[39]

The Lemon Test: Alton Lemon filed a taxpayer's suit against David Kurtzman, Pennsylvania superintendent of schools, to prevent implementation of a "parochiaid" plan. In *Lemon v. Kurtzman* and *Earley v. DiCenso,* a Rhode Island companion case, the Court invalidated laws subsidizing teacher salaries in church-connected schools. Although limited to those teaching "secular subjects," such as languages, science and mathematics, the Court nonetheless held that such laws constituted direct aid to religion and were therefore unconstitutional. An eight member majority, with only Justice White dissenting, found "excessive state entanglement with religion" in *Lemon.*[40]

Lemon is a landmark case because the Court developed a three-part test a law must pass to survive an Establishment Clause challenge.

(1) The statute must have a secular, rather than a religious purpose.
(2) The law must be neutral. It may neither advance nor inhibit religion.
(3) Government must avoid "excessive entanglement" with religion. This, as noted, was the test that the Pennsylvania and Rhode Island laws failed.

In a landmark 1973 ruling, the Court declared unconstitutional a New York state law providing **grants** to non-public schools **for maintenance and repair.** The statute also gave **tax credits** to parents of children attending church-connected schools, and **tuition reimbursement** to low-income parents. Justice Lewis Powell, writing for the majority, restated the Lemon test.[41]

To pass muster under the Establishment Clause, the law in question, first, must reflect a clearly secular legislative purpose...second, must have a primary effect that neither advances nor inhibits religion...and third, must avoid excessive government entanglement with religion.

Serious students of religion in America point to a frequently ignored dimension of these problems. While it is respectable to dress up one's arguments in constitutional language, it is nonetheless true that motives are not always pure. There remains in the U.S. a legacy of anti-Catholicism, anti-Semitism, anti-Mormonism. Some Americans are strongly opposed to "fundamentalism," as they define it. Many powerful interest groups argue that we must maintain the secular state and that aid to church-connected schools will put too much politics in religion or too much religion in politics, something the Founding Fathers did not intend.

Agostini et al. v. Felton et al., 521 U.S. 203 (1997)

For many years, one of the major aspects of the parochiaid debate has been whether public school teachers should be permitted to offer remedial and other special education to students enrolled in parochial schools. Under the *Lemon* test, the high tribunal struck down such aid in two 1985 companion cases, *Grand Rapids (Michigan) v. Ball*, 473 U.S. 373, and *Aguilar v. Felton*, 473 U.S. 402.

The New York City Board of Education was bound for 12 years by a Federal court injunction forbidding it from sending teachers into parochial schools to guide and instruct low-income, at-risk children. Although Congress specifically provided Federal funds for this purpose, the Supreme Court had ruled that providing this service inside a religious school violates the Establishment Clause of the First Amendment.

In June, 1997, the Supreme Court revisited this question and reversed its earlier rulings. At issue was a 1965 Federal funding program known as Title I, intended to educate all school children who need remedial help, including those in parochial schools. With the backing of the Clinton Administration, New York City schools asked the Court to free it from the requirements of its original 1985 ruling. It noted that a majority of current justices had complained about the 1985 ruling in subsequent decisions.

"Interaction between church and state is inevitable," Justice Sandra Day O'Connor wrote for a 5-4 majority. "We have always tolerated some level of involvement between the two." O'Connor noted that what had changed over the years was the Court's view of whether particular public aid to religion had "an impermissible effect," for example, requiring a government to get excessively involved in the workings of a church institution.

While Justice O'Connor's ruling emphasized the narrow scope of the Court's decision, focused on a Federal program that provides funds for remedial education nationwide, some religious leaders immediately declared that it could help their efforts to get government to pay for vouchers that could be used by parents to send their children to religious schools. In *Agostini v. Felton*, O'Connor said that the Court had expressly disavowed the idea that the First Amendment absolutely bars the placing of a public employee in a sectarian school. She noted that in a 1993 ruling, the Court had allowed a public school teacher to enter a Roman Catholic school as a sign-language interpreter for a deaf student.

Title I "does not result in any governmental indoctrination; define its recipients by reference to religion; or create an excessive entanglement between church and state," O'Connor wrote. And further:

Our cases subsequent to *Aguilar* have…modified in two significant respects the approach we use to assess indoctrination. First, we have abandoned the presumption…that placement of public employees on parochial school grounds inevitably results in the impermissible effect of state-sponsored indoctrination or constitutions a symbolic union between government and religion…

Second, we have departed from the rule relied on in *Ball* that all government aid that directly aids the educational function of religious schools is invalid…

O'Connor was joined in the majority by Chief Justice William Rehnquist and Associate Justices Antonin Scalia, Anthony M. Kennedy and Clarence Thomas.

Dissenting Justices John Paul Stevens, David Souter, and Ruth Bader Ginsburg said in a statement: "Constitutional lines have to be drawn and on one side of every one of them is an otherwise sympathetic case that provokes impatience with the Constitution and with the line. But constitutional liens are the price of constitutional government."

Mitchell v. Helms, 530 U.S. 793 (2000)

Parochial school systems scored a major victory on June 29, 2000, when the Supreme Court, overruling a decision of the U.S. Court of Appeals for the Fifth Circuit, broadened the kinds of public aid that can be given to religious schools. The High Tribunal ruled that governments may lend computers and other instructional materials to private schools without violating the First Amendment.

The case of *Mitchell v. Helms* originated nearly 15 years before the Court decision when a group of Louisiana taxpayers challenged a Federal law which provided library books and television sets to church-connected schools. Later the argument focused on computers and software, as educational technology changed.

In 1998, the Fifth Circuit ruled that this kind of parochiaid violated the First Amendment provision that "Congress shall make no law respecting an establishment of religion, or prohibiting the free exercise thereof."

The Federal aid questioned in *Mitchell* was authorized by the Elementary and Secondary Education Act, a Johnson-era (1965) statute that has become the major vehicle for dispensing U.S. aid to American schools.

The Supreme Court, by a vote of 6-3, used broad language that critics feared could be used to consider publicly funded tuition vouchers for parochial school students. Justice Clarence Thomas, writing for a plurality of four justices (Chief Justice Rehnquist, Associate Justices Antonin Scalia, Anthony Kennedy and himself), declared that providing computers and other materials to all types of schools in no way advances any single religion.

Thomas said:

If the religious, irreligious and areligious are all alike eligible for governmental aid, no one would conclude that any indoctrination that any particular recipient conducts had been done at the behest of the government.

The Thomas opinion departed from Supreme Court opinions of the 1970s that limited public aid to church-connected schools. Those standards distinguished between direct and indirect aid and barred public aid to "pervasively sectarian" schools. Justice Thomas traced this to an outburst of anti-Catholic sentiment in the 1870s. He added that, over the years, the Supreme Court itself has done its bit to keep anti-Catholicism alive.

Thomas concluded that it did not matter whether the computers could be diverted to sectarian uses because the equipment itself does not embody religion. "A government computer or overhead projector does not itself inculcate a religious message, even when it is conveying one," he said.

Two other justices who formed the majority would not go that far, writing in a concurring opinion that they found "troubling" the expansive view taken in the Thomas opinion. Justices Sandra Day O'Connor and Stephen Breyer warned that the opinion endorsed by the four justices "foreshadows the approval of direct monetary subsidies to religious organizations, even when they use the money to advance religious objectives."

O'Connor's concurring opinion reasoned that teachers in parochial schools could abide by the ban on using government-provided computers to impart religious lessons, just as they have long been trusted not to use textbooks for that purpose.

In a dissenting opinion, Justice David Souter argued that whether public aid was distributed evenhandedly to different types of schools should not be the only constitutional test of the program. If that were the case, he wrote, "religious schools could be blessed with government funding as massive as expenditures made for the benefit of their public school counterparts, and religious missions would thrive on public money."

The Clinton administration hoped to wire every school in the nation, public or private, to the Internet. That was a primary educational goal of the President. His education secretary, Richard Riley, applauded the Supreme Court ruling because it ensured that "all children have access to computers and advanced technologies."

Not everyone was pleased with the decision. Barry Lynn, executive director of Americans United for Separation of Church and State, said:

> At public expense, religious schools can now have students surf the Internet to read the Bible in religion classes, learn theology from Jerry Falwell or download crucifixes as screen savers…We can now expect religious schools to clamor for an ever-increasing number of services paid for with tax dollars.

The School Voucher Reform Case: *Zelman v. Simmons-Harris*, 536 U.S. 639 (2002)

In 1995, a time when Cleveland, Ohio, public schools were in a condition described by the *Washington Post* as "near breakdown," the Ohio General Assembly adopted the Pilot Project Scholarship and Tutoring Program, a school voucher plan.

By the year 2002, the plan provided residents of one of the nation's worst-rated public school systems with vouchers worth up to $2,250 for about 4000 children from low-income families. They can attend any of 56 participating schools of their choice. Almost all (96-99%) are church-related. Most are Catholic. Although the voucher amounts almost cover the cost of a church-subsidized education, they in no way cover the normal tuition at secular academies.

It should be noted that secular private schools and suburban public schools are eligible to participate in the program. The fact that most have not done so is not the fault of the voucher program itself, Ohio Assistant Attorney General Judith French argued to the U.S. Supreme Court.

The program twice was tested in the Ohio Supreme Court and was upheld both times.

But the U.S. Court of Appeals for the Sixth Circuit disagreed in 2001, setting the stage for the appeal to the U.S. Supreme Court, which accepted the case and heard oral arguments in February, 2002. Some four months late, on the last day of the term, it held, 5-4, that the Cleveland program does not offend the Establishment Clause.

In a nutshell, the Supreme Court ruled that use of tax funds to send disadvantaged students to religious schools is constitutionally valid, providing that choice is offered.

Chief Justice William Rehnquist, writing for the majority, said:

> The question presented is whether this program offends the Establishment Clause of the United States Constitution. We hold that it does not...In 1995, a Federal District Court declared a crisis of magnitude and placed the entire Cleveland school district under state control...The district had failed to meet any of 18 state standards for minimal acceptable performance. Only 1 in 10 ninth-graders could pass a basic proficiency examination and students at all levels performed at a dismal rate compared with students in other Ohio public schools. More than two-thirds of high school students either dropped or failed out before graduation. Of those students who managed to reach their senior year, one of every four still failed to graduate. Of those who did graduate, few could read, write or compute at levels comparable to their counterparts in other cities.

> ...We believe that the program challenged here is a program of true private choice...the Ohio program is neutral in all respects toward religion. It is part of a general and multi-faceted undertaking by the State of Ohio to provide educational opportunities to the children of a failed school district. It confers educational assistance directly to a broad class of individuals without reference to religion., i.e., any parent of a school-age child who resides in the Cleveland City School District. The program permits the participation of *all* schools within the district, religious and non-religious. Adjacent public schools also may participate and have a financial incentive to do so. <u>Program benefits are available to participating families on neutral terms, with no reference to religion. The only preference stated anywhere in the program is a preference for low-income families,</u> who receive greater assistance and are given priority for admission at participating schools. There are no financial incentives that skew the program toward religious schools.

> ...There is also no evidence that the program fails to provide genuine opportunities for Cleveland parents to select secular educational options for their school-age children. Cleveland school children enjoy a range of educational choices: They may remain in public school as before, remain in public school with privately-funded tutoring aid, obtain a scholarship and choose a religious school, obtain a scholarship and choose a non-religious private school, enroll in a community school, or enroll in a magnet school. That 45 of 56 private schools now participating in the program are religious schools does not condemn it as a violation of the Establishment Clause. The Establishment Clause question is whether Ohio is coercing parents into sending their children to religious schools, and that question must be answered by evaluating all options Ohio provides Cleveland school children, only one of which is to obtain a program scholarship and choose a religious school.

> ...In sum, the Ohio program is entirely neutral with respect to religion. It provides benefits directly to a wide spectrum of individuals, defined only by financial need and residence in a particular school district. It permits such individuals to exercise genuine choice among options, public and private, secular and religious. The program is therefore a program of true private choice. In keeping with an unbroken line of decisions rejecting challenges to similar programs, we hold that the program does not offend the Establishment Clause.

The judgment of the Court of Appeals is reversed.

The Chief Justice was joined in the majority by Associate Justices Sandra Day O'Connor, Anthony Kennedy, Antonin Scalia and Clarence Thomas.

Dissenters were Justices David Souter, John Paul Stevens, Ruth Bader Ginsburg and Stephen Breyer. Disputing the majority's view that the Cleveland program treats religion neutrally and that parents have a real choice among schools, Souter wrote: "There is... no way to interpret the 96.6% of current voucher money going to religious schools as reflecting a free and genuine choice by the families that apply for vouchers."

Among Supreme Court justices, church-state cases appear to be bitterly fought and frequently come down to a single vote.

The Cleveland program is one of only three voucher programs in operation that permit participation by church-sponsored schools. The largest program is in Milwaukee, which has 10,000 students in the plan. Florida, the newest and smallest program, has only a few dozen students enrolled.

Two other states, New Hampshire and Vermont, have voucher plans which permit high school students to attend non-public, but not church-sponsored schools.

Much of the interest in education vouchers in recent years has been stimulated by the crisis of inner-city public schools. In Cleveland, New York, and Milwaukee, for example, less than half of all Black students graduate from high school. Some supporters of voucher plans argue that it is a way for students and parents to opt out of failing public schools.

Ballot initiatives on educational vouchers were roundly defeated in 2000 in Michigan and California, but the idea remains viable, given the Supreme Court ruling.

At the national level, President George W. Bush supports the idea of vouchers. He was, however, unable to persuade Congress to enact a national voucher program.

State supreme courts have considered several challenges to vouchers. For example, the Florida Supreme Court ruled, in 2006, that vouchers violate the uniformity clause of the state constitution. Other state supreme courts, including Wisconsin, have held that such uniformity clauses do not rule them out.

Recent Cases: Unusual Religious Practices

The Supreme Court annually places on its docket a number of "cutting edge of the law" cases involving freedom of religion. Some of these involve groups who claim that their unusual religious beliefs and practices are protected against government action by the First and 14th Amendments.

In 1990, two members of the Native American Church, Alfred Smith and Galen Black, took peyote as part of a religious ceremony. Peyote contains the hallucinogen mescaline, but has been used in Native American religious ceremonies for centuries.

Smith and Black were not arrested for taking drugs. But they were fired by their employer, a drug rehabilitation center. When they sought unemployment benefits, Oregon denied the claim on grounds that they were discharged for "**work related misconduct**."

Smith and Black then sued the state, arguing that a ban on peyote for religious ceremonies, and subsequent denial of their unemployment claims, violated the Free Exercise Clause. When the Native Americans won in the Oregon Supreme Court, the state appealed that ruling to the U.S. Supreme Court.

The nation's highest tribunal upheld the Oregon law. Justice Antonin Scalia, writing for the Court, said:[42]

We have never held that an individual's religious beliefs excuse him from compliance with an otherwise valid law prohibiting conduct that the State is free to regulate. On the contrary, the record of more than a century of our free exercise jurisprudence contradicts that proposition.

Because respondents' ingestion of peyote was prohibited under Oregon law, and because that prohibition is constitutional, Oregon may, consistent with the Free Exercise Clause, deny respondents unemployment compensation when their dismissal results from use of the drug.

The Religious Freedom Restoration Act

The *Smith* ruling was very controversial. In its aftermath, Hmong families in Rhode Island failed to prevent autopsies of dead relatives. The Hmongs believe that such a procedure destroys the possibility of everlasting life. Catholic teaching hospitals in Maryland lost accreditation because they refused to perform abortions, which the Roman Catholic Church views as tantamount to murder.

A bipartisan coalition of legislative leaders, ranging from Liberals like Ted Kennedy to Conservatives like Orrin Hatch, chairman of the powerful Senate Judiciary Committee, led a move to overturn the High Court ruling. They believed that *Smith* improperly restricted religious liberty.

With the enthusiastic support of President Clinton, Congress enacted the **Religious Freedom Restoration Act of 1993**. The law, also supported by a broad coalition of religious groups, was passed by a near-unanimous vote. Leaders of some religious groups, especially those outside the "mainline" denominations, complained that some general state and local laws discriminated against their members. Adversaries like Americans United for Separation of Church and State and the Conservative Traditional Values Coalition set aside their differences because they agreed on an important principle.

That principle: government should not inhibit believers from practicing their faith, unless they can prove that there is a "compelling" reason for doing so. The statute provided that **governments can infringe on religious practices only if they have a health, safety or other "compelling interest" in doing so.**

After enactment of the RFRA, state and local officials complained that the law had gone too far. California officials were upset that a group of Jehovah's Witnesses successfully sued over having to take a loyalty oath as a condition of employment with the state. An Amish group in Wisconsin refused to post bright orange safety triangles on their horse-drawn buggies and escaped fines when the courts ruled in their favor. In New York state, a Native American prison guard won a lawsuit after refusing to cut his hair. In Washington, D.C., the Western Presbyterian Church in Foggy Bottom won its struggle to keep open a controversial homeless feeding program to which District officials had objected.

Other bitter and often emotional disputes arose. For example, prisoners in the District of Columbia used the law to claim that they needed special accommodations to fulfill their religious traditions. Visitors posing as missionaries had unsupervised "spiritual" meetings with inmates. It was later discovered that they were smuggling drugs into prison.

The law was tested in the case of *City of Boerne (Texas) v. Flores*, 521 U.S. 507 (1997), argued February 19,1997, and decided on June 25 of that year.

Flores, the Catholic archbishop of San Antonio, had applied for a building permit to enlarge a church in Boerne, Texas. After local zoning authorities denied the permit, relying on an ordinance governing historic preservation in a district which included the church, the archbishop sued under RFRA. The Federal District Court rejected the archdiocesan argument, concluding that Congress had exceeded the scope of its enforcement power under Section 5 of the 14th Amendment in enacting the statute. However, the trial court's decision was reversed by the Fifth Circuit Court of Appeals. The U.S. Supreme Court then took the case, setting the stage for a landmark decision.

The issue was whether the Religious Freedom Restoration Act violated the First and 14th Amendments, and whether Congress gave religion special privilege over other expressions of conscience in passing the statute.

The Supreme Court, by a 6-3 vote, struck down the law as an example of congressional overreaching.

RFRA, the majority held, is not a proper exercise of congressional enforcement power because it contradicts vital principles necessary to maintain separation of powers and the federal-state balance. The legislative record lacks examples of any instances of generally applicable laws passed because of religious bigotry in the past 40 years. Rather, the emphasis of the RFRA hearings was on laws like the one at issue that place incidental burdens on religion. It is difficult to maintain that such laws are based on animus or hostility to the burdened religious practices or that they indicated some widespread pattern of religious discrimination in this country.

RFRA's most serious shortcoming, the Court held, lies in the fact that it is so out of proportion to a supposed remedial or preventive objective that it cannot be understood as responsible to, or designed to prevent, unconstitutional behavior. Its sweeping coverage ensures its intrusion at every level of government, displacing laws and prohibiting official actions of almost every description and regardless of subject matter...All told, RFRA is a considerable congressional intrusion into the States' traditional prerogatives and general authority to regulate for the health and welfare of their citizens, and is not designed to identify and counteract state laws likely to be unconstitutional because of their treatment of religion.

Justice Anthony Kennedy, writing for the majority, concluded:[43]

> Numerous state laws, such as the zoning regulations at issue here, impose a substantial burden on a large class of individuals. When the exercise of religion has been burdened in any incidental way by a law of general application, it does not follow that the persons affected have been burdened any more than other citizens, let alone burdened because of their religious beliefs.

Impact of Boerne v. Flores: The Supreme Court ruling means that *Smith* remains the guiding legal principle. Experts in church-state law say that only blatant and clearly bigoted attempts by state and local governments to discriminate against religious practices will be illegal. Such attempts have been rare in modern U.S. history.

Although many religious leaders and members of Congress were displeased by the *Boerne* ruling, a group of state attorneys general argued that they did not need the power of a federal law to protect religious liberties. Some of them cautioned that the decision may not be as dire as some religious activists claimed.

Animal Rights Activists, Hialeah, Fla., and the Church of the Lukumi Babalu Aye

In 1993, the Supreme Court took the case of *Church of Lukumi Babalu Aye v. Hialeah*, 508 U.S. 520.

The city of Hialeah, Fla., in response to complaints from animal rights activists and others, enacted legislation following an emergency public session of Council. The ordinance noted residents' "concern" over religious practices of Haitian immigrants, deemed inconsistent with public morals, peace or safety, and declared the city's "commitment" to forbidding such practices. The ordinance incorporates Florida's animal cruelty law and broadly punishes whoever "unnecessarily or cruelly…kills any animal." The law further stipulates that "sacrifice" is "to unnecessarily kill…an animal in a…ritual…not for the primary purpose of food consumption" and forbids the "possession, sacrifice, or slaughter of an animal if it is killed in any type of ritual."

The Church of Lukumi Babalu Aye practices the Santeria religion, which uses animal sacrifice as one of its principal forms of devotion. The animals are killed by cutting their carotid arteries and are cooked and eaten following all Santeria rituals except healing and death rites. The city ordinance followed a decision by the church to lease land and establish a house of worship in Hialeah. The Santeria congregants then took their case to the Federal District Court, which ruled for the city. The tribunal held that, among other things, there was a compelling governmental interest in protecting public health and that cruelty to animals fully justified the absolute prohibition on ritual sacrifice. The 11th Circuit Court of Appeals affirmed the decision, but the Supreme Court took the case and reversed that judgment.

Justice Kennedy delivered the opinion of the Court, concluding that the laws in question were enacted contrary to free exercise principles and are, therefore, void. He reasoned that each of the ordinances pursues the city's governmental interests only against conduct motivated by religious belief and thereby violates the requirement that laws burdening religious practice must be of general applicability. They are not narrowly tailored to accomplish the asserted governmental interests. All are overbroad.

Gonzales v. O Centro Espirta Beneficiente Uniao Do Vegetal, 126 S. Ct. 1211 (2006)

Federal authorities staged a drug raid on Jeffrey Bronfan's Santa Fe, New Mexico, home in May, 1999, and seized some 30 gallons of hoasca tea. The tea contained dimethyltrypltamine (DMT), a hallucinogenic drug.

Bronfan, leader of the Brazil-based O Centro Espirita Beneficiente Uniao Do Vegetal (UDV), sued the Federal government, charging violations of the Religious Freedom Restoration Act and his church's First Amendment rights. He also asked for an injunction that would allow UDV members to consume the tea during religious services.

The government's position was that DMT is a Schedule I drug under the Controlled Substances Act, and has no recognized medical value. It also is banned under the 1971 United Nations Convention on Psychotropic Substances, a treaty signed by more than 160 countries, including the U.S.

A Federal District Court in New Mexico granted the UDV request for an injunction, noting that the group was likely to win its case under terms of the Religious Freedom Restoration Act. The U.S. Court of Appeals for the 10th Circuit ruled that the tea was protected under RFDA and that the government had failed to prove that hoasca tea endangers users' health, could be diverted to other users or violates the UN treaty.

The U.S. Supreme Court accepted review of the case in April, 2005, and, in its first religious freedom case under new Chief Justice John Roberts, ruled on February 21, 2006, that the small sect may use the hallucinogenic tea as part of a ritual intended to "connect" members with God. UDV members, who combine Christian beliefs and Brazilian customs, drink the tea twice a month at four-hour ceremonies.

The government had argued that the drug not only violates the Controlled Substances Act, but also a treaty in which the U.S. commits itself to prevent importation of DMT, a Schedule I drug under Federal law. It further contended that the U.S. had a legitimate interest in protecting practitioners' health and safety, preventing diversion of the drug to other users, and complying with an international treaty on psychotropic substances. As noted, lower Federal courts had ruled that the government had failed to demonstrate those interests.

Speaking for a unanimous 8-0 court (New Justice Samuel Alito did not participate in the case), the Chief Justice wrote:[44]

> The Government's argument echoes the classic rejoinder of bureaucrats throughout history: If I make an exception for you, I'll have to make one for everybody, so no exceptions...The Religious Freedom Restoration Act operates by mandating consideration, under the compelling interest test, of exceptions to rules of general applicability...Congress determined that the legislated test "is a workable test for striking sensible balances between religious liberty and competing prior governmental interests.

Justice Roberts also wrote:[45]

> The law already contains an exception that explicitly allows members of the Native American Church to use peyote in religious ceremonies, even though peyote is a Schedule I drug. If such use is permitted...for hundreds of thousands of Native Americans practicing their faith, it is difficult to see how those same findings alone can preclude any consideration of a similar exception for the 130 or so American members of the UDV who want to practice theirs.

The high court's ruling did not end the case. It ruled only on a preliminary injunction that barred the government from enforcing the federal drug law against the Brazil-based church. The case goes back to lower Federal courts, where the government is entitled to make its case more fully. The Supreme Court guidelines, however, may make it difficult for the government to prevail.

Religious Student Publications

University of Virginia, a public institution, authorized payments from its Student Activities Fund to outside contractors for printing costs of a wide variety of student publications called "Contracted Independent Organizations." Mandatory student fees supported a broad range of extracurricular student activities. The Contracted Independent Organizations (CIOs) were required to include a disclaimer in their dealings with third parties and in all written materials. It said that they were independent of the university and the university was not responsible for them.

One student organization, Wide Awake Productions, was denied funding because its newspaper "primarily promotes or manifests a particular belief in or about a deity or an ultimate reality," forbidden by the University of Virginia's Student Activity Fee Guidelines.

The Christian students sued the university, claiming that its refusal to pay their printing bill violated their First Amendment right to freedom of speech and press. Both the Federal District Court and the Fourth Circuit rulings supported the university's claim that to give financial aid to the group would violate the Establishment Clause of the First Amendment. The Supreme Court, however, saw it differently.

In *Rosenberger et al. v. Rector and Visitors of University of Virginia et al*, 515 U.S. 819 (1995), the highest court in the land held that guidelines used to deny Student Activity Fee support to the Christian group were a denial of their right of religious speech.

On the other hand, some Conservative Christian students at the University of Wisconsin objected to the use of money from their student activity fees for funding groups whose values they deemed contrary to Christian morality. They argued that they should not be compelled to pay that portion of their fees to subsidize 18 political or ideological groups.

Groups targeted by the suit included the International Socialist Organization, the Lesbian, Gay, Bisexual Campus Center and Amnesty International.

Both the U.S. District Court and the U.S. Court of Appeals for the Seventh Circuit agreed with the plaintiffs, stressing the fact that the First Amendment incorporates the right not to speak and the right not to be required to subsidize the speech of another.

The Supreme Court reversed in *Board of Regents of the University of Wisconsin System v. Southworth,* 120 S. Ct. 1346 (2000).

Justice Kennedy, author of the Court's unanimous opinion, asserted that the "First Amendment permits a public university to charge its students an activity fee used to fund a program to facilitate extracurricular student speech if the program is viewpoint neutral." He noted that the University of Wisconsin did administer the program in such a way, and that the "sole purpose of the fee was to facilitate the free and open exchange of ideas by, and among, its students."

Graduation prayers: It is settled constitutional law that required public school prayers violate the First and 14th Amendment. But what about a brief prayer as part of a baccalaureate program? The Court dealt with this issue in *Lee v. Weisman* (1992), ruling that public schools may not include nondenominational prayers, led by representatives of major faiths, at graduation ceremonies.

Religious Displays

In *Lynch v. Donnelly* (1984), the Court upheld the erection of a nativity scene as part of an official Christmas display by the city of Pawtucket, R.I. The city used a local park owned by a nonprofit organization to erect a holiday display, featuring both religious and secular Yuletide symbols.

Pawtucket had spent a small amount of money to buy a creche and to erect and dismantle the display each year. The Rhode Island Civil Liberties Union sued the city, arguing that these and other expenditures violated the Establishment Clause.

Writing for the Court, Chief Justice Burger said:[46]

> It would be ironic...if the inclusion of a single symbol of a particular historical religious event, as part of a celebration acknowledged in the Western World for 20 centuries, and in this country by the people, by the executive branch, by the Congress, and the courts for two centuries, would so "taint" the city's exhibit as to render it violative of the Establishment Clause. To forbid the use of one passive symbol—the creche—at the time people are taking note of the season with Christmas hymns and carols in public schools...would be a stilted overreaction contrary to our history and to our holdings.

32

Supreme Court critics labelled the Pawtucket decision the "Reindeer Rule." They were joined by some religious leaders who applauded the decision, but not its logic. They resented the fact that symbols of the infant Jesus, Mary and Joseph were exhibited next to reindeer and elves. These same leaders decried the commercialization of the season and the watering down of its religious message, the birth of a savior. Some of them echoed the familiar sermon: too many Americans have taken Christ out of Christmas and even use the term Xmas as a substitute for it.

Five years later, in *County of Allegheny v. ACLU*, the Court considered a challenge to Pittsburgh-area holiday exhibits erected on public property. A Roman Catholic group donated a creche, displayed on the main staircase inside the Allegheny County Courthouse. A banner read, "Glory to God in the Highest."

The Court held that the government could not erect this nativity scene in the courthouse because **it amounted to endorsement of Christian doctrine.**

At the same time, the Court upheld display of a 18 foot menorah, a Jewish symbol of Chanukah, placed next to a Christmas tree and accompanied by a sign extolling liberty. Writing for the majority, Justice Harry Blackmun noted that:[47]

> ...the display of the Chanukah menorah in front of the City-County Building may well present a closer constitutional question. The menorah, one must recognize, is a religious symbol: it serves to commemorate the miracle of the oil as described in the Talmud. But the menorah's message is not exclusively religious. The menorah is the primary visual symbol for a holiday that, like Christmas, has both religious and secular dimensions. Moreover, the menorah here stands next to a Christmas tree and a sign saluting liberty. While no challenge has been made here to the display of the tree and the sign, their presence is obviously relevant in determining the effect of the menorah's display. The necessary result of placing a menorah next to a Christmas tree is to create an "overall holiday setting" that represents both Christmas and Chanukah – two holidays, not one.

The mere fact that Pittsburgh displays symbols of both Christmas and Chanukah does not end the constitutional inquiry. If the city celebrates both Christmas and Chanukah as religious holidays, then it violates the Establishment Clause. The simultaneous endorsement of Judaism and Christianity is no less constitutionally infirm than the endorsement of Christianity alone.

Conversely, if the city celebrates both Christmas and Chanukah as secular holidays, then its conduct is beyond the reach of the Establishment Clause. Because government may celebrate Christmas as a secular holiday, it follows that government may also acknowledge Chanukah as a secular holiday. Simply put, it would be a form of discrimination against Jews to allow Pittsburgh to celebrate Christmas as a cultural tradition while simultaneously disallowing the city's acknowledgment of Chanukah as a contemporaneous cultural tradition.

Accordingly, the relevant question for Establishment Clause purposes is whether the combined display of the tree, the sign, and the menorah has the effect of endorsing both Christian and Jewish faiths, or rather simply recognizes that both Christmas and Chanukah are part of the same winter holiday season, which has attained a secular status in our society. Of the two interpretations of this particular display, the latter seems far more plausible and is also in line with *Lynch*.

Although the focus of this chapter is the First Amendment, it should be noted that a provision of the Constitution which has considerable political importance, although it is not a source of constitutional debate, is Article VI, Section 3, which provides in part that ..."no religious test shall ever be required as a Qualification to any Office or public Trust under the United States."

American history is filled with episodes of religious prejudice and voters unquestionably cast their ballots for or against candidates on the basis of their religious preferences. No Jew ever has been nominated for President of the United States and only one, Sen. Joe Liberman of Connecticut, has been nominated for Vice President by a major party.

When Roman Catholic Al Smith, then governor of New York, was nominated as the Democratic Party's presidential candidate in 1928, several southern states which had not voted for a Republican since the Civil War, split the "Solid South."

Not until John Kennedy was elected in 1960 did the U.S. have a Catholic as President.

There was considerable talk in 1968 about Michigan Gov. George Romney. Could a Mormon be chosen as President? In 2008, the same question was raised about his son, Mitt, the former governor of Massachusetts. Polls indicated, given the number of respondents who said they would not support Romney because of his faith, that religious prejudice is a long way from dead early in the 21st Century.

The Constitution may require no religious test, but some American voters apparently still do. Attention also will be given to related questions of racial and gender discrimination in Chapter IV, with specific reference to the 2008 presidential campaigns of Democratic Party Senators Hillary Clinton of New York and Barack Obama of Illinois.

FREEDOM OF SPEECH

Although freedom of speech is one of the most precious liberties guaranteed by the First Amendment, it is by no means absolute. Great philosophers, such as John Stuart Mill, long have argued that it is perilous to assume that only majorities are right. Minorities must be given freedom to express unpopular, even hateful viewpoints. In his classic essay, *On Liberty,* Mill wrote:[48]

> If all mankind, minus one, were of one opinion, and only one person were of the contrary opinion, mankind would be no more justified in silencing that one person, than he, if he had the power, would be justified in silencing mankind. Were an opinion a person possesses of no value except to the owner; if to be obstructed in the enjoyment of it were simply a private injury, it would make some difference whether the injury was inflicted on a few persons or on many. But the peculiar evil of silencing the expression of opinion is it is robbing the human race. If the opinion is right, they are deprived of the opportunity of exchanging error for truth; if wrong, they lose, what is almost as great a benefit, the clearer perception and livelier impression of truth, produced by its collision with error.

However, certain free expression guidelines are drawn and limits imposed in even the most democratic of governments.

America's Founding Fathers realized very well that political and moral "Truth" is elusive. Soon after the birth of the United States, therefore, the First Congress proposed the Bill of Rights to meet the universal criticism of the anti-Federalists to the new Constitution: lack of a written statement of unalienable rights.

The First Amendment provides in part that "Congress shall make no law...abridging the freedom of speech." State constitutions contain similar provisions, forbidding public officials from infringing free expression of ideas. Although one does have an absolute, unqualified right to one's thoughts and beliefs, certain "actions" may be restrained by government.

Freedom of expression also may collide with the **police power of the state.** This authority, that all levels of U.S. government have, enables them to enact laws which protect public health, welfare, morals and safety. When such conflicts occur, the U.S. and state constitutions protect the individual.

Courts also prevent state and local infringement of basic rights, such as free speech and press, by applying the Due Process Clause of the 14th Amendment to specific cases.

Since 1925, in the landmark case of *Gitlow v. New York*, the U.S. Supreme Court has "incorporated" this First Amendment freedom into the 14th Amendment, thereby restraining the states and their political subdivisions. The Court has declared unconstitutional a number of state and local laws designed to curb freedom of expression.

Liberty and License: It should be noted that the First and 14th Amendments protect the individual only against government encroachment of his or her rights. It has been necessary for states and communities to pass laws to forbid infringement of free expression by private individuals. State libel and slander laws illustrate this point.

There is a basic difference between liberty and license, a difference not always recognized during tumultuous periods in American history. Liberty means freedom under law. It is the right to do something, provided we do not thereby injure our fellow citizens. Freedom, some would argue, is not free. It demands responsibility and respect for the rights of others. It is not a blank check to do as one pleases. License is an abuse of liberty. Slanderous speech or libelous publications would illustrate the point. The line, however, between liberty and license may not always be easily drawn. Courts must answer difficult questions and draw lines when conflicts inevitably arise.

Proponents of democracy assume that citizens should be free to express their ideas, either by speaking or by writing. It does not matter that some opinions are of "low-quality:" foolish, ill-informed, prejudicial, radical or reactionary. **There is no such thing as being "politically correct."** All "heretics" are welcome in a free-wheeling, democratic debate.

Democrats assume, as totalitarians do not, that **no group, nation, or individual has a monopoly on Truth.** History shows that what once was regarded as Eternal Truth was merely the orthodoxy of the time. In the era of Christopher Columbus, for example, "everyone knew" that the Earth was flat. The ideal of free expression is held so vital in the U.S. that the principle of censorship, either on political or moral grounds, historically has been repugnant to the courts.

National Security

One of the major problems faced by the U.S. and other democracies is the problem of war, hot or cold. Many contend that civil liberties tend to "contract" during emergencies when the life of the nation itself may be at issue. Lincoln once asked, "If a nation loses her life, what remains of her liberty?" Serious students of U.S. history never have questioned the need to limit freedom of speech during national emergencies, such as war. Sedition statutes go back to the earliest days of the republic. Two landmark cases in the annals of the U.S. Supreme Court illustrate the point, *Schenck v. U.S.*, and *Dennis v. U.S.*

Schenck: clear and present danger doctrine: During World War I, Congress passed the **Espionage Act.** Among other things, the law forbade speeches which obstructed the Allied war effort. One could not interfere with armed forces recruiting. One could not encourage young men of military age to dodge the draft or to desert from the military services. Charles Schenck, general secretary of the Socialist Party of Philadelphia, admitted that he had violated the act.

He argued, however, that his conviction by a Federal District Court was a miscarriage of justice because the Espionage Act violated the free speech and press (printed handbills) guarantees of the Constitution. The U.S. Supreme Court, however, could find nothing in the First or 14th Amendments to justify Schenck's conduct. Speaking through Justice Oliver Wendell Holmes, the high tribunal upheld Schenck's conviction. Holmes wrote in part:[49]

> The character of every act depends upon the circumstances in which it is done...The most stringent protection of free speech would not protect a man in falsely shouting fire in a theatre and causing a panic...The question in every case is whether the words are used in circumstances and are of such a nature as to create a clear and present danger and that they will bring about substantive evils that Congress has a right to prevent. It is a question of proximity and degree. When a nation is at war many things that might be said in time of peace are such a hindrance to its effort that their utterance will not be endured so long as men fight and no Court could regard them as protected by any constitutional right.

Government, according to Holmes' opinion, must prove clearly that a specific speech or handbill presents an **imminent danger of substantive evil.** If it does, then government has the constitutional power to prevent it. Incitement to riot, property destruction, or attempts to overthrow the government clearly may be prevented by the powers of government.

The "**clear and present danger doctrine**" was a major judicial standard of regulation of free expression until 1925, when the Court adopted a less liberal stance. In that year, in *Gitlow v. New York*, the Court adopted what was known as the "**evil tendency test.**" The Court ruled, with Justices Holmes and Brandeis dissenting, that the Constitution did not protect those types of expression which created a tendency toward illegal actions. As a result of the Gitlow decision, government, for a time, was in a stronger position to suppress criticism.[50]

The Smith Act Cases

In 1940, Congress passed the **Smith Act,** the first peacetime sedition statute since the law of 1789. The law prohibited the advocacy of the overthrow of the U.S. government by force or violence, as well as conspiracies to accomplish this purpose. In 1951, the U.S. Supreme Court reviewed the convictions, under the Smith Act, of 11 leaders of the Communist Party, U.S.A., who had been convicted in lower Federal courts of conspiracy to organize the Communist Party for the purpose of having it teach and advocate the overthrow and destruction of the U.S. government by force and violence.

Their defense was that Articles II and III of the Smith Act were unconstitutional infringements of the First Amendment, contrary to certain other provisions of the Bill of Rights and were unconstitutionally vague under both First and Fifth Amendments. Speaking through Chief Justice Vinson, the Supreme Court rejected this argument and upheld the convictions. Vinson wrote:[51]

> Congress has the power to protect the United States government from armed rebellion, and the defendants were advocating the violent overthrow of the government. This law was not directed against the advocacy of discussion of the government, but against the advocacy of violence. These persons intended to overthrow the United States government as soon as conditions would permit. This represented a clear and present danger to the government. It was the existence of the highly organized conspiracy that created the danger.

In a concluding paragraph, Justice Vinson observed:[52]

Whatever theoretical merit there might be to the argument that there is a "right" to rebellion against dictatorial government is without force where the existing structure of the government provides for peaceful and orderly change. We reject any principle of governmental helplessness in the face of preparation for revolution, which principle, carried to its logical conclusion, must lead to anarchy.

Using this **grave and probable danger doctrine,** the U.S. government convicted more than 70 other Communists under the Smith Act in the early 1950s.

However, in 1957, the Warren Court ruled in *Yates v. U.S.,* that **mere theoretical advocacy of overthrow of the U.S. government by force and violence was a judicially protected freedom.**

Henceforth, the First Amendment protected all political expressions except those which urged one to do something, rather than merely to believe in something. *Yates* moved the Court back closer to Justice Holmes' "clear and present danger doctrine."[53]

In 1950, the Court had temporarily abandoned the clear and present danger doctrine in *American Communications Association v. Douds.* It ruled that government restrictions on freedom of speech and assembly must be balanced against the seriousness of the evil that government is attempting to prevent.

In *Douds,* the evil to be prevented was politically-inspired strikes by Communist-dominated labor unions. Thus, balancing of competing interests was added as a standard in judicial "line-drawing" between permissible and impermissible types of expression.[54]

Literalist view vs. "line drawing:" Two late Supreme Court justices, Hugo Black and William O. Douglas, the most "liberal" members of the Warren Court, rejected "**line-drawing**." They took a **literalist view** of the First Amendment. When it says "no law, it means no law," they argued. But few of their judicial colleagues have agreed. The Court continues its difficult task of "line-drawing" in this vital area.

In 1969, the U.S. Supreme Court further extended the limits of free speech in *Brandenburg v. Ohio.* Clarence Brandenburg, a "leader" of the Ku Klux Klan, had been convicted under a 1919 state criminal syndicalism statute for a speech he made at a Clermont County (Cincinnati area) Klan rally.

The scenario is familiar: a dozen figures, wearing white hoods, burning a cross, and listening to "hate speech," denouncing Blacks and Jews.

The Court reversed Brandenburg's conviction because Ohio had not proved that any real danger existed. Brandenburg's "threatening speech," the Court found, was protected by the First Amendment unless the state could show that such advocacy was "directed to inciting or producing imminent lawless action" and was likely to produce such action.

The Ohio law, the Court found, failed to make a distinction between "mere abstract teaching" of the need for the use of force and violence and actual preparation of a group for violence. It intruded, therefore, upon individual free expression of ideas and constitutionally protected liberties.

Hate Crimes and Hate Speech: In 1997, the Supreme Court considered a challenge to a St. Paul, Minn., statute which forbade the display of a symbol which one knows or has reason to know "arouses anger, alarm or resentment in others on the basis of race, color, creed, religion or gender."

Petitioner, Robert A. Viktora, a white teenager identified as R.A.V., and several other white youths were charged under the "Bias Motivated Crime Ordinance" but the trial (juvenile) court dismissed the charge on the ground that the ordinance was substantially overbroad and impermissibly content-based. The Minnesota Supreme Court reversed. The Supreme Court granted *certiorari*.

The nation's highest tribunal ruled that the city statute was unconstitutional on its face under the First Amendment's free speech guarantee. In this case , *R.A.V. v. City of St. Paul*, 505 U.S., 377 (1992), a burning cross had been placed on a the lawn of the only Black family in a St. Paul neighborhood as a gesture of hate. In essence, the Court found that "hate speech" cannot be silenced and that bigots have constitutional rights, too.

Justice Scalia, writing for the Court, found the ordinance was unconstitutional because it imposed special prohibitions on those speakers who express views on the disfavored subjects of "race, color, creed, religion or gender." He wrote:[55]

Displays containing abusive invective, no matter how vicious or severe, are permissible unless they are addressed to one of the specified disfavored topics. Those who wish to use "fighting words" in connection with other ideas—to express hostility, for example, on the basis of political affiliation, union membership or homosexuality—are not covered. The First Amendment does not permit St. Paul to impose special prohibitions on those speakers who express views on disfavored subjects. In its practical operation, moreover, the ordinance goes beyond even mere content discrimination, to actual viewpoint discrimination.

Displays containing some words—odious racial epithets, for example, would be prohibited to proponents of all views. But "fighting words" that do not themselves invoke race, color, creed, religion or gender—aspersions upon a person's mother, for example—would seemingly be usable...in the placards of those arguing in favor of race, color, tolerance and equality, etc., but could not be used by that speaker's opponents. One could hold up a sign saying, for example, that all "anti-Catholic bigots" are misbegotten, but not that all "papists" are, for that would insult and provoke violence on the basis of religion.

St. Paul has no such authority to license one side of a debate to fight free style, while requiring the other to follow Marquis of Queensbury Rules.

St. Paul has not singled out an especially offensive mode of expression...Rather, it has proscribed fighting words of whatever manner that communicate messages of racial, gender or religious intolerance. Selectivity of this sort creates the possibility that the city is seeking to handicap the expression of particular ideas. That possibility alone would be enough to render the ordinance presumptively invalid, but St. Paul's comments and concessions in this case elevate the possibility to a certainty.

In his concluding paragraph, Justice Scalia wrote:

Let there be no mistake about our belief that burning a cross in someone's front yard is reprehensible. But St. Paul has sufficient means at its disposal to prevent such behavior without adding the First Amendment to the fire.

A year later, the Supreme Court made it clear, however, that protection of violent *speech* does not extend to violent *crimes,* such as assault, that are motivated by racial, religious or other forms of prejudice. The Rehnquist Court turned its attention to laws in 28 states that provide for enhanced sentences for persons convicted of assault and battery or vandalism when the victim was chosen because of racial, religious, gender or ethnic bias.

In *Wisconsin v. Mitchell*, 113 S. Ct. 2194 (1993), a state statute that provided for increased sentences for these crimes was challenged as a violation of the First Amendment. In a unanimous ruling, the Court held that the law was aimed at "conduct unprotected by the First Amendment," rather than the defendant's speech.

The trial record shows that Todd Mitchell and several other Black youths were talking about a scene in the film, *Mississippi Burning*, in which a white man beats a young Black. Later, as Mitchell's group moved outside, he asked: "Do you feel hyped up to move on some white people?" Within a few moments, a young white boy appeared on the street and Mitchell said: "There goes a white boy; go get him."

After rushing the boy, Mitchell and the others beat him unconscious and stole his shoes. Mitchell subsequently was convicted of battery, which carries a maximum sentence of two years imprisonment under Wisconsin law. But the state "hate speech" law provided that an enhanced sentence may be given whenever the defendant "intentionally selects the person against whom the crime…is committed…because of the race, religion, color, disability, sexual orientation, national origin or ancestry of that person." Because Mitchell had intentionally chosen his victim because of his race, he was given a four-year sentence. The Wisconsin Supreme Court reversed, relying largely on *R.A.V. v. St. Paul*.

The U.S. Supreme Court, speaking through Chief Justice Rehnquist, unanimously held that Mitchell's First Amendment Rights were not violated by the application of the penalty enhancement provision in Wisconsin law. Sentencing judges, the high tribunal noted, traditionally consider a variety of factors, including a defendant's motive for committing an offense. Although a sentencing judge may not consider a defendant's abstract beliefs—even if obnoxious to most people—the Constitution erects no barrier to evidence of one's beliefs and associations simply because they are protected by the First Amendment.

Here, the Court noted, the ordinance is directed at conduct unprotected by the First Amendment. Moreover, Wisconsin's desire to redress what it perceives as the greater individual and social harm inflicted by bias-inspired conduct provides an adequate explanation for the provision over and above mere disagreement with the offender's beliefs or biases.

Rejecting the argument that the law had a "chilling effect" on free speech, and was, therefore, constitutionally overbroad, the Chief Justice wrote:[56]

> We find no merit in this contention. The sort of chill envisioned here is far more attenuated and unlikely that that contemplated in traditional overbreadth cases. We must conjure up a vision of a Wisconsin citizen suppressing his unpopular bigoted opinions for fear that if he later commits an offense covered by the statute, these opinions will be offered at trial to establish that he selected his victim on account of the victim's protected status, thus qualifying him for penalty-enhancement…This is simply too speculative a hypothesis to support Mitchell's overbreadth claim.

Virginia v. Black, 538 U.S. 343 (2003)

In 1975, Virginia amended an old law, originally enacted in 1952, to ban cross burning at a time when racial tensions were high in the state. Historically, cross burning was associated with the Ku Klux Klan, which preached white, Protestant supremacy and threatened Jews, Roman Catholics, "foreigners" and Blacks.

The revised statute made it <u>a felony for individuals to burn crosses with the intent of intimidating any person or group.</u> The state treated cross burning as *prima facie* <u>evidence of such intent.</u> The law provided that:

> ...It shall be unlawful for any person or persons, with the intent of intimidating any person or group of persons, to burn, or to cause to be burned, a cross on the property of another, a highway or other public place. Any person who shall violate any provision of this section shall be guilty of a felony.

<u>The maximum sentence for those convicted under the law is five years in prison and a $2500 fine.</u>

Virginia v. Black[57] involved two separate incidents. In one, Barry Black led a Ku Klux Klan rally of some 30 people in Carroll County, Virginia, which culminated in the burning of a 25-foot-high cross on private property with the owner's consent. At Black's trial, the court instructed the jury that the burning of a cross was by itself sufficient evidence from which it could infer the required threat.

<u>The all-white jury of six men and six women took less than half an hour to convict Black, who was given the maximum $2500 fine, but no jail time.</u>

The second incident involved teenagers Richard Elliott and Jonathan O'Mara, convicted of trying to burn a cross in a yard of James Jubilee, a Black man who lived next door to Elliot and whose white wife Susan was pregnant with twins at the time. Neither Elliott nor O'Mara was a Klansman. Elliott, however, had indicated that he was upset that the interracial family had moved into his neighborhood just four months earlier. Both of the teenagers were drinking before they constructed a four by two foot cross and transported it to Jubilee's home. They failed, possibly because they were drunk, to set the cross on fire with a lighter fluid. The charge against Elliott and O'Meara, therefore, was **attempted cross burning.**

Virginia's Court of Appeals upheld the three convictions in two separate cases, but the state Supreme Court struck down the law, 4-3, finding that it was in conflict with the First Amendment.

The U.S. Supreme Court granted review and handed down its decision on April 7, 2003. It was asked to decide two major questions: 1) Is that part of the Virginia law making it illegal to burn a cross for the purpose of intimidating individuals constitutional? 2) Is that part of the statute which requires that cross burning be considered *prima facie* evidence of intent to discriminate constitutional?

The Court answered the first question in the affirmative, 6-3, ruling that Virginia law did not run afoul of the First Amendment insofar as it banned cross burning with intent to discriminate. On the second issue, the Court held, 5-4, cross burning cannot be considered *prima facie* evidence of intent to intimidate. Black's conviction could not stand.

Justice O'Connor, writing for the majority, said that the court's opinion was not inconsistent with *R.A.V. v. City of St. Paul.* She wrote:[58]

> The provision permits the Commonwealth to arrest, prosecute, and convict a person based solely on the fact of cross burning itself...This is problematical because some individuals will burn the cross not to intimidate, but to show support for their ideology or as a "symbol of group solidarity.

Tracing the history of the Klan, O'Connor said that the organization came to use cross burning as a way to represent the Klan itself, its ideology and solidarity. In that sense, she concluded, cross burning can be protected speech.

She wrote:

> It may be true that a cross burning, even at a political rally, arouses a sense of anger or hatred among the vast majority of citizens who see a burning cross...But this sense of anger or hatred is not sufficient to ban all cross burnings.

The First Amendment permits Virginia to outlaw cross burning done with the intent to intimidate because burning a cross is a particularly virulent form of intimidation. This is instead of prohibiting all intimidating messages in light of cross burning's long and pernicious history as a signal of impending violence. Thus, just as a State may regulate only that obscenity which is the most obscene due to its prurient content, so too may a State choose to prohibit only those forms of intimidation that are most likely to inspire fear of bodily harm...the *prima facie* provision strips away the very reason why a State may ban cross burning with the intent to intimidate. The *prima facie* evidence provision permits a jury to convict in every cross-burning case in which defendants exercise their constitutional right not to put on a defense. And even where a defendant like Black presents a defense, the *prima facie* evidence provision makes it more likely that the jury will find an intent to intimidate, regardless of the particular facts of the case. The provision permits the Commonwealth to arrest, prosecute and convict a person based solely on the fact of cross burning itself.

It is apparent that the provision as so interpreted "would create an unacceptable risk of the suppression of ideas." The act of burning a cross may mean that a person is engaged in constitutionally proscribable intimidation. But that same act may mean only that the person is engaged in core political speech. The *prima facie* evidence provision in this statute blurs the line between these two meanings of a burning cross. As interpreted by the jury instruction, the provision chills constitutionally protected political speech because of the possibility that a State will prosecute – and potentially convict – somebody engaging only in lawful political speech at the core of what the First Amendment is designed to protect.

Justice Thomas, the only Black on the Supreme Court, dissented, saying that he would uphold the Virginia law in its entirety, even the part that allows a jury to draw an inference of intent to intimidate from the cross burning itself. Thomas also contended that the law prohibited only conduct, not free expression.

Thomas wrote:[59]

> In every culture, certain things acquire meaning well beyond what outsiders can comprehend. That goes for both the sacred...and the profane. I believe that cross burning is the paradigmatic example of the latter.
>
> I agree with the majority's conclusion that it is constitutionally permissible to ban cross burning carried out with the intent to intimidate, relying on one of the exceptions to the First Amendment's prohibition on content-based discrimination outlined in R.A.V. v. St. Paul...In my view, whatever expressive value cross burning has, the legislature simply wrote it out by banning only intimidating conduct undertaken by a particular means. A conclusion that the statute prohibiting cross burning with intent to intimidate sweeps beyond a prohibition on certain conduct into the zone of expression and overlooks not only the words of the statute, but also reality.

The Court ignores Justice Holmes' familiar aphorism that a page of history is worth a volume of logic. The world's oldest, most persistent terrorist organization is not European or even Middle Eastern in origin. Fifty years before the Irish Republican Army was organized, a century before Al Fatah declared its holy war on Israel, the Ku Klux Klan was actively harassing, torturing and murdering in the United States. Today…its members remain fanatically committed to a course of violent opposition to social progress and racial equality in the United States—M. Newton and J. Newton, The Ku Klux Klan: an Encyclopedia, vii (1991).

To me, the majority's brief history of the Ku Klux Klan only reinforces the common understanding of the Klan as a terrorist organization, which, in its endeavor to intimidate, or even eliminate those it dislikes, uses the most brutal of methods.

Such methods typically include cross burning, "a tool for the intimidation and harassment of racial minorities, Catholics, Jews, Communists and any other groups hated by the Klan."—*Capitol Square Review and Advisory Board v. Pinette,* 515 U.S. 753, 770 *(*1995).

For those not easily frightened, cross burning has been followed by more extreme measures, such as beatings and murder.

As the Solicitor General points out, the association between acts of intimidating cross burning and violence is well established in recent American history. Indeed, the connection between cross burning and violence is well ingrained, and lower courts have so recognized.

In our culture, cross burning has almost invariably meant lawlessness and understandably instills in its victims well-grounded fear of physical violence.

This statute prohibits only conduct, not expression. And just as one cannot burn down someone's house to make a political point and then seek refuge in the First Amendment, those who hate cannot terrorize and intimidate to make their point. In light of my conclusion that the statute here addresses only conduct, there is no need to analyze it under any of our First Amendment tests.

One of the major issues on state college campuses in recent years has been student speech codes. While courts concede that university administrators have good intentions, they frequently have ruled that these codes violate First Amendment freedoms.

University of Michigan, like many other public institutions, was concerned about so-called hate speech. It "outlawed" verbal attacks on other students for a variety of reasons, including race, ethnicity, sex or sexual orientation, religion, age, marital status, Vietnam veteran status or being handicapped. A Federal judge ruled in *Doe v. University of Michigan,* that the UM code violated basic First Amendment freedoms.[60]

Courts usually find that college-level speech codes are unconstitutional. Free speech on high school campuses is another matter. Given recent secondary school violence, including mass shootings, officials are concerned about hate speech and veiled threats. Principals, staff and teachers all are worried about student drug use, as well as t-shirts with sexist, racist and inflammatory ethnic political messages that may fan the flames of hatred..

In *Morse v. Frederick* (2007), the Roberts Court held that Juneau, Alaska, school principal Deborah Morse had not violated the First Amendment rights of Joseph Frederick, an 18-year-old senior, who displayed a banner which she regarded as promoting illegal drug use.[61]

On the morning of January 24, 2002, high school students and staff were allowed to leave classes to watch the "Olympic Torch Relay" pass on its way to Salt Lake City, Utah, site of the Winter Olympic. As TV cameras reported the event, Frederick and some of his friends unfurled a 14-foot banner, which said "BONG HITS 4 JESUS." Moore seized the banner and later suspended Frederick for violating the school's anti-drug policy. The Juneau superintendent of schools upheld the suspension, after which Frederick sued both Principal Morse and the school board for violating his First Amendment free speech rights.

The U.S. District Court for Alaska dismissed the case. It found that Supreme Court precedent permitted authorities to punish those kinds of student speech which would undermine the school's basic educational mission. However, the Court of Appeals for the Ninth Circuit reversed that decision. Morse and the board then petitioned the Supreme Court for a writ of *certiorari,* granted in December, 2006.

The Supreme Court ruled, 6-3, for Morse and the school board. The majority opinion, written by Chief Justice Roberts, was joined by Justices Scalia, Kennedy, Thomas, Alito and Breyer. It held that "schools may take steps to safeguard those entrusted to their care from speech that can reasonably be regarded as encouraging illegal drug use. Schools, in this case, did not violate the First Amendment by confiscating the drug banner and suspending Frederick."

Justice Stevens wrote a dissenting opinion, joined by Justices Ginsburg and Souter. Stevens was willing to give full First Amendment protection to "…student speech if the message itself neither violates a permissible rule nor expressly advocates conduct that is illegal and harmful to students…This nonsense banner does neither, and the Court does serious violence to the First Amendment in upholding – indeed, lauding – a school's decision to punish Frederick for expressing a view with which it disagreed," he said.

FREEDOM OF ASSEMBLY AND ASSOCIATION

What, if any, limits should Congress and state legislatures impose on freedom of assembly and association? Government has the power to protect public order. Protesters do not have constitutional rights to block traffic during rush hour, incite to riot or engage in fighting.

Such "expressions" are not protected by the First or 14th Amendments. Justice Holmes once observed, "Your right to swing your arms ends where my nose begins."

With the exceptions of Justices Black and Douglas, who argued that the First Amendment was an absolute, most jurists have accepted the difficulty task of "line-drawing," establishing a number of standards to guide them between permissible and impermissible forms of "free expression."

Although he held absolutist views regarding free expression, Justice Black carefully distinguished between speech and conduct, such as picketing. This, he agreed, was not an absolute right.

Some judges have argued that First Amendment freedoms should be given **preferential treatment** by the courts because they are essential in a democratic society. According to this theory, courts should take a very long and hard look at those laws regulating freedom of expression, assembly or association.

The theory of free expression has not always been honored in practice in the U.S. Shortly after ratification of the First Amendment, for example, Congress passed the **Alien and Sedition Acts of 1789** because it feared that the French Revolution would subvert the infant American Republic.

Periods of popular excitement followed both World Wars. The contagion of Communism was feared both after the Bolshevik Revolution of 1917 and the advent of the Cold War in 1946-47. "**McCarthyism**" was a major problem during the early and mid 1950s. The decade of the

1960s was characterized by massive protests by civil rights demonstrators, anti-war protestors, draft-card burners, student radicals who sometimes seized university buildings and many others. But Americans continued to pay attention to the need for free trade in ideas, even if those ideas were loathsome to many. What limits have courts traditionally imposed on free speech and assembly? Association?

Free Assembly Landmarks

Freedom of assembly first was "incorporated" into the liberties protected against state encroachment in 1937. The Court ruled, in *De Jonge v. Oregon*, that the right of "peaceable assembly" was a right as "equally fundamental" as those of free speech and press. It is a right, the Court found, that "cannot be denied without violating those fundamental principles of liberty and justice which lie at the base of all civil and political institutions—principles which the 14th Amendment embodies in the general terms of its Due Process Clause."[62]

In *Chaplinsky v. New Hampshire*, the U.S. Supreme Court held that one could not call a policeman a "damned Fascist" and "damned racketeer" without inviting a probable violent response. Consequently, such **"fighting words" were outside the protection of the First and 14th Amendments.** However, in *Terminello v. Chicago*, the Court set aside the conviction for breach of the peace of Arthur Terminello, who denounced Jews, Blacks, President Franklin D. Roosevelt and Communists. Although Terminello was virtually certain to cause turmoil wherever and whenever he spoke, the Court concluded that **those who responded violently, rather than the speaker, ought to be punished.**[63]

In a 1951 landmark case, *Feiner v. New York*, the high tribunal upheld the disorderly conduct conviction of Irving Feiner, a Black student at Syracuse University who denounced President Truman, the American Legion and the mayor of Syracuse, N.Y. He also urged Blacks to "rise up in arms and fight" for equal rights. Police asked Feiner to stop speaking. When he refused to do so, they arrested him. The Supreme Court concluded that the **arresting officers were not interested in suppressing his views, but only in preserving law and order. The guarantee of free speech, the Court held, does not include a license to incite to riot.**[64]

In 1963, the Warren Court reversed a breach of peace conviction of 187 Black high school and college students who marched on the capital of South Carolina with banners, "Down With Segregation," while chanting "We Shall Not Be Moved." The Court held, in *Edwards v. South Carolina*, that the 14th Amendment "does not permit a state to make criminal the peaceful expression of unpopular views." Justice Tom Clark dissented, reasoning that "to say that the police may not intervene until the riot has occurred is like keeping out the doctor until the patient dies."[65]

Further restrictions on picketing were upheld by the Court in 1965, when it ruled in *Cox v. Louisiana* that a state law which banned parades or picketing near courthouses was not an infringement of the First or 14th Amendments. The state legislature was **concerned with attempts to influence or intimidate judges, jurors and witnesses.**

In 1965, the Supreme Court upheld the trespass convictions of some 2100 Florida A&M College students who had marched on a jail to protest the arrest and imprisonment of fellow students. When they refused a police order to leave, they were arrested. Speaking for the Court, Justice Black held that a state, like a private individual, has "the power to preserve the property under its control for the use to which it is properly dedicated."[66]

Symbolic Free Expression

A new type of problem has come before the Court in recent years, that of "**symbolic free expression.**" Defense lawyers often have argued that their clients have a constitutional right to express ideas by silent, non-verbal communication.

In 1969, during the height of anti-war protests, the Supreme Court held, in *Tinker v. Des Moines*, that students could not be forbidden by public school authorities from wearing black armbands to class to protest the Vietnam conflict.[67]

A year earlier, the Court had ruled, however, that a draft registrant did not have a constitutionally protected right to burn his draft card. It held that David P. O'Brien "could have conveyed his message in many ways other than by burning his draft card."[68]

Freedom of speech and religion may sometimes overlap in the area of symbolic free expression. The placement of a religious symbol in a public forum, such as a cross in a public square, involves both freedom of religion and symbolic speech.

In *Capitol Square Review and Advisory Board v. Pinette*, 515 U.S. 753 (1995), the Supreme Court considered this question. Ohio law makes Capitol Square, the Statehouse Plaza in Columbus, a forum for discussion of public questions and gives the Square Review and Advisory Board responsibility to regulate access to the Plaza. A group must simply fill out an official application and meet several speech neutral criteria.

After the Board rejected, for Establishment Clause reasons, an application from the Ku Klux Klan to place a cross on the Square during the 1993 Christmas season, the Klan filed suit in Federal District Court. The Court ordered the board to issue the permit and the Sixth Circuit Court of Appeals affirmed the judgment. The U.S. Supreme Court granted *certiorari* because of conflicts between various Circuit courts on the question of whether a private, unattended display of a religious symbol in a public form violates the Establishment Clause.

It should be noted that the Supreme Court limited its review to the Establishment Clause issue. It refused to consider the Klan's argument that the only reason that Ohio authorities refused permission to erect the cross was the Klan's political views, rather than the sectarian religion issue.

Justice Scalia concluded that the display amounted to private religious speech that is as fully protected by the Free Speech Clause as secular private expression.

Flag Burning

Among the most "emotional" of recent cases involving symbolic free expression are those involving flag desecration. Gregory Johnson was among a group of demonstrators at the 1984 Republican National Convention in Dallas. He marched to city hall and burned the American flag. Johnson was arrested, tried and convicted under a Texas flag desecration statute.

In 1989, the U.S. Supreme Court struck down the law, ruling that flag burning was protected by First and 14th Amendment free expression guarantees. This decision sparked political flames, culminating in the presidential campaign of 1988. Vice President George Bush visited flag factories and urged Congress to amend the Constitution to halt flag desecration.

Although the Democrats controlled Congress, they were feeling considerable heat from an inflamed public opinion. Congress chose not to propose a constitutional amendment, but rather to pass the **Flag Protection Act of 1989.** The act made it a crime to "knowingly mutilate, deface, physically defile, burn, maintain on the floor or ground, or trample upon any flag of the United States."

Flag burning incidents in Seattle and Washington, D.C., led to a test of the law in the U.S. Supreme Court. As President Bush had predicted, the Supreme Court invalidated the law. It held that the statute, like the Texas law, violated First Amendment guarantees of free speech.[69]

In 1971, in *Coates v. Cincinnati*, the Supreme Court ruled unconstitutional a city ordinance forbidding three or more persons from assembling on sidewalks and there conducting themselves in a manner annoying to passersby. Speaking for the Court, Justice Stewart, a former member of Cincinnati's city council and son of James Garfield Stewart, a former Cincinnati mayor and Ohio Supreme Court justice, wrote:[70]

> The city is free to prevent people from blocking sidewalks, obstructing traffic, littering streets, committing assaults, or engaging in countless other forms of anti-social conduct. It can do so through the enactment and enforcement of ordinances directed with reasonable specificity toward the conduct to be prohibited. It cannot constitutionally do so through the enactment and enforcement of an ordinance whose violations may entirely depend upon whether or not a policeman is annoyed.

In short, the city had enacted a measure which was **unconstitutionally vague and too broadly drawn.**

Flag Protection Amendment

On several occasions after *Texas v. Johnson* and *U.S. v. Eichman*, Congress attempted to propose a Flag Desecration Amendment. The most recent effort came as Congress neared its summer recess in 2006 and it was obviously going to be a close call in the Senate. Historically, the House of Representatives has voted overwhelmingly for the amendment, far in excess of the constitutionally required 2/3. In the 109th Congress, the House supported the measure, 286-130.

The Senate began debate on the measure on June 26, 2006. The following day, the amendment, sponsored by Judiciary Chairman Orin Hatch of Utah, **fell one vote short** of the required 2/3 majority with 66 senators voting aye and 34 voting nay. Only three Republican senators, Lincoln Chafee of Rhode Island, Mitch McConnell of Kentucky and Bob Bennett of Utah, opposed the amendment.

A majority of Senate Democrats, including the party's possible presidential nominees, Barack Obama and Hillary Clinton, rejected the amendment. They said that, with mid-term 2006 congressional elections looming, this was, simply, a case of Republican political grandstanding.

With Democrats holding majorities in both House and Senate after the 110th Congress convened in January, 2007, it appeared unlikely that the Flag Protection Amendment would resurface any time soon. Pollsters said that Republican prospects of regaining control of Congress in the 2008 election were dim.

Free Speech For Whom?

Many, if not most Americans, if asked, probably would reply that they believe in freedom of speech, press, assembly and association. But, if pressed by more specific questions, as countless polls have indicated, they change their minds. Among questions of the post World War II era which sparked debate were the following:

Should a Communist speaker be permitted to speak or to teach at a state-supported university? Should the Central Intelligence Agency (CIA) be permitted to recruit at college placement centers? Should a scientist who believes that Blacks are genetically inferior to whites be permitted to express that view? Should a "liberal" faculty member be permitted to interrupt a speech by former South Vietnamese Premier Ky at Cornell University? Should universities outlaw "hate speech?"

For many Americans, including self-styled "liberal intellectuals," freedom of expression is apparently only for those who agree with them, and are, therefore "politically correct." The widely-known jurist, Judge Learned Hand, once summed up our ideal of free expression simply:

> The First Amendment presupposes that right conclusions are more likely to be gathered out of a multitude of tongues than through any kind of authoritative selection. To many that is and always will be folly; but we have staked upon it our all.

Rumsfeld v. Forum for Academic and Institutional Rights, 547 U.S. 47 (2006)

In one of the most closely followed cases of its 2005-06 term, the U.S. Supreme Court considered the case of *Rumsfeld v. Forum for Academic and Institutional Rights*. The case involved a challenge, on free speech grounds, from professors at 30 law schools who argued that they should not be compelled by the Solomon Amendment to associate with military recruiters or promote their appearances on campus.

The amendment, named after its sponsor, Rep. Gerald Solomon, (R., New York), withholds Federal funds from institutions of higher education that deny military recruiters the same access to campuses and students that they provide to other employers. Secretary of Defense Donald Rumsfeld was challenging a preliminary injunction issued by the U.S. Court of Appeals for the Third Circuit, as well as its ruling that the Amendment likely violates the First Amendment.

The law professors had formed a group called the Forum for Academic and Institutional Rights (FAIR) and argued that the Solomon Amendment violates their free speech rights under the First Amendment by compelling them to disseminate a message with which they disagree.

The case had its roots in a 1990 decision by the Association of Law Schools to add sexual orientation to its non-discrimination policy which previously had applied to race and gender. It forbade employers who discriminate from using law school career placement facilities.

The Clinton Administration had adopted a "Don't Ask, Don't Tell" policy, under which the armed services could not ask members of the military if they are homosexual. However, any evidence of homosexual conduct or orientation is grounds for discharge.

The military told law schools that it would not sign a non-discrimination statement that included sexual orientation. Some universities responded by closing their doors to armed services recruiters. This angered members of Congress, who then passed Representative Solomon's Amendment to a military appropriation bill in 1994.

Most law schools, faced with a cutoff of Federal funds, compromised. Some, like Harvard, permitted recruiters to talk to their students, but refused to allow them to use placement service offices. For a time, this appeared to satisfy the Defense Department. But, in 2003, the Pentagon told law schools that it would insist that the military be given the same access as other employers.

Because some $35 billion a year was involved, most schools allowed recruiters to return to their placement offices. This led to formation of FAIR, and its subsequent lawsuit, initially rejected by a Federal District Court in 2003. FAIR won its appeal in the Third Circuit and the U.S. Supreme Court granted review in May, 2005. The case was argued on December 6, 2005, and decided on March 6, 2006.

Chief Justice John Roberts rejected FAIR's arguments and ruled for the Defense Department (Rumsfeld). Concluding that the Solomon Amendment regulates conduct, and only incidentally affects First Amendment rights, he wrote for a unanimous Court (8-0):[71]

> A military recruiter's mere presence on campus does not violate a law school's right to associate, regardless of how repugnant the law school considers the recruiter's message...Students and faculty are free to associate to voice their disapproval of the military's message...Recruiters are, by definition, outsiders who come onto campus for the limited purpose of trying to hire students – not to become members of the school's expressive association....The Solomon Amendment neither limits what law schools may say nor requires them to say anything...In this case, FAIR has attempted to stretch a number of First Amendment doctrines well beyond the sort of activities these doctrines protect...Law schools remain free under the statute to express whatever views they may have on the military's congressionally-mandated employment policy, all the while retaining eligibility for Federal funds...As a general matter, the Solomon Amendment regulates conduct, not speech. **It affects what law schools must do –** afford equal access to military recruiters – **not what they may or may not say**...Accommodating the military's message does not affect the law schools' speech, because the schools are not speaking when they host interviews and recruiting receptions.
>
> ...The Solomon Amendment gives universities a choice: Either allow military recruiters the same access to students afforded any other recruiter or forgo certain Federal funds. And that choice is a constitutional exercise of Congress' spending power, one that does not run afoul of the First Amendment.

The Chief Justice filed the only opinion in the case. It was joined by every associate justice, except Samuel Alito, who was not on the bench when the case was argued.

The Puzzle of Obscenity

In a nation of more than 300 million people, characterized by ethical pluralism, it is only natural that vigorous and often bitter debate occurs when legislatures attempt to define moral standards and translate them into law. The problem is aggravated when a group attempts to impose its own moral concepts on the community. Sometimes what "Caesar" requires is not enough for these people and they set about trying to ban the distribution of books they consider indecent, immoral or obscene. In the 21st Century, with new technologies developing, the debate has come to include movies, television and most recently, the internet.

Americans vary considerably in their attitudes toward censorship. At one extreme are the hard-core blue-noses who blush at the mention of the word sex. Fortunately, we have come a long way since the heyday of the New York Society for the Suppression of Vice and the Boston Watch and Ward Society. At the other extreme are those who believe that "anything goes" and that freedom of expression ought to be absolute. Governments, they argue, should impose no restraints on press or speech in the name of public morality. History, they say, is filled with horror stories resulting from attempts of "good people" to purge moral heresy.

Few judges or U.S. Supreme Court justices have been First Amendment absolutists, with the notable exceptions of William O. Douglas and Hugo Black. No law, Black and Douglas contended, meant exactly that—no law!

While unwilling to accept the Black-Douglas view, many Liberal justices have concluded that First Amendment freedoms do merit preferential treatment by the courts. Consequently, they will not extend the usual "presumption of validity" rule to laws which regulate those precious liberties.

Most American courts have taken a middle course. While generally skeptical about censorship, they conclude the government may, perhaps even must, regulate certain types of expression, such as the seditious, libelous, slanderous and the obscene. But those who advocate censorship are faced with several basic questions. What kinds of books, magazines and pamphlets ought to be censored? Who should do the censoring and what should be the criteria for censorship?

Constitutional "experts" agree that obscene expressions are not entitled to the protection of the First Amendment. But the sticky problem of definition remains. What expressions are obscene? Perhaps even Solomon could not adequately define the term early in the 21st Century. It should be realized that obscenity is often entangled in human emotions. None of us can escape from the prison of his or her environment. Those with strong religious convictions of right and wrong, often instilled during childhood socialization, are likely to see films, books, magazines and television in a different perspective from one who has no such background.

Under American law, the print press is generally free from prior restraint on publication. However, post-publication restraints are permissible. State legislatures, which have written most censorship laws, can and do act against books and films after they have been produced and distributed. Courts have recognized that states may use their police powers to protect and promote public morals, as well as public health, safety and welfare. But their acts are subject to judicial review. Pre-publication restraint may not be imposed on printed words, but films have been considered in a different category.

The Federal government also plays a censorship role. Congress has empowered the Post Office to bar from the mails those publications deemed obscene. Customs officials may ban a book from the U.S., pending judicial review. James Joyce's famous *Ulysses* is a case in point. The book was not permitted to enter the U.S. until Judge Francis Woolsey found that it was not legally obscene.

In 1967, President Lyndon Johnson signed into law a bill creating an 18-member Commission on Obscenity and Pornography. Its duties as defined by Congress were fourfold:

(1) to analyze the obscenity laws and recommend definitions of obscenity;

(2) to explore the nature and volume of obscenity and ascertain its methods of distribution;

(3) to study the effects of obscenity and its relationship to criminal and other anti-social behavior;

(4) to recommend legislative, administrative and other action to regulate its flow.

In the fall of 1970, the Commission submitted its report. Richard Nixon was then President, and he rejected its findings. The report urged that censorship be ended for consenting adults, but continued for juveniles. Attacked for "libertine" proposals, strong opposition developed to the report. The U.S. Senate voted to condemn it, with only five members dissenting. The President said:

> As long as I am in the White House, there will be no relaxation of the national effort to control and eliminate smut…American morality is not to be trifled with. The Commission has performed a disservice and I totally reject its report.

American law frequently reflects its British ancestry. This was true for years in the area of "obscenity." It is a well-established principle of Anglo-Saxon justice that obscene publications are not entitled to constitutional protection. But the dilemma of definition again arises. What is obscene?

For purposes of convenience, one may divide the media into several categories when studying this problem. In general, print media enjoy the greatest protection under the First Amendment. Movies today appear to be in a largely "post-censorship" era. Radio and television are still under regulation of the Federal Communications Commission. The Internet is so new that problems unimagined by Framers of the First Amendment are only now beginning to emerge.

Printed Matter

British courts, speaking through Lord Cockburn in the 1868 case of *Regina v. Hicklin*, handed down a definition of obscenity that American courts followed well into the 20th Century. Lord Cockburn's test was "…whether the tendency of the matter charged as obscene is to deprave and corrupt those whose minds are open to such immoral influences and into whose hands a publication of this sort may fall."

This "**Hicklin Rule**" meant, in effect, that the starting point in the definition of obscenity was to be the moral level of a child. Furthermore, the court declared, obscenity was not only to be judged by the tendency of the whole book, but also by isolated passages in it.

Inspired by this approach, "obscenity hunters," like Anthony Comstock, went to great pains to impose Puritan moral standards on America. Using this broad rule, American courts held books by such noted writers as D.H. Lawrence, James Joyce, Henry Miller and even Aristophanes to be obscene.

The Roth-Alberts Test

In 1957, the U.S. Supreme Court, in the companion cases of *Roth v. U.S.* and *Alberts v. California*, rejected the Hicklin test and narrowed the meaning of obscenity. The Court, speaking through Justice Brennan, emphasized that sex and obscenity are not synonymous and that only those materials which deal with sex in a manner appealing to prurient interest (materials tending to excite lustful thoughts) may be judged obscene.

In addition to these criteria, the Court laid down four other tests. Books must be judged as a whole rather than on the basis of isolated passages. Their probable effect must be considered in terms of normal, adult persons, rather than a deviant or a child. Decency, or obscenity, is to be determined on the basis of contemporary community standards and materials must lack redeeming social importance before they can be adjudged obscene.

The Court also found that all ideas having even the slightest significance—unorthodox ideas, controversial ideas, even ideas hateful to the prevailing climate of opinion—have the full protection of the Constitution. Implicit in the history of the First Amendment, the Court found, is the rejection of obscenity as utterly without redeeming social importance. In both *Roth* and

Alberts, the Court found, trial courts had sufficiently followed proper standards and used the proper definition of obscenity. Consequently, their convictions stood.

The Supreme Court handed down another significant ruling in *Butler v. Michigan*. The state had made it a misdemeanor to sell to the general public any books containing obscene language "tending to the corruption of the morals of youth." A Detroit trial court judge convicted Alfred E. Butler and fined him $100 for selling John Griffin's *The Devil Rides Outside* to a Detroit policeman. The book, the judge concluded, would tend to corrupt the morals of youth.

The book is a story of a young American's visit to a French Benedictine monastery to study Gregorian chants. The youth, observing the monks, aspires to imitate their virtues, particularly chastity, although he is sex-obsessed and indulges in numerous illicit loves.

The Supreme Court reversed Butler's conviction, holding that the Michigan law was an unconstitutional infringement of the Due Process Clause of the 14th Amendment. Justice Frankfurter, speaking for the Court, wrote:[72]

> The state insists that, by thus quarantining the general public against books not too rugged for grown men and women in order to shield juvenile innocence, it is exercising its power to promote the general welfare. Surely this is to burn the house to roast the pig.

The Court held that Michigan could not arbitrarily curtail the liberties of adults by a requirement that permits them to read only what is fit for children. In short, if materials designed for public distribution are to be banned as obscene, the test of constitutionality must be their effect on adults.

The decade of the 1960s saw a cultural war erupt in the United States. The battle cry of the Liberal-left on campuses was, "If it feels good, do it!" Rules, they argued, were made to be broken. Authority was to be challenged, not respected. The "New Morality" was in vogue. So was "Situation Ethics," which holds that each of the 10 Commandments should be preceded by the word "ordinarily." Those who disagreed said the New Morality was merely the "Old Immorality" under a new label. Situation ethics, they argued, was nothing more than an elaborate rationalization for a wide variety of immoral behavior. Although the anti-Vietnam War protesters got much of the publicity, some collegians of the 1960s were also very much into experimentation with drugs and "free love."

It should, therefore, not be surprising that the Supreme Court, always on the cutting edge of the law, was flooded with cases involving pornography, obscenity and morality. Further attempting to clarify the meaning of *Roth-Alberts*, the Court handed down significant rulings in a half dozen cases.

In 1964, the Court set aside a ruling of the Ohio Supreme Court (*Jacobellis v. Ohio*) that a brief, nonexplicit love scene in the French film, *Les Amants*, was obscene. Justice Potter Stewart's comment was to live forever in Supreme Court history, when, attempting to define obscenity, he noted, "I know it when I see it and this isn't it."

In 1966, the Court heard three cases in this area. In *Memoirs v. Massachusetts*, the Court struck down Massachusetts ban on John Cleland's 1750 novel, Memoirs of a Woman of Pleasure—also known as Fanny Hill—on the grounds that it had some literary value.

In *Ginzburg v. U.S.*, the Court upheld the conviction of pornographer Ralph Ginzburg, found guilty in Federal court of mailing obscene publications, including the magazine Eros. The Court found that Ginzburg had been guilty of "pandering" or advertising his materials so as to "appeal to the erotic interests" of his potential customers.

In *Mishkin v. New York*, Mishkin argued that his materials were not obscene because they did not appeal to the average person, who would find them disgusting, but to sick deviates who enjoyed books dealing with sadomasochism and fetishism. The Supreme Court upheld the conviction and added the phrase "or the intended and probable and recipient group" to the "average person" test of *Roth*.

The Court took a step toward a consenting-adults view of obscenity by reversing convictions in *Redrup v. New York* (1967) of exhibitors who had sold non-explicit "girlie magazines." The Court found that there was no evidence of sale to juveniles or of pandering.

But the Court did uphold the concept of "variable obscenity" a year later when it upheld the conviction of a proprietor of a luncheonette who sold non-explicit girlie magazines to a juvenile. New York and other states, the Supreme Court ruled, could have a stricter standard for the dissemination of sexual materials to minors than to adults.

During the 1970s, the Supreme Court recognized that the *Roth-Alberts* definition of obscenity was legally unworkable. Chief Justice Warren Burger devised a new test in *Miller v. California*, 413 U.S. 15 (1973). The new test had the following four main elements:

(1) the average person finds that it violates community standards;
(2) the work, taken as a whole, appeals to a prurient interest in sex;
(3) the work shows patently offensive sexual conduct;
(4) the work lacks serious literary, artistic, political or scientific merit.

Civil libertarians insist that one person's "prurient interest" is another person's pleasure. *Miller*, therefore, has not been the definitive answer to the problem and obscenity remains an unsettled problem. The Burger and Rehnquist Courts, however, have been much more reluctant than the Warren Court to consider large numbers of such cases.

The Rehnquist Court has made it clear that states may outlaw private possession of child pornography in the home. In *Osborne v. Ohio*, 495 U.S. 103 (1990), it upheld a state ban on private possession of such materials because they encouraged a commercial demand for exploitation of children. The Ohio statute made it a crime to "possess or view any material or performance that shows a minor who is not the person's child or ward in a state of nudity." The law made exceptions for bona fide artistic, medical, scientific or educational materials related to legitimate study or research.

The Court made it clear that, *Stanley v. Georgia* notwithstanding, the need to protect children outweighs one's right to possess and view obscene materials in the privacy of one's home.

Is Pornography an Offense Against Women?

First Amendment values may conflict with others considered of basic importance in American society. During the 1980s and 1990s, a heated debate has developed between those who value free expression most and those who consider equality, particularly sexual equality, of pre-eminent importance. A number of feminist groups have argued that obscenity and pornography exploit and degrade women and should, therefore, be banned as a matter of civil rights for women. In a rather unusual political alliance, some militant feminists joined religious fundamentalists to pressure the Indianapolis, Indiana, City Council to enact an ordinance reflecting this viewpoint.

On May 1, 1984, the city enacted a censorship statute. Although the measure ostensibly was an anti-obscenity/pornography measure, it was so broadly drawn that it quickly drew the wrath of the American Civil Liberties Union, a group long noted for its sympathetic view of women's rights.

The statute was drafted by University of Michigan Law School professor Catherine MacKinnon and her feminist colleague, Andrea Dworkin. Dworkin reasoned that: [73]

52

Pornography is a discriminatory practice based on sex because its effect is to deny women equal opportunities in society. The bigotry and contempt it promotes, with the acts of aggression it fosters, harm women's opportunities for equality of rights in employment, education, access to and use of public accommodations, acquisitions of real property, and contribute significantly to restricting women in particular from full exercise of citizenship and participation in public life, including in neighborhoods.

The Indianapolis ordinance permitted women offended by the depiction of women as sex objects or objects of sexual violence or subordination to file a complaint with the municipal Equal Opportunity Office.

If a woman believed that an aggressive act had been committed against her because of the stimulation of such materials, she could sue the publisher or disseminator of the material, such as a bookstore or theater, for damages.

Civil libertarians pointed out that under the statute, a woman might purchase a novel which featured a female character who enjoyed rough or violent lovemaking. If she was offended by that depiction, she could complain to the city of Indianapolis that her civil rights were being jeopardized. If her husband read the book and had such sexual relations with her later, she could sue both the bookstore and the publisher.

Columnist Nat Hentoff said, "This law is so broad and vague that God could be in the docket for passages in the Old Testament." Thomas Emerson, a Yale University Law School professor who specializes in First Amendment issues, asked, "Is the solution to the harm done by pornography a law so 'nearly limitless' in its scope that it would outlaw a substantial portion of the world's literature?"

In its Friend of the Courts brief, the ACLU noted that books that would be banned by Indianapolis included Nabokobv's *Lolita*, Petronius' *Satyricon*, Fielding's *Tom Jones* and Gericault's *A Nude Being Tortured*. Movies considered objectionable would include the Janet Leigh shower scene in *Psycho* as well as scenes from *Jack the Ripper*, *Looking for Mr. Goodbar* and *The Godfather*.

Late in 1984, Sarah Evans Barker, first female Federal District Court judge in Indiana history, in her first case as judge, declared the ordinance unconstitutional because it suppressed free speech, contrary to the First Amendment, and because it was too vague, thereby denying a potential defendant due process of law.

Although efforts to restrict behavior that leads to humiliation and degradation of women may be necessary and desirable, Judge Barker said, "Free speech, rather than being an enemy, is a long tested and worthy ally. To deny free speech in order to engineer social change in the name of accomplishing a greater good for one sector of our society erodes the freedom of all." In this collision of values, between liberty and equality, liberty was protected by Judge Barker who noted:[74]

> To permit every interest group, especially those who claimed to be victimized by unfair expression, their own legislative exceptions to the First Amendment, so long as they succeed in obtaining a majority of legislative voters in their favor, demonstrates the potentially predatory nature of what defendants seek through this Ordinance.

An old saying is that "politics makes strange bedfellows." This is clearly illustrated in the Indianapolis case. Judge Barker was a Conservative, appointed by President Reagan. McKinnon and her usual allies are on the political left. In this case, however, some feminist civil libertarians opposed the McKinnon view while right-wing, fundamentalist preachers and other "crusaders" against obscenity and pornography supported McKinnon.

McKinnon and her allies took the case to the Seventh Circuit Court of Appeals (which sits in Chicago). It upheld Judge Barker and described the municipal statute as a form of thought control. Writing for the Appeals Court, Judge Frank Easterbrook said:[75]

> Under the ordinance, graphic sexually explicit speech is "pornography" or not, depending on the perspective the author adopts. Speech that "subordinates" women and also, for example, presents women as enjoying pain, humiliation or rape, or even simply presents women in "positions of servility, submission or display" is forbidden, no matter how great the literary or political value of the work taken as a whole.

> Speech that portrays women in positions of equality is lawful, no matter how graphic the sexual content. That is thought control. It establishes an "approved" view of women, of how they may react to sexual encounters, of how the sexes may relate to each other. Those who espouse the approved view may use sexual images; those who do not, may not.

In *American Bookstores v. Hudnut*, 475 U.S. 1001 (1986), the U.S. Supreme Court, without hearing oral arguments, summarily affirmed the decision of both District and Circuit Courts that the ordinance was unconstitutional. Professor McKinnon characterized civil libertarians who oppose censorship as "First Amendment Wimps."

The Censor Goes to the Movies

Early in the 20th Century, a new medium of communication emerged, the movies. Framers of the First Amendment hardly could have foreseen the technology which produced them. In considering the problem of film censorship, one must recognize the nature of the medium. Movies, particularly those shown now, are shown on large screens with advanced sound systems and highly developed special effects. They are more graphic (critics would say pornographic), vivid and have a greater impact on the viewer than does the printed word. Therefore, would-be censors argue, films have a much greater potential to damage the moral fabric of society.

Anthony Comstock's New York Society for the Suppression of Vice tried, as early as 1909, to censor movies. New York, Pennsylvania, Ohio and Kansas enacted film censorship laws before 1915. Movies, perhaps reflecting the moral confusion in the nation during World War I, were strongly assailed, and some critics proposed a Federal film censorship law.

Mutual Film v. Ohio Industrial Commission: In 1915, the U.S. Supreme Court had its first encounter with the issue of movie censorship. Ohio had established a commission in 1913 which was authorized to approve for public viewing only those films adjudged to be of a "moral, educational, amusing or harmless character." This type of prior restraint, applied to news press, would be clearly unconstitutional. But the Supreme Court, speaking through Justice McKenna, upheld the Ohio statute:[76]

> The exhibition of moving pictures is a business, pure and simple, originated and conducted for profit, like other spectacles, not to be regarded, nor intended to be regarded by the Ohio Constitution, we think, as part of the press of the country or as organs of public opinion. They are mere representations of events.

Between 1915-52, seven states and numerous local governments required film exhibitors to submit their movies to censors for licensing before they could be shown. During this period,

Hollywood attempted self-regulation to forestall increased government censorship. An office, headed by former Republican National Chairman Will Hayes, was established to review scripts and films. A production code was drawn, and the **Hayes Office** was empowered to fine a studio $25,000 if it released a film without the **industry seal of approval**.

The code, which outlawed nudity, glorification of crime and certain "taboo" topics, such as drug addiction, produced an era of happy endings. Moviegoers flocked into theaters to see child star Shirley Temple, cowboy stars like Gene Autry, comedians like the Marx Brothers and Abbott and Costello.

But the situation changed after World War II with the advent of television, which kept people from attending mediocre movies and the increasing appeal of foreign "adult" films which were not subject to the code. Foreign films were bolder and considerably more frank in their treatment of sex. Many Americans preferred them to domestic products, and this was clearly understood by Hollywood, which eventually relaxed its standards to compete with non-code films.

It was an Italian film, *The Miracle*, by Roberto Rossellini, which produced what some called the "Emancipation Proclamation of the Movies" in 1952. The Supreme Court, in *Burstyn v. Wilson*, 343 U.S. 495, overruled Mutual Film and brought movies under the protection of the Constitution.

New York censors had banned *The Miracle* on the grounds that it was "sacrilegious." Roman Catholics objected to it strongly, both in the pulpit and in the press. Cardinal Francis Spellman denounced it and the Legion of Decency condemned it. What was it all about?

The story was one of a simple-minded peasant girl who is approached by a bearded stranger one day as she minds her herd of goats. She believes that he is St. Joseph and has come to take her to heaven. The stranger plies her with wine, then ravishes her while she is in a state of religious ecstasy. Later, when the villagers discover that the girl is pregnant, they abuse her badly. At the end of the movie, the unfortunate girl goes to a mountain church where she bears her baby, and, in so doing, regains her sanity.

The Supreme Court struck down New York's ban, largely because it considered the term "sacrilegious" to be unconstitutionally vague. Censors, the high tribunal ruled, had abused their discretion by banning a film merely because it offended the religious sensibilities of some people. The term "sacrilegious" lacks precise meaning, the Court said.

Most significantly, the Supreme Court held that liberty of "expression by means of motion pictures is included within the free speech guarantee of the 14th Amendment."

Film censorship continued, however, in several states and municipalities after *Burstyn*. City governments denied licenses to show films for a wide variety of reasons. Memphis, Tenn., banned *Imitation of Life* because it did not approve of its treatment of racial matters. It also banned *The Southerner* because of its unflattering view of southern tenant farmers. Ohio and Kansas censored films which were pro-labor union. In Chicago, where films were licensed by the Office of the Commissioner of Police, a permit was denied to show a newsreel. It showed Chicago police shooting at labor pickets.

It was not until 1961, nine years after *The Miracle* case, that the Supreme Court agreed to hear a challenge to Chicago's censorship law, and by implication, all prior restraints on films. Times Film Corporation had applied for a license to show *Don Juan*, a movie based on Mozart's opera, *Don Giovanni*, but refused to submit the film with the application, as required by city ordinance. After Chicago refused to issue a permit, petitioner filed suit in U.S. District Court, seeking an order requiring the city to issue the permit without seeing the film.

It was a close call, 5-4, but the Supreme Court upheld the constitutionality of municipal film licensing, providing that the statute was properly drafted to avoid unconstitutional vagueness.

From the viewpoint of purely constitutional arguments, Times Film Corporation had put all of its eggs in one basket, and the Court held that the law was not invalid on its face. Speaking through Justice Clark, the majority denied that a film exhibitor had the right to show any and every movie at least once, "even if this film contains the basest type of pornography, incitement to riot or forceful overthrow of orderly government."

Chief Justice Warren, joined by Black, Douglas and Brennan, dissented, holding that if film censorship is valid, there is no reason why it cannot be extended to other forms of expression.

In *Freedman v. Maryland*, the Supreme Court held that laws calling for prior submission of all movies to a censorship board are valid only if the review board is required to grant the license promptly or go to court for a judicial hearing. The burden is on the censor to prove that a film is, in fact, obscene. Maryland's procedures failed this test.

By 1967, only Kansas, Virginia and Maryland had statewide censorship laws. Kansas and Virginia got out of the movie censorship business before the dawn of the 1980s. Maryland rewrote its prior restraint law to conform to Freedman. However, the legislature, in creating the State Film Censor Board, had enacted a "sunset law." Its authority expired in 1981 and Maryland became the last state to operate a film censorship body.

Voluntary Censorship: Do Ratings Serve A Useful Purpose?

For reasons of self-interest and good public relations, Hollywood has attempted—from the time of the Hayes Office—to deflect government censorship by a program of self-censorship, or, in more recent times, a rating system designed—so Hollywood says—to offer guidance to parents and others on the types of contemporary films being offered.

The ratings system has been revised a number of times. At present, it is as follows:

G - general audiences, all ages admitted

PG - parental guidance suggested; some material may not be suitable for children

PG-13 - parents are strongly cautioned to give special guidance for attendance of children under 13; some material may be inappropriate

R - under 17 requires an accompanying parent or guardian

NC - no one under 17 admitted

Gone is the old X rating, which was formerly reserved for hard-core pornography and films depicting explicit sexual scenes. Hollywood was embarrassed—if that is possible—when an X rated film, *Midnight Cowboy*, won the Academy Award for best picture. It promptly was re-edited and re-released with an R rating.

Although one could argue that the current ratings system does offer some guidance to parents, few critics believe that it is systematically enforced. How many teens under age 17 are admitted to R and NC films? As one cynic put it, watching "early teens" line up at the mall for the movies: "If you're old enough to reach up and put your money through the window, they'll sell you a ticket." Perhaps not in some places, but the enforcement of the code is, in the judgment of many ratings systems critics, a major problem.

In the summer of 1999, following shootings which killed students at Littleton, Colorado, and Conyers, Georgia, critics began to pressure Hollywood to enforce the code. President Clinton, who had many political friends in show business, pressured the movie industry to require I.D. cards for teens attending R-rated films.

Radio and Television

As noted above, broadcasters have less First Amendment protection than do print media. Indeed, Walter Cronkite, long-time CBS managing editor and news anchorman, has referred to broadcasters as the "stepchildren of the First Amendment."

The early impetus for Federal government control of broadcasting, however, came from the broadcasters themselves. There are a limited number of air wave frequencies and after hundreds of new stations went on the air, static and chaos reigned before Congress stepped in. It passed the Radio Act of 1927, followed by the Communications Act of 1934.

The Federal Communications Commission (FCC) was established to license stations for limited periods. Typically, television stations received licenses to broadcast for five years and radio stations for seven. Although it is clearly an extremely valuable piece of property, a broadcast license rests on two key assumptions: (1) the "airwaves belong to the public," not the stations using them, and (2) broadcasting is to serve the "public convenience, interest or necessity."

Members of the FCC are appointed by the President for a period of five years, with terms of office staggered. Not more than three commissioners may belong to any one political party. No individual who has a financial interest in industries regulated by the FCC may serve, and Senate confirmation of appointments is required.

Congress made it clear, as has the commission, that the FCC was never intended to be a censor of program content. It does have considerable authority, however, to regulate broadcasting in the "public interest, convenience and necessity." In the so-called "Seven Dirty Words Case," involving a monologue by comedian George Carlin, *FCC v. Pacifica Foundation*, 438 U.S. 726 (1978), the Supreme Court made it clear that the FCC has legal authority to punish stations who air "filthy words, even if those words are not legally obscene."

A disc jockey on a New York FM radio station owned by Pacifica Foundation played Carlin's 12-minute record, made in his nightclub act. The comedian repeated, in a variety of contexts, "the curse words and swear words...you couldn't say on the public airwaves." Carlin then said them and the station put them on the airwaves in the middle of a weekday afternoon when a listener, driving his small child home, heard them and was not amused. He filed a complaint with the FCC.

In an opinion by Justice John Paul Stevens, the Court upheld the FCC reprimand, finding that, while the terms used were not obscene, they were indecent—a problem magnified by the fact that the material was aired during the hours of the day when children might hear it. Noting that freedom of speech is not absolute and has been legally constrained in the U.S. for sedition, defamation, "fighting words" and obscenity, Stevens wrote:[77]

> We must consider its context in order to determine whether the Commission's action was constitutionally permissible...courts have long recognized that each medium of expression presents special First Amendment problems and that of all forms of communication, it is broadcasting that has received the most limited First Amendment protection.
>
> Patently offensive, indecent material presented over the airwaves confronts the citizen, not only in public, but also in the privacy of the home, where the individual's right to be left alone plainly outweighs the First Amendment rights of an intruder.
>
> Broadcasting is uniquely accessible to children, even those too young to read...The ease with which children may obtain access to broadcast material...amply justifies special treatment of indecent broadcasting.
>
> As Mr. Justice Sutherland wrote, a 'nuisance may be merely a right thing in the

wrong place—like a pig in a parlor instead of the barnyard…We simply hold that when the Commission finds that a pig has entered the parlor, the exercise of its regulatory power does not depend on proof that the pig is obscene.'

In 1993-95, the FCC fined some radio stations that broadcast Howard Stern's talk show a total of more than $1.5 million for what it considered airing of indecent radio programs. The ultimate weapon that the FCC can (but seldom does) exercise is its refusal to renew a broadcast license of a station which fails to program "in the public interest."

New Media: Cable TV and the Internet

In 1984, Congress wrote the Cable Communications Policy Act which incorporates regulation of cable systems into the 1934 Communications Act. The law sets up a legal framework for community regulation of cable systems under the supervision of the FCC. The statute also distinguishes between programs that were initially broadcast over the air and then retransmitted by cable and cable-only programming that is never sent over the airwaves. Local public access channels provided by the cable company and Home Box Office are examples of the later category.

The Cable Act permits local governments and cable systems to ban programs that are "obscene" or "indecent." As a matter of settled law, it is clear that "obscene" programs may be banned. "Indecent" programming, however, is another matter. Although there are relatively few cases in this new medium, several Federal courts have ruled that state and local "indecency" laws, as applied to cable, violate the First Amendment.

In Miami, Fla., for example, cable subscriber Ruben Cruz challenged the "indecency" provision of the Cable Act in Federal District Court, which found the provision unconstitutional. The U.S. Court of Appeals for the 11ᵗʰ Circuit agreed, ruling in an influential opinion:

> Cablevision…does not intrude into the home. The Cablevision subscriber must affirmatively elect to have cable service come into his home. Additionally, the subscriber must make the additional affirmative decision whether to purchase any 'extra' programming service, such as HBO. The subscriber must make a monthly decision whether to continue to subscribe to cable, and if dissatisfied with the cable service, he may cancel his subscription. The Supreme Court's reference to 'a nuisance rationale' is not applicable to the Cablevision system where there is no possibility that a non-cable subscriber will be confronted with materials carried only on cable.

Additionally, parents may obtain a "lockbox" or a parental key device enabling them to prevent children from gaining access to "objectionable" channels of programming. Cablevision provides these without charge to subscribers.

It should be noted that this case, *Cruz v. Ferre, 755 F.2d 1415 (11ᵗʰ Cir. 1985), was not appealed to the U.S. Supreme Court.*

A U.S. District Court in Salt Lake City, Utah, ruled that the Utah Cable Television Programming Decency Act violated the First Amendment because its "indecency" standards failed to meet U.S. Supreme Court guidelines under *Miller*. The U.S. Court of Appeals sustained the verdict and the U.S. Supreme Court affirmed without comment in *Wilkinson v. Jones*, 480 U.S. 926 (1987).

Communications Decency Act of 1996

Public concern over access to pornographic materials via the Internet led Congress to enact the Communications Decency Act . The statute is only one of six parts (Title V) of the Telecommunications Act of 1996, a 103-page law whose primary purpose has little to do with "decency." Its basic objective is to reduce regulation and encourage "the rapid deployment of new telecommunications technologies."

Most major provisions of the law deal, not with the Internet, but rather with promotion of competition in the local telephone service market, multichannel video market, and the market for over the air broadcasting. Six of the statute's seven titles were the result of extensive congressional hearings and reports prepared by Senate and House committees.

The Communications Decency Act, by contrast, featured provisions added in executive committee after hearings had concluded or were adopted as amendments during floor debate on the legislation. An amendment offered in the Senate was the source of two statutory provisions challenged in the case of *Reno v. American Civil Liberties Union,* 117 S. Ct. 2329, (1997).

The CDA established a variety of content-based restrictions on the Internet, ranging from "obscenity" and child pornography to "indecency" and the discussion of abortion services. Several First Amendment interest groups, led by ACLU, challenged the statute shortly after it was signed by President Clinton in February, 1996. ACLU did not dispute provisions banning "obscenity" and child pornography and the U.S. did not defend restrictions Congress placed on discussion of abortion on the Internet. Focus of the legal debate, therefore, was on the congressional ban on transmission of "indecent" material to minors via the Internet.

Two parts of the act were the center of the lawsuit. Section 223(a) (1) (B) forbade using a "telecommunications device" for making, creating, or soliciting "any comment, request, suggestion, proposal, image or other communication which is obscene or indecent, knowing the recipient of the communication is under 18 years of age, regardless of whether the maker of such communication placed the call or initiated the communication."

Section 223 (d) provided that whoever "uses any interactive computer service to display in a manner available to a person under 18 years of age, any comment, request, suggestion, proposal, image, or other communication that, in context, depicts or describes, in terms patently offensive, measured by contemporary community standards, sexual or excretory activities or organs, regardless of whether the user of such service placed the call or initiated the communication" would be fined, imprisoned or both.

In June, 1996, a special panel of three Federal District Court judges unanimously declared the Communications Decency Act unconstitutional. The tribunal stressed the fact that the term "indecent," mentioned nowhere in the statute, is inherently vague. The court also concluded that the law forbade speech that was legal for adults, and that the law's provisions to require age screening of Internet messages was technically impossible. It found the government's position "profoundly repugnant to First Amendment principles." The U.S. appealed the decision.

On June 26, 1997, the U.S. Supreme Court, by a vote of 7-2, sustained the lower court's judgment. The two dissenters, Chief Justice Rehnquist and Justice O'Connor, agreed that parts of the law were unconstitutional, although they would have upheld other parts of the statute.

Writing for the majority, Justice Stevens noted that the ultimate effect of the statute was to censor speech that was protected for adults under the First Amendment. He also noted the problem of vagueness and overbreadth.

Stevens, observing that the law prohibits communications that are (1) "indecent" and (2) patently offensive as measured by contemporary community standards, found an "absence of a definition of either term," and consequently, the law "will provoke uncertainty among speakers about how the two standards relate to each other and just what they mean...This uncertainty undermines the likelihood that the CDA has been carefully tailored to the goal of protecting minors." He continued:[78]

> In evaluating the free speech rights of adults, we have made it perfectly clear that sexual expression which is indecent, but not obscene, is protected by the First Amendment. Where obscenity is not involved, we have consistently held that the fact that protected speech may be offensive to some does not justify its suppression...It is true that we have repeatedly recognized the governmental interest in protecting children from harmful materials...But that interest does not justify an unnecessarily broad suppression of speech addressed to adults...Regardless of the strength of the government's interest in protecting children, the level of discourse reaching a mailbox simply cannot be limited to that which would be suitable for a sandbox.

Stevens then addressed the issue of overbreadth:[79]

> The breadth of the CDA's coverage is wholly unprecedented...Its open-ended prohibitions embrace all nonprofit entities and individuals posting indecent messages or displaying them on their own computers in the presence of minors. The general, undefined terms...cover large amounts of non-pornographic material with serious educational or other value...As a matter of constitutional tradition, in the absence of evidence to the contrary, we presume that governmental regulation of the content of speech is more likely to interfere with the free exchange of ideas than to encourage it. The interest in encouraging freedom of expression in a democratic society outweighs any theoretical but unproven benefit of censorship.

U.S. v. Playboy Entertainment Group, 120 S. Ct. 1878 (2000)

On May 23, 2000, the Court again ruled on a controversial provision (Section 505) of the Telecommunications Act of 1996. Designed to protect adults who find sexually-oriented programming offensive and to prevent such material from entering homes where children might see it against their parents' wishes, the law required cable TV operators to "fully scramble or otherwise fully block" channels devoted to "sexually-oriented programming" at hours when children were likely to view cable TV.

Playboy Entertainment Group challenged the provision, and a special Federal District Court in Delaware ruled that it violated the First Amendment by targeting a certain kind of speech based on its content, and banned that type of programming for adult subscribers for two-thirds of the day.

The three-judge panel suggested that children were protected by Section 504, which provides for voluntary blocking. Customers who wish to receive a blocking device could have one installed free of charge while those who wished to receive Playboy programming would be able to receive it 24 hours per day. The court enjoined the government from enforcing Section 505, but the U.S. appealed and the Supreme Court accepted the case.

In a 5-4 ruling, the Rehnquist Court affirmed the special panel's decision. Although all of the justices believed that the government's interests were legitimate, the majority concluded that there were **less restrictive means** for Congress to achieve the desired ends. Specifically, the majority held that cable operators could be required to provide free lockout devices to subscribers.

Justice Anthony Kennedy wrote:

> When the purpose and design of a statute is to regulate speech by reason of its content, special consideration of latitude is not accorded to the government merely because the law can somehow be described as a burden rather than outright suppression…an effective blocking system would provide parents the information needed to engage in active supervision. The government has not shown that this alternative, a regime of added communication and support, would be insufficient to secure its objective, or that any overriding harm justifies its intervention.

The majority opinion was joined by Justices John Paul Stevens, David Souter, Ruth Bader Ginsburg and Clarence Thomas.

Chief Justice William Rehnquist dissented, as did Sandra Day O'Connor, Antonin Scalia and Stephen Breyer. Justice Breyer, writing for the dissenters, said that the majority had not made a realistic assessment of the alternatives. He said that there is no evidence that allowing cable subscribers to request complete blocking of certain programming would be equally effective in shielding children.

Justice Breyer noted that millions of children are left alone at home after school, and that the restrictions struck down by the Court offered more certain protections for a "large number of families."

By finding "adequate alternatives" where there are none, the Court reduces Congress's protective power to the vanishing point, he said.

Child Online Protection Act

After the Supreme Court held that provisions of the Communications Decency Act threatened freedom of speech, Congress responded by passing the Child Online Protection Act in 1998. COPA was limited in scope to content on commercial web sites, not e-mail or chat rooms, both of which had been covered in the CDA.

The CDA had applied to "any person," but COPA prohibited the knowing dissemination of material that is "harmful to minors." This was defined, based on language used by the High Tribunal in *Miller v. California* (1973), as those sexually explicit materials that would seem inappropriate to "the average person, applying contemporary community standards." Minors were defined as those under the age of 17. Each violation carried a penalty of a $50,000 fine and six months in jail.

The CDA did not allow defendants an "affirmative defense," that is, to claim that they had tried to uphold the law. Under COPA, Web sites could avoid prosecution by showing that they had made good-faith efforts to prevent children from gaining access to sexual material, through the use of a credit card or special access code.

Predictably, the American Civil Liberties Union, the Electronic Frontier Foundation, and the Electronic Privacy Information Center, among others, called the statute "son of CDA," and challenged it in Federal courts. In fact, they filed the initial lawsuit the day after the bill was signed into law by President Clinton.

Although they scored legal victories at the District Court level and in the U.S. Court of Appeals for the Third Circuit, the "coalition" faced another challenge when the nation's Highest Tribunal agreed to review the case.

During its 2001-2002 term, the Supreme Court reviewed two cases in which lower Federal courts had struck down provisions of COPA and the Child Pornography Prevention Act (CPPA).

Ashcroft v. Free Speech Coalition, 535 U.S. 234 (2002)

In *Ashcroft v. Free Speech Coalition*, decided April 16, 2002, the Supreme Court struck down a congressional ban on "virtual" child pornography, holding that the law was constitutionally overbroad. The statute, the Court held, would suppress not only images harmful to children, but also legitimate artistic or political expression.

At issue was a provision in the Child Pornography Prevention Act aimed at cracking down on computer-generated child pornography which displayed images that "appear to be" those of minors engaging in sexually explicit conduct.

In July, 1997, the Free Speech Coalition, a trade association of businesses involved in production and distribution of "adult" entertainment, filed suit in the Northern California U.S. District Court, contending that sections of the new law were unconstitutionally vague.

District Judge Samuel Conti rejected those claims, upholding the constitutionality of CPPA. "Even if no children are involved in the production of sexually explicit materials, the devastating...effect that such materials have on society and the well-being of children merits the regulation of such images," he ruled.

The Free Speech Coalition appealed Judge Conti's ruling to the Ninth Circuit Court of Appeals. It overruled the lower court's decision, holding that parts of the CPPA were unconstitutionally vague and also unconstitutionally overbroad.

The tribunal held that the statute banned material that is protected by the First Amendment: visual depiction of adults and computer-generated non-persons that "appear to be" minors and promotional materials that "convey the impression" that they are minors. Congress, the appeals court said, "cannot regulate virtual child pornography because it does not require the use of actual children." The Ninth Circuit's ruling was taken on appeal to the Supreme Court by U.S. Attorney General John Ashcroft. Affirming the lower Federal court and writing for a 7-2 majority, Justice Anthony M. Kennedy said:[80]

Few legitimate movie producers or book publishers, or few other speakers in any capacity would risk distributing images in or near the uncertain reach of this law. The Constitution gives significant protection from overbroad laws that chill speech within the First Amendment's vast and privileged sphere.

Legitimate artistic expression that might have been deterred by law, Kennedy noted, included award-winning films such as "American Beauty" and "Traffic," both of which include sexual scenes involving minors. The justice also commented that some modern versions of Shakespeare's *Romeo and Juliet*, a literary classic about two teenage lovers, might run afoul of the law.

Kennedy's opinion recognized the seriousness of child sexual abuse. He stressed, however, that when the Court has upheld bans on pornography, it has based its rulings on concern for real victims. The 1996 statute, he said, "prohibits speech that records no crime and creates no victims by its production."

62

Justices John Paul Stevens, David Souter, Ruth Bader Ginsburg and Stephen Breyer supported Kennedy's opinion. Justice Clarence Thomas wrote a concurring opinion, explaining his reasons for reaching the same conclusion. He indicated that he was open to regulation of virtual images.

Chief Justice William H. Rehnquist, joined by Associate Justices Antonin Scalia and Sandra Day O'Connor, voted to uphold fully the contested provisions of the law. They said the statute could have been narrowly read to cover only computer images "virtually indistinguishable" from actual children.

The Free Speech Coalition did not challenge one major provision of the law and it remains intact. That is the congressional ban on "morphing," in which a photograph of an actual child is manipulated on a computer to make it appear that the child is engaged in sex. This could be seen as precisely the kind of child exploitation the Court had outlawed in 1990 in *Osborne v. Ohio*.

Less than two weeks after the Supreme Court ruling in *Ashcroft v. Free Speech Coalition*, the attorney general, supported by angry members of Congress, was outlining proposals that he hoped would pass constitutional muster and ban computer simulations of teenagers or children having sex.

Ashcroft v. ACLU, 535 U.S. 564 (2002)

Soon after Congress enacted the Child Online Protection Act in 1998, the American Civil Liberties Union challenged its validity in the U.S. District Court for the Eastern District of Pennsylvania. Joining the ACLU were several Web publishers and free speech groups, including American Booksellers, Foundation for Free Expression, the Electronic Frontier Foundation and the Philadelphia Gay News, which feared that the adult content appearing on their sites would make them liable for prosecution under COPA.

The District Court granted a preliminary injunction preventing the government from enforcing the statute. The court found that the high costs of implementing age verification systems would lead Web publishers to quit publishing objectionable materials, and would lead to unnecessary censorship. It concluded that COPA imposed too heavy a burden on First Amendment freedoms in its attempt to shield minors from harmful Web content.

A panel of the Third Circuit Court of Appeals unanimously upheld the District Court ruling. Web publishers, it held, would have to censor material that might be considered harmful by the nation's most Puritan communities, but might be considered permissible in communities with more liberal notions of sexual morality.

Looking ahead to future technologies, the Appeals Court expressed its confidence that developing technology will soon render the "community standards" challenge moot, making congressional regulation to protect minors from harmful material on the Web constitutionally practicable.

Attorney General John Ashcroft appealed for a writ of *certiorari,* which the U.S. Supreme Court granted on May 21, 2001.

In *Ashcroft v. ACLU*, decided May 14, 2002, the Supreme Court handed down what Justice Clarence Thomas characterized as a "very limited decision." The High Tribunal concluded that reliance of the Child Online Protection Act on a notion of "community standards" to define what material in cyberspace is "harmful to minors" does not necessarily violate the First Amendment.

In overruling the Third Circuit, the Supreme Court noted that other potential free speech issues surrounded COPA. These included whether government could have found a **less**

restrictive means to protect children, an issue raised at District Court trial, but not considered by the appellate court. Without deciding those issues, the U.S. Supreme Court ordered the Third Circuit to review those questions, but left its ban on enforcement of COPA in place pending the ultimate outcome.

In a concurring opinion, joined by Justices Ruth Bader Ginsburg and David Souter, Justice Anthony Kennedy noted that there was a "very real likelihood" that COPA was unconstitutional on its face. However, Kennedy recognized that, given the fact that the law was enacted in response to the Court's striking down of the Communications Decency Act, "the Judiciary must proceed with caution and identify overbreadth with care before invalidating the Act."

Only Justice John Paul Stevens dissented, writing that he would have affirmed the Third Circuit's decision. "In the context of the Internet," Stevens wrote, "community standards become a sword, rather than a shield. If a prurient appeal is offensive in a Puritan village, it may be a crime to post it on the World Wide Web."

In March, 2003, the Third Circuit again found the law unconstitutional because, in its efforts to shield minors from some web sites, it had restricted access of adults to the material. Meanwhile, the Supreme Court barred the government from enforcing the law.

In Ashcroft v. ACLU (542 U.S. 656 (2004), known as Ashcroft II, the Supreme Court held, 5-4, that COPA was unenforceable because imposing criminal penalties was not the least restrictive means of achieving congressional objectives. It upheld the Third Circuit's injunction, preventing the statute from taking effect.

However, it again sent the case back for further review. It instructed the lower Federal tribunal to consider whether filters are a less restrictive and more effective means to protect children, while protecting First Amendment rights of adults.

As of mid-2006, the COPA was not being enforced and neither Congress nor the courts seemed ready to clarify the law's ultimate status.

Public Libraries, the Internet, and Material Harmful to Children

Congress made a third attempt to regulate internet speech with the Children's Internet Protection Act (CIPA). The law requires public libraries to install filters to block access to obscene material, child pornography, or other materials "harmful to minors." This was a condition of receiving Federal funding under the Library Services and Technology Act.

A Federal District Court in Philadelphia ruled that the filtering act was unconstitutional and issued an injunction barring enforcement. The government, however, used a provision in the statute that permitted a direct appeal to the Supreme Court, bypassing the Court of Appeals.

In *U.S. v. American Library Association*, 539 U.S. 194 (2003), the Supreme Court reversed the District Court, upholding CIPA, 6-3. Chief Justice Rehnquist wrote:[81] "Congress has wide latitude to attach conditions to the receipt of Federal assistance in order to further its policy objectives." He also rejected the District Court's view that libraries are public forums, noting that internet access in public libraries is neither a traditional nor a designated public forum. "Filters," Chief Justice Rehnquist said, "are a reasonable way for libraries to exclude certain categories of content, without making individualized judgments that everything that they do make available has requisite and appropriate quality."

Justices Kennedy and Breyer, in concurring opinions, reasoned that there was "little to this case" because adults could ask librarians to unblock filtered material, and CIPA imposed a small burden on the adult library patrons. "I cannot say," Justice Breyer wrote, "that any speech-related harm that the act may cause is disproportionate, when considered in relation to the Act's legitimate objectives."[82]

Justices Stevens, Souter and Ginsburg, finding limited adult access to constitutionally protected materials objectionable, dissented.

U.S. v. Williams

In May, 2008, the Roberts Court reviewed a decision of a U.S. Court of Appeals which held that the pandering provision of Prosecutorial Remedies and Other Tools to end the Exploitation of Children Today (PROTECT) Act were overbroad, vague and unconstitutional.

The "pandering clause" of the act imposes criminal liability on anyone who knowingly "advertises, promotes, presents, distributes, or solicits through the mails, or in interstate or foreign commerce by any means, including by computer, any material or purported material that reflects the belief, or that is intended to cause another to believe, that the material or purported material is, or contains an obscene visual depiction of a minor engaging in sexually explicit conduct, or a visual depiction of an actual minor engaging in sexually explicit conduct."

The 11th Circuit found that the pandering clause of the PROTECT Act was not limited to child pornography and could not be invoked to reach beyond illegal content and target protected speech.

The question before the nation's highest tribunal was whether part of the act is overly broad, impermissibly vague or punishes constitutionally protected free speech.

Justice Scalia, writing for the majority in a 7-2 decision, upheld the latest congressional attempt to halt the spread of child pornography on the Internet. The justices found that the PROTECT Act applies regardless of whether the materials offered exist or involve real children. Scalia said that the statute was a constitutional effort by Congress to protect innocent children from abuse:[83]

> We hold that offers to provide or requests to obtain child pornography are categorically excluded from the First Amendment...The law punishes speech seeking to conclude illegal transactions...Such speech does not get First Amendment protection...Offers to give or receive what is unlawful to possess have no social value and thus, like obscenity, enjoy no First Amendment protection.

Chief Justice Roberts and Justices Stevens, Kennedy, Thomas, Breyer and Alito joined in the majority opinion. Justices Souter and Ginsburg dissented, largely on grounds that past Supreme Court decisions held that only pornographic photographs of actual children could be prohibited and that virtual child pornography retains First Amendment protection.

FREEDOM OF THE PRESS

Freedom of the press may be one of the nation's most vital civil liberties. It also is a source of a great amount of controversy because many Americans, private citizens and public officials, do not understand the meaning of this basic freedom. The press in a democratic society serves not as a cheerleader for those in positions of public authority, but as a "watchdog" and critic of their conduct of the public's business. The press is the means by which citizens are given information on which they can make intelligent decisions about public policies and public leaders, or would-be leaders. In a widely-quoted letter to Edward Carrington, Thomas Jefferson wrote:[84]

> The basis of governments being the opinion of the people, the first object should be to keep that right....were it left to me to decide whether we should have a government without newspapers, or newspapers without a government, I should not hesitate a moment to prefer the latter.

Jefferson believed that the watchdog function of the press was vital to a democratic political system. It must, he said, voice alarm, when liberty is threatened or individual rights are endangered. By shining the spotlight of pitiless publicity upon public officials who abuse the public trust, peaceful change could occur.

Libel and Press Responsibility

Although the Constitution mandates a free press, it does not require a responsible one. Indeed, heated theoretical debate has ranged for generations over the problem of an "irresponsible" press. Although most publishers and their editorial staffs at least pay lip service to the notion of **"social responsibility,"** not all media people agree what constitutes responsibility in particular situations. They are quite reluctant to insist on it as a matter of professional ethics.

Of all the serious legal issues facing the American press in the 21st Century, the most common may well be that of libel. This, however, is hardly new. Libel has been a source of concern to reporters, editors and publishers for more than 200 years.

There have been thousands of libel decisions but the mere threat of a lawsuit may lead some timid editors to kill or "water down" a story that otherwise might run. The so-called "chilling effect" of libel is always a source of concern in the newsroom. Perhaps the most important development in libel law in recent decades has been the **vast sums of money awarded to plaintiffs by juries.** Some examples:

A Wyoming jury awarded one Kimberli Pring, a former Miss Wyoming beauty contest winner, $26.5 million for a *Penthouse* magazine article in which she never was named. Although the award was overturned on appeal, *Penthouse's* legal fees were reported to be several hundred thousands of dollars.

The *Alton Telegraph* in Illinois lost a $9.2 million verdict on the basis of an interoffice memo, although no newspaper article even appeared in print. The *Telegraph* at the time was worth about $3 million. If the award had not been substantially reduced, the *Telegraph,* probably now would be out of business.

Show business celebrity Carol Burnett won a verdict of $1.6 million against the *National Enquirer* for an article which, although clearly slipshod journalism, may not have damaged Ms. Burnett's reputation very much. California courts eventually decided on a $150,000 award and Burnett donated the money to the University of Hawaii to establish a program for responsible journalism.[85]

Bruce Sanford, a widely-known Washington libel lawyer, argues that the punishment levied against the *National Enquirer* in the Burnett case did not fit the crime. "That kind of an award in a libel case for a story about being boisterous in a restaurant has an intimidating effect on the responsible press when they are printing far more serious allegations," Sanford said in a speech on May 13, 1981, at Northwestern University. The *Enquirer* had said that Burnett was rowdy and drunk in a restaurant while dining near Henry Kissinger.

"She has done for the libel suit what President Reagan has done for the jelly bean," Sanford said. She's given it popularity and plausibility.

Sanford notes that **20 years ago, libel verdicts seldom exceeded $20,000, but that typical verdicts today exceed six figures.**[86]

What is Libel? Slander?

What is **libel?** How does it differ from **slander?** Libel is a false printed or broadcast statement about a person which tends to bring one into public hatred, contempt or ridicule or to injure one in business or occupation. Slander consists of oral defamation.

Libel law is state law. The problem in the 1990s was much more complicated than it was in the 1890s. During the 19th Century, a printed communication was dealt with more harshly than slander because libel then was considered more permanent, more people saw it and it was generally considered to be intentional.

Broadcasting has made past distinctions almost meaningless. Comedian Jay Leno or one of his guests could defame someone on his TV show before an audience of millions. Although not printed, this defamation could have an greater impact on one's reputation than any print medium in the nation.

Four Elements of Actionable Libel

In order for a plaintiff to have a real case, rather than simply a nuisance suit, four elements must be proved. These are defamation, identification, publication and fault.[87]

Defamation: The words complained of must injure one's reputation. Some words, by their very nature, are harmful. This type of libel is called libel *per se* (direct libel). One cannot falsely call someone a "thief," "liar," "murderer," or "whore."

"Red flag words" like communist, fascist and atheist, must be avoided in news copy unless a publication is prepared to go to court. Veteran editors and reporters know that there is a very real difference between truth and **provable truth.** What a journalist knows in his/her heart is true may not be truth to a judge or a jury.

Another kind of libel is libel *per quod* (indirect). Here a statement requires reference to extrinsic circumstances to give it a defamatory meaning. For example, a false story that Jane Roe of 1234 Blessed Event Blvd. has just given birth to twins at Midwest City Hospital can be a problem if Mrs. Roe has been married for only two weeks and several of her friends and neighbors know this fact.

Identification: One cannot sue a newspaper for libel unless one can establish that he/she was the defamed party. Because of its landmark importance in another area, some people may tend to forget that *New York Times v. Sullivan* (1964) was reversed by the U.S. Supreme Court in part because Montgomery , Ala., Police Commissioner L.B. Sullivan had not been identified specifically. No "southern violator" was named in the *New York Times* ad.

One can be identified , however, in a number of ways other than by name, such as by photo, initials, or from the context of a story involving only a small number of people.

Jack Lait discovered this when his book, *Dallas Confidential,* was found to have libeled a number of Niemann-Marcus personnel. He had referred to male employees as "flaming faggots" and women workers as " high-priced call girls." Because Niemann-Marcus then had only six women and men in their respective clothing departments, this was considered to be libelous.

Publication: Any story which appears in print or goes over the airwaves is, as a practical matter, published. It is presumed to be seen or heard by a "third party." From a strictly legal viewpoint, printing and distribution of a story are not required for a successful libel suit.

Publication occurs, therefore, whenever a third party hears or sees a defamatory statement.

Fault: Fault is the fourth element in libel. It depends, to a large extent, on who the plaintiff is to determine what one must prove. If the plaintiff is a private citizen, he or she generally must prove only press negligence. But state laws do differ, and the Burger Court in 1974 gave them freedom to adopt varying liability standards in *Gertz v. Welch.*

"Actual malice:" The concept of fault has been changed considerably by the U.S. Supreme Court since 1964. In that year, the Warren Court, in *New York Times v. Sullivan*, ruled that the press had a First Amendment right to be mistaken in publishing false reports about public officials:

> Erroneous statement is inevitable in free debate and...it must be protected if the freedoms of expression are to have the 'breathing space' that they need...to survive.

In this case, the Court held that a public official could collect damages for a libelous remark about his public role only if he proved it was made with "**actual malice**." This the Court defined as "with knowledge that it was false or with reckless disregard of whether it was false or not."[88]

In companion cases in 1967, the Warren Court extended this actual malice test to **public figures.** In *Curtis Publishing Co. v. Butts* and *Associated Press v. Walker,* the high tribunal reviewed libel verdicts against the *Saturday Evening Post* and Associated Press.

The Court voted, 5-4, to uphold Butts' $460,000 libel judgment, but unanimously overruled Walker's $500,000 judgment against AP. The Court compared the two situations to illustrate the meaning of reckless disregard for the truth. The Court agreed that both Walker and Butts were public figures and should be subject to the **Sullivan Rule**, although neither of the men was a public official.[89]

Both *Walker* and *Butts* were involved in issues "in which the public has a justified and important interest." In the years since *Walker* and *Butts,* the precedent has stood. Neither the Burger nor Rehnquist courts has retreated from this concept and it appears to be settled law. **Public figures, as well as public officials, must prove reckless disregard for truth to win libel suits.**

The Butts award stood because of what many editors and publishers would characterize as slipshod, sloppy journalism. A cardinal rule, learned in most basis writing courses in Journalism schools, is "check your sources!"

Experienced reporters and editors always try to confirm stories by checking with multiple sources. Ben Bradlee, former Executive Editor of the *Washington Post,* claims that his newspaper never published any of Bob Woodward or Carl Bernstein's Watergate stories without confirming information from a second source.

In the Butts case, the former football coach and athletic director at University of Georgia had been accused in a May 23, 1963, cover story in the *Saturday Evening Post* of conspiring with Alabama coach Paul "Bear" Bryant to fix a college football game between the two Southeastern

Conference schools. The story was based on an affidavit, signed by one George Burnett who claimed to have accidentally overheard a telephone conversation between Butts and Bryant.

The information was not checked thoroughly. The single source turned out to be a convicted felon, then on probation for writing bad checks. Clearly, the *Post* should have been more careful. Fred Graham, who wrote the story, was a free-lancer, rather than a *Post* staffer. Indeed, he knew comparatively little about the fine points of intercollegiate football. Alabama, a 14-point favorite, won, 35-0, behind sophomore quarterback Joe Namath.

The Supreme Court in *Butts* cited what has come to be known as the **"Prudent Publisher Rule."** In a nutshell, the rule holds that publishers must follow the professional standards of journalism. This includes verification of facts, particularly where deadline pressures are less than monumental. Unlike wire services and multiple deadline daily newspapers, monthly magazines have comparatively "relaxed" deadline pressures.

The Walker case involved the integration of University of Mississippi during the fall of 1962. James Meredith, a Black senior transfer student, had been ordered admitted to Ole Miss by the U.S. Court of Appeals. It was **"hot news."** Associated Press was on the scene, filing updated stories throughout an evening filled with bloodshed and violence.

Major Gen. Edwin Walker, a retired tank commander active in right-wing causes, was on the Ole Miss campus. He had actively fought racial integration. A group of white students attacked U.S. marshals who were protecting Meredith. Walker conceded that he had been there and had addressed the students, but emphatically denied having led the charge, as AP had reported. A jury returned a verdict of $500,000 in his favor.

The Court compared the cases, noting tremendous deadline pressures facing a wire service, compared to almost leisurely deadlines faced by magazines. In *Walker,* there was insufficient time for checking; in *Butts,* there was.

What kinds of libel suits are doomed? As a practical matter, government, political parties and pressure groups cannot sue for libel because the citizen has a fundamental right to criticize such groups.

A municipal corporation has been held to have no legal personality capable of being defamed. Utterance directed against a government or city have been considered absolutely privileged. In 1920, the City of Chicago sued the *Chicago Tribune* for libeling its credit in the bond market and impairing its functioning as a municipality.

But the Illinois Supreme Court ruled against the city, noting that "no court of last resort in this country has ever held, or even suggested, that prosecutions for libel on government has any place in the American system of jurisprudence...Assuming that there was a temporary damage to the city and a resultant increase in taxes, it is better than an occasional individual newspaper that is so perverted in judgment or so misguided in his or its civic duty should go free than that all of the citizens should be put in jeopardy of imprisonment or economic subjugation if they venture to criticize an inefficient or corrupt government."[90]

Prior Restraint: The Near Doctrine

Traditionally, freedom of the press has meant freedom from **"prior restraint,"** or pre-publication censorship. This is an old principle of Anglo-Saxon law, noted by the great British jurist, Sir William Blackstone. It was stated in the U.S. Supreme Court in *Near v. Minnesota* (1931).

Samuel Near hardly was a heroic publisher, battling for Truth and Justice. He was, rather, violently anti-Semitic. He published several articles in his Minneapolis-based *Saturday Press,* charging that public officials had been guilty of neglect of duty and misconduct in office. In his November 19 edition, Near wrote:

> I say that 90% of the crimes committed against society in this city are committed by Jew gangsters...I am launching no attack against the Jewish people AS A RACE. I am merely calling attention to a FACT. And if the people of that race and faith wish to rid themselves of the odium and stigma THE RODENTS OF THEIR OWN RACE HAVE BROUGHT UPON THEM, they need only to step to the front and help decent citizens of Minneapolis rid the city of these criminal Jews.

Floyd B. Olson, a victim of Near's poison pen, also was county attorney of Hennepin County. He entered a complaint under a state law which permitted the state to forbid distribution of "malicious, scandalous and defamatory newspapers."

The trial court found Near guilty of publishing such a newspaper and issued a permanent injunction against further publication. The Minnesota Supreme Court upheld Near's conviction. It denied that the state law violated the U.S. First Amendment, applicable to the state by virtue of the due process clause of the 14th Amendment, or the Minnesota Constitution.

Near's attorneys took the case to the U.S. Supreme Court. The high tribunal found that **Minnesota's "press gag law" was an unconstitutional infringement of freedom of the press.** Speaking for the Court, Chief Justice Charles Evans Hughes wrote:[91]

> It is no longer questioned that liberty of the press is one of the personal freedoms protected by the 14th Amendment...Liberty of the press in the meaning of the Constitution is principally immunity from previous restraint. The statute cannot be justified by giving a publisher an opportunity to present his evidence. It would be only a step to a complete system of censorship. The fact that liberty of the press may be abused by miscreant purveyors of scandal does not make any the less necessary the immunity of the press from previous restraint in dealing with official misconduct.

"Subsequent punishment," the Chief Justice continued, "is the appropriate remedy, consistent with constitutional privilege." In short, if charges are false, one has the legal remedy of a libel action. The legal **doctrine of "no prior restraint" is not an absolute.** But the history of government-press relations in America is such that prior restraints have not been necessary.

Special problems do arise during wartime. When they do, the press has engaged in "self-censorship," after consultation with government leaders. The press did not jeopardize American national security during the first two World Wars, in Korea, or in Vietnam. Little evidence suggests that editors are less patriotic than other citizens.

The Pentagon Papers Case

In the 1971 Pentagon Papers case, the Nixon Administration challenged publication of classified materials by the *New York Times, Washington Post* and other newspapers on the grounds that such publication jeopardized U.S. national security and was not, therefore, protected by the First Amendment.

Leaked to the press by one Daniel Ellsberg, the Pentagon Papers were a study of U.S. decision-making during the Vietnam War. Among other things, these papers were highly embarrassing to President Lyndon Johnson and other public officials who appear to have misled the American public about their motives and intentions in Southeast Asia. Ellsberg was a heroic figure to the extreme left in American politics, but perhaps to few others. He very well may have been convicted of stealing secret documents and leaking them to the press, had an overzealous group of "plumbers" in the Nixon White House not raided his psychiatrist's office, seeking evidence to discredit him. His conviction was prevented by this over-zealotry of Nixon Administration officials.

But the case of the *New York Times-Washington Post v. U.S.* was more important. After the U.S. District Court had granted a temporary restraining order, the U.S. Supreme Court lifted it. The Court, with each of the nine justices giving a separate opinion—a most unusual procedure—ruled that the government had failed to show that publication of the documents jeopardized national security.

News media people and journalism educators disagreed on the outcome of the Pentagon Papers case. While some saw it as strengthening of the "no prior restraint" rule, others believed the decision was no great victory for the press. A number of newspapers had been censored for several days by court injunction. It would have been a great victory, some argued, if the *Times* or others had gone on publishing Neil Sheehan's series and then won its case in the Supreme Court.[92]

Watergate: Americans are deeply divided on their political preferences. Some citizens apparently believe that the press ought to report the "superiority" of their favorite party and candidates on its news pages, as well as on its editorial pages.

Consequently, whose ox is being gored at a given moment has much to do with the popularity (or lack of it) of specific newspapers. When the *Washington Post* took the lead in investigating the Watergate affair, many conservatives were angry. After all, they reasoned, the Graham family which published the paper were Democrats and long-time "Nixon haters." This overlooked the fact that news and editorial policies differ.

While a newspaper is free to print whatever political advice it wishes to offer on its editorial page, it ordinarily is restrained in its news columns by professional standards of objective reporting. Eventually the *Post*, the *New York Times* and others unmasked the ugly and painful story of the Watergate matter. Two young reporters, Carl Bernstein and Bob Woodward, won a Pulitzer Prize for their efforts and Richard M. Nixon became the first president in U.S. history to be forced to resign his office.[93]

Without a free press, the truth of the Watergate matter may never have come out. In most other nations of the world, the press never could have served as a critic of the administration, unmasking its wrongdoing. In Iron Curtain countries of the time, editors and reporters were virtual auxiliaries of the Communist Party and printed only those criticisms of party and government that were "officially inspired."

Right to reply: Some public officials and candidates for public office argue that the press should be required to give them news space to reply to critical articles and editorials. Florida enacted such a **"right to reply law,"** unanimously struck down by the Burger Court in 1974. In *Miami Herald Publishing Company v. Tornillo,* the Chief Justice said that a newspaper involves a "crucial process" of editorial judgment that may not be regulated by the state. Justice Burger wrote:[94]

A responsible press is an undoubtedly desirable goal, but press responsibility is not mandated by the Constitution and like many other virtues, it cannot be legislated.

Collision Of Constitutional Values: Free Press-Fair Trial

For a number of years, journalists, lawyers and judges have debated the merits of competing constitutional values. Although no sweeping philosophical statements have been forthcoming from the bar or bench, it is clear that sometimes the rights guaranteed in the First and Sixth Amendments can collide.

The right of a defendant in a criminal case to a fair trial by an impartial jury of his or her peers is guaranteed by the Constitution. Sometimes, judges have concluded, the press has conducted "trial by newspaper."

Another issue involves reporters keeping certain information from government officials. Although these problems may be of paramount and immediate concern to reporters, editors, lawyers, judges and public officials, they also have a major impact on the free flow of information and the public's "right to know."

Press privilege: Although reporters long have had considerable freedom to comment on public affairs, they have not yet been given a right to withhold identity of news sources from grand juries investigating crime. In companion cases, *Branzburg v. Hayes, In Re Pappas* and *U.S. v. Caldwell,* the Court reviewed three related cases of reporters who refused to disclose confidential information to public authorities.

Paul Branzburg, a *Louisville Courier-Journal* reporter, refused to give information regarding his news sources to officials investigating drug use in Clay County, Ky. Also involved in the 1972 cases were the militant Black Panthers.

Reporters traditionally protect their news sources for either ethical or practical reasons. Who will supply information unless he or she can be assured the source will not be identified? A reporter or editor known for "burning the source" is hardly likely to attract news sources. However, the reporter's understandable desire to remain silent may conflict with the defendant's right to compel testimony on his/her behalf in a criminal case. Sustaining contempt rulings against the reporters, the U.S. Supreme Court held:[95]

> We perceive no basis for holding that the public interest in law enforcement...is insufficient to override the consequential, but uncertain burden on news gathering which is said to result from insisting that reporters, like other citizens, respond to relevant questions put to them in the course of a valid grand jury investigation or criminal trial.

Justice Stewart dissented, commenting:[96]

> The court's crabbed view of the First Amendment reflects a disturbing insensitivity to the independent press in our society...the right to gather news implies a right to a confidential relationship between a newsman and his informants.

Paul Branzburg lost his case, but he did not disclose his sources. He left the *Courier-Journal* and took a job with the *Detroit Free Press.* When Kentucky attempted to extradite Branzburg, Michigan Gov. William Milliken refused. Many reporters have gone to jail, rather than identify their sources.

Shield laws: One response to Branzburg and related cases is a demand from some newsmen for **"shield laws,"** protecting them from any need to supply law enforcement agencies with information. Some reporters resent "doing their work for them."

Not all editors, publishers and reporters agree on the need for shield legislation. Most states already have such legislation, giving reporters a limited privilege to withhold information under specified conditions.

While some journalists press for shield laws, others believe that the First Amendment is good enough for them. They argue that the amendment, if correctly interpreted (from their viewpoint), is superior to mere statutory law. **Some journalists also argue that it is a mistake to admit for a moment that government can grant immunity.**

This implies that the state also can withdraw it, something most of them find an appalling idea. It also smacks of "press licensing," contrary to the First and 14th Amendments and American democratic values.

If the issue of shield laws is complex, so too is the problem of Free Press-Fair Trial. Although some students of the problem believe it is as old as the printing press, it has received much attention in recent years.

Newspaper editors admit that some papers, usually not their own, have abused freedom of the press. The American Newspaper Publishers Association and the American Society of Newspaper Editors long have warned, however, that any judicial reforms must preserve freedom of the press.

A dramatic case recently has stimulated Congress to consider a Federal shield law. In 2003, retired U.S. ambassador Joseph Wilson strongly disputed claims of the Bush administration that Saddam Hussein's Iraq had tried to purchase uranium from Niger to manufacture nuclear weapons. Subsequently, news stories and reports by syndicated columnist Robert Novak identified Wilson's wife, Valerie Plame, as a Central Intelligence Agency covert agent. Federal law makes such "outing" a crime.

Ambassador Wilson accused the administration of leaking his wife's identity as an act of revenge for his criticism. A Federal probe resulted, and reporters Judith Miller of the *New York Times* and Matthew Cooper of *Time* magazine were served with subpoenas. Neither would identify their sources. Found in contempt by Federal Judge Thomas Hogan, both were given time to appeal. Hogan also ordered *Time* to pay a fine of $1000 a day until it complied.

Despite the fact that some 34 state attorneys general supported review, the U.S. Supreme Court denied *certiorari,* so the ruling of a three-judge panel of the U.S. Court of Appeals stood. Cooper's editor-in-Chief at *Time* angered many journalists by turning over his notes. The *New York Times* stood behind Miller, who never published anything she had received from her source, although she later spent 85 days in jail.

Special Federal prosecutor Patrick Fitzgerald insisted that he needed the reporters to testify before a Grand Jury. Faced with going to prison, Cooper yielded. He said, however, that his source had freed him from his promise of confidentiality. Miller refused to budge and Judge Hogan ordered her imprisoned for contempt in July, 2005.

Many journalists and journalism organizations began to pressure Congress to enact a Federal shield law in the aftermath of the Plame case. It proved, they maintained, that such a statute was essential.

The *New York Times* editorialized: "...the specter of reporters being imprisoned merely for doing their jobs is something that should worry everyone who cherishes the First Amendment and the essential role of a free press in a democracy."

Ultimately, Miller was freed after her source, Lewis "Scooter" Libby, Vice President Richard Cheney's chief of staff, released her from her promise of confidentiality. She later reached an agreement with the Federal prosecutor to give limited testimony to the Grand Jury.

Reporters Committee for Freedom of the Press and the Society of Professional Journalists, among others, were able to get Congress to consider enacting a shield law. Early efforts failed, but a revived measure had a chance of being passed by a Democratic-controlled Congress late in 2008.

Even if Congress enacted such a statute, it appeared likely that President Bush would veto it. The President believes that it would encourage leaks of classified information, but journalists may be optimistic about the future.

The three most likely persons to succeed Bush, presumptive Republican nominee John McCain and Democratic hopefuls Hillary Clinton and Barack Obama all had endorsed a Federal Shield law by the spring of 2008.

Closing Courtrooms

Are there inherent, serious dangers to the American public in restricting news at its source? Could this lead to the danger, as some suggest, of secret arrest and ultimately secret trials?

In 1979, this became a real and major source of concern to the media and civil libertarians. The U.S. Supreme Court held that a New York judge had acted properly in excluding the press from a preliminary hearing, at which suppression of evidence in a murder case was at issue. Judge DePasquale excluded both spectators and the press from these proceedings.

The Gannett Corporation appealed DePasquale's ruling since its Rochester, N.Y., paper was involved. All legal efforts in New York failed, but the U.S. Supreme Court granted a hearing.

In *Gannett v. DePasquale,* Justice Stewart held that the **right to a public trial,** like a right to trial by jury, **is for the defendant's benefit, not the media's**. Defendants who opt to waive jury trial, or be tried in private may do so, if the trial judge approves.[97]

State trial court judges began to use *Gannett* as a legal excuse to close down actual criminal trials. The Supreme Court, much to the relief of the media, ruled in 1980 that lower court judges had misinterpreted their ruling. In *Richmond Newspapers v. Virginia,* the **Court ruled against closing actual trials, stressing that the Gannett ruling involved a "pretrial" proceeding.** Chief Justice Burger, speaking for a 7-1 majority, wrote:[98]

> ...the First Amendment guarantees of speech and press, standing alone, prohibit government from summarily closing courtroom doors which had long been open to the public at the time that amendment was adopted.
>
> It is not crucial whether we describe this right to attend criminal trials to hear, see, and communicate observations concerning them as a 'right of access,' or a 'right to gather information,' for we have recognized that 'without some protection for seeking out news, freedom of the press could be eviscerated.'
>
> Subject to the traditional time, place, and manner restrictions...streets, sidewalks, and parks are places traditionally open, where First Amendment rights may be exercised...a trial courtroom also is a public place where the people generally—and representatives of the media—have a right to be present.
>
> We hold that the right to attend criminal trials is implicit in the guarantee of the First Amendment; without the freedom to attend such trials, which people have exercised for centuries, important aspects of freedom of speech and of the press could be eviscerated.

Is the press always a negative influence in a defendant's fair trial? Or can it be a positive one?

Can the press rid the community of fear, suspicion and ugly rumors by reporting facts about crime?

Or can a publisher, intent on convicting a defendant, and probably hyping circulation at the same time, deny him a basic Sixth Amendment right to a fair trial?

Sheppard v. Maxwell: One of the most highly publicized episodes in the annals of the Free Press-Fair Trial controversy was that involving Dr. Sam Sheppard, a Cleveland, Ohio, osteopath convicted in 1954 of murdering his pregnant wife, Marilyn Reese Sheppard. A highly publicized trial in the Cuyahoga County Common Pleas courtroom of Judge Edward Blythin, followed by Sheppard's subsequent legal battles, personal misfortunes, and eventual acquittal at a second trial in 1966, made for one of the more dramatic cases in this troublesome area.

Cleveland media, particularly the *Cleveland Press*, led by Louis B. Seltzer, unleashed a chain of publicity virtually unprecedented in the annals of American jurisprudence. Front page editorials said that somebody was getting away with murder. The *Press* and others argued facts of the case in editorials, pointed out discrepancies in Sheppard's testimony, stressed his extra-marital adventures and quoted *Time* magazine's reference to Sheppard as the "Romeo of the rubbing table."

Convicted of second degree murder, Sheppard was sentenced to life in the Ohio penitentiary. After a long legal battle, the case reached the U.S. Supreme Court, which ruled the pre-trial and trial press publicity interfered with the trial itself. The Court also criticized Judge Blythin's failure to control the courthouse and trial. The jurist was a candidate for re-election and the vote took place only two weeks after Sheppard's trial began.

Judge Blythin gave reporters free reign in the courthouse and lost control. The Court ultimately placed blame squarely on Blythin's shoulders for permitting this situation to occur. The Court also stressed that the remedy for cases such as Sam Sheppard's was not restraint of the press. The Court opinion states:[99]

> Nothing proscribes the press from reporting events that transpire in the courtroom. But where there is reasonable likelihood that prejudicial news prior to trial will prevent a fair trial, the judge should continue the case until the threat abates, or transfer it to another county not so permeated with publicity. In addition, sequestration (locking up) of the jury was something the judge should have raised.

Over the years, publishers have argued that, if the U.S. Supreme Court considered existing procedural remedies adequate to cope with the Sheppard case, it is difficult to conceive of any situation where those safeguards could not adequately protect any defendant. Bar and bench, as well as press groups, have studied the problem for decades.

Countless university seminars and panels have discussed the issue. Some editors fear that the American courts may be moving in the direction of a British-type system where Fair Trial supersedes Free Press.

Reacting to the Sheppard case, a number of trial judges issued "gag orders," restricting press coverage of criminal trials. In 1976, the Supreme Court reviewed a Nebraska judge's order barring the press from reporting the alleged confession of a suspect about to be tried in a sensational multiple murder case. Some 17 newspapers, magazines, radio and television stations filed a joint Friend of the Court *(amicus curiae)* brief on the Nebraska gag order. In *Nebraska Press Association v. Stuart*, 427 U.S. 539 (1976), the Court held that such "gag orders" were unconstitutional prior restraints on the press, contrary to the commands of the First and 14th Amendments. **Chief Justice Burger commented that "...prior restraints...are the most serious and least tolerable infringements on First Amendment rights."**

Newsroom searches: Despite the Court's ruling in the Nebraska case, professional journalism organizations remained unconvinced that the Burger Court was a friend of the press and its constitutional freedoms. They pointed to the 1977-78 term of the Court as a particularly dark chapter in press freedom. They were most upset by rulings in *Zurcher v. Stanford Daily* and *In Re Farber.*

In April, 1971, police officers from Palo Alto, California, entered the newsroom of the *Stanford Daily,* campus newspaper at Stanford University. Armed with a valid search warrant, they sought photos of a clash between police and demonstrators at University Hospital, covered the previous day in a special edition. The *Daily* filed a civil action, alleging violations of the First, Fourth, and 14th Amendments. A U.S. District Court ruled in favor of the students, but the police appealed and the Supreme Court ruled, 5-3, in May, 1978, that such searches were legal.

The Court rejected the argument that the First Amendment combined with the Fourth Amendment rights of persons not suspected of crime, justified requiring Police Chief Zurcher or prosecutors to use **subpoenas** rather than **search warrants** to obtain information from newsmen and newspapers. Justice Stewart dissented:[100]

> It seems to me self-evident that police searches of newspaper offices burden the freedom of the press. The most immediate and obvious First Amendment injury caused by such a visitation by the police is physical disruption of the operation of the newspaper. Policemen occupying a newsroom and searching it thoroughly for what may be an expanded period of time will inevitably interrupt its normal operations and thus impair or even temporarily prevent the processes of news gathering, writing, editing and publishing. By contrast, a subpoena would afford the newspaper itself an opportunity to locate whatever material might be requested and produce it.

In its January 7-8, 1978, editions the *New York Times* carried stories by Myron Farber on a number of mysterious deaths at Riverdell Hospital, Oradell, N.J. Following the stories, Dr. Mario E. Jascalevich was indicted on charges of poisoning five patients.

The trial started early in 1978. In May, Judge William Arnold ordered reporter Farber and the *Times* to turn over notes and documents on the case to the defense. They refused.

On June 30, Judge Arnold directed Farber and the *Times* to let him inspect the materials *in camera* (in his chambers, office or home). Again, Farber and the *Times* refused to comply, citing both the First Amendment and the New Jersey shield law.

On July 25, Judge Arnold found Farber and the *Times* in contempt of court. The *Times* was ordered to pay a fine of $100,000 plus an additional $5000 a day until it complied with the judge's order. Farber was fined $1000 and sentenced to six months in jail for criminal contempt.

On August 31, the New Jersey Supreme Court agreed to hear the case after Farber had spent 27 days in jail and the *Times* had paid $130,000 in fines. It ruled against Farber and ordered him back to jail, a step delayed until October 6, when the U.S. Supreme Court ordered Farber either to hand over his files or return to jail. Farber was released only after conclusion of Jascalevich's trial. The doctor was acquitted.[101]

Although the Burger Court had its media detractors—CBS once referred to it as "Nixon's Revenge on the Press"—the Chief Justice made it clear that "The First Amendment does not belong to any definable category of persons or entities: it belongs to all who exercise its freedoms."

Justice Burger and his successors, Chief Justices Rehnquist and Roberts, have made it clear that freedom of the press, as they view it, grants no special privileges to media beyond those available to ordinary citizens seeking to communicate ideas.

Problems of the Student Press

Tinker v. Des Moines may have been the high water mark for student free speech. Optimism was widespread after that 1969 Warren Court decision But passing of the years and changes in Supreme Court justices resulted in the high tribunal taking a more conservative position on student rights under the First Amendment. One area of concern was that of the rights of scholastic journalists, high school and college journalists and their advisers.

During the spring of 1983, a group of high school journalists at Hazelwood East High School near St. Louis, Mo., were preparing an issue of *Spectrum,* the school newspaper.

It should be emphasized that the paper was a journalism class project, taught for academic credit by regular faculty members during regular school hours. The outcome in Hazelwood may have been different had the paper been published as an extracurricular activity where any student could contribute articles.

Editor Kathy Kuhlmeier and staffers Leslie Smart and Lee Ann Tippett prepared a six-page edition, which included two pages of material on controversial topics, including teenage pregnancy, abortion, and the impact of their parents' divorces on students. Three (unnamed) students told student reporters how they had been affected by unwanted pregnancies. Birth control was mentioned in the interviews.

Faculty adviser Howard Emerson left page proofs with school Principal Robert Reynolds, who routinely approved each issue of the *Spectrum* before publication. Reynolds called Emerson to inform him that he was deleting the pages because of privacy law concerns and a lack of editorial balance.

These stories, the principal said, were "inappropriate for some of the school's younger students." He also was concerned that, although students were quoted anonymously in the articles on teen problem pregnancies, they could be identified. Reynolds further objected to the lack of journalistic objectivity involved in the divorce story. Parents of students should have had an opportunity to rebut critical remarks of their children, he said.

After being told that the articles were "inappropriate, personal, sensitive and unsuitable" for student consumption, *Spectrum* staffers called a local branch of the American Civil Liberties Union. They subsequently filed suit in the U.S. District Court, which ruled against school officials restricting student speech activities that are "an integral part of the school's educational function," such as a school-sponsored newspaper. Furthermore, the court held, Principal Reynolds' actions were justified to show that Hazelwood did not support the "sexual norms of students" and to protect privacy concerns raised by the articles.

A three-judge panel of the Federal Court of Appeals for the Eighth Circuit reversed on the grounds that the *Spectrum* was a public forum, intended to be a conduit for student viewpoints. It deserved First Amendment protection. Only a showing of substantial interference with the mission of the school would justify censorship. Hazelwood School District then petitioned the U.S. Supreme Court, which ruled on the case in January, 1988.

In a nutshell, the nation's highest tribunal ruled against the students, 5-3, holding that school authorities may exercise control over student expression that occurs in school-sponsored programs, provided that they have a valid educational purpose for doing so. Their actions must also be reasonable in achieving that educational purpose. Justice White wrote for the majority:

> ...we conclude that the standard articulated in *Tinker* for determining when a school may punish student expression need not also be the standard for determining when a school may refuse to lend its name and resources to the dissemination of student expression. Instead, we hold that educators do not offend the First Amendment by

exercising editorial control over the style and content of student speech in school-sponsored expressive activities, so long as their actions are reasonably related to legitimate pedagogical concerns...It is only when the decision to censor a school-sponsored publication, theatrical production or other vehicle of student expression has no valid educational purpose that the First Amendment is so "directly and sharply implicated" as to require judicial intervention to protect students' constitutional rights.[102]

Hazelwood Extended by U.S. Court of Appeals

Hazelwood, a significant victory for school administrators and a defeat for scholastic journalists, was limited to public elementary and secondary schools. The Court did not consider First Amendment protection for public colleges and universities.

It should be noted that the Constitution does not ban censorship of private colleges and universities.

For many years, journalists and educators worried about the perceived conservative shift of Federal courts on First Amendment issues. They wondered when one of them would apply *Hazelwood* to higher education. That happened in 1994, when Kentucky State University confiscated all copies of the school's yearbook on grounds of poor quality. *The Thorobred* was a student publication, supported by student fees, and was no part of the school's curriculum. Yearbook editor Capri Cotter and others sued KSU in Federal District Court.

In 1997, the court, citing *Hazelwood,* held that the yearbook was not a public forum and was subject to administrative control. The U.S. Court of Appeals for the Sixth Circuit voted, 2-1, to uphold this decision.

A coalition of college journalism education and media groups, as well as civil rights organizations, then petitioned the judges of the Sixth Circuit to hear the case *en banc.* The request was granted and the tribunal decided, 10-3, that KSU had violated student First Amendment rights.

The court noted that the yearbook was not a classroom activity in which students were assigned grades, but a designated public forum created by the university to exist in an atmosphere of free discussion and intellectual exploration

More disturbing to the college journalism community was *Hosty v. Carter.*[103]

Hosty permits administrators to review school-sponsored newspapers before they are printed and distributed.

The case began when Dean Patricia Carter of Governors State University, a public institution near Chicago, halted publication of the *Innovator* and demanded that she approve each future issue of the paper before it could be issued. Student journalists, including Margaret Hosty, had written both news stories and editorials critical of the university administration Three students, Hosty, Steven Barba, and Jeni Porche, sued, claiming that the dean was infringing the students' First Amendment rights.

The students won important First Amendment victories in both the Federal District Court and before a three-judge panel of the Chicago-based U.S. Court of Appeals for the Seventh Circuit. The latter tribunal held that *Hazelwood* was an inappropriate standard to censor university publications, citing more than 30 years of case law and traditions which protected college journalists. Illinois Attorney General James Ryan, who argued for Carter, said that *Hazelwood* should be applied to public colleges and universities.

Lisa Madigan, Ryan's successor as Attorney General, filed a petition on behalf of Dean Carter for a rehearing *en banc* before the Seventh Circuit. The petition was granted and the three-judge panel's decision was vacated. An 11-judge panel heard oral arguments and handed down its decision favoring the university on June 20, 2005.

The Seventh Circuit ruled that in this case, *Hazelwood* applied. If the *Innovator* was a clearly designated public forum, students would have authority to make content decisions. But the mere fact that the paper was an extracurricular activity, not published in a journalism class, did not clearly establish it as a public forum.

The tribunal also ruled that, even if the paper was a public forum, Dean Carter was entitled to qualified immunity from damages for infringing on student rights because she could not reasonably have known that *Hazelwood* did not apply to university publications. Qualified immunity is a doctrine that protects officials from liability in civil rights actions when they do not violate clearly established legal principles.

Lawyers for the student journalists filed a petition for a writ of *certiorari* with the U.S. Supreme Court. They were supported by many groups which filed friend of the court (*amicus*) briefs in the case. However, the U.S. Supreme Court announced on February 21, 2006, that it would not hear an appeal.

One should note that *Hosty v. Carter* applies only in states within the jurisdiction of the Seventh Circuit, Wisconsin, Illinois and Indiana. Perhaps student journalists should be apprehensive, but the case had limited application.

First Amendment freedoms, religion, speech, assembly and association, present difficult legal and philosophical problems. Problems of freedom of the press and government relations present profound questions of law and public policy which will have far-reaching consequences in America's quest for a free society well into the 21st Century.

We now turn our attention to those provisions of the Bill of Rights which protect the individual accused of crime.

1. John Courtney Murray, *We Hold These Truths* (New York: Sheed and Ward, 1960)

2. Although the focus of this study is the Bill of Rights, Article VI of the original Constitution stipulates that "...no religious Test shall be required as a Qualification to any Office or public Trust under the United States."

3. Quoted in H. Frank Way, *Liberty in the Balance*, fifth ed., (New York: McGraw-Hill, 1981), p. 71

4. *Ibid.*

5. In a nutshell, the doctrine of incorporation currently holds that most, but not all, provisions of the Bill of Rights are applicable to the states through the 14th Amendment.

6. *Reynolds v. U.S.*, 98 U.S. 145 (1878)

7. *Ibid.*

8. *West Virginia State Board of Education v. Barnette*, 319 U.S. 624 (1943)

9. *Minersville, Pa., School District v. Gobitis*, 310 U.S. 586 (1940)

10. Supra, Note 8, at pp. 641-2

11. *Elk Grove Unified School District v. Newdow*, 542 U.S. 1 (2004)

12. *Hein v. Freedom From Religion Foundation*, 551 U.S. — (2007)

13. *Ibid.*

14. *Ibid.*

15. *U.S. v. Seeger*, 380 U.S. 163 (1965)

16. *Welsh v. U.S.*, 398 U.S. 333 (1970)

17. *Gillette v. U.S.*, 401 U.S. 437 (1971)

18. See *McGowan v. Maryland*, 366 U.S. 420 (1961); *Two Guys from Harrison-Allentown, Inc. v. McGinley*, 366 U.S. 582 (1961); *Gallagher v. Crown Kosher Super Market*, 366 U.S. 617 (1961) and *Braunfeld v. Brown*, 366 U.S. 599 (1961).

19. *Sherbert v. Verner*, 374 U.S. 398 (1963) is the landmark case. See also, *Thomas v. Review Board of the Indiana Employment Security Division*, 450 U.S. 707 (1981); *Estate of Thornton v. Caldor, Inc.*,

472 U.S. 703 (1985), and *Hobbie v. Unemployment Appeals Commission of Florida*, 480 U.S. 136 (1987).

20. *Wisconsin v. Yoder*, 406 U.S. 295 (1972)

21. *Walz v. Tax Commission of the City of New York*, 397 U.S. 664 (1970) at p. 673

22. *Everson v. Board of Education*, 330 U.S. 1 (1947)

23. *McCollum v. Board of Education*, 333 U.S. 203 (1948)

24. *Zorach v. Clauson*, 343 U.S. 306 (1952)

25. *Ibid.* at p. 315

26. *Engel v. Vitale*, 370 U.S. 421 (1962)

27. *Ibid.* at pp. 431-2

28. *Abington, Pa., School District v. Schempp*, 374 U.S. 203 (1963)

29. *Ibid.* at pp. 224-5

30. In 1964, some Republicans, disenchanted with Nelson Rockefeller and Barry Goldwater, the party's two front-runners, wanted to "draft" Justice Stewart to run for President. The God-fearing justice indicated that he had no desire to leave the Court. Perhaps Stewart remembered the past: Justice Charles Evans Hughes resigned from the Court to run for President against Woodrow Wilson in 1916. He lost. He was, however, later reappointed as Chief Justice.

31. *Wallace v. Jaffree*, 472 U.S. 38 (1985). A good account of the case is found in Peter Irons, *The Courage of Their Convictions* (New York: The Free Press, 1988), pp. 355-378.

32. *McCreary County, Kentucky, v. ACLU of Kentucky*, 545 U.S. — (2005)

33. *Ibid.*

34. *VanOrden v. Perry*, 545 U.S. — (2005)

35. *Ibid.*

36. See *Widmar v. Vincent*, 454 U.S. 263 (1981) and *Board of Education v. Mergens*, 110 S. Ct. 2356 (1990).

37. *Good News Club, et. al, v. Milford Central School*, 533 U.S. 98 (2001)

38. *Board of Education v. Allen*, 392 U.S. 236 (1968). For related cases, see *Meek v. Pittenger*, 421 U.S. 349 (1975) and *Wolman v. Walter*, 433 U.S. 229 (1977).

39. *Tilton v. Richardson*, 403 U.S. 672 (1971)

40. *Lemon v. Kurtzman*, and *Early v. DiCenso*, 403 U. S. 602 (1971). The Court reaffirmed Lemon in 1985. See also *Grand Rapids School District v. Ball*, 473 U.S. 373 and *Aguilar v. Felton*, 473 U.S. 402 (1985).

41. *Committee for Public Education and Religious Liberty v. Nyquist*, 413 U.S. 756 (1973)

42. *Employment Division v. Smith*, 494 U.S. 872 (1990)

43. *City of Berne, Texas v. Flores*, 521 U.S. 507 (1997)

44. *Gonzales v. O. Centro Espirta Beneficente Uniao Do Vegetal*, No. 04-1084 (2006)

45. *Ibid.*

46. *Lynch v. Donnelly*, 465 U.S. 471 (1984)

47. *County of Allegheny v. ACLU*, 492 U.S. 573 (1989)

48. John Stuart Mill, *On Liberty*, 1859. Edited by Alburey Castell, (New York: F.S. Crofts and Co., 1947) p. 16.

49. *Schenck v. U.S.*, 249 U.S. 47 (1919)

82

---

50. *Gitlow v. New York*, 268 U.S. 652 (1925). The landmark importance of Gitlow lies in the fact that it was the first time that the Court applied the free speech guarantee of the First Amendment to the states. Free speech was thus "incorporated" into the liberties protected against state infringement by the 14th Amendment's Due Process Clause.

51. *Dennis v. U.S.*, 341 U.S. 494 (1951)

52. *Ibid.* at p. 501

53. *Yates v. U.S.*, 354 U.S. 298 (1957)

54. *American Communications Association v. Douds*, 339 U.S. 382 (1950)

55. *R.A.V. v. City of St. Paul*, 505 U.S. 377 (1992)

56. *Wisconsin v. Mitchell*, 113 S. Ct. 2194 (1993)

57. *Virginia v. Black*, 538 U.S. 343 (2003)

58. *Ibid.* Justice O'Connor's opinion may be found on pp. 347-368

59. *Ibid.* Justice Thomas' dissent may be found on pp. 388-400

60. *Doe v. University of Michigan*, 71 F. Supp. 852 (1989)

61. 551 U.S. — (2007)

62. *DeJonge v. Oregon*, 299 U.S. 353 (1937)

63. *Chaplinsky v. New Hampshire*, 315 U.S. 568 (1942) and *Terminello v. Chicago*, 337 U.S. 1 (1949)

64. *Feiner v. U.S.*, 340 U.S. 315 (1951)

65. *Edwards v. South Carolina*, 372 U.S. 229 (1963)

66. *Cox v. Louisiana*, 379 U.S. 536 (1965)

67. *Tinker v. Des Moines*, 393 U.S. 503 (1969)

68. *U.S. v. O'Brien*, 391 U.S. 367 (1968)

69. *Texas v. Johnson*, 491 U.S. 397 (1989) and *U.S. v. Eichman*, 110 S. Ct. 2404 (1990)

70. *Coates v. Cincinnati*, 402 U.S. 611 (1971)

71. *Rumsfeld v. Forum for Academic and Institutional Rights*, No. 004-1152 (2006)

72. *Butler v. Michigan*, 352 U.S. 380 (1957)

73. Quoted in Nat Hentoff, *Free Speech for Me – But Not for Thee*, New York: Harper-Collins, 1992, p. 339.

74. *American Booksellers v. Hudnut, 11 Media Law Reporter*, 1105 (1984)

75. *American Booksellers v. Hudnut*, 771 F. 2nd 323 (1985)

76. *Mutual Film Corporation v. Industrial Commission of Ohio*, 236 U.S. 230 (1915)

77. *FCC v. Pacifica Foundation*, 438 U.S. 726 (1978)

78. *Reno v. ACLU*, 117 S. Ct. 2329 (1997)

79. *Ibid.*

80. *Ashcroft v. Free Speech Coalition*, 505 U.S. 2354 (2002)

81. *U.S. v. American Library Association*, 539 U.S. 194 (2003)

82. *Ibid.* at p. 220

83. *U.S. v. Williams*, No. 06-694 (2008)

84. This widely-quoted Jefferson statement, carried daily on several newspaper editorial page mastheads, was made while he was out of office. Jefferson's views of the press, while President, were quite to the contrary. See Fred S. Siebert, Theodore Peterson and Wilbur Schramm, *Four Theories of the Press* (Urbana, Ill.: University of Illinois Press, 1956). See especially Chapter 2, The Libertarian Theory.

84

85. For a good brief discussion of the Burnett case, see Rodney A. Smolla, *Suing the Press: Libel, The Media & Power* (New York: Oxford University Press), pp. 100-117.

86. *Chicago Tribune*, May 14, 1981

87. For a good discussion of libel, see Ralph Holsinger and John Paul Dilts, *Media Law*, 3rd ed. (New York: McGraw-Hill, 1994), pp. 106-211.

88. *New York Times v. Sullivan*, 376 U.S. 254 (1964)

89. *Curtis Publishing Company v. Butts* and *Associated Press v. Walker*, 388 U.S. 130 (1967)

90. *City of Chicago v. Tribune Company*, 307 Ill. 595 (1923)

91. *Near v. Minnesota*, 283 U.S. 697 (1931). For an excellent in-depth study of the case, see Fred Friendly, *Minnesota Rag* (New York: Random House, 1981).

92. *New York Times v. U.S.* and *U.S. v. Washington Post*, 403 U.S. 713 (1971)

93. For an account of their investigative reporting, see Bob Woodward and Carl Bernstein, *All the President's Men* (New York: Simon and Schuster, 1974).

94. *Miami Herald Publishing Company v. Tornillo*, 418 U.S. 241 (1974)

95. *Branzburg v. Hayes*, 408 U.S. 665 (1972)

96. *Ibid.* at p. 725

97. *Gannett v. DePasquale*, 443 U.S. 368 (1979)

98. *Richmond Newspapers v. Virginia*, 448 U.S. 555 (1980)

99. *Sheppard v. Maxwell*, 384 U.S. 333 (1966)

100. *Zurcher v. Stanford Daily*, 436 U.S. 547 (1978)

101. *In re Farber*, 394 A. 2d 330 (N.J. 1978)

102. *Hazelwood School District v. Kuhlmeier*, 484 U.S. 260 (1988). Justice White's remarks may be found on pp. 270-273.

103. *Hosty v. Carter*, 412 F. 3d 731 7th Cir. (2005)

CHAPTER II: RIGHTS OF THE ACCUSED

Regular viewers of television network news are well aware of the fact that the U.S. has one of the highest crime rates in the world. Americans are reminded constantly of major increases in crime, particularly violent crime, over the past generation.

An FBI "crime clock" report, for example, shows that while a college student is attending a typical 50-minute class, about three persons will be murdered. Another 10 people will be raped. Some 65 persons will be robbed. About 100 persons will become victims of aggravated assaults. Some 1500 property crimes will be committed. About 150 Americans will have their cars stolen before the student moves on to his or her next class.[1]

The statistics are shocking, despite the fact that Americans may have become desensitized by overexposure to TV mayhem and violence. The three major news networks (ABC, NBC and CBS) regularly supply us with stories of murder, rape, arson, child abuse and crimes against the elderly.

Local community stations do likewise. An old slogan in local TV broadcasting is, "If it bleeds, it leads." The featured story often is about crime and violence. Monitoring public safety broadcasts, some assignment editors and news anchors in middle and small TV markets apparently love to use their scarce resources to send reporters and camera crews in pursuit of fire engines and police cruisers.

The result is that viewers sometimes may get a distorted impression of what actually goes on in their community. How secure one really is and how secure one feels may be entirely different matters. One also should note that crime statistics are understated. Only a fraction of crimes is reported to police. Some victims fear reprisal by criminals. Others simply believe that police do not respond to 911 calls in a timely manner. Still others "don't want to get involved."

Given the nation's high crime rates, it should not surprise anyone that Americans have strong opinions about "cops," courts and criminals. When judges free a defendant because of a "technicality," especially if he or she has confessed to a crime, many people are angry. They feel that the rights of the accused are receiving a higher priority than the rights of victims.

Some Americans have little faith in the criminal justice system. Too often they read stories about courts putting felons back on the streets where they again beat, rape and murder law-abiding citizens. A guilty person ought not to go free just because of blunders by law enforcement officials, they conclude.

In *People v. Defoe,* 242 N.Y. 21 (1926), Judge Benjamin Cardozo, later a U.S. Supreme Court justice, remarked, "The criminal is to go free because the constable has blundered."

American courts must deal daily with the problem of balancing competing liberties. We do have a Bill of Rights. Americans don't want individuals deprived of life, liberty or property without Due Process of Law. They believe in the concept of Fair Trial with all of the its essential procedural rights.

This chapter will focus on those provisions in the Fourth, Fifth, Sixth and Eighth Amendments which are fundamental to the American system of criminal justice. At the end, we also will consider Article I provisions of the U.S. Constitution. These forbid Congress from suspending the writ of *habeas corpus* during peacetime or enacting *ex post facto* laws or bills of attainder.

Defense attorneys admit that some of their clients have done horrible things. A.C. Peruto, a New York attorney specializing in criminal law, once referred to a defendant as "a creeping, crawling crud." Why? He had raped a nun and then carved crosses on her breast with a knife.[2]

Why do we extend constitutional rights to even "a creeping, crawling crud?" We do so because of the doctrine of presumption of innocence. We want to protect innocent defendants. We give **all** citizens rights. Justice William O. Douglas once remarked, "...respecting the dignity even of the least worthy citizen...raises the stature of all of us."[3]

Constitutional amendments four through six and eight deal explicitly with the rights of the accused. They make up 40% of the Bill of Rights and cannot, therefore, be ignored. The framers of these amendments, aware of tragic human mistakes in European history, considered defendant's rights of fundamental importance. They hoped to prevent horrors of the past from happening here.

NATION AND STATES

It should be noted at the outset that the American political system is Federal, rather than unitary. There is none of the centralization of power and authority found in Great Britain, for example. In the U.S., to a very large degree, nation and state both are autonomous. In our decentralized political system, areas such as foreign policy, national security, regulation of interstate and foreign commerce, the monetary system and fiscal policy all clearly are matters of national responsibility. At least in theory, the U.S. government is one limited by constitutionally delegated powers.

But many areas of public policy, under the 10th Amendment, are reserved to the states. Most Americans are preoccupied with their daily lives: earning a living, getting an education for themselves or their children, getting married or divorced. They want their garbage collected, their streets cleaned of snow, their neighborhood kept well lighted – and their taxes kept low!

In the early years of the 21st century, a high priority is public safety. Americans want to be secure in their homes and communities. Historically, state and local governments have had primary responsibility for education of youth and maintaining public health and safety. An overwhelming majority of criminal cases always has been tried in state and local courts. Cases usually begin there and end there.[4]

In *Barron v. Baltimore,* 32 U.S. 243 (1833), the U.S. Supreme Court held that the protections of the Bill of Rights applied only to the U.S. government, not to the states. Until the 20th Century, state supreme courts had the very last word on how citizens within their jurisdiction should be treated by police and inferior state courts. Cases could go no further. *Barron* meant that defendants could not appeal state rulings to Federal courts on grounds that rights had been infringed under the U.S. Bill of Rights. Diversity of criminal procedures between state and Federal government became inevitable.

Ratification of the 14th Amendment supplied the legal basis for change. Of primary significance was its Due Process Clause. Change, however, was slow in coming. For example, in 1900, the Supreme Court held that states did not have to meet the same standards in jury trials as did the Federal government. The 14th Amendment, it ruled, did not require state trial juries to be composed of 12 citizens. In 1908, it held that the 14th Amendment did not protect individuals against self-incrimination in state criminal proceedings.[5]

Over time, on a case-by-case basis, the U.S. Supreme Court has "incorporated" most of the provisions found in the Bill of Rights. It has not, however, incorporated all of them, refusing to rule that, invariably, state courts must use the same standards as Federal courts. The **doctrine of "selective incorporation"** refers to the process by which some provisions of the Bill of Rights have become applicable to the states through the 14th Amendment. The **"total incorporation"** view, argued by many civil libertarians, would have applied the entire Bill of Rights to the states. This perspective never has commanded majority support from the Court.

The Palko Rule

In *Palko v. Connecticut,* the Court, through Justice Cardozo, said that states were free to adopt any standards so long as they were not in conflict with "the concept of ordered liberty," and did not violate principles of justice so rooted in the traditions and conscience of our people to be ranked as fundamental.

At his first trial for killing two policemen, Frank Palko was found guilty of second-degree murder and sentenced to life imprisonment. Because of errors in his first trial, Connecticut tried Palko again. It decided to go for the death penalty at the second trial. Palko was convicted and sentenced to die. He argued that his second trial constituted double jeopardy, forbidden by the Fifth Amendment.

Was Palko's "hardship" the kind that was "so acute and shocking that our polity will not endure it?" Justice Benjamin Cardozo concluded that Palko's right to immunity from double jeopardy was not "fundamental."

Cardozo wrote:[6]

> Is that kind of double jeopardy to which the statute has subjected him a hardship so acute and shocking that our polity will not endure it? Does it violate those 'fundamental principles of liberty and justice which lie at the base of all our civil and political institutions?' The answer surely must be 'no.' What the answer would have to be if the state were permitted, after a trial free from error, to try the accused over again or to bring another case against him, we have no occasion to consider. We deal with the statute before us and no other. The state is not attempting to wear the accused out by a multitude of cases with accumulated trials. It asks no more than this, that the case against him shall go on until there shall be a trial free from the corrosion of substantial legal error.
>
> This is not cruelty at all, nor even vexation in any immoderate degree. If the trial had been infected with error adverse to the accused, there might have been review at his instance, and as often as necessary to purge the vicious taint. A reciprocal privilege, subject at all times to the discretion of the presiding judge...has now been granted to the state.

The **Palko Rule** created some serious problems of definition. Although Justice Cardozo denied Palko's claims, he tried to explain why some rights are absorbed into Due Process while others are not. Certain of the rights stipulated in the Constitution, such as freedom of speech, press and religion, he said, were *"the very essence of a scheme of ordered liberty,"* and must be protected against state encroachment. Others, such as grand jury indictment and double jeopardy, were not fundamental.

The Court would have to decide later just which procedures were necessary to ordered liberty and which ones were not. Eventually, it would largely abandon different tests for state and Federal courts. This was a result of the "Warren Court Revolution," to be discussed in reviewing specific amendments and cases that follow.

THE FOURTH AMENDMENT

The Fourth Amendment provides:

The right of the people to be secure in their persons, houses, papers, and effects, against unreasonable searches and seizures, shall not be violated, and no warrants shall issue, but upon probable cause, supported by oath or affirmation, and particularly describing the place to be searched, and the persons or things to be seized.

"The poorest man may in his cottage bid defiance to all the forces of the Crown. It may be frail, its roof may shake, the wind may blow through it, the storms may enter, the rain may enter—but the King of England cannot enter."
—William Pitt, Earl of Chatham.[7]

The Fourth Amendment was intended to give some measure of privacy and real meaning to the ancient English maxim, quoted above. The authors of the amendment detested actions of the British Parliament, which violated the "rights of Englishmen" when it authorized **writs of assistance.** These writs permitted customs officials to search for contraband, goods colonists had imported without paying taxes to the Crown. After the Revolution, an aroused public opinion against general search warrants led to the Fourth Amendment.

Since the late 19th Century, the Federal law of arrest, search and seizure has become one of the most complicated in the Constitution. There has been much debate during the past four decades over the Supreme Court's interpretation of Fourth Amendment guarantees. A study of some of the liberal Warren Court rulings and the somewhat more conservative approach of the Burger and Rehnquist courts will follow.

The Amendment forbids only **"unreasonable" searches and seizures.** But what is "reasonable?" Judges constantly are called upon, in exercising their power of judicial review, to consider laws and acts of both executive and legislative authorities which are claimed to be "unreasonable." Courts daily are attempting to balance the needs of society for effective law enforcement and "domestic tranquillity" against claimed privacy rights of the individual. What are some of the guidelines that have evolved in this area?

In defining reasonableness, the Fourth Amendment relies heavily upon the requirement of a **search warrant,** issued "upon **probable cause,** supported by oath or affirmation, and particularly describing the place to be searched, and the persons or things to be seized."

Courts must protect the public against police excesses. Evidence which is obtained illegally generally cannot be used in criminal trials. This is the so-called **"exclusionary rule."** Yet many democracies, including Great Britain, permit police to introduce evidence, irrespective of how it was obtained. If, after trial, it is shown that evidence was obtained by police misconduct, officials can be held accountable.

Critics of the American system of justice often argue that too many criminals go free because of "mere technicalities." Minor police errors ought not to prevent criminals from being convicted, they contend. This, it is argued, is particularly true in the America of the early 21st century where violent crime is a source of major social problems.

Supporters of the American approach argue that only by demanding exclusion of "tainted evidence" can police be punished. Only evidence which is "above reproach" ought to be used, they insist.

The **"Fruit of the Poisonous Tree Doctrine"** holds that evidence which is the direct result of illegal conduct on the part of an official is inadmissible at trial. This, the Supreme Court ruled in *Nardone v. U.S.*, 302 U.S. 379 (1937), denies the accused his or her constitutional rights under the Due Process Clause of the 14th Amendment.

The doctrine draws its name from the idea that once a tree is poisoned (primary evidence is illegally obtained), the fruit of the tree (secondary evidence otherwise unobtainable) is likewise poisoned and is, therefore, inadmissible.

The Exclusionary Rule

Several landmark cases clarify the meaning of the Fourth Amendment within the context of the **exclusionary rule.** The U.S. Supreme Court first issued the rule for Federal courts in *Weeks v. U.S.* (1914). It first considered application of the rule to the states in 1949, holding that, although the Fourth Amendment ban on unreasonable searches and seizures applied to the states, the exclusionary rule did not. Evidence obtained by illegal police conduct could be used in state criminal prosecutions. The Court specifically noted in *Wolf v. Colorado,* 338 U.S. 25 (1949), that other nations did not exclude evidence improperly obtained from their criminal trials. Ultimately, the Court's difficulty in justifying this difference between Federal and state standards led it, in 1961, to reverse *Wolf* in *Mapp v. Ohio.* A recent landmark case is *U.S. v. Leon.*

Weeks v. U.S.

Fremont Weeks was indicted for several crimes, including illegal use of the mails to conduct a lottery. Police went to his home without a warrant. With the help of a neighbor, they found a key, entered and searched his home, and seized incriminating evidence. They gave this material to a Federal marshal, who went to Weeks' residence later that day and carried off additional boxes of papers and documents to use as evidence.

At trial, Weeks' attorney objected to the use of illegally-obtained evidence against his client. The objection was overruled. The Supreme Court granted review to consider the Fourth Amendment issue of evidence obtained without a search warrant.

Justice Day's opinion: Writing for the Court, Justice William Rufus Day traced the history of the Fourth Amendment. He noted that it had been adopted to prevent the use of general search warrants and writs of assistance. Day also noted that opposition to these practices established the principle which was enacted into the fundamental law in the Fourth Amendment – that a man's house was his castle and not to be invaded by any general authority to search and seize his goods and papers.

A U.S. marshal had been involved in exactly that kind of denial of constitutional rights, and the courts, Day concluded, would not be a party to such an act. He wrote:[8]

> The effect of the Fourth Amendment is to put the courts of the United States and Federal officials, in the exercise of their power and authority, under limitations and restraints as to the exercise of such power and authority, and to

forever secure the people, their persons, houses, papers, and effects, against all unreasonable searches and seizures under the guise of law.

If letters and private documents can thus be seized and held and used in evidence against a citizen accused of an offense, the protection of the Fourth Amendment, declaring his right to be secure against such searches and seizures, is of no value, and, so far as those thus placed are concerned, might as well be stricken from the Constitution. The efforts of the courts, and their officials to bring the guilty to punishment, praiseworthy as they are, are not to be aided by the sacrifice of those great principles established by years of endeavor and suffering which have resulted in their embodiment in the fundamental law of the land.

The Court ordered items seized by the U.S. marshal to be returned. Because, however, Weeks pre-dated the wholesale "incorporation" of rights into the Due Process Clause of the 14th Amendment, evidence seized by local police did not have to be returned and remained admissible in state courts.

This Fourth Amendment "loophole" led to a series of further landmark decisions. Two of them are considered below.

Mapp v. Ohio

Cleveland police officers were seeking a suspect in the bombing of Don King's home. King, an alleged numbers racketeer, later became a prominent boxing promoter. The officers, believing that Dollree Mapp was harboring a fugitive, went to her home on May 23, 1957. On advice from her attorney, whom she called immediately, Mapp refused to admit police without a search warrant. Their superiors instructed the officers to place the home under surveillance. Three hours later, they again tried to gain access. When Mapp did not answer the door, they broke into her home.

Mapp objected to the police presence and demanded to see their warrant. When Sgt. Carl Delau held out a piece of paper, Mapp grabbed it and stuck it in her blouse. A struggle followed, police recovered the paper and handcuffed Mapp for being "belligerent." The search produced "lewd and lascivious" books, pictures and photographs found in Mapp's bedroom. She later was convicted of possession of obscene material. Under the Weeks rule, such material could not be used in a Federal criminal case. The Ohio Supreme Court upheld Mapp's conviction because it found no "use of brutal or offensive physical force against the defendant."

The U.S. Supreme Court reversed Mapp's conviction. It held that Cleveland Police had conducted an unreasonable search and seizure because they had not obtained a search warrant, although they had time to do so. Such illegally obtained evidence could not be used in her trial, the Court held, **extending the Federal rule to the states**.

Justice Clark's opinion: Justice Tom Clark wrote the Court opinion, noting that after 1949 more than half of the states had wholly or partly adopted or adhered to the Weeks rule. He wrote:[9]

The ignoble shortcut to conviction left open to the State tends to destroy the entire system of constitutional restraints on which the liberties of the people rest. Having once recognized that the right to privacy embodied in the Fourth Amendment is enforceable against the States, and that the right to be secure against rude invasions of privacy by state officers is, therefore, constitutional in origin, we can no longer permit that right to remain an empty promise. Because it is enforceable in the same manner and to like effect as other basic rights secured by the Due Process Clause, we can no longer permit it to be revocable at the whim of any police officer who, in the name of law enforcement itself, chooses to suspend its enjoyment. Our decision, founded on reason and truth, gives to the individual no more than that which the Constitution guarantees him, to the police officer no less than that to which honest law enforcement is entitled, and, to the courts, the judicial integrity so necessary in the true administration of justice.

All evidence obtained by searches and seizures in violation of the Constitution is, by that same authority, inadmissible in a state court. If the Fourth Amendment is enforceable against the states, as has been repeatedly held, it is enforceable against them by the same notion of exclusion as is used against the Federal government.

Harlan dissents: Justice John Marshall Harlan dissented on the grounds that the 14th Amendment permits states to determine specifics of their own trial procedures. He also expressed concern that the Supreme Court placed its own integrity in jeopardy by making a decision on an issue not really central to the issue before it. Harlan wrote:[10]

A state conviction comes to us as the complete product of a sovereign judicial system. Typically, a case will have been tried in a trial court, tested in some final appellate court, and will go no further. In the comparatively rare instances when a conviction is reviewed by us on due process grounds, we deal then with a finished product in the creation of which we are allowed no hand, and our task, far from being one of overall supervision, is, speaking generally, restricted to a determination of whether the prosecution was Constitutionally fair. The specifics of trial procedure, which in every mature legal system will vary greatly in detail, are within the sole competence of the States. I do not see how it can be said that a trial becomes unfair simply because a State determines that evidence may be considered by the trier of fact, regardless of how it was obtained, if it is relevant to the one issue with which the trial is concerned, the guilt of innocence of the accused.

In the last analysis, I think this Court can increase respect for the Constitution only if it rigidly respects the limitations which the Constitution places upon it, and respects as well the principles inherent in its own processes. In the present case I think we exceed both, and that our voice becomes only a voice of power, not of reason.

The Burger Court, in 1984, created an exception to the Mapp rule, holding that evidence obtained illegally could be used against the defendants because police had acted in "good faith" to acquire it. The landmark case is *U.S. v. Leon.*

Good Faith Exception: In August, 1981, Burbank, Ca., police, acting on a tip relating to a narcotics sale five months earlier, began a drug investigation. Their informant said that Leon and two others, "Patsy and Armando," known drug dealers, were selling cocaine from their homes. Police then placed the suspects under surveillance. A veteran detective, deciding that he needed a search warrant to deal with this drug smuggling operation, drew up an affidavit. After reviewing the evidence, a judge issued warrants, authorizing a search of three homes and several cars owned by Alberto Leon, Armando

Sanchez, Patsy Stewart and Ricardo Del Castillo. The search netted a large quantity of drugs and the suspects were indicted.

In their U.S. District Court trial, the defendants' lawyer then moved to suppress evidence obtained under the warrant. He argued that police had failed to establish the informants' credibility. Although he saw it as a close question, the trial judge threw out the case because of the defective affidavit. The document was, he ruled, insufficient to establish probable cause.

Conceding that police had acted in good faith to obtain the warrant, the court found nonetheless that this did not satisfy Fourth Amendment requirements and the evidence had to be suppressed. The U.S. Court of Appeals for the Ninth Circuit affirmed the decision.

The U.S. asked the Supreme Court to review the issue and consider making an exception to the operation of the exclusionary rule. In a landmark decision, the Court held by a 6-3 vote that evidence obtained by police in a "reasonable, good faith reliance" on a search warrant may be used at trial even if the warrant later proves to be defective.

The Court reviewed recent cases that had raised difficult questions about social costs of the exclusionary rule. It said that it had held that application of the rule was a separate issue from whether the police had infringed upon Fourth Amendment rights. The Court was trying to measure probable cause by the "**totality of the circumstances**" in which information was evaluated.

Justice White delivered the opinion of the Court, writing:[11]

> We have concluded that, in the Fourth Amendment context, the exclusionary rule can be modified somewhat without jeopardizing its ability to perform its intended functions.
>
> The substantial social costs exacted by the exclusionary rule for the vindication of Fourth Amendment rights have long been a source of concern. Indiscriminate application of the exclusionary rule, therefore, may well generate disrespect for the law and the administration of justice.
>
> The balancing approach that has evolved during the years of experience with the rule provides strong support for the modification currently urged upon us...our evaluation of the costs and benefits of suppressing reliable physical evidence seized by officers reasonably relying on a warrant issued by a detached and neutral magistrate leads to the conclusion that such evidence should be admissible in the prosecution's case.
>
> We conclude that the marginal or nonexistent benefits produced by suppressing evidence obtained in objectively reasonable reliance on a subsequently invalidated search warrant cannot justify the substantial costs of exclusion.

White's opinion concluded that no justification exists for excluding evidence if it will not deter police misconduct. He wrote:[12]

> If exclusion of evidence obtained pursuant to a subsequently invalidated warrant is to have any deterrent effect...it must alter the behavior of individual law enforcement officers or the policies of their departments.
>
> We have frequently questioned whether the exclusionary rule can have any deterrent effect when the offending officers acted in the objectively reasonable belief that their conduct did not violate the Fourth Amendment. But even assuming that the rule effectively deters some police misconduct and provides incentives for

the law enforcement profession as a whole to conduct itself in accord with the Fourth Amendment, it cannot be expected, and should not be applied, to deter objectively reasonable law enforcement activity.

This is particularly true, we believe, when an officer acting with objective good faith has obtained a search warrant from a judge or magistrate and acted within its scope. In most such cases, there is no police illegality and thus nothing to deter. It is the magistrate's responsibility to determine whether the officer's allegations establish probable cause and, if so, to issue a warrant comporting in form with the requirements of the Fourth Amendment. In the ordinary case, an officer cannot be expected to question the magistrate's probable cause determination or his judgment that the form of the warrant is technically sufficient. Penalizing the officer for the magistrate's error, rather than his own, cannot logically contribute to the deterrence of Fourth Amendment violations.

A year before *Leon,* in *Illinois v. Gates,* 462 U.S. 213 (1983), the Court considered standards for obtaining a warrant based on an anonymous letter. It then also ruled that judges who issue warrants should consider the "totality of the circumstances" in deciding whether probable cause exists to search a person or place involved in a crime. Magistrates need to use "common sense."

In the Gates case, Bloomingdale, Ill., police received a tip that Lance and Sue Gates of the suburban Chicago community were engaged in drug dealing, and pinpointed where and when, as well as how, they conducted their "business." The letter concluded: "Presently, they have over $100,000 worth of drugs in their basement. They brag about the fact they never have to work, and make their entire living on pushers. I guarantee if you watch them carefully you will make a big catch. They are friends with some big drug dealers, who visit their house often."

Bloomington police verified the information and obtained a search warrant based on probable cause. The search netted 350 pounds of marijuana. Illinois courts suppressed the evidence, as did the Illinois Supreme Court. The U.S. Supreme Court agreed to the state's request for review and handed down this major decision, effectively enhancing the power of law enforcement officials.

Stop and Frisk: Terry v. Ohio

When can police search a citizen without it being "unreasonable?" Generally, under two conditions, when they lawfully place a suspect under arrest and when they have a search warrant. The test for a lawful arrest is "probable cause." A person may be arrested if a judge issues a warrant for the arrest, or if one commits a crime in the presence of a police officer. An officer may also arrest a suspect if he or she has probable cause to believe that a person has committed a felony.

In a warrantless arrest, police still must follow the "rules." In general, they may search suspects, things in plain view and things or places under the suspect's immediate control. An arrested person may be searched to find concealed weapons or evidence of crime. Even when there is no probable cause for arrest, police may stop, question and search a suspect's outer clothing.

A search warrant is a judicial order permitting law enforcement officers to search a specific place. It describes what or who is to be searched and seized. The court may issue a warrant only if it is convinced that good reason (probable cause) exists to believe that a crime has been committed and that the evidence related to it will be found. Police also may search a building after receiving permission from the occupant.

Constitutional scholars, lawyers and judges all consider *Terry v. Ohio* one of the Supreme Court's landmark rulings. In *Terry,* the Warren Court added to a list of permissible warrantless searches when it upheld an Ohio "stop and frisk" law.

Officer Martin McFadden, a 39-year veteran Cleveland policeman, observed three men acting "suspiciously" in the downtown area. Their actions led McFadden to conclude that they were "casing" a store for a robbery. McFadden walked up to the men, identified himself as a policeman and frisked Terry. He felt a pistol in Terry's pocket and arrested him on concealed weapons charges. Terry later was convicted and sentenced to one to three years.

At trial, the prosecutor argued that McFadden's warrantless search was incidental to the arrest. The judge rejected this argument, holding that no probable cause existed. He did, however, rule for the state, finding that police officers have the right to stop and frisk when they believe that their lives are in jeopardy.

Chief Justice Warren wrote the opinion of the Court. He said:[13]

Unquestionably, petitioner was entitled to the protection of the Fourth Amendment as he walked down the streets in Cleveland. The question is whether in all the circumstances of this on-the-street encounter, his right to personal security was violated by unreasonable search and seizure.

We conclude that the revolver seized from Terry was properly admitted in evidence against him. At the time he seized petitioner and searched him for weapons, Officer McFadden had reasonable grounds to believe that petitioner was armed and dangerous, and it was necessary for the protection for himself and others to take swift measures to discover the true facts and neutralize the threat of harm if it materialized. The policeman carefully restricted his search to what was appropriate to the discovery of the particular items which he sought. Each case of this sort will, of course, have to be decided on its own facts. We merely hold today that where a police officer observes unusual conduct which leads him reasonably to conclude in light of his experience that criminal activity may be afoot and that the person with whom he is dealing may be armed and presently dangerous, where in the course of investigating his behavior he identifies himself as a policeman and makes reasonable inquiries, and where nothing in the initial stages of the encounter serves to dispel his reasonable fear for his own or other's safety, he is entitled for the protection of himself and others in the area to conduct a carefully limited search of the outer clothing of such persons in an attempt to discover weapons which might be used to assault him.

Such a search is a reasonable search under the Fourth Amendment and any weapons seized may properly be introduced in evidence against the person from whom they were taken.

Justice Douglas dissented, writing:[14]

The infringement of personal liberty of any 'seizure' of a person can only be 'reasonable' under the Fourth Amendment if we require police to possess 'probable cause' before they seize him. Only that line draws a meaningful distinction between an officer's mere inkling and the presence of facts...which could convince a reasonable man that the person seized has committed, is committing, or is about to commit a particular crime.

In sum, the key test in "stop and frisk" searches is whether a prudent person, given the circumstances, would be warranted in the belief that his or her safety or that of others was in danger. Police can use "stop and frisk" searches only when they see a threat, not merely to gather evidence.

The U.S. Supreme Court decided two "stop and frisk" cases during the 1999-2000 term.

In one landmark decision, it ruled that police may not stop and frisk someone merely on an anonymous tip that he is carrying a gun, *Florida v. J.L.,* 529 U.S. 266 (2000).

The case began in 1995, when an unnamed informant told Miami police that one of three young Black men at a bus stop was carrying a gun, adding that he was wearing a plaid shirt. Officers saw nothing suspicious, but patted down the youth in plaid and found a gun.

The Florida Supreme Court ruled the search unconstitutional. It noted that the U.S. Supreme Court has allowed police to stop a person—even though there is no probable cause for arrest—if the officer has reason to believe that a crime is about to be committed. But, the Court held, nameless telephone tips, without verification by the police, are not sufficient to justify a stop and frisk search and violate the Fourth Amendment's protection against unreasonable searches.

In affirming the Florida ruling, the Supreme Court ruled that the Miami tip was not sufficiently reliable to justify police action. Speaking for a unanimous Court, Justice Ruth Bader Ginsburg said:

> The anonymous call concerning J.L. (the defendant in this case) provided no predictive information and therefore left the police without means to test the informant's knowledge or credibility...That the allegation about the gun turned out to be correct does not suggest that the officers, prior to the frisks, had a reasonable basis for suspecting J.L. of engaging in unlawful conduct. The reasonableness of official suspicion must be measured by what the officers knew before they conducted their search.

Answering the argument that police should be given more leeway when an anonymous informant claims a firearm is involved, Justice Ginsburg wrote:

> Such an exception (for firearms) would enable any person seeking to harass another to set in motion an intrusive, embarrassing police search of the targeted person simply by placing an anonymous call falsely reporting the target's unlawful carriage of a gun.

In *Illinois v. Wardlow,* 528 U.S. 119 (2000), the Supreme Court held unanimously that police may stop and frisk someone who runs at the mere site of an officer. Sam Wardlow was stopped in 1995 by Chicago police in an area of heavy narcotics trafficking on the city's West Side. Two officers patrolling this high-crime area saw Wardlow run as they appeared. The officers pursued and apprehended him.

He was carrying an illegal handgun and was arrested for unlawful possession of a firearm. Before Wardlow's trial, his lawyer moved to suppress the evidence, arguing that police must point to "specific reasonable inferences" why the stop was necessary. The trial judge denied the motion, and in a bench trial, found the defendant guilty. Wardlow, who had a prior felony record, was sentenced to two years in prison.

But the Illinois Supreme Court overturned the conviction, ruling that Wardlow's sudden flight was insufficient to justify an arrest.

Sometimes the Supreme Court, acting as the ultimate "umpire" in the nation's judicial system, tries to eliminate confusion when state court interpretations of the Federal Constitution are in conflict. In the year 2000, some 10 states, including Illinois, had ruled that fleeing at the sight of an officer does not create sufficient suspicion to warrant such a stop. Judges in seven other states said that it does. The Supreme Court granted Illinois' request for *certiorari* in May, 1999, and handed down its decision on January 12, 2000.

In overruling the Illinois Supreme Court, Chief Justice Rehnquist, writing for a 5-4 majority, said:

> ...Nervous, evasive behavior is a pertinent factor in determining reasonable suspicion...Headlong flight—whenever it occurs—is the consummate act of evasion. It is not necessarily indicative of wrongdoing, but it is certainly suggestive of such.

The Chief was joined by Justices Antonin Scalia Clarence Thomas, Sandra Day O'Connor and Anthony Kennedy.

Justice John Paul Stevens wrote a dissenting opinion, signed by Justices David Souter, Ruth Bader Ginsburg and Stephen Breyer.

Police Intrusions Into the Human Body

Intrusions into the human body are perhaps the most invasive kinds of police "searches." The Supreme Court has been called upon, in several cases, to draw the line between constitutionally permissible and impermissible searches. Some examples:

Rochin v. California, 342 U.S. 165 (1952) – Police broke into a suspected drug dealer's house, "invaded" his bedroom and took Rochin to the hospital after he swallowed two capsules, rather than let police seize them. Physicians pumped his stomach and its contents (illegal drugs) later were used to get a conviction.

The Supreme Court excluded this "evidence" on grounds that such police methods violated the defendant's right to Due Process of Law. Justice Frankfurter, in writing the opinion, developed the *shocked conscience rule.* He wrote, "The proceedings by which this conviction was obtained do more than offend some fastidious squeamishness or private sentimentalism about combating crime too energetically. This is action that shocks the conscience...methods too close to the rack and the screw to permit of constitutional differentiation."

Schmerber v. California, 384 U.S. 757 (1966) – The Supreme Court was asked to rule on the question: can police force a person to take a blood test, administered in a hospital? Defendant's lawyers argued that such blood tests violate the "shocked conscience rule" and that they also constitute an illegal search and seizure of the human body.

The Court, divided 5-4, disagreed. Justice Brennan ruled that the tests did not violate *Rochin* because they were routine and minor intrusions, conducted by trained physicians in the safety of a hospital. The test also was reasonable, Brennan said, because police saw evidence of drunkenness and a "loss of evidence exception" was in effect. Had police waited to obtain a warrant, the evidence would have disappeared.

Winston v. Lee, 470 U.S. 753 (1985) – Can a defendant, shot in an attempted robbery, be forced to undergo surgery? Can the bullet be removed and then used as evidence against him? Rudolph Lee had a gunshot wound in the chest when caught by police. Prosecutors requested a court order to force Lee to undergo surgery, have the bullet removed and used as evidence that he had shot a store owner—who returned the fire. Lee would have to undergo general anesthesia. His lawyers objected to all of this.

The Supreme Court ruled unanimously that compulsory surgery would intrude on Lee's Fourth Amendment privacy rights. It held that the dangers involved in undergoing general anesthesia and surgery constituted an "unreasonable" search. The state, the Court concluded, also had failed to prove that the bullet was absolutely necessary to prove its case.

In *Sell v. U.S.,* 539 U.S. 166 (2003*)*, the Supreme Court reviewed a decision of the Eighth Circuit Court of Appeals that Dr. Charles Sell could be required to take medication to become competent to stand trial. Sell, a dentist, faced several charges, ranging from Medicaid fraud and money laundering, to conspiracy to kill a witness and an FBI agent. He had refused to take antipsychotic medications.

In a 6-3 ruling, the Supreme Court upheld the lower court, but provided that four criteria must be met.

(1) There must be an important government interest at stake. Prosecution of a crime to determine the defendant's guilt or innocence is such an interest.

(2) The medication must be likely to enable the defendant to become competent to stand trial without producing serious side effects.

(3) The prescription must be medically appropriate.

(4) It medication must be necessary and less intrusive procedures must be unlikely to produce the same result.

Related Cases

As a practical matter, "things in plain view" or "under immediate control" mean the room in which an arrest occurs, not other rooms in the house. If police want to conduct a more extensive search, they must get a warrant.

After a campus police officer spotted a student carrying a liquor bottle outside his dormitory, he placed the youth under arrest on charges of suspected underage drinking. When the student failed to produce identification, police accompanied him back to his room so that he could prove that he was 21. From an open doorway, an officer saw some marijuana and drug "equipment." He entered the room without the student's permission and arrested him for drug possession. The youth was tried and convicted, but the case was appealed all the way to the U.S. Supreme Court. The Court ruled, in *Washington v. Chrisman,* 455 U.S. 1 (1982), that officers could seize drugs that were in plain view.

The Court also found, in *Oliver v. U.S.,* 466 U.S. 170 (1984), that police may enter an open field where marijuana is growing in plain view. Oliver, the Court held, in order to conceal his criminal activities, planted marijuana on secluded land and erected fences and "No Trespassing" signs. This failed to demonstrate, however, that the expectation of privacy was *legitimate* in the sense required by the Fourth Amendment.

In *Chimel v. California,* 395 U.S. 752 (1969), the Court held that police may, in making a lawful warrantless arrest in a home or office, seize evidence of crime which is in plain sight. There is, however, a question of scope. Police may not search the entire house. A **spatial limits test** was devised by Justice Stewart.

In *U.S. v. Matlock,* 415 U.S. 164 (1974), the Court admitted evidence seized in a warrantless search of a room occupied by a suspected bank robber and the female with whom he lived. When police arrested the suspect in front of the house, he was not asked to agree to a search. His co-occupant, however, admitted police officers to the room. Justice White held for the majority that permission for a warrantless search may be obtained from "a third party who possessed common authority or other sufficient relationship to the premises or effect sought to be inspected."

Auto searches: Searches of automobiles present special problems. Cars are mobile and warrants may not be required for a search, although there must be probable cause. In *Carroll v. U.S.,* 267 U.S. 132 (1925), the Court held that automobiles are "moving vehicles," not entitled to the same degree of protection as people, houses and papers. During the past 30 years, the Court heard a number of auto search cases, considering such questions as the following:

What are the limits of auto searches? May police search areas other than where driver and passengers sit? What about glove compartments, trunks, baggage and boxes? The Court's decisions were not always consistent, sometimes pleasing Liberals, sometimes pleasing Conservatives. The ideological loser, as always, is angry with the Supreme Court.

For example, the Court held, in *Arkansas v. Sanders,* 422 U.S. 753 (1979), that police could not search a suitcase taken from an arrested person's car. They extended this protection in *Robbins v. California,* 453 U.S. 420 (1981), to any closed container found during a lawful auto search. The container was protected in the same way as closed luggage.

But in *U.S. v. Ross,* 456 U.S. 798 (1982), the Court overruled *Robbins. Ross* is now the current leading case in this area. If police have probable cause to search a car, the **search may extend to every part of the vehicle, including all packages and containers that may conceal the object of the search,** the Court held. *Ross* is considered a landmark judicial effort to clarify rules which will guide police and courts in their day-to-day work. It came after years of contradictory lower court rulings.

In *Michael A. Whren and James L. Brown v. U.S.,* 517 U.S. 806 (1996), the Supreme Court unanimously upheld the felony drug conviction of a Washington, D.C., motorist stopped for a minor traffic violation – turning a corner without signaling. Vice Squad Police were patrolling a "high drug area" of D.C. when their suspicions were aroused by Brown's erratic driving.

When officer Ephraim Soto approached the driver's window, he observed two large plastic bags of what appeared to be crack cocaine in Whren's hands. Brown and Whren were arrested, several types of illegal drugs were retrieved from the car and they were charged with violating various Federal drug laws.

Petitioners argued that officers lacked "probable cause" that they were involved in drug dealing and used the traffic violation as a pretext to stop them and search the vehicle. The trial court rejected a motion to suppress the evidence and Whren and Brown were convicted. The Court of Appeals for the District of Columbia affirmed the conviction, holding that "regardless of whether a police officer subjectively believes that the occupants of an automobile may be engaging in some other illegal behavior, a traffic stop is permissible as long as a reasonable officer in the same circumstances could have stopped the car for the suspected traffic violation." The Supreme Court granted *certiorari.*

The Supreme Court held that the temporary detention of a motorist upon probable cause to believe that he has violated traffic laws does not violate the Fourth Amendment's prohibition against unreasonable seizures, even if a reasonable officer would not have stopped the motorist, absent some additional law enforcement objective. Detention of a motorist, the Court found, was reasonable where probable cause exists to believe that a traffic violation has occurred. The officer's motive was irrelevant as long as police, in some situations, might reasonably stop a vehicle for the infraction that occurred. Therefore, this stop and search of a motorist was considered to meet the Fourth Amendment's "reasonableness" standard.

However, in December, 1998, the Court held, in *Knowles v. Iowa,* 525 U.S. 113 (1998), that issuing a speeding ticket does not automatically give police authority to search a car. An Iowa law, the only one of its kind in the nation, gave police virtually blanket authority to search a car after issuing the driver a citation for speeding or other routine traffic offenses. The Iowa Supreme Court had upheld the law, 5-4, and the Rehnquist Court granted *certiorari.*

Patrick Knowles, the defendant in this case, was driving 43 miles per hour in a 25 mile per hour zone when a police officer stopped him in Newton, Iowa. The officer gave Knowles a speeding ticket after determining that his license was valid and that there were no outstanding warrants for his arrest. The officer then searched the car, found marijuana and a pipe, and arrested Knowles.

At a hearing after his arrest for marijuana possession, Knowles challenged the constitutionality of the search. The officer testified that he had no basis for suspecting a crime other than speeding, but had conducted the search under the Iowa law authorizing searches "incident to the citation." The ACLU and the National Association of Criminal Defense Lawyers filed a brief for Knowles, while the National Association of Police Officers entered the case on Iowa's behalf, stressing the danger presented to police officers, from even routine traffic stops.

If Iowa prevailed in the case, it appeared evident that the practice of conducting searches after such traffic stops would become widespread. Rehnquist made it clear that, far from ignoring the issue of police safety, the Court had taken adequate account of it in previous decisions, such as *Maryland v. Jerry Lee Wilson,* 519 U.S. 408 (1997), when the Court ruled that police may routinely order passengers out of a car they have stopped for a traffic violation.

Although the Court did not declare the Iowa law unconstitutional in all possible applications, it did hold that for a simple speeding offense, justifications for the Court's doctrine permitting a "search incident to arrest" simply do not apply.

The Chief Justice said that the threat faced by police in issuing a traffic ticket, which he called a "relatively brief encounter," was "a good deal less than in the case of a custodial arrest." There is no further evidence to discover in a speeding case, he noted, because once the driver has been stopped for speeding, "...all the evidence necessary to prosecute the offense has been obtained." He wrote:

> While concern for officer safety...may justify the minimal additional intrusion of ordering a driver and passengers out of the car, it does not by itself justify the often considerably greater intrusion attending a full field-type search.

Bond v. U.S., 529 U.S., 334 (2000)

On April 17, 2000, the Supreme Court weighed another Fourth Amendment question. Can a law enforcement officer manipulate a bus passenger's personal carry-on baggage to determine its contents?

Steven Bond was on board a Greyhound bus passing through Texas when it was stopped at a border patrol checkpoint for a routine immigration inspection.

Border patrol agent Cesar Cantu verified the immigration status of each passenger, but stopped to feel and squeeze all carry-on luggage stored in the overhead storage bins. Cantu asked Bond for permission to open his bag, and was told "go ahead." Inside the luggage, the agent discovered a "brick" of methamphetamine wrapped in a pair of trousers. Under questioning, Bond admitted that he was taking the drugs to be sold in Little Rock, Ark. Bond was indicted on charges of conspiracy to possess and possession with intent to distribute methamphetamine.

Before trial, Bond 's lawyer moved to suppress the evidence, arguing that the search was illegal. A Federal judge denied the motion, and Bond later was convicted of both charges and sentenced to 57 months in prison. The Court of Appeals for the Fifth Circuit unanimously affirmed the convictions.

The Supreme Court ruled (7-2) that the Fourth Amendment's protection against unreasonable searches was violated when the agent physically manipulated the carry-on bag.

The Court rejected the government's argument that in exposing his luggage to the public, Bond lost any reasonable expectation that his bag would not be physically manipulated by agent Cantu.

Speaking through Chief Justice William Rehnquist, the majority ruled that physically invasive inspections are more intrusive than purely visual ones and that, although bus passengers may expect their bags to be handled by other passengers and bus line employees, they do not expect them to feel the bag in an exploratory manner.

Justices Stephen Breyer and Antonin Scalia dissented.

In *U.S. v. Drayton*, 536 U.S. 194 (2002), the Supreme Court ruled that police need not advise bus passengers that they are free to refuse permission to be searched when officers are looking for drugs or weapons.

Two seatmates, Christopher Drayton and Clifton Brown, Jr., gave police permission to search a bag they shared. No contraband was found.

When, however, Drayton and Brown consented to a check of their persons, the result was different. Both men had taped cocaine to their thighs.

A Federal Court of Appeals held the search was unconstitutional because of the "coercive" atmosphere, but the Supreme Court disagreed.

Justice Anthony Kennedy noted, for a 6-3 majority, that neither man was seized and both freely consented to the search. Under the "totality of circumstances" rule, the Court reinstated the convictions of Drayton and Brown.

Michigan's Sobriety Checkpoint Law

Fatal auto accidents often involve the (mis)use of alcohol. Groups like MADD (Mothers Against Drunk Driving) and SADD (Students Against Drunk Driving) exist only because of an epidemic misuse of alcohol in today's society. When most Americans think of the "drug problem," they often forget that they themselves use one of the most common recreational drugs in America today – alcohol.

Courts have long held that driving an automobile is a privilege, not a right. Judges can and do suspend or revoke drivers' licenses. When a police officer sees a motorist driving erratically, it is reasonable for him or her to stop the car, order the motorist to get out and, if necessary, conduct a Breathalyzer test.

State standards vary, but any physician will tell you quite simply: if your reading is .010, you're unable to function. If it's .015, and you get home without killing yourself or another person, it's only because of (take your choice) your Guardian Angel or good luck.

Such police actions clearly do not violate the Fourth Amendment.

However, the Michigan legislature, at Gov. James Blanchard's urging, enacted a sobriety checkpoint law in 1986. Police established roadblocks that stopped *all* passing cars without a warrant and without any suspicion that the driver had broken the law. Did this amount to an unreasonable search and seizure?

A number of groups thought that it did, among them the ACLU. Six state legislators challenged the statute because they thought that it was unconstitutional to stop drivers who showed no signs of being "impaired" or drunk. The Michigan Council on Alcohol Problems, noting that about 25,000 Americans are killed annually by drunken drivers, supported the law as a worthwhile effort to save potential victims.

The Michigan Court of Appeals agreed with the ACLU position. Evidence showed that the sobriety checkpoint program, in effect for only one night while a court challenge was pending, netted only two intoxicated motorists of the 126 persons stopped. The appellate court noted that police remained free to stop any car if an officer had reason to do so.

However, in *Michigan v. Sitz*, 496 U.S. 444 (1990), the Supreme Court upheld the constitutionality of the sobriety checkpoints. Drivers passing certain roadside points were stopped and, although they generally could remain in their cars, were briefly examined for signs of intoxication. The Court held that, although the checkpoints were a "seizure," they were nonetheless **"reasonable."** The Court found that the intrusion of a brief stop was slight, and since every car was stopped, no one was being singled out in a discriminatory manner.

Critics complained that police should not have been authorized to search 98% of the innocent motorists, only the 2% guilty who could have been detected by their erratic driving. Indeed, law enforcement officers complained about the program being a huge waste of time, money and manpower. They believed that, given scarce resources, Michigan should focus on erratic drivers.

Sitz was the first case in which the U.S. Supreme Court upheld the right of law enforcement officers to detain persons without any suspicion of wrongdoing. Before this case, some legal basis for police action was required.

The Michigan sobriety checkpoint program, which was involved in a seven-year legal battle, came to an end on September 14, 1993, when the Michigan Supreme Court killed it, 5-2, ruling that it violates the state constitution. In an opinion by Justice Patricia J. Boyle, the court held that the law amounted to an illegal search and seizure.

In a brief "lecture" on Federalism, the Michigan Supreme Court noted that although the U.S. Supreme Court had upheld the program under the Federal Constitution, *the state is free to give greater protection to individual rights than the U.S. Constitution provides.*

"We may not disregard the guarantees that our constitution confers on Michigan citizens merely because the U.S. Supreme Court has withdrawn or not extended such protection," Justice Boyle wrote.

Justices James H. Brickley and Robert P. Griffin dissented. Brickley said that the program was reasonable and its public safety-related benefits outweighed any interference with individual liberty.

"The intrusion on motorists is minimal," he wrote, echoing the U.S. Supreme Court view of 1990.

For the record, it should be noted that Michigan Gov. John Engler opposed the program and some legislators resolved to block funding, had the Michigan Supreme Court upheld the program.[15]

The Roberts Court, Police Searches and the Fourth Amendment

In *Hudson v. Michigan*, 547 U.S. 586 (2006), a case upholding the conviction of a Michigan man for drug possession, the U.S. Supreme Court narrowed the individual's Fourth Amendment protection against improper police procedure. Although armed with a valid search warrant, Detroit officers entered a home without first following the traditional practice known as "knock and announce."

Booker Hudson was tried and convicted after police found five rocks of crack cocaine. Both prosecution and defense agreed that officers announced their presence, but waited only a few seconds before barging into Hudson's home.

On June 15, 2006, a deeply-divided (5-4) court ruled that evidence obtained by such a search can be used at trial despite a constitutional violation. Writing for a 5-4 majority, Justice Antonin Scalia said that individuals subject to an improper entry remained free to file civil rights lawsuits against police.

Scalia noted that, had police waited 20 seconds, a traditional, court-approved procedure, they would have found the evidence anyway. That made, he said, the connection between improper entry and discovery of evidence "too attenuated" to justify the "massive remedy of suppressing evidence of guilt."

Justice Scalia noted that the purpose of the landmark decision, *Mapp v. Ohio*, was to deter constitutional violations by making them costly for the prosecution. Today, he said, there is less need for such deterrence when police are better trained and when the ability to bring civil rights suits against government has greatly expanded.

In his dissent, Justice Breyer described the majority's decision as "an argument against the Fourth Amendment's exclusionary principle itself...an argument that this court until now has consistently rejected."

Wiretapping

Wiretapping and electronic eavesdropping were unknown in 1791. The Supreme Court has had a number of problems reconciling modern technology and constitutional rights. The issue first arose in 1928.

In *Olmstead v. U.S.*, the U.S. Supreme Court heard its first wiretapping case. It arose during the Prohibition era when Federal agents tapped the telephone of suspected bootlegger Roy Olmstead. Using then-new technology, agents installed equipment on wires in an apartment building's basement. *Olmstead* raised the question whether the use of "noninvasive eavesdropping devices" to gather incriminating evidence was a search and seizure under the Fourth Amendment.

There was no physical entry into Olmstead's home or office. He was convicted strictly on the basis of the wiretap evidence. Olmstead's lawyer argued in the Supreme Court that the wiretaps were a search without a warrant and without probable cause, and that evidence against his client should have been excluded because it was illegally obtained. It also was argued that Olmstead's Fifth Amendment right not to incriminate himself had been violated.

A Court divided, 5-4, held that a search and seizure must be physical. Something tangible must be searched and seized. Wiretapping, the Court held, did not involve actual physical trespass. There was no search and seizure because evidence was obtained by hearing. The Court also rejected Olmstead's Fifth Amendment argument, holding that he had not been forced to talk on the phone, but had done so voluntarily.

Justice Brandeis dissented, rejecting the government's view that enforcement of prohibition was a good enough reason to justify the government's actions. He wrote:[16]

> Experience should teach us to be most on our guard to protect liberty when the government's purposes are beneficent. The greatest dangers to liberty lurk in insidious encroachment by men of zeal, well-meaning but without understanding. Our government is the potent, the omnipresent teacher. For good or for ill, it teaches the whole people by its example.

For 40 years, *Olmstead* and Federal statutes exempted wiretapping and electronic surveillance or "bugging" from the law. In 1967, in a similar case involving gambling, the Warren Court overruled *Olmstead*.

The Supreme Court found, in *Katz v. U.S.,* that the Fourth Amendment applied to search and seizure of words and that it protected individuals, not places. Federal agents had obtained evidence against Charles Katz, a gambler who made interstate calls from Los Angeles to Miami and Boston bookmakers to bet on horse races and college basketball games.

FBI agents bugged a public telephone booth habitually used by Katz. Because the FBI acted without a warrant, the Court held that Katz's constitutional rights had been violated. He was, the tribunal noted, in a public phone booth, entitled under the Constitution to make a private phone call that would not be monitored by Federal agents.

The Warren Court, in creating an **expectation of privacy doctrine**, was catching up with modern technology. Overruling *Olmstead,* it held that a conversation was something tangible and could not be seized electronically. Placing a "bug" or tap did not have to involve physical "trespass" to violate the Fourth Amendment. Writing for the Court, Justice Stewart said:[17]

> The Government does not question...basic principles. Rather, it urges the creation of a new exception to cover this case. It argues that surveillance of a telephone booth should be exempted from the usual requirement of advanced authorization by a magistrate upon a showing of probable cause. We cannot agree. Omission of such authorization 'bypasses the safeguards provided by an objective predetermination of probable cause, and substitutes instead the far less reliable procedure of an after-the-event justification for the...search, too likely to be subtly influenced by the familiar shortcomings of hindsight judgment.'

And by passing a neutral predetermination of the scope of a search leaves individuals secure from Fourth Amendment violations only in the discretion of the police.

These considerations do not vanish when the search in question is transferred from the setting of a home, an office or a hotel room, to that of a telephone booth. Wherever a man may be, he is entitled to know that he will remain free from unreasonable searches and seizures. The government agents here ignore the procedure of antecedent justification...that is central to the Fourth Amendment, a procedure that we hold to be a constitutional precondition of the kind of electronic surveillance involved in this case. Because the surveillance here failed to meet that condition, and because it led to the petitioner's conviction, the judgment must be reversed.

In a dissenting opinion, Justice Black said:[18]

If I could agree with the Court that eavesdropping carried on by electronic means ...constitutes a 'search' or 'seizure,' I would be happy to join the Court's opinion.

My basic objection is twofold: (1) I do not believe that the words of the Amendment will bear the meaning given them by today's decision, and (2) I do not believe that it is the proper role of this Court to rewrite the Amendment in order 'to bring it into harmony with the times' and thus reach a result that many people believe to be desirable.

Congress, in enacting the Omnibus Crime Control and Safe Streets Act of 1968, gave Federal judges authority to issue wiretap orders to Federal agents in their war against organized crime. National security cases also are covered.

In 1969, the Nixon Administration contended that it had the power and authority to tap and bug domestic groups that it considered a threat to U.S. national security, even without a court order. In 1972, a unanimous Supreme Court ruled otherwise in *U.S. v. U.S. District Court for the Eastern District of Michigan,* 407 U.S. 297 (1972). President Nixon also admitted in 1973 that, in an effort to plug news "leaks" and protect U.S. national security, he had authorized wiretaps on some White House aides, officials and reporters. Nixon, however, was not the first President to authorize wiretapping and bugging. Both John F. Kennedy and Lyndon B. Johnson, his immediate predecessor, had done so.

Congress also got into the "bugging" and wiretapping game when it passed the Foreign Intelligence Surveillance Act in 1978. The law requires a court order for these activities, even in national security probes. But that has proved to be "no problem." Congress set up a special court to authorize these warrants. The law contains a sole exception, permitting the U.S. to eavesdrop, without a warrant, on foreign governments. According to Federal records, judges had approved nearly 6000 wiretapping applications without rejecting a single one by the end of 1990.

During the past generation, with the exception of national security cases, most wiretapping and electronic surveillance by both Federal and state officials has involved either gambling or drug dealing.

Some groups, like the American Civil Liberties Union, see other threats to loss of privacy, such as random urine tests of workers by their employers. Although many workers have no objections to taking these tests, some do. ACLU has contended that, where random tests are administered to everyone without any specific reason or probable cause, innocent people suffer a humiliating invasion of privacy.

Justice Scalia, generally considered one of the more conservative members of the Rehnquist Court, has denounced these tests as "an immolation of privacy and human dignity in symbolic opposition to drug use."[19]

FIFTH AMENDMENT

The Fifth Amendment provides:

No person shall be held to answer for a capital or otherwise infamous crime, unless on a presentment or indictment of a Grand Jury, except in cases arising in the land or naval forces, or in the militia, when in actual service in time of war or public danger; nor shall any person be subject for the same offence to be twice put in jeopardy of life or limb; nor shall be compelled in any criminal case to be a witness against himself, nor be deprived of life, liberty or property, without due process of law; nor shall private property be taken for public use, without just compensation.

Grand Jury Indictment

The Fifth Amendment requires a grand jury indictment for capital and "otherwise infamous" crimes. This restrains prosecutors who must persuade a citizen grand jury that there is real evidence of crime before a defendant can be tried. A **grand jury** simply determines whether there is enough evidence to warrant the time and expense of prosecution. It is intended to protect individuals from those prosecutors who may be either politically ambitious or simply overzealous.

However, grand jury proceedings are secret, evidence presented to them is one-sided *(ex parte)* and prosecutors tend to dominate them. If a grand jury finds that there is enough evidence to try a person, it returns a "**true bill**" or indictment. If not, it returns "**no bill.**" If the latter occurs, the state may prosecute later, if new evidence is developed. There is no double jeopardy possibility until a **petit jury** reaches a verdict. A petit jury decides whether a defendant is guilty or not guilty.

Reprosecution is ruled out if the petit jury acquits the defendant. If a trial ends with a guilty verdict and the defendant wins an appeal, the state may reprosecute since the **defendant is entitled only to a fair trial, not acquittal.** The terms "grand" and "petit" come from French words for large and small. Federal grand juries may be composed of as many as 23 citizens, of whom any 12 may return an indictment. A petit jury traditionally consists of a dozen citizens who determine whether an individual is guilty or not guilty of a particular crime. In recent years, some states have used smaller petit juries, as noted below.

The U.S. Constitution establishes an "**accusatorial,**" rather than an "**inquisitional**" system. It is based on the theory that it is better that a guilty person go free than that an innocent person be convicted. It should be noted that the Supreme Court refused, in *Hurtado v. California,* 110 U.S. 516 (1884), to require states to use grand juries. Even in 1999, states more commonly than not charge individuals by means of an "information," a prosecutor's affidavit.

Double Jeopardy

The Fifth Amendment prohibits defendants from "twice being put in jeopardy of life or limb" for the same offense. Without this constitutional guarantee, the government could exhaust a person, both physically and financially, even if he or she had been found not guilty of a crime.

Double jeopardy remains the subject of much debate because it has not been interpreted to bar separate Federal and state prosecutions where **one criminal act offends two sovereigns.** Courts also do not consider it double jeopardy when a state decides to retry a defendant when a jury is "hung" or divided and fails to reach a verdict. If a first trial verdict is set aside because of error, another trial also is permitted. **Where state juries have refused to convict in some cases,** such as that of Rodney King in California, **the Federal government has later indicted, tried and convicted the same defendants for civil rights law violations.** The brutal beating of King, a Black man, by several Los Angeles police officers, was watched by millions of Americans in one of the most (in)famous TV "replays" in history. Those officers involved were found not guilty by a California jury, but later were convicted, under U.S. civil rights law, in Federal court for the same offense.

Major decisions on double jeopardy include the following:

1. *Palko v. Connecticut,* 302 U.S. 319 (1937): As previously noted, the Court upheld a state's right to appeal a second-degree murder verdict. Palko was retried, convicted of first-degree murder and sentenced to die. Because double jeopardy is not "implicit in a scheme of ordered liberty," the Court found no constitutional violation. In this case, all the state sought was "a trial free from the corrosion of substantial legal error." The Palko decision later was overruled by *Benton v. Maryland,* as noted below.

2. *Louisiana ex. rel. Francis v. Resweber,* 329 U.S. 459 (1947): Willie Francis, a convicted killer, "escaped execution" because of a mechanical failure of the state's electric chair. Francis tried to prevent Louisiana's second effort to execute him on grounds of double jeopardy and cruel and unusual punishment. The Court held, 5-4, that the state's second try to execute him does not violate the Constitution and Francis was executed.

3. *Benton v. Maryland,* 395 U.S. 784 (1969): overruled Palko. The Court held that the Fifth Amendment guarantee against double jeopardy is enforceable against the states through the 14th Amendment. Tried on burglary and larceny charges, Benton was acquitted of larceny but convicted of burglary. Retried because of errors in the burglary conviction, the defendant was convicted of both charges. The Court held that the larceny conviction subjected the defendant to double jeopardy.

Self-Incrimination

The framers of the Bill of Rights wrote the Fifth Amendment primarily to protect defendants against torture. Horrible treatment of defendants was common throughout Europe, and notable in England during the era of **"Star Chamber."** This "court," so named because its ceiling was covered with stars, sat without a jury and could impose nearly any penalty. Its abuses led framers of the Bill of Rights to include the no self-incrimination stipulation in the Fifth Amendment.

Until the end of the 16th Century, English criminal courts required all persons accused, or even suspected of crime, to testify against themselves. This characterized the **"inquisitional system,"** dating back to ancient times. History records that the Romans charged persons with crime on the basis of mere rumor. Individuals were brought before secret tribunals and made to "tell the truth." Torture commonly was used to force confessions. There was no right to confront one's accusers, no right to try to rebut "evidence." The "deck" was stacked, against the individual as **power and authority were combined in the hands of ONE, who served as prosecutor, judge and jury.**

In England, ecclesiastical courts were used to prosecute "heretics" for holding of "incorrect" beliefs. Some civil libertarians reflect on this today, when it is in vogue to be "politically correct."

Puritan "radical" John Lilburne was hauled before the court of Star Chamber in 1637. He refused to be questioned under oath, arguing that it violated the **Magna Carta.** Found in contempt of court, Lilburne was whipped, fined and jailed. But he eventually won his point when, in 1641, the British Parliament abolished Star Chamber. Parliament also forbade church courts from administering oaths requiring people to accuse themselves.

In writing the Fifth Amendment, the framers intended to prevent the use of torture to force confessions of crime. Although the idea would have been considered "radical" in the 17th Century, the concept of fairness had evolved by the time of the Bill of Rights. Anyone accused of crime was considered entitled to "presumption of innocence" until government, by the weight of the evidence, proved its case beyond a reasonable doubt.

Although not binding on state governments until *Malloy v. Hogan,* 378 U.S. 1 (1964), the right to remain silent is today applied to all criminal proceedings in the nation: federal, state and local. Police use of the so-called "third degree"—to force confessions of crime—was common earlier in U.S. history. A basic principle of Anglo-American liberty is that individuals need not help government convict them of crime.

Not until 1936 did the Court invalidate confessions obtained through physical brutality. In *Brown v. Mississippi,* 297 U.S. 278 (1936), the Court threw out the murder convictions of three Blacks because police brutality and torture forced them to confess. Police had stripped, whipped and hanged them until they were nearly dead. This, the Court ruled, was a denial of Due Process of Law.

After *Brown,* police resorted to more "sophisticated techniques." They held suspects incommunicado, so that they could not notify family or friends of their arrests. They "delayed" bringing them before a judge who could warn them of their rights. Suspects were forced to undergo marathon questioning without food or sleep. In *Ashcraft v. Tennessee,* 322 U.S. 143 (1944), police used relay teams to "grill" a suspect non-stop for 36 hours. The Court ruled that these techniques of psychological coercion, used to force a confession, were inadmissible.

Under the Fifth Amendment, defendants need not testify and judges may not comment to juries on their failure to take the witness stand. This protection also extends to witnesses called to testify before congressional committees and who appear before grand juries. Public employees who use the Fifth Amendment cannot be fired for doing so.

In the 1960s, civil libertarians were concerned primarily about uneducated, sometimes illiterate or functionally illiterate suspects, who were ignorant and unaware of their rights. These suspects were particularly unaware of their right to remain silent and not incriminate themselves. Although the U.S. Supreme Court long had banned involuntary confessions in Federal courts, they had permitted them in state trials. The Warren Court, however, handed down two landmark decisions in this area in *Escobedo v. Illinois* and *Miranda v. Arizona,* among the most controversial cases of the time.

Escobedo v. Illinois

In January, 1960, Chicago police arrested Danny Escobedo for the fatal shooting of his brother-in-law, Manuel Valtierra. When they attempted to question him, Escobedo refused on advice of his lawyer, and was released. About a week later, a man in police custody told them that Escobedo had shot his brother-in-law because he had mistreated his sister. Police again arrested Escobedo.

They told him, en route to headquarters, that they knew the whole story and that he might as well confess. Escobedo again refused. At the police precinct, Escobedo asked to see his lawyer, who was in an adjacent room, but was refused. Escobedo was questioned, without benefit of counsel, for more than 14 hours. Eventually, he made an incriminating statement.

Tried and convicted of murder, Escobedo appealed, claiming that he was denied his right to counsel. He also argued that his lawyer should have been present during police questioning. Illinois courts upheld his conviction, but the U.S. Supreme Court then took the case.

In one of its most hotly-debated rulings, a divided (5-4) Warren Court, reversed Escobedo's conviction and sent the case back to Illinois for retrial. Justice Arthur J. Goldberg wrote for the majority:[20]

The critical question in this case is whether, under the circumstances, the refusal by the police to honor petitioner's request to consult with his lawyer during the course of an interrogation constitutes a denial of 'the Assistance of Counsel' in violation of the Sixth Amendment to the Constitution as 'made obligatory upon the States by the 14th Amendment,' and thereby renders inadmissible in a state criminal trial any incriminating statement elicited by the police during the interrogation.

We granted a writ of *certiorari* to consider whether the petitioner's statement was constitutionally admissible at trial. We conclude, for the reasons stated below, that it was not and, accordingly, we reverse the judgment of conviction.

The interrogation here was conducted before petitioner was formally indicted. But in the context of this case, that fact should make no difference. When petitioner requested, and was denied, an opportunity to consult with his lawyer, the investigation had ceased to be a general investigation of 'an unsolved crime.' Petitioner had become the accused, and the purpose of the interrogation was to 'get him' to confess his guilt despite his constitutional right not to do so. At the time of his arrest and throughout the course of the interrogation, the police told petitioner that they had convincing evidence that he had fired the fatal shots. Without informing him of his absolute right to remain silent in the face of this accusation, the police urged him to make a statement.

Petitioner, a layman, was undoubtedly unaware that under Illinois law an admission of 'mere' complicity in the murder plot was legally as damaging as an admission of firing the fatal shots. The 'guiding hand of counsel' was essential to advise petitioner of his rights in this delicate situation. This was the 'stage when legal aid and advice' was most critical to petitioner.

What happened at this interrogation could certainly 'affect the whole trial,' since 'rights' may be irretrievably lost, if not then and there asserted, as they are when an accused represented by counsel waives a right for strategic purposes. It would exalt form over substance to make the right to counsel, under these circumstances, depend on whether at the time of the interrogation, the authorities had secured a formal indictment. Petitioner had, for all practical purposes, already been charged with murder.

It is argued that if the right to counsel is afforded prior to indictment, the number of confessions obtained by the police will diminish significantly, because most confessions are obtained during the period between arrest and indictment, and 'any lawyer worth his salt will tell the suspect in no uncertain terms to make no statement to police under any circumstances.' This argument, of course, cuts two ways. The fact that many confessions are obtained during this period points up its critical nature as a 'stage when legal aid and advice' are surely needed. The right to counsel would indeed be hollow if it began at a period when few confessions were obtained. There is necessarily a direct relationship between the importance of stage to the police in their quest for a confession and the criticalness of that stage to the accused in his need for legal advice. *Our Constitution, unlike some others, strikes the balance in favor of the right of the accused to be advised by his lawyer of his privilege against self-incrimination* (emphasis added).

We have learned the lesson of history, ancient and modern, that a system of criminal law enforcement which comes to depend on the 'confession' will, in the long run, be less reliable and more subject to abuses than a system which depends on extrinsic evidence independently secured through skillful investigation.

We hold, therefore, that where, as here, the investigation is no longer a general inquiry into an unsolved crime, but has begun to focus on a particular suspect, the suspect has been taken into police custody, the police carry out a process of interrogations that lends itself to eliciting incriminating statements, the suspect has requested and been denied an opportunity to consult with his lawyer, and the police have not effectively warned him of his absolute constitutional right to remain silent, the accused has been denied 'the Assistance of Counsel' in violation of the Sixth Amendment to the Constitution as 'made obligatory upon the States by the 14th Amendment,' and that no statement elicited by the police during the interrogation may be used against him at a criminal trial.

Nothing we have said today affects the powers of the police to investigate 'an unsolved crime' by gathering information from witnesses and by other 'proper investigative efforts.' *We hold only that when the process shifts from investigatory to accusatory—when its focus is on the accused and its purpose is to elicit a confession—our adversary system begins to operate, and, under the circumstances here, the accused must be permitted to consult with his lawyer* (emphasis added).

Postscript: Escobedo, who had been in and out of trouble with police nearly all of his life, did not take advantage of his "second chance" to reform himself. Not long after the landmark U.S. Supreme Court ruling, he was arrested, charged and convicted of burglary. He died an early death and will be remembered primarily, if not exclusively, for the landmark case that bears his name.

If an individual indicates that he wishes the assistance of counsel before any interrogation occurs, the authorities cannot rationally ignore or deny his request on the basis that the individual does not have or cannot afford a retained attorney. The financial ability of the individual has no relationship to the scope of the rights involved here. The privilege against self-incrimination secured by the Constitution applies to all individuals. A need for counsel in order to protect the privilege exists for the indigent as well as the affluent.

Denial of counsel to the indigent at the time of interrogation while allowing an attorney to those who can afford one would be no more supportable by reason or logic than the similar situation at trial and on appeal struck down in *Gideon*.

Postscript: Miranda was retried and convicted. The most damaging evidence was supplied by his girlfriend, who testified that he had told her that he was guilty. Some 13 years later, four after being released from prison, Miranda got into a barroom brawl in Phoenix on February 1, 1976. He was stabbed to death. As police arrested one Rodriguez Zamora, they read him his rights from a "Miranda Card."

The Supreme Court later extended *Miranda* rights to police lineups in *Gilbert v. California*, 388 U.S. 263 and *Kirby v. Illinois*, 406 U.S. 682 (1972). In *Estelle v. Smith*, 451 U.S. 454 (1981), *Miranda* rights were given to defendants undergoing psychiatric examinations to determine mental competency to stand trial.

One is not, however, entitled to *Miranda* rights, if, while in jail, he or she confesses a crime to another inmate who turns out to be an undercover police officer. This was the Court's ruling in *Illinois v. Perkins*, 496 U.S. 292 (1990). Justice Anthony M. Kennedy, writing for the majority, observed: "*Miranda* forbids coercion, not mere strategic deception."

Miranda Modified By Burger, Rehnquist Courts

The end of an era in the Court's history came in 1969, when the Chief Justice retired. President Nixon appointed Warren Burger as Earl Warren's successor. Nixon also had the opportunity to name three more justices within four years. As a group, they were perhaps more conservative than their predecessors, particularly in the criminal law area. The Burger Court era, in turn, ended in 1986 when President Ronald Reagan elevated Associate Justice William Rehnquist to Chief. Under both men, the Court handed down some decisions which limited the impact of *Miranda*. Of greatest significance were the following:

- *Harris v. New York*, 401 U.S. 222 (1971): The Burger Court held that if a statement were made by a suspect without proper *Miranda* warnings, it still could be used to discredit a defendant's trial testimony. Harris, charged with sale of heroin, had testified at his trial that he had sold "baking soda" to an undercover narcotics agent. The state then read a statement Harris had made, without full *Miranda* warnings, just after his arrest. He had admitted the heroin sale and made no reference to "baking soda." Chief Justice Burger observed, "The shield of *Miranda* cannot be perverted into a license to use perjury by way of defense."

- In *Michigan v. Tucker*, 417 U.S. 433 (1974): The Court further modified *Miranda*, ruling that leads from statements made to police after an incomplete *Miranda* warning could nevertheless be used to develop the case against a defendant.

114

- In *Jenkins v. Anderson,* 447 U.S. 2312 (1980): The Court ruled that, if a defendant took the stand at trial, he or she could be questioned about pre-arrest silence.

- In *Brewer v. Williams,* 430 U.S. 387 (1977): The court reaffirmed the right to counsel. The suspect in a gruesome Iowa murder case, one Robert Williams, with no attorney present, led police to a body of Pamela Powers, a 10-year-old girl. This happened after a detective drew him into conversation about the crime during a 160-mile auto ride from Davenport to Des Moines. In what became known as the "Christian burial speech," one of the detectives said: "I feel that we should stop and locate the body, that parents of this little girl should be entitled to a Christian burial for the little girl who was snatched away from them on Christmas Eve and murdered." Williams, an escapee from a mental hospital, who was known to be "deeply religious," then led them to the child's body.

By a narrow 5-4 margin, the Burger Court reversed the conviction. When, however, Williams was found guilty of the crime at a second trial, the Court upheld his conviction, holding that the body would have been discovered even without his help.

Miranda Revisited

In *Dickerson v. U.S.,* 530 U.S. 428 (2000), delayed application of the 1968 Omnibus Crime Control Act reopened matters that the Court appeared to have settled in *Miranda v. Arizona.* Most of the Congress in 1968 had opposed *Miranda,* and Section 3501 of their crime bill attempted to overrule *Miranda* by substituting the pre-*Miranda* standard of voluntariness in place of the specific warnings required by that decision.

In Federal prosecutions, confessions that the trial judge considered voluntary on the basis of the totality of circumstances would be admissible, even in the absence of *Miranda* warnings.

Between 1968 and 1997, a series of Attorneys General refused to enforce the congressional statute. But the Court of Appeals for the Fourth Circuit held that Charles Dickerson's confessions that he had been involved in seven bank robberies in Maryland and Virginia were admissible because they had been given voluntarily to FBI agents. Dickerson's attorney sought to suppress the statements because they had been given without *Miranda* warnings.

Dickerson v. U.S. thus became a direct challenge to *Miranda* when the Fourth Circuit ruled that the *Miranda* decision was not mandated by the Fifth Amendment to the U.S. Constitution, and was effectively overruled by Congress when it passed Section 3501 of the Omnibus Crime Control Act of 1968.

U.S. Attorney General Janet Reno argued that "in the years since *Miranda* was handed down, it has become embedded in the law" and has developed into "a constitutional foundation" that cannot be reversed by legislation.

The Justice Department also argued that *Miranda* was "workable" and "in many respects beneficial to law enforcement" because it provided a clear rule for police to follow. The warnings, familiar to almost all viewers of television police shows or crime movies, were keys to public confidence in the criminal justice system, Reno argued.

Because Reno and the Justice Department refused to defend the 1968 congressional statute, the U.S. Supreme Court appointed Professor Paul Cassell of the University of Utah Law School to undertake the job as *amicus curiae.* A noted critic of *Miranda,* Cassell recruited victims' rights and police organizations to join in his efforts.

Law enforcement groups argued that police should no longer be required to recite the *Miranda* list and obtain signed waivers before taking statements from suspects. The abusive interrogations and police brutality prior to the 1966 *Miranda* ruling have been curtailed, they argued, so the rule is no longer necessary.

Professor Cassell argued that while *Miranda* rights flowed from the Fifth Amendment, they were not required by it. He said that briefs from law enforcement agencies showed "the real world costs" of *Miranda* and argued that the decision recommended procedural safeguards, not a constitutional mandate. He cited the case of a Washington state man who had not been read his rights and escaped conviction in the rape of a 12-year-old girl, despite the fact that prosecutors said that he declared that "she got what she deserved."

A 7-2 majority, speaking through Chief Justice Rehnquist, rejected Cassell's arguments. Rehnquist wrote that it was clear that the original *Miranda* majority "thought that it was announcing a constitutional rule and that subsequent Supreme Court opinions that recognized exceptions to the *Miranda* rule did not change that."

"These decisions illustrate the principle—not that *Miranda* is not a constitutional rule—but that no constitutional rule is immutable," Rehnquist said. The Chief Justice adopted the Justice Department's argument that law enforcement agencies have become comfortable operating under *Miranda* constraints. He wrote:

> …We hold that *Miranda*, being a constitutional decision of this Court, may not be in effect overruled by an Act of Congress, and we decline to overrule *Miranda* ourselves. We therefore hold that *Miranda* and its progeny in this Court govern the admissibility of statements made during custodial interrogation in both state and federal courts…the principles of *stare decisis* weight heavily against overruling…
>
> The disadvantage of the *Miranda* rule is that statements made may be by no means involuntary, made by a defendant who is aware of his 'rights,' may nonetheless be excluded and a guilty defendant go free as a result. But experience suggests that the totality of circumstances test which Section 3501 seeks to revive is more difficult than *Miranda* for law enforcement officers to conform to, and for courts to apply in a consistent manner.

Scalia Dissents:

Justice Antonin Scalia, joined by Justice Clarence Thomas, dissented. Calling the *Miranda* decision preposterous, Scalia wrote an opinion eight pages longer than the majority's ruling. Among other things, Scalia accused the majority of expanding the Constitution in a display of frightening anti-democratic power. He wrote:

> I am not convinced by the petitioner's argument that *Miranda* should be preserved because the decision occupies a special place in the 'public's consciousness.' As far as I am aware, the public is not under the illusion that we are infallible. I see little harm in admitting that we made a mistake in taking away from the people the ability to decide for themselves what protections (beyond those required by the Constitution) are reasonably affordable in the criminal investigatory process…

Today's judgment converts *Miranda* from a milestone of judicial overreaching into the very Cheops' Pyramid (or perhaps the Sphinx would be a better analogue) of judicial arrogance in imposing its Court-made code upon the States; the original opinion at least asserted that it was demanded by the Constitution. Today's decision does not pretend that it is—and yet still asserts the right to impose it against the will of the people's representatives in Congress.

I dissent from today's decision and until Section 3501 is repealed, will continue to apply it in all cases where there has been a sustainable finding that the defendant's confession was voluntary.

Eminent Domain

The last provision in the Fifth Amendment focuses not on criminal defendants, but rather on those who own property that government wants for a public purpose. Most countries recognize a right of **eminent domain** in cases where land is required to build roads or parks. The Fifth Amendment is intended to guarantee that just compensation be paid when land is taken for a public purpose.

The Supreme Court has defined "**public purpose**" very broadly. Property owners seldom can contest governmental "takings" except to argue for what they believe is "**just compensation**" in their particular cases. Some examples of landmark eminent domain rulings include the following:

Penn Central Transportation Co. v. City of New York, 438 U.S. 104 (1978): The Court held that "diminution in property value, standing alone," does not establish a "taking." Government may designate a building as a "historic landmark" and restrict its subsequent use, such as for construction of an office tower. This, despite the fact that owners of Grand Central Terminal in New York could have made greater rental profits with modification of the structure.

U.S. v. Sioux Nation of Indians, 448 U.S. 371 (1980): The Court held that the U.S. government acted in bad faith and exceeded its powers in abrogating Indian treaties and taking the Black Hills from the Sioux. The Indians, the Court held, were entitled to receive about $100 million in compensation.

Hawaii Housing Authority et al v. Midkiff, 467 U.S. 229 (1984): The Court upheld a 1967 land reform statute authorizing the state to take residential property even though the land was not to be owned or operated by government or be open to public use. The law transferred ownership from large landowners to tenants and then lent tenants money to buy the lands. The Court found that transferring property to private beneficiaries does not invalidate a taking.

In *Lucas v. South Carolina Coastal Council,* 505 U.S. 1003 (1992), the Supreme Court ruled for plaintiff David Lucas and overturned a decision of the South Carolina Supreme Court. In 1986, Lucas had bought two residential lots on a South Carolina barrier island for nearly $1 million. At the time, it was legal for him to build single-family homes on each of the lots without special permits.

Subsequently, the state passed the Beachfront Management Act, which required the South Carolina Coastal Council to set a baseline for seashore development. This made it impossible for Lucas to develop his property. Justice Scalia, writing for the majority, said:[22]

We think... that there are good reasons for our frequently expressed belief that the owner of real property has been called upon to sacrifice all economically beneficial uses in the name of the common good, that is, to leave his property economically, he has suffered a taking...The trial court found Lucas' two beachfront lots to have been rendered valueless by respondent's enforcement of the coastal zone construction ban.

In a case some legal scholars consider the most important eminent domain ruling in a generation, *Kelo v. City of New London*, 125 S. Ct. 2655 (2005), the Supreme Court upheld a "taking" by New London, Connecticut, for economic development purposes.

The city argued that it had the power to take land for the public purpose of creating jobs, increasing tax revenues and rejuvenating the downtown and waterfront areas.

Unwilling property owners countered that this "taking" had neither a public purpose nor constituted a public use.

The Supreme Court of Connecticut said that if an economic development project promises to create jobs, increase government revenues and revitalize a depressed urban area, it qualifies as a "public use." The state's highest tribunal also held that government may constitutionally delegate eminent domain power to a private enterprise if it serves as its authorized agent.

The U.S. Supreme Court, in a 5-4 decision, found for New London. Justice Stevens wrote for the majority which included Justices Kennedy, Souter, Ginsburg and Breyer. He emphasized that the high court would show judicial restraint toward decisions of state and local legislative bodies concerning their powers of eminent domain.

Speaking through Justice O'Connor, the dissenters (Chief Justice Rehnquist and Justices Scalia and Thomas), suggested that the use of eminent domain power approved by the Court was a kind of Robin Hood in reverse story—give to the rich, take from the poor.

After *Kelo*, legislatures began to consider demands of aroused citizens that states limit property seizures by government agencies. Many property owners, including Norwood, Ohio, residents Jay and Carl Gamble and Joseph Horney, filed suits challenging eminent domain statutes.

The Ohio Supreme Court ruled unanimously, just a year after *Kelo*, that economic development alone does not justify taking of private homes. Conceding the U.S. Supreme Court's authority to rule that bulldozing private homes for private development does not violate the U.S. Constitution, it reminded us that, in the American Federal system, state Supreme Courts have final authority over interpretation of state laws and constitutions.

Ohio's highest tribunal struck down part of the state eminent domain law and criticized Norwood, a Cincinnati enclave, for its unconstitutionally vague description of targeted residential areas as "deteriorated."

Many of the homes involved, the court observed, were structurally sound. Tearing them down to construct the $150 million Rookwood Project, office buildings, apartments and retail stores, violated Ohio law, the court said.

Property owners hailed the ruling in *City of Norwood v. Horney et. al*, as a great victory.

Voters in Michigan went to the polls in November, 2006, and overwhelmingly (more than 80%) approved a proposed constitutional amendment. It provided that, if a person's home is seized for public use, the amount of just compensation shall not be less than 125% of fair market value. It also stipulated that public use does not include transferring private property to another private entity for economic development, or for the purpose of generating enhanced tax revenues.

Some critics of the Michigan amendment argued that it was redundant because the state Supreme Court had ruled in 2004 *(County of Wayne v. Hathcock)* that Michigan governments may not use eminent domain to take private property because another use of it might be more profitable. That decision represented a major shift in legal struggles between developers and homeowners.

It was applauded by many because it overruled a famous (perhaps infamous) 1981 decision of the court in the *Poletown* case that the state could use its power of eminent domain for economic development and to increase tax revenues. In that case, the City of Detroit bulldozed an entire neighborhood of some 1000 homes, 600 businesses and historic churches to give the property to General Motors for an auto plant.

Ralph Nader, then considered a leading reformer in American politics, joined the Poletown Neighborhood Council and the Archdiocese of Detroit in battling GM and Detroit Mayor Coleman Young. He referred to Young as a petty dictator. The mayor responded that Nader had a psychotic hatred of GM.

National media covered the story, particularly the closing drama when police evicted 20 protesters from Immaculate Conception Church (founded in 1921) to end a 29-day sit-in there. Members of St. John the Evangelist Church (established 1890) also had to find a new place to worship as their church was razed.

THE SIXTH AMENDMENT

The Sixth Amendment provides:

In all criminal prosecutions, the accused shall enjoy the right to a speedy and public trial, by an impartial jury of the State and district wherein the crime shall have been committed, which district shall have been previously ascertained by law, and to be informed of the nature and cause of the accusation; to be confronted with the witnesses against him; to have compulsory process for obtaining witnesses in his favor; and to have the assistance of counsel for his defense.

Right To Legal Counsel

In the beginning of the 21st Century, no other right guaranteed to one accused of crime is perhaps more important than the right to consult a lawyer. Representing a defendant at trial is clearly only a small part of the defense lawyer's task. It begins with interrogation of a suspect. Defense attorneys must protect their clients' constitutional rights from arrest through final appeal.

Historically, it has been the defendant's responsibility to hire an attorney and to pay for his or her services. But in the past 30 years, both courts and legislatures have substantially enlarged the right to counsel. Many persons accused of crimes have little or no money, and the problem of indigent defendants has been a real dilemma for American democracy.

Civil libertarians and others who urge reform of the U.S. legal system long have argued that only those with money fully enjoy their rights to counsel. "How many rich people go to jail?" they asked. These reformers contended that the only way to change the system would be through a U.S. Supreme Court ruling forcing government to appoint free legal counsel for indigent defendants.[23]

In March, 1931, nine young Black males, seven white males and two white females were riding on a freight train in Alabama. The youths got into a fight and the whites were thrown from the train. The white girls, Ruby Bates and Victoria Price, said that the Blacks, who ranged in age from 12-20, had raped them. When the train reached Paint Rock, Ala., the Blacks were arrested and jailed in Scottsboro. The *New York Times* reported that only the presence of national guardsmen prevented a mass lynching.

When the largely uneducated defendants were brought into the courtroom, they obviously were frightened. They were away from their homes, family and friends. At the preliminary hearing, the presiding judge, Alfred Hawkins, showed no sympathy. But because they were charged with a capital crime, he was required under state law to appoint legal counsel to represent them.

In the Alabama of the 1930s, as well as in a number of other Southern states, rape was a crime punishable by flexible sentencing, commonly 20 years or death. A Black defendant, convicted of raping a white woman, faced a genuine possibility of a death sentence. Such laws remained on the statute books until the U.S. Supreme Court ruled, in *Coker v. Georgia*, 433 U.S. 58 (1977), that the death penalty for rape was unconstitutional.

Judge Hawkins took the peculiar step of naming all the members of the town bar association as co-counsel for the defendants. He set a trial date for less than a week after their indictment. When the day arrived, one Stephen Roddy, an out-of-town attorney, appeared to represent the "Scottsborough Boys," as the media called them. He immediately asked the judge for more time to prepare an adequate defense, but Hawkins denied his request.

Judge Hawkins granted a change of venue, and the case was tried in Decatur, Ala., 50 miles west of Scottsboro. Judge James Horton was named to preside in the first of two trials held there. Perhaps predictably, all the defendants, including Ozie Powell, were convicted. After the Alabama Supreme Court had upheld the convictions, the U.S. Supreme Court agreed to review the case.

The principal question in *Powell v. Alabama* was simply: **Do the indigent defendants in this capital case have the right to legal counsel at state expense?** As it often does, the U.S. Supreme Court decided the case on narrow grounds. It refused to make any broad, sweeping statements or to decide if the Sixth Amendment guarantees every defendant the right to legal counsel. But, as Justice George Sutherland's opinion makes clear, in cases involving unusual situations, such as capital crimes, or young, illiterate and uneducated defendants, a lawyer's participation is essential to ensure fundamental fairness. *Powell* made one point very clear: **In capital cases, such as Powell, defendants are entitled to legal counsel, at state expense.**

Justice Sutherland, speaking for the majority, said:[24]

It is hardly necessary to say that the right to counsel being conceded, a defendant should be afforded a fair opportunity to secure counsel of his own choice. Not only was that not done here, but such designation of counsel as was attempted was either so indefinite or so close upon the trial as to amount to a denial of effective and substantial aid in that regard.

Until the very morning of the trial, no lawyer had been named or definitely designated to represent the defendants. Prior to that time, the trial judge had 'appointed all members of the bar' for the limited 'purpose of arraigning the defendants.' Whether they would represent the defendants thereafter, if no counsel appeared in their behalf, was a matter of speculation only, or as the judge indicated, of mere anticipation on the part of the court. Such a designation, even if made for all purposes, would, in our opinion, have fallen far short of meeting, in any proper sense, a requirement for the appointment of counsel.

The defendants, young, ignorant, illiterate, surrounded by hostile sentiment, hauled back and forth under guard of soldiers, charged with an atrocious crime, regarded with especial horror in the community where they were to be tried, were thus put in peril of their lives within a few moments after counsel, for the first time charged with any degree of responsibility, began to represent them.

We think that the failure of the trial court to give them reasonable time and opportunity to secure counsel was a clear denial of due process.

We are of the opinion that, under the circumstances just stated, the necessity of counsel was so vital and imperative that the failure of the trial court to make an effective appointment of counsel was likewise a denial of due process within the meaning of the 14th Amendment.

All that is necessary now to decide, as we do decide, is that in a capital case, where the defendant is unable to employ counsel, and is incapable adequately of making his own defense because of ignorance, feeble-mindedness, illiteracy or the like, it is the duty of the court, whether requested or not, to assign counsel for him as a necessary requisite of due process or law; and that duty is not discharged by an assignment at such a time or under such circumstances as to preclude the giving of effective aid in the preparation and trial of the case. To hold otherwise would be to ignore the fundamental postulate, already adverted to...'that there are certain immutable principles of justice which inhere in the very idea of free government which no member of the Union may disregard.'

Postscript: In 1938, some six years after *Powell*, the Supreme Court heard the case of *Johnson v. Zerbst,* 304 U.S. 458 (1938). It ruled that indigent defendants being tried in Federal criminal courts must be represented by legal counsel. But the decision, limited only to the Federal government, failed to recognize that most prosecutions occur in state courts. Civil libertarians and others urged the U.S. Supreme Court to apply *Zerbst* to the states.

In *Betts v. Brady,* 316 U.S. 455 (1942), the Court refused to do so. Writing for the majority, Justice Owen J. Roberts considered the intent of the framers. They had, he concluded, never intended the right to counsel to be defined as a fundamental guarantee, merely that it apply to extreme situations such as *Powell*. Betts, Roberts noted, was neither helpless nor illiterate and he could not be executed for a Maryland robbery.

The years in which former California Attorney General and Governor Earl Warren served as Chief Justice of the United States were characterized by storms of controversy. Some might contend that the Court always is in the center of a storm, but the Warren years clearly exceeded the norm for turmoil.

It was ahead of the country in several areas, notably civil rights. The *Brown* decision, to be discussed in chapter four, was reached 10 years before Congress passed the Civil Rights Act of 1964. The school prayer decisions were most unpopular, as indicated by every poll taken at the time. The decisions in free speech cases also irritated a considerable number of Americans. Some thought that the Court was coddling Communists and jeopardizing U.S. national security. Billboards, sponsored by some of the more

Conservative interest groups, were erected on interstate highways. They advised: "Impeach Earl Warren, Save Our Republic."

The Warren Court criminal law rulings sparked a national debate on "the rights of criminals." Phrasing the issue that way, of course, assumes that all defendants are guilty. Many police, prosecutors and other law enforcement officials were unhappy with the Warren Court. Clearly, it made their jobs more difficult. Some civil libertarians would say it merely required greater professionalism and the end of old, but inexcusable, police methods.

The Gideon Case

One decision, however, which was not extremely controversial, but clearly a landmark, was *Gideon v. Wainwright.* It reversed *Betts v. Brady* and established the right of indigent defendants, charged with felonies in state courts, to be represented by legal counsel.

Clarence Earl Gideon was charged with breaking and entering the Bay Harbor Poolroom in Panama City, Fla. When he appeared for trial, he asked presiding Judge Robert McCrary to appoint a lawyer to defend him since he had no money to hire one. The judge denied the request, commenting, according to the U.S. Supreme Court record: "Mr. Gideon, I am sorry, but I cannot appoint Counsel to represent you in this case. Under the laws of the State of Florida, the only time the Court can appoint counsel to represent a Defendant is when the person is charged with a capital offense. I am sorry, but I will have to deny your request to appoint Counsel to defend you in this case."

The state of Florida apparently had neither the inclination nor the funds to provide legal counsel for indigents charged with non-capital crimes. It also apparently paid no heed to folk wisdom: "He who hath himself for his counsel hath a fool for a client."

Gideon, a poor, uneducated, alcoholic white drifter, had to defend himself as best he could. His best was not good enough. He was sentenced to five years in Florida State Prison at Raiford after being convicted of stealing beer, wine and change from vending machines.

Gideon was a loser, but he had been a loser all of his life. He ran away from home at 14, served a year in reform school, and was convicted four separate times for burglary and larceny. He received 33 years in prison sentences, although he only served 17.

At Raiford, Gideon spent much of his time in the prison library, studying law. One might call this motivation! He eventually filed a petition in longhand, on prison stationery with Division of Corrections correspondence regulations at the top of the page. He asked the U.S. Supreme Court to grant a petition for a *writ of certiorari.* If granted, such a writ would order Florida to deliver up the case record so that the justices could be certain that the correct decision had been reached below.

The Court granted Gideon's petition, ordered the state of Florida to respond, and scheduled submission of briefs and oral arguments. Because he had no money, Gideon was permitted to proceed *in pauperis.*

If one needs an occasional reminder that much is RIGHT with the American judicial system, consider these facts. The Supreme Court appointed attorney Abe Fortas of a prominent Washington law firm to represent Gideon. This is the same Mr. Fortas who later served as associate justice of the U.S. Supreme Court and was nominated by President Lyndon B. Johnson to succeed Earl Warren as Chief Justice of the United States. When the Senate resisted, Fortas resigned from the Court, giving Richard Nixon the chance to appoint Warren Burger.

Some 22 states, according to the record, supported Gideon with an *amicus curiae* brief, written by Minnesota Attorney General Walter Mondale. Mondale later served as U.S.

122

Senator, Vice President of the United States under Jimmy Carter and the Democratic presidential nominee in 1984! The major question before the Court was: can a state court fairly try a felony defendant who is unable to afford a lawyer?

In a unanimous, 9-0, opinion, written by Justice Black, the U.S. Supreme Court said:[25]

> Since 1942, when Betts v. Brady was decided by a divided court, the problem of a defendant's federal constitutional right to counsel in a state court has been a continuing source of controversy and litigation in both state and federal courts. To give this problem another review here, we granted certiorari. Since Gideon was proceeding in forma pauperis, we appointed counsel to represent him and requested both sides to discuss in their briefs and oral arguments the following: 'Should this Court's holding in Betts v. Brady be reconsidered?'
>
> The facts upon which Betts claimed that he had been unconstitutionally denied the right to have counsel appointed to assist him are strikingly like the facts upon which Gideon here bases his federal constitutional claim.
>
> Since the facts and circumstances of the two cases are so nearly indistinguishable, we think that the Betts v. Brady holding, if left standing, would require us to reject Gideon's claim that the Constitution guarantees him the assistance of counsel. Upon full reconsideration, we conclude that Betts v. Brady should be overruled.
>
> We accept Betts v. Brady's assumption, based as it was on our prior cases, that a provision of the Bill of Rights which is 'fundamental and essential to a fair trial' is made obligatory upon the States by the 14th Amendment. We think that the Court in Betts was wrong, however, in concluding that the Sixth's Amendment's guarantee of counsel is not one of these fundamental rights.
>
> Reason and reflection require us to recognize that in our adversary system of criminal justice, any person haled into court who is too poor to hire a lawyer cannot be assured a fair trial unless counsel is provided for him. This seems to us to be an obvious truth. Governments, both state and federal, quite properly spend vast sums of money to establish machinery to try defendants accused of crime. Lawyers to prosecute are everywhere deemed essential to protect the public's interest in an orderly society. Similarly, there are few defendants charged with crime, few indeed, who fail to hire the best lawyers they can get to prepare and present their defenses. That government hires lawyers to prosecute and defendants who have the money to hire lawyers to defend are the strongest indications of the widespread belief that lawyers in criminal courts are necessities, not luxuries. The right of one charged with crime to counsel may not be deemed fundamental and essential to fair trials in some countries, but it is in ours.
>
> The Court in *Betts v. Brady* departed from the sound wisdom upon which the Court's holding in *Powell v. Alabama* rested. Florida, supported by two other States, has asked that *Betts v. Brady* be left intact. Twenty-two States, as Friends of the Court, argue that Betts was 'an anachronism when handed down' and that it should now be overruled. We agree.

Postscript: Gideon, a "jailhouse lawyer," was very upset when he discovered that he would be retried by the state of Florida. He thought that this constituted double jeopardy. Fortas advised him to consult the local branch of the ACLU for help. He did, but refused their aid. With the assistance, however, of court-appointed counsel, Gideon eventually was acquitted by a jury. Anthony Lewis, who covered the case for the *New York Times,* published a popular book, *Gideon's Trumpet,* which later was the basis for a TV movie, starring Henry Fonda in the role of Gideon.

Gideon was a felony case. What about misdemeanors or crimes which are petty, ordinarily punishable by less than a year in prison?

In 1972, the Burger Court considered the case of Jon Argersinger, a Tallahassee, Fla. gas station attendant who had no lawyer when he pleaded guilty to carrying a concealed weapon, a misdemeanor under Florida law. It held, in *Argersinger v. Hamlin,* 407 U.S. 25 (1972), that state courts must provide a lawyer to indigent defendants in all criminal cases, including misdemeanor cases, involving possible imprisonment. Misdemeanor cases, the Court held, may be no less complex than felony cases. The Court, expanding its *Gideon* rule, also took note of the "assembly line" character of many misdemeanor proceedings. It held that, absent a "knowing and intelligent waiver," no defendant may be sent to prison unless he or she has been represented by an attorney.

Nearly every student has seen the statue of a blindfolded "Maiden Justice" with nicely balanced scales in her hands, representing the ideal of a judicial system which is blind to social class distinctions. Only the most naive of citizens would argue that there is anything resembling the ideal that "justice is blind" in contemporary society. Having a court-appointed lawyer does not necessarily mean that one receives good legal advice. Some of these lawyers are young and just out of law school. Some are downright incompetent. Others simply are so overburdened with work that they lack the time to prepare an effective defense. Equal justice under law remains, however, an ideal goal which American society always hopes to reach.

Considerably more controversial than Gideon were *Escobedo v. Illinois* and *Miranda v. Arizona,* which involved the question, WHEN is a defendant entitled *to counsel? Escobedo* expanded the right to legal counsel to include pre-trial, investigative stages. In *Miranda,* the Court bolstered *Escobedo* by requiring police to inform suspects of their constitutional rights. Virtually every student who has seen a crime movie or TV show is familiar with the arrest scene, in which the detective reads the "villain" his *Miranda* rights. Because these cases involve the element of self-incrimination and the Fifth Amendment, they are discussed above, under that heading.

Trial By Jury

Trial by jury is a distinctive feature of the Anglo-American system of liberty. Believing that fair trials were most likely with juries, U.S. Constitution writers incorporated, in Article III, a provision that "The Trial of all Crimes, except in Cases of Impeachment, shall be by Jury."

Architects of the Bill of Rights added the Fifth Amendment Grand Jury provision and the Sixth Amendment guarantee of a "speedy and public trial by an impartial jury." Defendants, under the Sixth Amendment, enjoy "speedy and public" trials.

While a 12-member jury has been the norm under Anglo-American law, the Constitution does not demand it. Nor does it require unanimous verdicts. In recent years, the Supreme Court has permitted states to experiment in this area.

It also should be noted that defendants need not exercise their right to a trial by a petit jury. They may enter into a **plea bargain,** pleading guilty in exchange for a less severe sentence than would be given if the case went to trial.

It is of fundamental importance that juries be unbiased. Lawyers very carefully screen them *(voir dire)* before trial. Both defense counsel and prosecutors may exercise a number of **peremptory challenges** (no reason needed to excuse a juror) as well as **challenges for cause,** which relate to juror bias.

Some examples of the Supreme Court's important rulings in this area are as follows:

- *Strauder v. West Virginia,* 100 U.S. 303 (1880): The Supreme Court declared unconstitutional a law requiring juries to be made up exclusively of white males. The statute, the Court held, deprived Blacks of their rights under the Equal Protection Clause of the 14th Amendment and denied them Due Process of Law.

- *Maxwell v. Dow,* 176 U.S. 581 (1900): The Court ruled that a state may use eight-person juries, rather than the 12 required in Federal courts.

- *Patton v. U.S.,* 281 U.S. 276 (1930): The Court upheld a verdict reached by 11 jurors in a Federal court. The 12th juror became ill after the trial started, and both defense and prosecution agreed to proceed without him. Just as a defendant in Federal court may waive a jury trial altogether, he or she also may agree to trial by 11 jurors, the Court held. Otherwise, Federal courts must use 12-member juries.

- Unanimous verdicts in state criminal trials, while commonly the rule, are not required. The Court, in *Johnson v. Louisiana,* 406 U.S. 356 (1972), upheld a state law requiring only a 9-3 jury vote for a guilty verdict.

- *Norris v. Alabama,* 294 U.S. 587 (1935): The Court reversed the conviction of a Black youth for rape because of a "long-continued, unvarying and wholesale exclusion of Negroes from jury service" in the county in which the trial occurred. The Supreme Court found that no Black ever had been called for jury duty and no Black names ever had been placed on the lists of potential jurors. Many, however, were qualified to be jurors and some had served in that role in Federal trials.

- *Duncan v. Louisiana,* 391 U.S. 145 (1968): The Warren Court reversed a judge's guilty verdict in a case for which the maximum sentence was two years in prison. Although Duncan got only 60 days, the Court held that the defendant has a right to trial by jury in "serious" state criminal cases. "Serious" was defined as those crimes punishable by a prison term of six months or longer. The Court, in *Witherspoon v. Illinois,* 391 U.S. 510 (1968), prohibited a death sentence when the jury that imposed it excluded prospective jurors who were opposed to capital punishment.

- *Taylor v. Louisiana,* 419 U.S. 522 (1975): The Court reversed a rape conviction because state law excluded women from the pool from which juries were chosen. Defendants, the Court ruled, were denied their right to trial by an impartial jury drawn from a representative section of the community. Sex no longer could be a valid basis for determining eligibility for jury service. *Taylor* overruled *Hoyt v. Florida*, 368 U.S. 57 (1961), which had upheld the exemption of women from jury duty on grounds that "woman is still regarded as the center of home and family life."

- *Ballew v. Georgia*, 435 U.S. 223 (1978), and *Burch v. Louisiana*, 441 U.S. 130 (1979): The numbers question arose again. The Court held in the Georgia case that conviction by a jury of less than six members deprives the accused of the right to trial by jury. In the Louisiana case, it ruled that a state cannot constitutionally convict a person of a non-petty offense by a non-unanimous vote of a six-member jury.

- *Lockhart v. McCree*, 476 U.S. 1 (1986): Dealt with the question, can persons opposed to the death penalty be excluded from juries that determine the guilt as well as the sentence of persons accused of a capital offense? The Supreme Court ruled that states may exclude such persons. The practice, it held, creates neither a biased jury nor one that fails to represent a fair cross-section of the community. Excluded jurors are a distinctive group, and a state has the right to impanel a single jury that can impartially decide all the issues in a case.

THE EIGHTH AMENDMENT

The Eighth Amendment provides:

Excessive bail shall not be required, nor excessive fines imposed, nor cruel and unusual punishments inflicted.

The issue of excessive bail seldom has gone all the way to the U.S. Supreme Court. In *U.S. v. Salerno*, 481 U.S. 739 (1987), the Rehnquist Court held that pretrial detention without bail of persons deemed a threat to public safety does not violate the Eighth Amendment. The majority noted that the amendment "says nothing about whether bail shall be available at all."

Anthony Salerno was the boss of the Genovese crime family. At his bail hearing, Federal attorneys asked the court to deny bail because Salerno would commit murder if freed. Before 1984, such a motion probably would not have been made. But in that year, Congress enacted the Bail Reform Act, permitting Federal judges to refuse bail to defendants to protect the "safety of any other person and the community."

After hearing the government's evidence, the judge denied bail. Salerno then appealed successfully to the U.S. Court of Appeals, which ruled that the 1984 law was unconstitutional. The Supreme Court reversed, not only upholding the Federal statute, but also implying that 24 similar state laws were valid.

The Capital Punishment Debate

Although the Eighth Amendment prohibits **cruel and unusual punishment,** it fails to define it. Over the years, the courts have defined it as torture or any punishment which is grossly disproportionate to the offense. The U.S. Supreme Court seldom used the provision until the 1970s, when it heard a number of death penalty cases.

A long-standing topic of debate in American law has been the issue of capital punishment. College students have been arguing about this, as have professors, lawyers, judges, civil libertarians and others for more than 50 years.

In early England, most felons were hanged. For the crime of treason, one could be drawn and quartered. Historic techniques of execution have included stoning, crucifixion and starvation. The firing squad, the electric chair, the gas chamber, the gallows and lethal injection have been prescribed by American state laws.

A fundamental question, of course, is whether capital punishment is cruel and unusual under the Eighth Amendment. Until the 1970s, the Supreme Court chose to hear only a few, narrowly-focused capital punishment cases. It did uphold death by firing squad as a "humane" form of execution in *Wilkerson v. Utah,* 99 U.S. 130 (1878), and permitted electrocution as a mode of execution in *In re Kemmler,* 136 U.S. 436 (1890).

Landmark rulings in this area came almost exclusively from the Burger Court, which ruled, in *Furman v. Georgia,* that capital punishment, under then-existing state laws, was so infrequent and randomly imposed that it no longer credibly deterred crime. It was, a 5-4 majority held, cruel and unusual.

But the majority was very "shaky." It never found any agreed-upon logic to support its ruling against the death penalty. The five did agree that the Eighth Amendment prevented states from executing convicts then on death row. But only two justices, Marshall and Brennan, voted against the death penalty *per se.*

Douglas voted against it because he considered it racially discriminatory. White and Stewart considered it unconstitutional because it was imposed in an arbitrary and capricious manner. One could not predict who would be sentenced to death. In short, this was a very fragmented majority. A solid minority of four, Chief Justice Burger and Justices Powell, Blackmun and Rehnquist, disagreed.

There was no single majority opinion in *Furman.* Each of the nine justices wrote a separate opinion. Some 133 pages of views, including dissents, are a matter of record.[26]

Justice Potter Stewart said, "The death penalty has in fact been imposed on a capriciously selected handful."

Justice William Brennan commented, "It is uniquely degrading and is tolerated only because of its disuse."

Justice Byron White said, "The threat of execution is too attenuated to service criminal justice."

Justice Thurgood Marshall commented, "The death penalty falls disproportionately on the poor and minorities."

Justice William O. Douglas said, "Capital punishment has no application to society at large, but only to some selected outcasts."

Although dissenting justices disagreed about the value of the death penalty, all of them said that if it were abolished, abolition should result from popular action, not judicial decree.

Furman had the effect of overturning 40 state capital punishment statutes. Death sentences of more than 600 inmates were commuted. But because of the fact that the Court had not ruled that the death penalty *per se* was unconstitutional, about three-fourths of the states wrote new laws to meet the Supreme Court objections. New laws were written to give judges and juries less discretion, to be less arbitrary and discriminatory. The Court reinstituted the death penalty in *Gregg v. Georgia,* 428 U.S. 153 (1976). It found that capital punishment was constitutional if it is not imposed capriciously or arbitrarily, if the sentencing authority follows strict guidelines, and if it is not mandated for any particular crime.

The new Georgia death penalty law was crafted carefully to meet Supreme Court objections in *Furman*. It provided for two jury trials, the first to determine guilt or innocence, the second, if necessary, to determine the punishment. A second trial could include evidence ruled out at the first and provide additional protection for the accused.

Juries, in deciding whether to impose a death sentence, would have limited discretion. They would have to consider a set of guidelines which spell out "aggravating circumstances." The law also provided for state supreme court review of each death sentence. The court would consider if the sentence was imposed because of prejudice and passion, or some other arbitrary factor. It also could consider the "proportionality" of the death sentence, that is, determine if the sentence is excessive or disproportionate when compared to other sentences imposed by Georgia juries.

Both the Burger and Rehnquist Courts have taken a strong stand against mandatory death sentences. In *Woodson v. North Carolina*, 428 U.S. 280 (1976), the Burger Court held that the mandatory approach was "unduly harsh and unworkably rigid." North Carolina provided no standards by which a judge or jury could decide "which murderer shall live and which shall die." There also was no opportunity for judge or jury to consider "mitigating circumstances."

Capital punishment resumed in the United States on the morning of January 17, 1977, when Gary Gilmore, convicted of the murders of a motel owner and filling station attendant, was executed by a firing squad in Draper, Utah. Gilmore was convicted of killing both men by shooting them in the head after forcing them to lie face down on the floor.

Writer Norman Mailer won a 1980 Pulitzer Prize for *The Executioner's Song*, his book on the Gilmore case. It later became a made-for-TV movie.

In 1984, North Carolina executed Velma Barfield. She became the first woman convicted of murder to die since capital punishment was reinstated

The Rehnquist Court considered *Sumner v. Shuman*, 483 U.S. 66 (1987). Nevada prisoners serving life terms without hope of pardon or parole were to receive automatic death sentences if they committed a first degree murder (guard or fellow inmate in most cases) while incarcerated. The Court restated its *Woodson* rule. There can be no exceptions to the ban on mandatory capital punishment.

The use of the death penalty was limited when the Court held in *Coker v. Georgia*, 433 U.S. 584 (1977), that the death penalty could not be imposed for nonfatal rape of an adult woman.

Can the state execute a person who has gone insane while awaiting execution on death row? In *Ford v. Wainright*, 91 L. Ed. 2d 339 (1986), the Burger Court handed down its last capital punishment decision. It held that the Constitution bars execution of killers who become insane on death row. If, however, a condemned killer regains sanity, he or she may be executed.

An interesting question growing out of this ruling is one of professional and ethical responsibility of a psychiatrist. **Should one "help" a patient to become sane so that the state can execute him or her?**

Opponents of capital punishment launched another major attack with a 1986 study of 2000 Georgia murder cases tried in the 1970s by Professor David C. Baldus and others.

Known as the Baldus report, Iowa professors cited statistics to try to show that executions were racially discriminatory. They noted that:

- Prosecutors sought the death penalty in 70% of their cases involving Black defendants and white victims while they sought such a penalty in only 32% of cases involving white defendants and white victims.

- Defendants accused of killing whites were 11 times more likely to receive the death penalty than if they murdered Blacks.

- Defendants charged with killing whites were 4.3 times as likely to receive the death penalty as defendants charged with killing Blacks.

Armed with the Baldus study, anti-capital punishment lawyers for the NAACP Legal Defense and Educational Fund tried to persuade the Rehnquist Court that death penalty laws violated the Equal Protection and Due Process Clauses.

But in *McCleskey v. Kemp*, 481 U.S. 279 (1987), the Court ruled that statistical evidence demonstrating that the death penalty was imposed more often on killers of whites than of Blacks failed to adequately demonstrate unconstitutional discrimination. McCleskey failed to prove discriminatory intent in his specific case. Neither the Eighth nor 14th Amendments were violated, the Court ruled.

McCleskey, according to testimony of one of his accomplices, had shot and killed an Atlanta police officer during an attempted robbery. He had confessed to robbery and, according to prosecution evidence, bragged about the killing. The Court handed down two capital punishment decisions in 1989.

In *Penry v. Lynaugh*, 106 L. Ed. 2d 256 (1989), it held that the death sentence for mentally retarded persons is not unconstitutional *per se*. Such persons, however, are entitled to instructions that jurors may treat evidence of mental retardation as mitigating the effect of the murder. In companion cases, *Stanford v. Kentucky* and *Wilkins v. Missouri*, 492 U.S. 361 (1989), the Court held that persons as young as 16 years old may be sentenced to death.

In *Atkins v. Virginia*, 536 U.S. 304 (2002), a Supreme Court majority overruled *Penry*, holding that a national consensus now rejects execution of mentally retarded offenders as excessive punishment, contrary to the Eighth Amendment. Only two states barred such executions in 1989, while 18 of the 38 states that had the death penalty in 2002 do so.

Atkins, a Virginia man with an IQ of 59, was convicted of abducting Eric Nesbitt, robbing him of his money, and driving him to an Automated Teller Machine, where cameras recorded withdrawal of additional cash. Nesbitt was then taken to an isolated location, shot eight times and killed.

Writing for the six-member majority, Justice John Paul Stevens said:

...It is not so much the number of these states that is significant, but the consistency of the direction of change...Even most states that nominally allow executing the retarded are not actually carrying out such executions. The practice, therefore, has become truly unusual and it is fair to say that a national consensus has developed against it.

Some characteristics of mental retardation undermine the strength of the procedural protections that our capital jurisprudence steadfastly guards...as a result, mentally retarded defendants in the aggregate face a special risk of wrongful execution.

Stevens noted that retarded defendants have diminished capacities to understand and process information, to reason logically and to control impulsive behavior. He concluded that they should face criminal punishment for their acts, but have reduced "personal culpability."

Stevens was joined in his opinion by Justices Sandra Day O'Connor, Anthony Kennedy, David Souter, Ruth Bader Ginsburg and Stephen Breyer.

Chief Justice William Rehnquist and Associate Justices Antonin Scalia and Clarence Thomas dissented. Scalia disputed that there is a real national consensus against executing the retarded, pointing out that 18 of 38 states is less than half. He wrote:

> In the absence of an authentic consensus, the majority has simply enshrined its own views as constitutional law...The arrogance of this assumption of power takes one's breath away. There is something to said for popular abolition of the death penalty; there is nothing to be said for its incremental abolition by this court.

In *Ring v. Arizona*, 536 U.S. 584 (2002), decided only four days after *Atkins*, the Supreme Court held that juries, rather than judges, must make life-or-death decisions in capital cases. The decision effectively invalidated death penalty statutes in five states, Arizona, Colorado, Idaho, Montana and Nebraska.

In all of these states, judges consider the existence of "aggravating factors" that separate convicted killers eligible for death sentences from those who are not.

Timothy Ring was convicted of killing an armored car driver when committing a robbery in Phoenix in 1994. Lawyers challenged his death sentence on grounds that his constitutional right to a jury trial was violated when a judge held a separate sentencing hearing after the jury that convicted him of murder had been dismissed.

The Supreme Court ruling had no effect in the 29 states whose capital punishment laws conformed to the requirements it announced on June 24, 2002. Legislatures in the states impacted by *Ring* had to rewrite their sentencing procedures.

In *Williams v. Taylor*, 529 U.S. 362 (2000), the Supreme Court held, 5-4, that a Federal judge's authority to overrule a state court decision in death penalty cases is limited. The decision was the first major interpretation of a 1996 Federal law designed to limit inmate appeals and hasten executions.

The statute was adopted in the wake of the 1995 Oklahoma City bombing, in part to deal with the public concern that condemned prisoners were circumventing the judicial system by dragging out their appeals for many years.

The case also arose during a renewed national debate over the fairness of capital punishment and whether innocent people have been wrongly condemned to death. In one of the most dramatic demonstrations of concern, Illinois Gov. George H. Ryan (R.), in January, 2000, imposed a moratorium on executions in his state after concluding that 13 persons had been unjustly sentenced to death. Before leaving office in January, 2004, Ryan commuted the death sentences of 167 Illinois death row inmates.

Speaking for the majority, Justice Sandra Day O'Connor said that even if a Federal judge believes that a state court has erred in rejecting an inmate's claim, he or she can reverse only if the state court used an "unreasonable" interpretation of Federal law. O'Connor's opinion was joined by Chief Justice William Rehnquist and Associate Justices Antonin Scalia, Clarence Thomas and Anthony Kennedy.

Dissenting were Justices John Paul Stevens, David Souter, Ruth Bader Ginsburg and Stephen Breyer.

Despite the tough new standard, the Court, in a separate 6-3 vote, threw out the death sentence of convicted killer Terry Williams and ruled that he deserved a new hearing because his lawyers so mishandled his sentencing trial that it violated his Sixth Amendment **right to effective counsel**.

Among other things, lawyers failed to investigate the facts thoroughly and also failed to present substantial mitigating evidence to the sentencing jury. They failed to produce evidence of Williams' 'borderline' mental retardation and routine beatings suffered as a child. They did not show that Williams functioned well in structured environments, such as correctional centers. Significant facts gathered in interviews with the defendant's wife and 11-year-old daughter also were ignored by his attorneys.

Williams' lead counsel, E.L. Motley, Jr., suffered from a debilitating mental illness and subsequently was banned from the practice of law.

What constitutes effective counsel may be subject to debate, but clearly the Supreme Court will not tolerate the kind of legal representation given a Texas death row inmate, Calvin Burdine. On June 3, 2002, the Court opened the way for a new trial in a case that focused attention on the quality of legal counsel in capital cases. Without comment, the Court let stand a ruling by the U.S. Court of Appeals for the Fifth Circuit in the infamous "sleeping lawyer case."

Although the state of Texas argued that the performance of the late attorney Joe Frank Cannon, who allegedly slept through parts of his client's murder trial, had not made it impossible for Burdine to receive a fair trial, the full Fifth Circuit ruled otherwise. Roe Wilson, assistant district attorney for Harris County, indicated that Burdine probably would be retried for the fatal stabbing of W.T. Wise, his former gay lover, during a burglary. There was, Wilson reminded a news conference, a confession in the case.

The Court reversed its *Stanford* ruling in 2005, holding in *Roper v. Simmons* that the Eighth and 14th Amendments prohibit the death penalty for those under the age of 18 when their crimes were committed. In a 5-4 decision, Justice Kennedy, writing for the majority, stressed three points…"evolving standards of decency," the fact that this kind of brutal juvenile crime makes it likely that mitigating factors may be overlooked and, finally, the overwhelming weight of international opinion against capital punishment. Joining Kennedy in the majority were Justices Stevens, Souter, Ginsburg and Breyer.[27]

Justice Scalia, in a ringing dissent, joined by Thomas and Chief Justice Rehnquist, criticized the majority for finding a "moral consensus" against executing those who commit murder before reaching the age of 18. "By what conceivable warrant can nine lawyers presume to be the authoritative conscience of the nation?" he asked.

Scalia accused the majority of citing sociological studies it liked, and effectively looking over the heads of the American people. He also rejected the concept "that American law should conform to the laws of the rest of the world." He wrote:[28]

…The Court proclaims itself sole arbiter of our Nation's moral standards—and in the course of discharging that awesome responsibility purports to take guidance from the view of foreign courts and legislatures….Because I do not believe that the meaning of the Eighth Amendment, any more than the meaning of other provisions of our Constitution, should be determined by the subjective views of five members of this Court and like-minded foreigners, I dissent.

In a more restrained dissent, Justice O'Connor said, "...The evidence before us fails to demonstrate conclusively that any such consensus has emerged in the brief period since we upheld this practice in *Stanford v. Kentucky*...I would not substitute our judgment about the moral propriety of capital punishment for 17-year-old murderers for the judgment of the Nation's legislatures."

The Roberts Court and Capital Punishment

After John Roberts replaced the late William Rehnquist as Chief Justice of the United States and Samuel Alito was confirmed as Sandra Day O'Connor's successor, court watchers assumed that the nation's highest tribunal would be headed in a more conservative direction. To some, this meant that it would be "tougher" on crime and more deferential to legislatures, including those which had enacted capital punishment laws. There had been much talk during Roberts and Alito's confirmation hearings about "judicial activism" and "judicial self-restraint."

In rulings during its 2006-07 term, the nation's highest tribunal considered several significant capital punishment cases.

It held in *Panetti v. Quarterman (No. 06-6407)* that a delusional, mentally ill convicted killer could not be executed because he had no "rational understanding" of why Texas had sentenced him to die.

Four conservatives, Chief Justice Roberts and Justices Scalia, Thomas and Alito dissented. Justice Kennedy, who appears to some court watchers to be O'Connor's successor as the "swing, centrist vote," authored the majority opinion. He was joined by Justices Stevens, Souter, Breyer and Ginzburg.

In *Uttecht v. Brown* (No. 06-413), the tribunal made it easier for states to remove potential jurors in capital cases when they express reservations about the death penalty. Justice Kennedy again wrote for a 5-4 majority. This time he "swung" to the conservatives, holding with Chief Justice Roberts and Justices Scalia, Thomas and Alito that appellate courts must yield to a trial judge's decision that a juror would be able to overcome misgivings and be able to vote to impose a death penalty. Dissenting Justices Stevens, Souter, Ginsburg and Breyer felt that this would tilt jury panels in the direction of those most likely to vote for death.

In its 2007-08 term, the Roberts Court considered the question of whether lethal injection as a method of execution violated the Eighth Amendment ban on cruel and unusual punishment.

All American states which exact the ultimate penalty of death for murder, with the exception of Nebraska, use lethal injection as the method of execution.

Nine states had suspended such punishment in 2006 after it took Florida 34 minutes, twice the "normal time" to execute convicted killer Angel Diaz.

The U.S. Supreme Court accepted two Kentucky cases in September, 2007. This effectively imposed a *de facto* nationwide moratorium on executions pending its decision. The Court ruled (7-2) on April 16, 2008, in *Baze v. Rees* that the three-drug lethal injection protocol used to execute prisoners in most states does not violate the Eighth Amendment's prohibition on cruel and unusual punishment.

The legal challenge was brought by Kentucky inmates, Ralph Baze and Thomas Bowling. Baze had been convicted of killing a sheriff and deputy sheriff in Powell County, Ky., while Bowling was convicted of the shooting murders of a Lexington, Ky., couple. He also wounded their two-year-old son.

Neither of the condemned men questioned the death penalty *per se*. Rather, they argued, the method of execution was "cruel and unusual" because it might subject them to an unacceptable level of pain and suffering.

Under the three-drug protocol used in Kentucky, a barbiturate is administered to make the inmate unconscious. He then receives a drug intended to cause total paralysis. Finally, potassium chloride is injected to stop the heart.

If the first drug fails to work properly, the condemned man will remain mentally aware as the other drugs are injected. This could cause unbearable pain and suffering from the injection of potassium chloride. But the inmate will be unable to show any pain because he has been paralyzed by the second drug. Those witnessing the execution may conclude that the prisoner has gone peacefully to sleep. In fact, those opposed to lethal injection argue, he may have been fully conscious and in agony during the final moments of life.

Some states, including Florida and Missouri, have ensured that this will not happen by requiring verification that the prisoner is unconscious prior to the administration of the other two drugs.

In his controlling opinion, Chief Justice Roberts said that Kentucky had established safeguards to prevent botched executions. Members of the injection team must have a year or more of professional experience as paramedics or certified medical assistants. The warden and deputy warden also must be present. Roberts wrote:

> In light of these safeguards, we cannot say that the risks identified are so substantial or imminent as to amount to an Eighth Amendment violation...Much of the case rests on the contention that they have identified a significant risk of harm that can be eliminated by adopting alternative procedures... But the Eighth Amendment does not require the invalidation of execution methods whenever a slightly or marginally safer alternative is identified. This court has ruled that capital punishment is constitutional and so there must be a means to implement it...

Justices Kennedy and Alito fully joined the Chief Justice's opinion. Concurring in the judgment only were Justices Stevens, Scalia, Thomas and Breyer. Justices Ginsburg and Souter dissented, saying that they would return the case to lower courts to consider whether Kentucky's failure to include available safeguards created an "...untoward, readily avoidable risk of inflicting severe and unnecessary pain."

Although concurring in the result, largely because it conformed to Supreme Court precedents, Justice Stevens said the nation should re-examine the death penalty. "The time for dispassionate, impartial comparison of the costs that death penalty litigation imposes on society with the benefits that it produces has surely arrived," he said.

Another major capital punishment case on the Supreme Court's agenda remained undecided in late spring, 2008. The question was whether the state of Louisiana could impose the death penalty on those who rape children. The nation's highest tribunal ruled in *Coker v Georgia* than non-capital rape of an adult victim could not be punished by death.

The U.S. criminal justice system goes a very long way to protect the defendant. We have inherited from our British ancestors a system which requires the state to prove that John or Jane Q. Citizen has committed a crime before punishing him or her.

The system is stacked. The individual need not prove anything. Burden of proof is on the state. It must demonstrate, by weight of clear and convincing evidence, that an individual is guilty beyond "**reasonable doubt**." The theory behind the system is that it is better that a guilty person go free than that an innocent person be jailed.

"Three Strikes and You're Out" Laws

In recent years, several states, including California, Virginia and Washington, have adopted tough, anti-crime laws called, "Three Strikes and You're Out" statutes.

They provide a lifetime sentence without hope of parole for anyone convicted of a third felony, even though it may be a relatively minor offense. Some states require that the felonies must be crimes of violence. In others, like California, any three felonies will do.

In *Ewing v. California*, 538 U.S. 11 (2003), the Supreme Court considered a challenge to the California recidivism statute. The defendant, Gary A. Ewing, had been sentenced to 25 years to life for stealing three golf clubs, valued at about $1200, from a pro shop. He had previously been convicted of four serious or violent felonies. At trial, the court reviewed Ewing's prior offenses before imposing sentence. It noted that he had committed his last crime while on parole. Both the California Court of Appeals and the state Supreme Court denied review.

The U.S. Supreme Court held that the statute did not violate the Eighth Amendment's ban on "cruel and unusual" punishment.

In the year before *Ewing*, the Supreme Court reviewed the case of *Lockyer v. Andrade*, 538 U.S. 63 (2003). California courts had concluded that two consecutive terms of 25 years to life in prison for Leandro Andrade was not "cruel and unusual punishment" for the crime of petty theft of about $150 worth of videotapes from a K-Mart store. He had been caught stealing for the third and fourth times.

The Ninth Circuit U.S. Court of Appeals overturned these state rulings, holding that the sentence was grossly disproportionate to the crime committed. The Supreme Court, in turn, rejected that finding, 5-4. Justice O'Connor, author of the majority opinion, focused on "gross disproportionality." She wrote:

> The gross disproportionality principle reserves a constitutional violation for only the extraordinary case. In applying this principle...it was not an unreasonable application of our clearly established law for the California Court of Appeals to affirm Andrade's sentence of two consecutive terms of 25 years to life in prison.

ARTICLE I PROVISIONS

Although, as noted, Amendments 4-6 and 8 comprise 40% of the Bill of Rights and focus largely on the rights of the accused, some of the greatest of America's freedoms are found in Article I of the Constitution itself, which spells out the powers and authority of Congress and what it may do.

From the perspective of limited government, it also spells out what Congress may NOT do. The framers of the Constitution specifically insisted that Congress:

- may not pass bills of attainder;
- may not enact *ex post facto* laws or:
- suspend the writ of *habeas corpus* during peacetime.

Bills of Attainder

A **bill of attainder** is a legislative act which inflicts punishment on an individual without giving him or her a judicial trial. Congress may define certain kinds of anti-social conduct as criminal. It may prescribe punishment. But it cannot sentence anyone. This is the task of Federal trial judges.

Bills of attainder, rare in the nation's history, represent raw exercise of judicial power and authority by the legislature. The Court seldom has ruled that Congress has violated the Constitution in this respect. One such case, *U.S. v. Lovett*, 328 U.S. 303 (1946), involved three Federal government officials whose political views were disliked by Martin Dies, then chairman of the House Committee on Un-American Activities. Dies charged that Lovett, an undersecretary of state in the Truman administration (later secretary of defense) was a "subversive." The House, at the committee's urging, then passed a **"rider"** to an appropriations bill, forbidding payment of salary to Lovett and others named in the statute, unless they were renominated by the President and confirmed by the Senate.

The Court ruled that this was an unconstitutional bill of attainder because the men involved had been tried, in effect, on charges of subversion by the House committee. Congressional efforts to bar them from government service constituted punishment with the meaning of a bill of attainder.

The Court also ruled against Congress in *U.S. v. Brown*, 381 U.S. 437 (1965). Congress had provided, in the Labor-Management Reporting and Disclosure Act of 1959, that no Communist Party member should be allowed to serve as a labor union official. Brown, a San Francisco longshoreman, had been an active party member for 25 years.

A jury convicted Brown on charges of knowingly and willfully serving as a union officer while a Communist Party member. But the U.S. Court of Appeals for the Ninth Circuit reversed his conviction. The Supreme Court granted the government's request for review, and found that Brown was the victim of an unconstitutional bill of attainder. In several other cases, the Court has rejected arguments that Federal laws amounted to unconstitutional bills of attainder.

Ex Post Facto Laws

The term *ex post facto* comes from the Latin: after the fact. It means essentially that no one may be prosecuted for an act done before a law subsequently defines it to be criminal. Any act which aggravates a crime, increases punishment for it or alters the rules of evidence to the disadvantage of the defendant also is prohibited. *Ex post facto law* applies only to criminal, not civil law, *Calder v. Bull,* 3 Dallas 386 (1798).

Habeas Corpus

The term *habeas corpus* comes from the Latin: you have the body. The writ commonly refers to a procedure for getting a judge to consider whether an individual is being illegally detained. Technically, it is an order to the jailer to bring the body of the prisoner before the court.

Without this "great writ of Anglo-American liberty," those exercising power and authority would be unrestrained. People literally could be left to "rot" in prison, not unknown in human history.

In recent decades, defense attorneys have sought Federal writs of *habeas corpus* to challenge constitutionality of state criminal convictions. U.S. District Court judges increasingly have been asked to determine whether state convictions are consistent with Due Process of Law. State judges resent this and their criticism may have been a factor in Supreme Court decisions limiting the writ's usage.

In *Felker v. Turpin,* 518 U.S. 651 (1996), the Supreme Court upheld an Act of Congress which severely restricts Federal *habeas corpus* appeals by state prison inmates who have already filed one. Rejecting the argument that the statute effectively violated the Constitution's Suspension Clause (Article I, Section 9, Clause 2), which provides that "the Privilege of the Writ of *Habeas Corpus* shall not be suspended," Chief Justice Rehnquist wrote:

> The Act does not violate the Constitution's Suspension Clause. The new restrictions on successive *habeas corpus* petitions constitute a modified...rule, a restraint on what is called in *habeas* practice 'abuse of the writ.' The doctrine of abuse of the writ refers to a complex and evolving body of equitable practices principles informed and controlled by historical usage, statutory developments and judicial decisions. The new restrictions are well within the compass of this evolutionary process and do not amount to a 'suspension' of the writ.

In *O'Sullivan v. Boerckel* 526 U.S. 838 (1999), the Court held that **state prisoners generally cannot pursue claims in Federal courts which were not raised on direct appeal to the state's highest court**. Writing for the majority in a 6-3 decision, Justice O'Connor said, "State prisoners must give the state Courts one full opportunity to resolve any constitutional issues by invoking one complete round of the state's established appellate review process."

Darren Boerckel was convicted in 1976 of raping an 87-year-old woman when he was 17. He received prison sentences of 20-60 years on counts of burglary, aggravated battery and rape.

In *Rasul v. Bush,* 542 U.S. 466 (2004), and *Hamdi v. Rumsfeld,* 542 U.S. 507 (2004*),* the Supreme Court rejected President Bush's view that he could hold foreign nationals and U.S. citizens called "enemy combatants" indefinitely in its war on terrorism. Detainees, held at Guantanamo Bay, Cuba, the Court found, have a right to an independent tribunal determination of the validity of their detention.

U.S. District Courts were opened to detainees. These tribunals will consider the legality of individual detentions, and what kind of hearings will be required.

136

Hamdan v. Rumsfeld, No. 05-184

One of the most significant cases on the U.S. Supreme Court docket in 2006 was *Hamdan v. Rumsfeld.* It involved the question of the president's authority to establish military commissions to try enemy combatants at Guantanamo Bay. Also at issue was the question whether Congress could block the Supreme Court from hearing cases before military commissions. Finally, the Court was asked to rule on whether U.S. courts can enforce articles of the 1949 Geneva Convention.

Salim Ahmed Hamdan, Osama bin Laden's chauffeur, was captured by U.S. forces in Afghanistan in April, 2004. He filed a petition for *habeas corpus* to challenge his confinement at the U.S. Guantanamo Bay Naval Base after being charged with several counts of terrorism and designated for trial before a military commission.

Hamdan was given a formal hearing before a Combatant Status Review Tribunal, which determined that he was an enemy combatant, "either a member of or affiliated with Al Qaeda, and could, therefore, be held by the U.S."

In November, 2004, however, U.S. District Court Judge James Robertson granted Hamdan's petition for *habeas corpus*, finding that he could not be tried by a military commission, unless he first was found not to be a prisoner of war under the 1949 Geneva Convention.

The U.S. Court of Appeals for the District of Columbia Circuit reversed Judge Robertson, rejecting Hamdan's argument that the President violated the separation of powers inherent in the Constitution when he established the military commissions. The Court also held that Congress had authorized the President to establish the commission in 2001, and that the Geneva Convention cannot be judicially enforced in Federal Court.

The U.S. Supreme Court granted *certiorari* in November, 2005, and the case was argued on March 28, 2006.

Chief Justice John Robert recused himself because he had been a member of the three-judge panel which had ruled for the government. This left open the possibility of a 4-4 tie vote, which would have the effect of affirming the Court of Appeals decision without establishing a major precedent.

However, in late June, 2006, the Supreme Court held, 5-3, that Hamdan's trial before a military commission could not proceed. The commissions were not authorized by Congress, and a trial by a military tribunal also would violate the Uniform Code of Military Justice and the four Geneva Conventions signed by the U.S. in 1949. The Court specifically rejected the President's view that the Geneva Conventions did not apply to detainees in the war on terror.

Justice Stevens wrote the majority opinion. He was joined by Justices Souter, Ginsburg, Breyer and Kennedy. Justices Scalia, Thomas and Alito each wrote a dissenting opinion. They argued that the Court lacked jurisdiction to hear the case because the Detainee Treatment Act provided that "no court, justice or judge shall have jurisdiction to hear or consider an application for a writ of *habeas corpus* filed by or on behalf of an alien detained by the Department of Defense at Guantanamo, Cuba.

After the court's ruling, President Bush asked Congress for legislation to effectively overturn it. It responded by passing the Military Commissions Act of 2006. The statute provided for military trials for unlawful enemy combatants and stripped Federal courts of authority to consider *habeas corpus* petitions filed by detainees. The law further provided that non-U.S. citizens, including permanent residents of the U.S., may not invoke the Geneva Conventions as a source of rights.

The new law was challenged almost immediately by lawyers for detainees in nearly 200 pending cases. Their argument was that the Act violates Article I, Section 9 (2) of the U.S. Constitution, which forbids suspension of *habeas corpus* except in cases of rebellion or invasion.

The Supreme Court handed down a major decision on June 12, 2008, in the consolidated cases of *Lakhdar Boumediene, et. al.v. George Bush* (No. 06-1195) and *Khaled Al Odah v. U.S.* (No. 06-1196). Boumediene, an Algerian national, was arrested in Bosnia in 2001 in a suspected plot to attack the U.S. Embassy in Sarajevo. Al Odah , a citizen of Kuwait, was taken captive in Pakistan in 2002

The deeply-divided Court ruled, 5-4, that part of the Military Commission Act of 2006 was unconstitutional. It struck down the congressional remedy of military tribunals without trial access to the U.S. Supreme Court system for Guantanamo detainees.

Justice Kennedy, writing for the majority which included Justices Stevens, Souter, Ginsburg and Breyer, said, "The laws and the Constitution are destined to survive, and remain in force, in extraordinary times. Liberty and security can be reconciled, and in our system they are reconciled within the framework of the law."

Kennedy noted that several of the detainees had been held as prisoners for six years without review of their claims. "The cost of delay can no longer be borne by those who are held in custody...Their access to the writ is a necessity," he wrote.

Detainees have rights under the U.S. Constitution, he said, but the system the administration put in place to classify them as enemy combatants and the review procedures are inadequate.

President Bush had argued that the Guantanamo detainees had no rights, and that the classification and review process was an adequate substitute for civilian court hearings.

Chief Justice Roberts and Justices Scalia, Thomas and Alito dissented. Scalia accused the majority of usurping the "mandate of the political branches" in the case of the Guantanamo law, enacted by Congress and signed by President Bush.

Judges, he said, "simply have no competency to second guess" military officials on which foreigners picked up on the battlefield should be imprisoned. He observed that the Court would "live to regret" its decision.

In a separate dissent, Chief Justice Roberts said the majority offered no practical solutions for military officials. He wrote, "For all its eloquence about the detainees' right to the writ, the Court makes no effort to elaborate how exactly the remedy it prescribes will differ" from existing procedures.

Accusing the majority of judicial activism, the Chief Justice said the decision "is not really about the detainees at all, but about control of federal policy regarding enemy combatants." The result of the case, he concluded, was that the American public would "lose a bit more control over the conduct of the nation's foreign policy to unelected, politically unaccountable judges."

We now turn our attention to the heated debate over the right to privacy. Do Americans have such a right? If so, where did they get it—from the Constitution or from "imaginative judges?"

138

1. Adapted from *Crime in the United States*, 1991, Uniform Crime Reports, Federal Bureau of Investigation (Washington, D.C., U.S. Government Printing Office, 1992), p. 4.

2. George McKenna, *A Guide to The Constitution: That Delicate Balance* (New York: Random House, 1984). p. 107. See also, Friendly and Elliott, *The Constitution: That Delicate Balance* (New York: Random House, 1984).

3. *Stein v. New York*, 346 U.S. 156 (1953)

4. For cases to reach a Federal court, a substantial "Federal question" must be raised. State law or administrative practices must conflict with U.S. law or the American Constitution.

5. *Maxwell v. Dow*, 176 U.S. 581 (1900) and *Twining v. N.J.*, 211 U.S. 78 (1908)

6. *Palko v. Connecticut*, 302 U.S. 319 (1937). Palko later was executed.

7. Quoted in Way, *Liberty in the Balance, op. cit.*, p. 103.

8. *Weeks v. U.S.*, 232 U.S. 383 (1914)

9. *Mapp v. Ohio*, 367 U.S. 643 (1961)

10. *Ibid.* at pp. 673-686

11. *U.S. v. Leon*, 468 U.S. 899 (1984)

12. *Ibid.* at pp. 918-921

13. *Terry v. Ohio*, 392 U.S. 1 (1968)

14. *Ibid.* at p. 38

15. "State high court rules sobriety checkpoint law unconstitutional," *The Detroit News,* September 15, 1993, p. 7-B

16. *Olmstead v. U.S.,* 277 U.S. 438 (1928)

17. *Katz v. U.S.,* 389 U.S. 347 (1967)

18. *Ibid.* at p. 365

19. Quoted in Ira Glasser, *Visions of Liberty* (New York: Arcade Publishing, 1991), p. 177.

20. *Escobedo v. Illinois,* 378 U.S. 478 (1964)

21. *Miranda v. Arizona,* 384 U.S. 436 (1966)

22. *Lucas v. South Carolina Coastal Council,* 505 U.S. 1003 (1992)

23. *Powell v. Alabama,* 282 U.S. 45 (1932)

24. *Ibid.* at pp. 53-73; For an excellent account of the case, see Dan T. Carter, *Scottsboro: A Tragedy of the American South,* revised edition (Baton Rouge, Louisiana State University Press, 1979). Carter was called in 1977 as an expert witness in Victoria Price Street's libel suit against NBC television for its 1976 movie, based to some extent on Carter's book, his Ph.D. dissertation.

25. *Gideon v. Wainwright,* 372 U.S. 335 (1963)

26. See *Furman v. Georgia,* 408 U.S. 238 (1972)

27. *Roper v. Simmons,* 543 U.S. 551 (2005)

28. *Ibid.*

CHAPTER III: THE RIGHT TO PRIVACY

The word privacy appears nowhere in the U.S. Constitution or the Bill of Rights. Yet a right to privacy has been recognized, first by courts, and more recently by Congress and state legislatures. Long ago, Justice Louis Brandeis, in a dissenting opinion in *Olmstead v. U.S.*, 277 U.S. 438 (1928), wrote that the architects of the Constitution had tried to give Americans "the right to be let alone...the right most valued by civilized men." For more than 30 years, Brandeis' opinion was the only serious mention of a right to privacy. Then, in 1961, Justice John Marshall Harlan, dissenting in *Poe v. Ullman*, 367 U.S. 497 (1961), indicated that other justices thought that the right to privacy existed.

The question before the Court in *Poe* was the constitutionality of a Connecticut law forbidding the use of birth control. It applied even to **married** couples. A physician, Dr. Lee Buxton, challenged the act on behalf of two female patients who wanted to use contraceptives for health reasons. One, aged 26, had three congenitally abnormal children who had died shortly after birth. Buxton felt that another pregnancy would threaten her mental, as well as physical health. The second woman, aged 25, nearly had died after her last pregnancy. She was unconscious for weeks, left partially paralyzed, and suffered impaired speech. Buxton felt that another pregnancy probably would kill her. Both women, known in the legal proceedings as Poe and Doe, agreed to test the statute.

When the Court refused to hear the case on procedural grounds, Harlan was furious. He argued that the Due Process Clause of the 14th Amendment could be used to invalidate the law. He contended that it "unduly burdened liberty" and constituted "an intolerable and unjustifiable invasion of privacy."

Before his appointment to the Court, Brandeis had co-authored with his Boston law partner Samuel Warren one of the earliest articles on privacy in the *Harvard Law Review*.[1]

In essence, Warren's prominent Boston family was the topic of "lurid" press accounts of their social activities. This happened during an era that historians call the age of "yellow journalism." Warren responded by teaming with Brandeis to propose a new **tort,** the invasion of privacy. The article reasoned that the law should recognize a right to an "inviolate personality" that would protect "thoughts, emotions, and sensations...whether expressed in writing, in conduct, in conversation, in attitudes or in facial expression."

Brandeis and Warren further contended that courts could create privacy rights rather than wait for the legislature to act. Their argument for privacy law was to have great influence.

The press, Brandeis and Warren said, was "overstepping in every direction the obvious bounds of propriety and of decency; idle gossip was crowding out real news," causing great "mental pain and distress" to innocent people who found the "sacred precincts of their private and domestic life" invaded by the prying press. They sought a legal remedy for unwanted and unjustified public exposure of intimate personal facts.

In recent decades, the U.S. Supreme Court has created, defined and protected a right to privacy. Both Congress and state legislatures have enacted privacy statutes. We live, early in the 21st Century, in the age of the data bank and advanced surveillance techniques. Government agencies, banks, credit companies, corporations, schools, the ever-prying press and other institutions all intrude into the individual's solace and desire to be left alone. Americans are understandably concerned about the potential impact of modern, sophisticated technology on their privacy.

When the Bill of Rights was adopted in 1791, the national government quite explicitly was forbidden to infringe upon certain liberties. But James Madison, principal author of the Ninth Amendment, assumed that other rights not specified in Amendments 1-8 also could not be violated by the national government. The Ninth Amendment stipulates:

> *The enumeration in the Constitution, of certain rights, shall not be construed to deny or disparage others retained by the people.*

The amendment expresses two basic premises of American Constitutional Law: that the Federal government is one of limited, enumerated powers, and that expression of those powers is a guarantee that the American people enjoy unstated, innumerable rights against the Federal government.

In introducing his proposal for a Bill of Rights on the floor of the House, Madison said:[2]

> It has been objected also against the bill of rights, that, by enumerating particular exceptions to the grant of power, it would disparage those rights which were not placed in that enumeration; and it might follow, by implication, that those rights which were not singled out were intended to be assigned into the hands of the General Government, and were consequently insecure. This is one of the most plausible arguments I ever heard urged against the admission of rights into this system; but I conceive, that it may be guarded against. I have attempted it, as gentlemen may see by turning to the last clause of the fourth resolution (Ninth Amendment).

The clause to which Madison referred read as follows:[3]

> The exceptions here or elsewhere in the constitution, made in favor of particular rights, shall not be so construed as to diminish the just importance of other rights retained by the people, or as to enlarge the powers delegated by the constitution; but either as actual limitations of such powers, or as inserted merely for greater caution.

In sum, Madison said that the wording of his original proposal and the Ninth Amendment were merely two ways of saying the same thing. Where the U.S. government lacked delegated power, the American people remained free to do as they wish.

There are, however, several different views regarding interpretation of the Ninth Amendment. It may simply protect unenumerated rights. Or it may protect state governments against Federal usurpation of power.

The Ninth Amendment was comparatively dormant, if not forgotten, until 1965, when the U.S. Supreme Court used it to find a right of privacy. Justice Arthur Goldberg found this right in the Ninth Amendment, although his Brethren found it elsewhere, as noted below.

LEGAL ORIGINS: THE BIRTH CONTROL CASES

The U.S. Supreme Court first established the right to privacy in *Griswold v. Connecticut,* 381 U.S. 479 (1965). The case involved Estelle T. Griswold, executive director of Connecticut's Planned Parenthood League and the previously mentioned Dr. Buxton, head of the gynecology department at Yale University Medical School. Buxton had tried to challenge the law in *Poe* and *Doe* earlier, only to have the Court refuse to hear the case. Plaintiffs, the Court noted, did not face any realistic threat of prosecution.

Deliberately setting out to challenge the 1879 state law, Dr. Buxton opened a birth control clinic from November 1 to November 10, 1961. He prescribed contraceptives and provided birth control advice to married couples. At the time, Connecticut banned birth control, even for the married.

The law provided: "any person who uses any drug, medicinal article or instrument for the purpose of preventing conception shall be fined not less than $50 or imprisoned not less than 60 days nor more than one year or be both fined and imprisoned."

Fred Friendly and Martha J. H. Elliott describe the police "raid" on the birth control clinic:[4]

> It was one of the easiest types of investigations you could get involved in, Detective Berg remembers. Mrs. Griswold and Dr. Buxton gave the detectives a guided tour of the clinic, pointing out the condoms and vaginal foam they were dispensing. It wasn't one of those investigations where you have to dig out the information...it was sort of: Here it is; Here we are; Take us in; We want to test this.

Griswold and Burton were charged under a Connecticut statute which provided: "Any person who assists, abets, counsels, causes, hires or commands another to commit any offense may be prosecuted and punished as if he were the principal offender." Griswold and Buxton were found guilty of being accessories and fined $100 each. Appeals in Connecticut courts failed, but the U.S. Supreme Court agreed to review the case.

Griswold's lawyer, Professor Thomas Emerson of Yale Law School, argued that the Connecticut law was unconstitutional because it infringed on an individual "right to privacy." This right, he argued, could be found in five amendments: the First, Third, Fourth, Ninth and 14th. Emerson was among a group of Yale law and medical school professors who "created" Griswold.

They did so only after many failures to get the Connecticut legislature to repeal the law. The act was largely unenforced, and the lawmakers apparently had other priorities. There also was a history of failed lawsuits. Four cases had been taken to the Connecticut Supreme Court of Errors within a period of about two decades.

Justice Black is reported to have dismissed Professor Emerson's First Amendment argument that the law violated a married couple's right of assembly and association with the remark: "The right of a husband and wife to assemble in bed is a new right of assembly for me."

Developing the so-called **"penumbra doctrine,"** the Court held that guarantees in the Bill of Rights cast "penumbras" or shadows that may encompass other rights not specifically mentioned. Speaking for the Court, Justice Douglas wrote:[5]

> Specific guarantees in the Bill of Rights have penumbras, formed by emanations from those guarantees that help give them life and substance. Various guarantees create zones of privacy. The right of association contained in the penumbra of the First Amendment is one, as we have seen. The Third Amendment in its prohibition against the quartering of soldiers 'in any house' in time of peace without the consent of the owner is another facet of that privacy. The Fourth Amendment is another. The Fifth Amendment in its Self-Incrimination Clause enables the citizen to create a zone of privacy which government may not force him

to surrender to his detriment. The Ninth Amendment provides: 'The enumeration in the Constitution of certain rights, shall not be construed to deny or disparage others retained by the people.'

We recently referred in *Mapp v. Ohio* to the Fourth Amendment as creating a 'right to privacy, no less important than any other right carefully and particularly reserved to the people.'

We have had many controversies over these penumbral rights of 'privacy and repose'...the right to privacy which presses for recognition here is a legitimate one.

The present case, then, concerns a relationship lying within the zone of privacy created by several constitutional guarantees. And it concerns a law which, in forbidding the *use* of contraceptives rather than regulating their manufacture or sale, seeks to achieve its goals by means of having a maximum destructive impact upon that relationship. Such a law cannot stand in light of the familiar principle, so often applied by this Court, that a 'governmental purpose to control or prevent activities constitutionally subject to state regulation may not be achieved by means which sweep unnecessarily broadly and thereby invade the area of protected freedoms.'

Would we allow the police to search the sacred precincts of marital bedrooms for telltale signs of the use of contraceptives? The very idea is repulsive to the notions of privacy surrounding the marriage relationship.

We deal with a right of privacy older than the Bill of Rights—older than our political parties, older than our school system. Marriage is a coming together for better or worse, hopefully enduring, and intimate to the degree of being sacred. It is an association that promotes a way of life, not causes; a harmony in living, not political faiths; a bilateral loyalty, not commercial or social projects. Yet it is an association for as noble a purpose as any involved in our prior decisions.

Although *Griswold* is considered a landmark case, the Court failed to speak clearly or with unity. Seven justices found that a right to privacy exists. But they found it in three different areas of the Constitution: zones of privacy emanating from the First, Third, Fourth, Fifth and Ninth Amendments, the Ninth Amendment alone and the 14th Amendment. Douglas, author of the majority opinion quoted above, stressed the penumbra doctrine. But Goldberg, Chief Justice Warren and Brennan, supported a separate concurring opinion, stressing the Ninth Amendment. Goldberg wrote:[6]

The concept of liberty protects those personal rights that are fundamental, and is not confined to the specific terms of the Bill of Rights. My conclusion that it embraces the right of marital privacy, though that right is not mentioned explicitly in the Constitution, is supported both by numerous decisions and by the language and history of the Ninth Amendment...it was proffered to quiet expressed fears that a bill of specifically enumerated rights could not be sufficiently broad to cover all essential rights and the specific mention of certain rights would be interpreted as a denial that others were protected.

While this Court has had little occasion to interpret the Ninth Amendment, it cannot be presumed that any clause in the Constitution is intended to be without effect...to hold that a right so basic and fundamental and so deep-rooted in our society as the right to privacy in marriage may be infringed because that right is not guaranteed in so many words by the first eight amendments to the Constitution is to ignore the Ninth Amendment and to give it no effect whatsoever.

The Ninth Amendment shows a belief of the Constitution's authors that fundamental rights exist that are not expressly enumerated in the first eight amendments and an intent that the list of rights included there not be deemed exhaustive.

In sum, the Ninth Amendment simply lends strong support for the view that the 'liberty' protected by the Fifth and 14th Amendments from infringement by the Federal Government or the States is not restricted to rights specifically mentioned in the first eight amendments.

The Government, absent a showing of a compelling subordinating state interest, could not decree that all husbands and wives must be sterilized after two children have been born to them. Yet by such reasoning an invasion of marital privacy would not be subject to constitutional challenge because, while it might be 'silly,' no provision of the Constitution specifically prevents the Government from curtailing the marital right to bear children and raise a family. If upon a showing of a slender basis of rationality, a law outlawing voluntary birth control by married persons is valid, then, by the same reasoning, a law requiring compulsory birth control also would seem to be valid. In my view, however, both types of law would unjustifiably intrude upon the rights of marital privacy which are constitutionally protected.

Two dissenting justices, Black and Stewart, could find no constitutional right to privacy at all. They argued that, in the absence of some specific prohibition, the Bill of Rights and the 14th Amendment do not permit courts and judges to veto state legislative policies they may dislike.

Black is generally considered to be one of the most Liberal justices in Supreme Court history. He was usually on the same side as the Liberal Douglas. But Black, joined by Stewart, wrote a rigorous dissent. Noting that the law was every bit as offensive to him as to the majority, he did not see the case as one involving fundamental First Amendment freedoms.

It was, he held, merely one in which defendants had supplied devices that the state had a right to restrict. He complained of privacy as an invented right that the Court treated as though there is some constitutional provision or provisions forbidding any law ever to be passed which might abridge the "privacy" of individuals.

He wrote:[7]

I think it belittles (the Fourth) Amendment to talk about it as though it protects nothing but 'privacy.' The average man would very likely not have his feeling soothed any more by having his property seized openly than by having it seized privately and by stealth. He simply wants his property left alone...a person can be as much, if not more, irritated, annoyed and injured by an unceremonious public arrest by a policeman as he is by a seizure in the privacy of his office or home.

I like my privacy as well as the next one, but I am nevertheless compelled to admit that government has a right to invade it unless prohibited by some specific constitutional provision.

Black also found no logical connection between the Ninth or 14th Amendments and rights claimed in *Griswold*. He complained that Goldberg was, in his interpretation of the Ninth Amendment, allowing courts to overturn laws, when the Amendment, properly interpreted, only reserved rights to the people.

Using the 14th Amendment to claim a right to privacy was an abuse of the Due Process Clause, Black reasoned. It was a dangerous path to take, he suggested, creating a standard which would allow future justices to make a personal "appraisal of what laws are unwise or unnecessary."

He wrote:[8]

I do not believe that we are granted power by the Due Process Clause or any other constitutional provision or provisions to measure constitutionally by our belief that legislation is arbitrary, capricious or unreasonable, or accomplishes no justifiable purpose or is offensive to our own notions of 'civilized standards of conduct.' Such an appraisal of the wisdom of legislation is an attribute of the power to make laws, not of the power to interpret them. The use by Federal courts of such a formula or doctrine or what not to veto federal or state laws simply takes away from Congress and the States the power to make laws based on their own judgment of fairness and wisdom and transfers that power to this Court for ultimate determination—a power which was specifically denied to federal courts by the convention that framed the Constitution.

Black was particularly concerned about relying on "people's collective conscience" or the "principles they hold most fundamental." That, he said, was simply asking too much of a justice. He wrote:[9]

I realize that many good and able men have eloquently spoken and written, sometimes in rhapsodical strains, about the duty of this court to keep the Constitution in tune with the times. The idea is that the Constitution must be changed from time to time and that this Court is charged with a duty to make those changes. For myself, I must with all deference reject that philosophy. The Constitution makers knew the need for change and provided for it. Amendments suggested by the people's elected representatives can be submitted to the people or their selected agents for ratification. The method of change was good for our Fathers, and being somewhat old-fashioned, I must add it is good enough for me. And so, I cannot rely on the Due Process Clause or the Ninth Amendment or any mysterious and uncertain natural law concept as a reason for striking down this state law.

Justice Stewart remarked:[10]

I think this is an uncommonly silly law. As a practical matter, the law is obviously unenforceable, except in the oblique context of the present case. As a philosophical matter, I believe the use of contraceptives in the relationship of marriage should be left to personal and private choice. As a matter of social policy, I think professional counsel about methods of birth control should be available to all, so that each individual's choice can be meaningfully made. But we are not asked whether we think this law is unwise, or even asinine. We are asked to hold that it violates the United States Constitution. And that I cannot do.

Eisenstadt: Contraceptives For Singles?

Students should note that *Griswold* dealt only with the issue of *marital privacy*. What about sexually active single people? State laws, including those of Massachusetts, were written in an age when legislatures considered pre-marital intercourse both sinful and criminal. The sin of "fornication" was abominable in the sight of God. It also was a crime, deserving of punishment by the state.

In an age when condoms are freely distributed to public school children, it may surprise some students to learn that not until 1972 did the U.S. Supreme Court declare unconstitutional a state law which prohibited the sale of contraceptives to unmarried people.

Eisenstadt v. Baird, 405 U.S. 38 (1972), arose after William Baird, a 40-year-old former medical student and planned parenthood enthusiast, gave a lecture on birth control at Boston University. He displayed several kinds of contraceptives during his presentation to students and faculty. He also urged them to work for repeal of the Massachusetts birth control laws. At the end of his lecture, Baird gave a woman a package of vaginal foam.

Massachusetts law permitted contraceptives to be distributed for the sole purpose of preventing the spread of disease. If a person wanted contraceptives to avoid pregnancy, the law limited availability to the married. Even then, a licensed physician was required to write a prescription.

Baird was charged and convicted of the crime of illegally distributing contraceptives. He had no medical license and, therefore, no authority to distribute them. The Massachusetts Supreme Judicial Court upheld his conviction. It did, however, set aside, on First Amendment Free Speech grounds, a second conviction for exhibiting contraceptives.

Baird then filed a Federal *habeas corpus* petition, which was dismissed by the U.S. District Court. It was, however, reviewed favorably by the U.S. Court of Appeals for the First Circuit. The Circuit Court found that the purpose of the law "was to limit contraception in and of itself," which it found in conflict with the "right to marital privacy," declared in *Griswold.*

Thomas Eisenstadt, sheriff of Suffolk County, pursued an appeal. The U.S. Supreme Court granted review. The argument now shifted from the sanctity of marriage to the sanctity of individual sexual desires.

Writing for a six-member majority, Justice William Brennan concluded that the law violated the "rights of single people" under the Equal Protection Clause of the 14th Amendment. The Supreme Court found that enforcement of the law would "materially impair the ability of single persons to obtain contraceptives." The question, the Court asked, is "whether there is some ground of difference that rationally explains the different treatment accorded married and unmarried persons" under the law.[11]

Brennan wrote that a suggested purpose of the law is to promote marital fidelity. He rejected this on grounds that "contraceptives may be made available to married persons without regard to whether they are living with their spouses or the uses to which the contraceptives are to be put."

The majority opinion also rejected the notion that the law was intended to discourage premarital sexual intercourse. The law, the Court said, "...has at best a marginal relation to the proffered objective, and by allowing the distribution of contraceptives to any married person, it fails to deter married persons from engaging in illicit sexual relations with unmarried persons."

Brennan noted that the law is "so riddled with exceptions that deterrence of premarital sex cannot reasonably be regarded as its aim."

The Court concluded, "It would be plainly unreasonable to assume that Massachusetts has prescribed pregnancy and the birth of an unwanted child as punishment for fornication." Fornication, under Massachusetts law, was defined as the crime of sexual intercourse between unmarried persons. The penalty provided was 90 days in jail and a $30 fine.

The law under which Baird was convicted carried a maximum sentence of five years!

The Supreme Court found this entirely unreasonable. The law exposed "the aider and abettor" who simply gives away a contraceptive to 20 times the 90-day sentence of the offender himself.

The Court also rejected arguments that the law was a proper public health statute. This, it held, would make the statute "both discriminatory and overbroad," since whatever health reasons exist are as great for single couples as for married couples. Brennan concluded that "whatever the rights of the individual to access to contraceptives may be, the rights must be the same for the unmarried and the married alike."

Justice Brennan noted:[12]

> If, under *Griswold*, the distribution of contraceptives to married persons cannot be prohibited, a ban on distribution to unmarried persons would be equally impermissible. It is true that in *Griswold* the right to privacy in question inhered in the marital relationship. Yet the marital couple is not an independent entity with a mind and heart of its own, but an association of two individuals each with separate intellectual and emotional makeup. If the right of privacy means anything, it is the right of the individual, *married or single,* to be free from unwarranted governmental intrusion into matters so fundamentally affecting a person as the decision whether to bear or beget a child.

Chief Justice Burger dissented, concluding that the law was a legitimate use of the police power of the state to regulate public health. He wrote:[13]

> If the Constitution can be strained to invalidate the Massachusetts statute underlying Baird's conviction, we could quite as well employ it for the protection of a 'curbstone quack,' reminiscent of the 'medicine man' of times past, who attracted a crowd of the curious with a soap box lecture and then plied them with 'free samples' of some unproved remedy. Massachusetts presumably outlawed such activities long ago, but today's holding seems to invite their return.

Critics of *Eisenstadt* argued that it improperly took a decision that related to the sanctity of the marital bedroom and turned it into a general right of sexual relations.

Related Cases: In *Carey v. Population Services International,* 431 U.S. 678 (1977), the Court held unconstitutional a New York law making it a crime to sell or distribute contraceptives to anyone under the age of 16. The statute also permitted the sale of contraceptives to anyone over the age of 16 only by a registered pharmacist.

In *Carey*, the Court, speaking through Justice Brennan, followed the logic of *Eisenstadt*. It held that the right to privacy in procreation matters extends to minors as well as to adults. Restricting sales of contraceptives to registered pharmacists also burdens the right of individuals to use contraceptives, should they choose to do so.

In *Planned Parenthood Federation of America v. Heckler*, 712 F. 2d 650 (D.C. Cir. 1983), a rule promulgated by Margaret Heckler, Secretary of Health and Human Services under President Reagan, was challenged. The so-called **"squeal rule"** required family planning services officials to notify parents or guardian of an unmarried minor when it provided federally funded contraceptives to the child. The Court of Appeals for the District of Columbia held that Congress had not authorized such a rule, and struck it down.

THE ABORTION DEBATE AND THE RIGHT TO PRIVACY

During the past generation, abortion has become one of the more controversial issues on the American agenda. Unlike most other divisive issues, it offers little or no room for compromise.

Ardent "pro-choice" advocates argue that a woman should be granted a constitutional right to choose to terminate a pregnancy. She should, they say, have the right to control her own body. She never should be forced to bear an unwanted child or to have an illegal or unsafe abortion.

Equally ardent "pro-life" advocates argue that giving a woman freedom of choice to abort a fetus is tantamount to giving her the right to kill a child.

Before 1973, individual states were free to decide if females could have legal abortions. If a state permitted them, it determined conditions under which abortions could be performed. In New York state, for example, abortion on demand was permitted during the first 24 weeks of pregnancy. Other states, such as Texas, banned all except therapeutic abortions (those necessary to save the life of the expectant mother). Michigan's law was similar to that of Texas. In fact, Michigan voters, after a very heated and emotional campaign, went to the polls in 1972 and voted overwhelmingly (61%) against "liberalization" of the state abortion statutes. The voters' decision was nullified within a matter of months when the Supreme Court handed down its *Roe* decision.[14]

Roe v. Wade

In 1969, Norma McCorvey, a 21-year-old waitress, became pregnant as the result of an affair. At the time, she said that she had been attacked and raped by three men one night while returning to her motel room. The men, she claimed, left her lying on a country road. Later she admitted that this story was a lie. Divorced and already the mother of a five-year-old daughter, McCorvey sought an abortion. However, she lived in Texas which, as noted, forbade all abortions except those necessary to save the life on an expectant mother. The Texas law was passed in 1856.

Although her name (she was Jane Roe of *Roe v. Wade)* lives in legal history, McCorvey never had an abortion. The gestation period of a baby is shorter than that of a lawsuit. She gave birth to a daughter in June, 1970, and then put her up for adoption. But McCorvey still was upset by the Texas statute. With the help of two young female attorneys just out of law school, she used her case to challenge the abortion statute.

Attorneys Linda Coffee and Sarah Weddington, who had an illegal abortion in a Mexican border town when a law student at University of Texas, filed suit in the U.S. District Court for the Northern District of Texas. For purposes of the lawsuit, McCorvey, as noted, adopted the pseudonym "Jane Roe."[15]

Defendant in the case was Henry Wade, district attorney for Dallas County. A three-judge Federal panel in Dallas ruled that the Texas statute did, in fact, violate McCorvey's right to obtain an abortion. The panel based its decision on the Ninth Amendment to the Constitution.

In a *per curiam* ruling, an opinion "by the court" which expresses its decision, but whose author is unidentified, the Court held that the Texas Abortion Laws must be declared unconstitutional because they deprive single women and married couples of their right, secured by the Ninth Amendment, to choose whether to have children.

McCorvey also asked the Court to issue an injunction restraining enforcement of the law so that she could procure a legal abortion in Texas. It was clear to the three-judge panel that its decision was going to be appealed to the U.S. Supreme Court. Therefore, it refused to accompany its declaratory judgment with an injunction. McCorvey's attorneys prepared to take their case to the nation's highest tribunal.

The Supreme Court Rules

In one of the most controversial cases in the annals of modern constitutional law, the Burger Court handed down its ruling in *Roe v. Wade,* 410 U.S. 113 (1973). It held (7-2) that the concept of privacy included the right to a legal abortion.

"The Constitution does not explicitly mention any right of privacy," Justice Harry Blackmun wrote for the majority. But "the Court has recognized that a right of personal privacy, or a guarantee of certain areas of zones of privacy, does exist under the Constitution."[16]

Individual justices disagreed on what part of the Constitution gave women such a right to privacy. The majority argued that the Due Process Clause of the 14th Amendment implies a "right to privacy" that protects a woman's freedom to choose, during the first three months of pregnancy, whether to have an abortion.

During this first trimester, a decision to terminate a pregnancy is one to be made, the Court said, by a woman, in consultation with her physician. She has a constitutional right to privacy during this time that may not be infringed by state laws. During the second trimester, states were permitted to regulate abortion procedures to protect the mother's health. During the last three months of pregnancy, states might ban abortions entirely.

The Court, while recognizing a broad right to abortion, *did not grant any absolute right to abortion on demand at any time.* Justice Blackmun, author of the majority opinion, took 51 pages to deliver one of the most controversial rulings in the Court's history. He said in part:[17]

> The Texas statutes that concern us here make it a crime to 'procure an abortion' as therein defined, or to attempt one, except with respect to 'an abortion procured or attempted by medical advice for the purpose of saving the life of the mother.' Similar statutes are in existence in a majority of the states.
>
> It perhaps is not generally appreciated that the restrictive criminal abortion laws in effect in a majority of states are of relatively recent vintage...instead, they

derive from statutory changes effected, for the most part, in the latter half of the 19th Century.

When most criminal abortion laws were first enacted, the procedure was a hazardous one for the woman. This was particularly true prior to the development of antisepsis.

The Constitution does not explicitly mention any right of privacy. In a line of decisions, however, the Court has recognized that a right of personal privacy, or a guarantee of certain areas or zones of privacy, does exist under the Constitution.

This right of privacy, whether it be founded in the 14th Amendment's concept of personal liberty and restrictions upon state action, as we feel it is, or as the District Court has determined, in the Ninth Amendment's reservation of rights to the people, is broad enough to encompass a woman's decision whether or not to terminate her pregnancy.

The detriment that the state would impose upon the pregnant woman by denying this choice altogether is apparent. Specific and direct harm medically diagnosable even in early pregnancy may be involved. Maternity, or additional offspring, may force upon the woman a distressful life and future. Psychological harm may be imminent. Mental and physical wealth may be taxed by child care.

There is also the distress, for all concerned, associated with the unwanted child, and there is the problem of bringing a child into a family already unable, psychologically and otherwise, to care for it.

On the basis of elements such as these, appellants and some *amici* argue that the woman's right is absolute and that she is entitled to terminate her pregnancy at whatever time, in whatever way, and for whatever reason she alone chooses. With this we do not agree.

The Court's decision recognizing a right to privacy also acknowledges that some state regulation in areas protected by that right is appropriate. A state properly asserts important interest in safeguarding health, in maintaining medical standards and in protecting potential life.

At the same point in pregnancy, these respective interests become sufficiently compelling to sustain regulation of the factors that govern the abortion decision. The privacy right involved, therefore, cannot be said to be absolute.

The appellee and certain *amici* argue that the fetus is a 'person' within the language and meaning of the 14th Amendment. In support of this, they outline at length and in detail the well-known facts of fetal development. If this suggestion of personhood is established, the appellant's case, of course, collapses, for the fetus' right to life is then guaranteed specifically by the amendment.

The Constitution does not define 'person' in so many words. The use of the word is such that it has application only postnatally.

All this, together with our observation that throughout the major portion of the 19th Century, prevailing legal abortion practices were far freer than they are today, persuades us that the word 'person,' as used in the 14th Amendment, does not include unborn.

Texas urges that, apart from the 14th Amendment, life begins at conception and is present throughout pregnancy, and that, therefore, the state has a compelling interest in protecting that life from and after conception.

We need not resolve the difficult question of when life begins. When those trained in the respective disciplines of medicine, philosophy and theology are unable to arrive at any consensus, the judiciary, at this point in the development of man's knowledge, is not in a position to speculate as to the answer.

The unborn have never been recognized in the law as persons in the whole sense. With respect to the state's important and legitimate interest in the health of the mother, the 'compelling' point, in the light of present medical knowledge, is at approximately the end of the first trimester. This is so because of the now established medical fact that until the end of the first trimester, mortality in abortion is less than mortality in normal childbirth.

It follows that, from and after this point, a state may regulate the abortion procedure to the extent that the regulation reasonably relates to the preservation and protection of maternal health.

With respect to the state's important and legitimate interest in potential life, the 'compelling' point is at viability. This is so because the fetus then presumably has the capability of meaningful life outside the mother's womb. If the state is interested in protecting fetal life after viability, it may go so far as to proscribe abortion during the period except when it is necessary to preserve the life or health of the mother.

White Dissents

Justices White and Rehnquist dissented, arguing for judicial self-restraint. The Court, they charged, had reached its decision on the basis of its own preferences, rather than following clear precedent and guiding principles of constitutional law. Majority justices, they implied, were acting as a superlegislature, substituting their own views for those of elected state legislatures whose abortion regulations they were invalidating. Justice White wrote:[18]

At the heart of the controversy in these cases are those recurring pregnancies that pose no danger whatsoever to the life or health of the mother but are nevertheless unwanted for any one of more of a variety of reasons—convenience, family planning, economics, dislike of children, the embarrassment of illegitimacy, etc. The common claim before us is that for any one of such reasons, or for no reason at all, and without asserting or claiming any threat to life or health, any woman is entitled to an abortion at her request if she is able to find a medical adviser willing to undertake the procedure.

The Court for the most part sustains this position: during the period prior to the time the fetus becomes viable, the Constitution of the United States values the convenience, whim or caprice of the putative mother more than life or potential life of the fetus.

The upshot is the legislature of the 50 states are constitutionally disentitled to weigh the relative importance of the continued existence and development of the fetus on the one hand against a spectrum of possible impacts on the mother on the other hand. As an exercise of raw judicial power, the Court perhaps has authority to do what it does today; but in my view its judgment is an improvident and extravagant exercise of the power of judicial review which the Constitution extends to this Court.

I find no constitutional warrant for imposing such an order of priorities on the people and the legislatures of the states. In a sensitive area such as this, involving as it does issues over which reasonable men may easily and heatedly differ, I cannot accept the Court's exercise of its clear power of choice by interposing a constitutional barrier to state efforts to protect human life and by investing mothers and doctors with the constitutionally protected right to exterminate it. The issue, for the most part, should be left with the people and to the political processes the people have devised to govern their affairs.

Reaction to Roe: Abortion Politics

The Court denied that it was attempting to define when life begins, as some of its critics complained. Some theologians, philosophers and others argue that life begins at the moment of conception. Others argue that "real" human life does not begin until a child has been delivered. Still others argue that life begins somewhere between conception and birth, such as when a fetus becomes "viable." Viability occurs when a fetus has the ability to survive outside the mother's womb.[19]

Those who believe that life begins at the moment of conception have argued that the human fetus is a "person" entitled to the Equal Protection of the Laws, guaranteed by the 14th Amendment. They identify themselves as "**pro-life**" or leaders of the "right-to-life" movement. Any intentional abortion, they argue, is an act of murder.

Those who support *Roe* feel quite differently. No one, they contend, can say precisely when life begins. Women are, they argue, entitled to choose whether or not to have a baby. These people identify themselves as "**pro-choice**."

In the last presidential election preceding *Roe v. Wade* (Nixon v. McGovern in 1972), delegates to the Democratic National Convention were prepared to write a pro-choice plank into the party's platform. Although this is common for Democratic conventions in recent years, it definitely was not the case before *Roe*. McGovern directly intervened to prevent that plank from being adopted. The Democratic Party Platform remained silent on the issue.

Nixon, for the record, publicly condemned abortion and opposed repeal of existing state abortion statutes. But the Republican Party Platform also took no stand on abortion that year.

American politics since *Roe v. Wade* has, to some degree, become "abortion politics," with presidential candidates and national political party platforms winning or losing votes, depending on their stance on abortion. Clearly, no one thought, before 1973, that what a presidential candidate thought about abortion was at all relevant. Americans elected Presidents primarily to deal with economic policy and foreign and national security issues.

The effect of *Roe v. Wade* was to invalidate not only the Texas law but also all similar state laws. At the time, some 45 states, including Michigan, had such statutes. The case was not the end, but rather only the beginning, of the heated abortion debate. It stimulated enormous local, state and national political activity on the part of "True Believers." These political activists believe that they cannot compromise on this issue. Perhaps no other single issue has aroused as much intense moral and political passion as has abortion.

Pro-life forces, led by Roman Catholics, fundamentalist Protestants, some Conservative Jews and others, pressured Congress to propose a constitutional amendment to overturn *Roe v. Wade*. They were, however, unable to do so. Nor were they able to withdraw abortion cases from the original jurisdiction of lower Federal courts, or from the appellate jurisdiction of the Supreme Court.

Senator Jesse Helms (R., N. Carolina) and Rep. Henry Hyde (R., Ill.) introduced the **"Human Life Statute"** in 1981. It stipulated that, "The Congress finds that the life of each human being begins at conception" and that "no inferior federal court...shall have jurisdiction to issue any...injunction ...or declaratory judgment in any case involving...any state law or municipal ordinance that....prohibits, limits or regulates...the performance of abortions." The measure never passed.

The most direct way to overturn a Supreme Court decision is by a constitutional amendment. The 16th (Income Tax) Amendment is an example. Anti-abortion legislators began in 1973 to try to do this and, a decade after *Roe,* such a measure, supported by President Reagan, reached the U.S. Senate floor. Sen. Orrin Hatch (R., Utah) sponsored an amendment that said simply, "A right to abortion is not guaranteed by the Constitution." The Senate voted, 50-49, against the amendment. As deeply divided as possible, possibly reflecting the views of the nation, the Senate was a long way from the two-thirds vote required to formally propose a constitutional amendment.

A two-thirds House vote, also required by the Constitution for amendments, is purely academic since the matter has never come before that chamber for a vote.

The Hyde Amendment, Harris v. McRae

The "pro-life" lobby did succeed, however, beginning in 1976, in barring the use of Federal funds to pay for elective abortions. This so-called **Hyde Amendment,** named after Rep. Henry Hyde (R., Ill.), denied the use of Federal Medicaid funds to pay for abortions. Title XIX of the Social Security Act established the Medicaid program to give Federal aid to states choosing to reimburse costs of medical treatment for the needy. A number of states had chosen to fund Medicaid elective abortions. Although the Federal statute was challenged, the U.S. Supreme Court, speaking through Justice Stewart, upheld the amendment in *Harris v. McRae,* 448 U.S. 297 (1980). Stewart wrote:[20]

It simply does not follow that a woman's freedom of choice carries with it a constitutional entitlement to the financial resources to avail herself of the full range of protected choices...although government may not place obstacles in the path of a woman's exercise of her freedom of choice, it need not remove those not of its own creation. Indigency falls in the latter category. The financial constraints that restrict an indigent woman's ability to enjoy the full range of constitutionally protected freedom of choice are the product not of governmental restrictions on access to abortions, but rather of her indigency. Although Congress has opted to subsidize medically necessary services generally, but not certain medically necessary abortions, the fact remains that the Hyde Amendment leaves an indigent woman with at least the same range of choice in deciding whether to obtain a medically necessary abortion as she would have if Congress had chosen to subsidize no health care costs at all. We are thus not persuaded that the Hyde Amendment impinges on the constitutionally protected freedom of choice recognized in *Wade.*

154

Brennan Dissents

Justice Brennan dissented, joined by Justices Marshall and Blackmun. He wrote, in part:[21]

>A poor woman in the early stages of pregnancy confronts two alternatives: she may elect either to carry the fetus to term or to have an abortion. In the abstract, of course, this choice is hers alone, and the Court rightly observes that the Hyde Amendment places no governmental obstacle in the path of a woman who chooses to terminate her pregnancy.

>But the reality of the situation is that the Hyde Amendment has effectively removed this choice from the indigent woman's hands. By funding all of the expenses associated with childbirth and none of the expenses incurred in terminating pregnancy, the government literally makes an offer that the indigent woman cannot afford to refuse. It matters not that in this instance the government has used the carrot rather than the stick. What is critical is the realization that as a practical matter, many poverty-stricken women will choose to carry their pregnancy to term simply because the government provides funds for the associated medical services, even though these same women would have chosen to have an abortion if the government had also paid for that option.

Federally funded abortions dropped from just under 300,000 in 1976 to 2400 in 1979.

Several states also have restricted the use of tax funds for abortion. In *Maher v. Roe,* 432 U.S. 464 (1977), the Supreme Court upheld a Connecticut law that permits Medicaid funds to be used for childbirth but not for abortion. At the end of 1992, some 31 states withheld Medicaid funds for all abortions except those necessary to protect the life of the expectant mother.

In 1988, the U.S. Supreme Court upheld the **Adolescent Family Life Act,** which forbade Federal funding of organizations involved with abortions. That same year, Dr. Louis Sullivan, secretary of Health and Human Services, issued new regulations that prohibited any agency receiving Federal family planning funds from providing counseling concerning the use of abortion or referral to abortion services.

Some outraged "pro-choice" health professionals, including Dr. Irving Rust, working at a New York planned parenthood clinic, charged that Sullivan's regulations amounted to a gag rule. It infringed on their obligation to offer patients complete professional advice, was tantamount to enforced malpractice and suppressed freedom of speech, they argued.

A number of clinics and physicians receiving Title X funds under the **Public Health Service Act,** then filed suit against Sullivan, seeking injunctive relief from the new regulations. A Federal District Court, however, granted **summary judgment** to the secretary, removing the issue from jury consideration, and this decision was affirmed on appeal. The U.S. Supreme Court granted *certiorari* because of conflicting conclusions of Federal appeals courts on the validity of these regulations.

In *Rust v. Sullivan,* 111 S. Ct. 1759 (1991), the Court, divided 5-4, upheld the regulations. This was, the tribunal found, a government-funded program, and government could control what doctors said to their patients.

Congress tried to overturn the Court's ruling by legislation. It was vetoed by President Bush who later revised the regulations, permitting physicians, but not other health professionals, to discuss abortion. The President believed that this was a good compromise, but opponents were not satisfied. They still talked about the "gag rule."

After the election of 1992, President Clinton rescinded the "gag rule."

POST-ROE RULINGS

For nearly two decades, although constantly opposed by pro-life forces, the Supreme Court reaffirmed and even broadened *Roe v. Wade.* For example, it struck down, in *Planned Parenthood of Missouri v. Danforth,* 28 U.S. 52 (1976), a state law requiring a woman to obtain spousal consent before undergoing an abortion. It also invalidated a provision requiring an unmarried woman under age 18 to obtain her parents' consent.

It declared unconstitutional a statute requiring an underage girl who was "emancipated" to have parental consent before obtaining an abortion and laws requiring a woman to be advised by a doctor as to the facts about abortion.

The Burger Court invalidated many state laws limiting abortion rights. It held that states cannot require a waiting period or counseling designed to change a woman's mind. States cannot require abortions to be performed in hospitals, rather than clinics, where they are less expensive.

In *Akron v. Akron Center for Reproductive Health,* 462 U.S. 416 (1983), the Rehnquist Court struck down five provisions of an ordinance regulating abortions. The law required:

1. All abortions, after the first trimester, must be performed in a hospital. The Court held that abortions may be performed as safely in an outpatient clinic as in a full-service hospital, citing the fact that the American College of Obstetricians and Gynecologists no longer suggests that all second semester abortions be performed in a hospital.

2. A ban on abortions on unmarried minors under the age of 15 without consent of a parent or a judge. The Court said, "We do not think that the Akron ordinance, as applied to Ohio juvenile proceedings, is reasonably susceptible of being construed to create an opportunity for case-by-case evaluations of the maturity of pregnant minors."

3. Informed consent, requiring a physician to inform the patient of the physical and emotional complications that may result from an abortion. Much of the information, the Court held, "...is designed not to inform the woman's consent but rather to persuade her to withhold it altogether...by insisting upon recitation of a lengthy and inflexible list of information, Akron unreasonably has placed obstacles in the path of the doctor upon whom the woman is entitled to rely for advice in connection with her decision."

4. A mandatory 24-hour waiting period after the woman signs a consent form. This provision, the Court held, increases cost of obtaining an abortion by requiring a woman to make two separate trips to the abortion facility. "...if a

woman after appropriate counseling, is prepared to give her written informed consent and proceed with the abortion, a State may not demand that she delay the effectuation of that decision."

5. Physicians performing abortions must "insure that the remains of the unborn child are disposed of in a humane and sanitary manner." This provision, the Court held, suggests some sort of "decent burial" of an embryo at the earliest stage of formation. This level of uncertainty is fatal where criminal liability is imposed.

In 1986, in *Thornburg v. American College of Obstetricians and Gynecologists,* 476 U.S. 747 (1986), the Court, while divided, 5-4, reaffirmed *Roe* and struck down a Pennsylvania law designed to discourage women from having abortions. The statute provided detailed instructions on how a woman must give her "informed consent" and set forth a number of reporting procedures for physicians to follow. A second physician was also required to be present in all cases where viability was possible.

The Court Changes Directions

In the late 1980s and early 1990s, the Supreme Court's approach to legislative restrictions on abortion changed. In 1989, by a 5-4 vote, the Court upheld a Missouri law that requires physicians to conduct tests to determine whether a fetus is viable if the physician has reason to believe the fetus is 20 or more weeks gestational age.

In a concurring opinion, Justice Antonin Scalia said that the time had come to reconsider *Roe v. Wade.* This landmark case is *Webster v. Reproductive Health Services,* discussed below. In 1990 and 1991, the Court again indicated it had changed some of its thinking on abortion.

In 1990, a 5-4 majority upheld Ohio and Minnesota laws requiring that both parents of an "unemancipated minor" must be notified before an abortion can be performed. The laws also provided "judicial bypass" substitutions for parental notification. Juvenile Court judges could permit abortion if, in their judgment, parental consent was not in the minor's best interest.[22]

Webster and Casey

Two landmark decisions of the Supreme Court are *Webster v. Reproductive Health Services,* 492 U.S. 990 (1989), and *Planned Parenthood of Southeastern Pennsylvania v. Casey,* 112 S. C. 2791 (1992).

The Supreme Court does not operate in a political vacuum, and changes in its personnel caused enormous media speculation as *Webster* worked its way to the top rung of the American judicial ladder. This was to be the first test of the positions of Justices Kennedy and Scalia since they had joined the Court. Scalia, a law professor, had opposed *Roe* before his appointment. Kennedy, also a law professor and a conservative, was something of as question mark. O'Connor had never called for *Roe's* reversal, but her position also was uncertain. Pro-life factions hoped that *Webster* would be the death knell of *Roe.* Pro-choice factions, with the probability of only four solid votes, feared that this might be the case.

In *Webster*, the Supreme Court signaled a clear change in direction. It upheld a Missouri law limiting a woman's right to an abortion. The statute required physicians to conduct pre-abortion viability tests to determine whether the fetus could survive outside the womb whenever there was reason to believe that the woman was 20 or more weeks pregnant. Since the 20-week period falls within the second trimester, the Court, by upholding the statute, placed its *Roe* trimester scheme in doubt.

The law also denied use of public facilities for abortions or the use of public funds for abortion counseling. It enjoined public employees from performing abortions. The preamble to the statute said that "the life of each human being begins at conception."

Although the Rehnquist Court did not overturn *Roe*, it clearly was willing to permit states to restrict abortion. Four justices clearly believe that the trimester scheme, developed in *Roe*, is both unworkable and unacceptable. Webster may stimulate states to enact additional restrictive abortion laws. In fact, hundreds of bills related to abortion were introduced in state legislatures after the decision.

Many pro-choice advocates feared that a constitutionally protected right to abortion would not survive another challenge. They expected *Roe* to be overturned when a Pennsylvania law was tested in *Planned Parenthood of Southeastern Pennsylvania v. Casey.* The Supreme Court decided the case on June 29, 1992, during the charged presidential election year environment.

The Pennsylvania statute required that:
- Females under the age of 18 obtain parental consent, or a court order substituting for parental consent before procuring an abortion.
- "Informed consent" precede all abortions. Mandatory counseling followed by a 24-hour waiting period were required.
- Married women must notify their husbands before undergoing an abortion.

The Court's decision in *Casey* reaffirmed *Roe v. Wade,* stressing the importance of *stare decisis* (maintaining settled law), but it also permitted more state restrictions on abortion.

The Supreme Court upheld the parental consent and informed consent provisions of the law, while a 5-4 majority voted to overturn the spousal notification provision.

Perhaps of greatest importance, the Court discarded its *Roe* trimester scheme. In its place, the Court adopted an "**undue burden test**," devised by Justice O'Connor. An undue burden is any law which "has the purpose or effect of placing a substantial obstacle in the path of a woman seeking an abortion of a nonviable fetus."

A majority held that courts "must protect all of the most fundamental personal liberties, whether or not these are specifically mentioned in...the Constitution."

No One Satisfied

Neither pro-life nor pro-choice elements were satisfied with the Casey ruling. Pro-choice activists were disappointed because *Casey* imposed further restrictions on abortion. It was, some of them feared, a warning that *Roe v Wade* eventually would be overturned. Pro-life activists also were disappointed. They had hoped that the Court would overturn *Roe* and return the issue to the states.

They did, in fact, come close to achieving this. Four justices—Rehnquist, White, Scalia and Thomas—said that they were ready to overrule *Roe*. Three justices, O'Connor, Kennedy and Souter, refused to overrule *Roe* because of the principle of *stare decisis*.

They noted, in a plurality opinion, that "to overrule under fire in the absence of the most compelling reason to reexamine a watershed decision would subvert the Court's legitimacy beyond any serious question."

Only two justices, Blackmun (author of the Roe opinion) and Stevens, voiced support for the substance of *Roe*. Some legal scholars suggest that the only clear outcome of *Casey* is that the Supreme Court will face more abortion rulings as it seeks to clarify the meaning of "undue burden."

The "undue burden" test, as noted, was formulated by Justice Sandra Day O'Connor. When President Reagan nominated O'Connor in 1981 to become the first female justice ever to serve on the Court, her qualifications were seriously questioned.

Attention focused on her views on abortion. The issue dominated public debate. Although pro-life groups opposed O'Connor, they did not have sufficient political "clout" to block her appointment. Justice O' Connor's subsequent abortion views have satisfied neither pro-choice nor pro-life lobbies.

Subsequent hearings before the U.S. Senate Judiciary Committee also have focused on Supreme Court nominees' views on abortion and the right to privacy. Although it is a firmly-rooted tradition that candidates should not be expected to indicate (pre-judge) how they would rule on specific issues, senators nonetheless have pressured them to do so.

The hearings on U.S. Appeals Court Judge Robert Bork's nomination to the Supreme Court were called a "witch-hunt" by those who were appalled at the conduct of Senators Edward Kennedy, Howard Metzenbaum and Joseph Biden during Bork's testimony. All three had announced their opposition to Bork before the hearings began. Biden was an announced candidate for the Democratic Party's presidential nomination. So was Paul Simon of Illinois, another committee member. Some viewed the Bork hearing as an "inquisition." Because Bork, once a noted Yale Law School professor, had written so much, his views on the topic were widely known. The Senate rejected President Reagan's Bork nomination on October 23, 1987.[23]

Bork wrote:[24]

> The subject of abortion has been fiercely debated in state legislatures for many years. It raises profound moral issues upon which people of good will can and do disagree depending upon whether they view a fetus as fully human, and therefore not to be killed for anyone's convenience, or whether they think the fetus less than human so that the desires of the pregnant woman should be paramount. Whatever the proper resolution of the moral debate...few people imagined that the Constitution resolved it. In 1973, a majority of the Supreme Court did imagine just that in *Roe v. Wade*.
>
> The discovery...that the question was not one for democratic decision but one of constitutional law was so implausible that it certainly deserved a 51-page explanation. Unfortunately, in the entire opinion, there is not one line of explanation, not one sentence that qualifies as a legal argument.

The Senate Judiciary Committee also pressured Judges David Souter, Clarence Thomas, Ruth Bader Ginsburg, Stephen Breyer, and, most recently, John Roberts and Samuel Alito, on the "privacy" issue. But they were able to dodge the issue. None of them had written as much about privacy rights as Bork. Some scholars note, perhaps sarcastically, that only unpublished law professors have a chance of being confirmed to the Supreme

Court when a Liberal Senate Judiciary Committee makes this "right to privacy" issue a "litmus test" for a Supreme Court nominee.

Future Court appointments are critical in the area of "abortion politics." The retirement of Justice White and his replacement by Ginsburg, a noted feminist and ACLU lawyer, may have given a bit of breathing space to pro-choice elements. Clearly, they supported Bill Clinton for President in the elections of 1992 and 1996 and expected him to appoint pro-choice judges.

Roe provided *Federal* constitutional protection against state regulation of abortion. As the Supreme Court narrows the scope of *Roe,* the question of abortion now moves to each of the 50 states. One must remember that in a Federal system, diversity of public policy is possible.

Even should the Supreme Court overrule *Roe,* individual states would not be compelled to do so. There is, in other words, a public policy component, as well as an element of constitutional law, involved in the issue. Activists on both sides of the fence are trying to elect "friendly" candidates to state legislatures. They also are pressuring legislatures to enact abortion laws that reflect their views.

Stenberg v. Carhart

On June 28, 2000, the Rehnquist Court handed down one of its most emotional decisions of the term in the so-called "partial birth" abortion case, *Stenberg v. Carhart,* 530 U.S. 914 (2000).

Nebraska was one of 31 states to enact bans on an abortion procedure known as dilation and extraction (D&E). The medical technique involves dilating a pregnant woman's cervix to allow a fetus to emerge into the vagina feet first. The physician then suctions out the fetal brain, collapsing the skull and permitting delivery of the head. Anyone convicted of performing the procedure faced up to 20 years in prison.

Dr. Leroy Carhart, a Bellevue, Nebraska, surgeon, was at the time the only physician in the state who performed abortions after 16 weeks. He challenged the statute in Federal District Court, arguing that the law violated the U.S. Constitution. He also asked for an injunction prohibiting its enforcement. Nebraska Attorney General Donald Stenberg's office defended the measure.

Following a highly-publicized trial in which several "expert witnesses" testified, as they usually do, on both sides of the issue, District Court Judge Richard Kopf struck down the law as unconstitutional. He also enjoined its enforcement and awarded attorney fees to Dr. Carhart. Nebraska appealed, but a panel of the Eighth Circuit unanimously affirmed the ruling.

The Supreme Court took the Nebraska case because the Eighth Circuit effectively invalidated abortion laws in Iowa, Arkansas and Nebraska. But the Seventh Circuit, only a month later, upheld laws banning partial birth abortion in Illinois and Wisconsin, creating an obvious conflict and considerable judicial confusion. Ten states asked the Supreme Court to grant *certiorari* in the Nebraska case.

In striking down Nebraska's law, the Eighth Circuit had declared that the statute would also effectively forbid the most common method of second-trimester abortions, known as dilation and evacuation (D&E). In that procedure, a fetus is removed in pieces from the uterus. An arm or leg of the fetus may be pulled into the vagina.

A sharply divided U.S. Supreme Court voted, 5-4, to affirm the Eighth Circuit's ruling. There were eight separate opinions in the case. Only Justice David Souter failed to explain his reasoning in his own words. The majority opinion, by Justice Stephen Breyer, was joined by Justices John Paul Stevens, Sandra Day O'Connor and Ruth Bader Ginsburg. Breyer wrote:

> ...The question before us is whether Nebraska's statute, making criminal the performance of a 'partial birth abortion,' violates the Federal Constitution, as interpreted in *Casey* and *Roe v. Wade*. We conclude that it does for at least two independent reasons. First, the law lacks any exception 'for the preservation of the ...health of the mother.' Second, it 'imposes an undue burden' on a woman's ability to choose a D&E abortion, thereby unduly burdening the right to choose abortion itself...
>
> Nebraska has not convinced us that a health exception is 'never necessary to preserve the health of women.' Rather, a statute that altogether forbids D&E creates a significant health risk. The statute consequently must contain a health exception. This is not to say that a State is prohibited from proscribing an abortion procedure whenever a particular physician deems the procedure preferable. By no means must a State grant physicians 'unfettered discretion' in their selection of abortion methods.
>
> ...Even if the statute's basic aim is to ban D&E, its language makes clear that it also covers a much broader category of procedures. The language does not track the medical differences between D&E and D&X—though it would have been a simple matter, for example, to provide an exception for the performance of D&E and other abortion procedures...
>
> ...Using this law, some present prosecutors and future Attorneys General may choose to pursue physicians who use D&E procedures, the most commonly used method for performing pre-viability second trimester abortions. All those who perform abortion procedures using that method must fear prosecution, conviction and imprisonment. The result is an undue burden upon a woman's right to make an abortion decision. We must consequently find the statute unconstitutional. The judgment of the Court of Appeals is: Affirmed.

Justice Breyer's opinion clearly recognized the deeply divisive nature of the abortion issue in contemporary America. He said:

We understand the controversial nature of the problem. Millions of Americans believe that life begins at conception and consequently an abortion is akin to causing the death of an innocent child; they recoil at the thought of a law that would permit it. Other millions fear that a law that forbids abortion would condemn many American women to lives that lack dignity, depriving them of equal liberty and leading those with least resources to undergo illegal abortions with the attendant risks of death and suffering. Taking account of these virtually irreconcilable points of view, aware that constitutional law must govern a society whose different members sincerely hold opposing views, and considering the matter in light of the Constitution's guarantees of fundamental individual liberty, this Court, in the course of a generation, has determined and then re-determined that the Constitution offers basic protection to the woman's right to choose.

In a ringing dissent, Justice Antonin Scalia said:

I am optimistic enough to believe that one day, *Stenberg v. Carhart* will be assigned its rightful place in the history of this Court's jurisprudence beside *Korematsu* and *Dred Scott*...The Court must know (as most state legislatures banning this procedure have concluded) that demanding a 'health exception'—which requires the abortionist to assure himself that, in his expert medical judgment, this method is, in the case at hand, marginally safer than others (how can one prove the contrary beyond a reasonable doubt?) is to give live birth abortion free reign...The method of killing a human child—one cannot even accurately say an entirely unborn human child—proscribed by this statute is so horrible that the most clinical description of it evokes a shudder of revulsion... The notion that the Constitution of the United States, designed, among other things, 'to establish Justice, insure domestic Tranquility...and secure the Blessings of Liberty to ourselves and our Posterity,' prohibits the States from simply banning this visibly brutal means of eliminating our half-born posterity is quite simply absurd.

Associate Justices Anthony Kennedy and Clarence Thomas, joined by Chief Justice Rehnquist, also contributed to the dissent. Kennedy wrote:

The Court's failure to accord any weight to Nebraska's interest in prohibiting partial birth abortion is erroneous and undermines its discussion and holding...The majority views the procedures from the perspective of the abortionist, rather than from the perspective of a society shocked when confronted with a new method of ending human life...

D&X is effective only when the fetus is close to viable or, is in fact, viable; thus the State is regulating the process at the point where its interest in life is nearing its peak. Courts are ill equipped to evaluate the relative worth of particular surgical procedures. The legislatures of several States have superior fact-finding capabilities in this regard...Ignoring substantial medical and ethical opinion, the Court substitutes its own judgment for the judgment of Nebraska and some 30 other States and sweeps the law away...

The decision nullifies a law expressing the will of the people of Nebraska that medical procedures must be governed by moral principles having their foundation in the intrinsic value of human life, including life of the unborn. Through their law, the people of Nebraska were forthright in confronting an issue of immense moral consequence. The State chose to forbid a procedure many decent and civilized people find so abhorrent as to be among the most serious of crimes against human life, while the State still protected the woman's autonomous right of choice as reaffirmed in *Casey*. The Court closes its eyes to these profound concerns. From the decision, the reasoning and judgment, I dissent.

Today some of the more militant "pro-life" activists picket abortion clinics to call attention to their cause. They also try to discourage women from having abortions.

In 1991 and 1992, "Operation Rescue" held several large, disruptive demonstrations outside clinics. Court injunctions and arrests followed. Demonstrators contended that government was violating their free speech rights. Judges said they are only trying to protect legitimate property interests of clinic owners.

Some constitutional scholars suggest that, absent a strong moral consensus on this issue, efforts to ban abortion may parallel the 1920's Prohibition movement. Pro-choice advocates fear that social costs would be high, perhaps even a return to "back alley" abortions if the procedure is again made illegal.

In the often overheated debate between pro-life and pro-choice elements, one should note that few favor abortion *per se*. But any solution to the problem, some social scientists contend, will require stronger families, better education and family planning.

Roe v. Wade was decided 30 years ago. But militant pro-choice and pro-life factions continue to debate whether taxpayers should fund abortions. State legislatures still argue about spousal and parental consent. In the election of 2000, pressure groups seemed to be obsessed about the positions of "pro-life" Texas Gov. George W. Bush and "pro-choice" Vice President Al Gore. Both were constantly asked to restate their already clear position on the issue. The same situation occurred in the 2004 presidential contest between Bush and Senator John Kerry.

Stenberg v. Carhart was decided just before the Democratic and Republican National Conventions met to choose their presidential and vice presidential candidates and to adopt their respective party platforms.

Gonzales v. Carhart et al. and Gonzales v. Planned Parenthood

In response to *Stenberg v. Carhart*, Congress passed the Partial Birth Abortion Ban Act in 2003. The statute, similar to the Nebraska law struck down in *Stenberg*, did not include an exception to protect the health of a woman.

Congress found that there was a moral, medical and ethical consensus that partial birth abortion is a gruesome and inhumane procedure that is never medically necessary. It prohibited physicians from using this particular method of ending fetal life in the later stages of pregnancy.

The law forbids physicians from "knowingly performing a partial birth abortion...that is not necessary to save the life of a mother." It defines "partial birth abortion" as a procedure in which a doctor "deliberately and intentionally vaginally delivers a living fetus until, in the case of a head-first presentation, the entire fetal head is outside of the mother's body...or, in the case of breech presentation, any part of the fetal trunk past the navel is outside the mother's body...for the purpose of performing an overt act that the person knows will kill the partially delivered living fetus."

Several abortion doctors, including LeRoy Carhart, challenged the Act in the U.S. District Court for the District of Nebraska. Judge Richard Kopf granted a permanent injunction prohibiting Attorney General Alberto Gonzales from enforcing the law. His finding was based on the failure of Congress to provide an exception where necessary to protect the mother's health.

A three-judge panel of the U.S. Court of Appeals for the Eighth Circuit reviewed a challenge to the District Court's decision and affirmed Judge Kopf's ruling. It also found that there was a lack of consensus in the medical community as to the banned procedure's necessity and that *Stenberg* required legislatures to err on the side of protecting women's health by including an exception.

In another case, Federal District Judge Phyllis Hamilton of the Northern District of California ruled the law unconstitutional because it unduly burdened a woman's ability to choose a second trimester abortion, was impermissibly vague, and lacked a health exception required by Supreme Court precedent. The U.S. Court of Appeals for the Ninth Circuit affirmed that decision.

The Attorney General appealed and the Supreme Court granted *certiorari* and consolidated appeals in *Gonzales v. Carhart* and *Gonzales v. Planned Parenthood.*

In its decision of April 18, 2007, the nation's highest tribunal was deeply divided as it upheld the constitutional validity of the Partial Birth Abortion Ban Act, 5-4.

Speaking for the majority, Justice Kennedy wrote:

We conclude that the Act is not void for vagueness, does not impose an unreasonable burden from any overbreadth, and is not invalid on its face....the Act expressed respect for the dignity of human life. The findings in the Act explain:

"Partial birth abortion...confuses the medical, legal and ethical duties of physicians to preserve and promote life, as the physician acts directly against the physical life of a child, whom he or she has just delivered, all but the head, out of the womb, in order to end that life."

There can be no doubt that the government has an interest in protecting the integrity and ethics of the medical profession...Under our precedents, it is clear that the State has "a significant role to play in regulating the medical profession.

Government may use its voice and its regulatory authority to show its profound respect for the life within the woman.

The Act's ban on abortions that involve partial delivery of a living fetus furthers the government's objectives...

...For many, D&E is a procedure itself laden with the power to devalue human life. Congress could...conclude that the type of abortion proscribed by the Act requires specific regulation because it implicates additional ethical and moral concerns that justify a special prohibition. Congress determined that the abortion methods it proscribed had a disturbing similarity to the killing of a newborn infant...

Joining the majority were Chief Justice Roberts and Justices Alito, Thomas and Scalia.

Justice Ginsburg, joined by Justices Stevens, Souter and Breyer, strongly dissented. She said:

... the notion that the Partial–Birth Abortion Ban Act furthers any legitimate governmental interest is, quite simply, irrational. The court's defense of the statute provides no saving explanation...the Act cannot be understood as anything other than an effort to chip away at a right declared again and again by this Court..

Mass demonstrations continue every January 22, the anniversary of the landmark *Roe v. Wade* ruling. One can see no end to this conflict as the nation moves well into the 21st Century.

It sometimes is argued that privacy rights collide with other constitutional freedoms, such as the right to free expression, guaranteed by the First Amendment. Rights, as noted previously, are not absolute. Individuals may think what they wish but, when their actions have an impact on others, they may be restrained or prohibited. Abortion protesters can be arrested if they violate laws or court orders that forbid them from protesting within a certain distance of abortion clinics. Neither may they physically interfere with a woman who wants to enter a clinic.

Responding to several situations where "peaceful" protests at abortion clinics turned violent, Congress in 1994 passed the **Freedom of Access to Clinic Entrances Act**. The law made it a Federal crime to block the entrance to abortion clinics or otherwise to prevent people from entering them. Although the statute has reduced the level of violence, it has not eliminated it; witness the killings of clinic employees in Massachusetts and Florida in recent years. One should note that responsible leaders within the pro-life movement have condemned these senseless acts of violence and murder.

Jane Madsen et al. v. Women's Health Center, Inc., et al., 512 U.S. 753 (1994), involved anti-abortion demonstrators who were targeting both a clinic and the homes of those who worked in the clinic. A Florida state court judge had issued an injunction that prohibited, among other things, "picketing, demonstrating, or using sound amplification equipment within 300 feet of the residences of clinic staff." The Supreme Court struck down this part of the injunction, ruling that "...the 300-foot zone around residences in this case is much larger than necessary." A smaller, more focused area would accomplish the desired result of protecting the home, the Court found.

In 1997, the Supreme Court, in *Paul Schenck and Dwight Saunders v. Pro Choice Network of Western New York et al.*, 519 U.S. 357 (1997), upheld the constitutionality of a law prohibiting protesters from entering a fixed 15-foot "buffer zone" around abortion clinics and from giving unwanted counseling to those entering the clinics. But the Court invalidated a "floating buffer zone." Chief Justice Rehnquist wrote:

> We conclude that the floating buffer zones burden more speech than necessary to serve the relevant governmental interest.

Pro Choice Network of Western New York, a provider of abortion services, three doctors and four medical clinics filed a complaint in Federal District Court, naming 50 individuals and three organizations—Operation Rescue, Project Rescue of Western New York and Project Life of Rochester. The groups, it was alleged, consistently engaged in illegal blockades, conspired to deny women seeking abortions equal protection of the laws, trespass, interference with business, harassment, false imprisonment and intentional infliction of emotional harm. The complaint asked the court for an order to restrain these activities and those of "sidewalk counselors" who handed women headed toward the clinic literature and talked to them in an attempt to persuade them not to get an abortion.

After a temporary restraining order was issued, Pro Choice Network again went into District Court alleging contempt of court because of failure of the pro-life groups to "cease and desist" from the activities named in their complaint.

Rejecting arguments that the injunction violated free speech rights of pro-life groups, the court held that the injunction served three governmental interests: (1) public safety, (2) ensuring that abortions are performed safely and (3) ensuring that a woman's constitutional rights to travel interstate and to choose to have an abortion are not sacrificed in the interest of defendant's First Amendment rights. The 15-foot "buffer zones" around entrances, people and vehicles seeking access are necessary to ensure that people and vehicles seeking access to the clinics will not be impeded and will be able to determine, by reading, where the entrances are located.

The injunction, the District Court ruled, also left defendants ample alternative channels for communication: "picket, carry signs, pray, sing or chant in full view of people going into the clinics." The verdict, reviewed by a full panel of the Court of Appeals, affirmed the District Court ruling before the Supreme Court granted review, affirming its decision in part and reversing it in part.

Chief Justice Rehnquist, in striking down the "floating" buffer zones, wrote that leafletting and "commenting on matters of public concern are classic forms of speech that lie at the heart of the First Amendment, and speech, in public areas, is at its most protected on public sidewalks, a prototypical example of a traditional public forum. The floating buffer," he added, "prevented protesters from communicating a message from a normal conversational distance or handing leaflets to people entering or leaving the clinics."

"Attempts to stand 15 feet from someone entering or leaving a clinic and to communicate a message...will be hazardous if one wishes to remain in compliance with the injunction...this type of buffer burdens more speech than is necessary to serve the relevant governmental interests," the Chief Justice concluded.

Hill v. Colorado

In *Hill v. Colorado*, 530 U.S. 703 (2000), the Supreme Court decided a case involving a law restricting protesters near facilities performing abortions. A 1993 Colorado law forbade "sidewalk counselors" within 100 feet to an entrance to any health care facility to approach within eight feet of another person without that person's consent. "Speakers" could not display signs, distribute anti-abortion leaflets or engage in oral protests, education or counseling with such other person without obtaining that person's consent.

Leila Jeanne Hill, Audrey Himmelmann and Everitt Simpson Jr. argued that the law imposed an unconstitutional burden on protected rights of free expression in a public forum.

They also argued that the statute was unconstitutional because it was too broad, vague and constituted a prior restraint on freedom of speech.

The trial court granted summary judgment for the state and the Colorado Court of Appeals affirmed. The Colorado Supreme Court also upheld the statute, ruling that "the First Amendment can accommodate reasonable government action intended to effectuate the free exercise of another fundamental right, an individual's right to privacy." It also found that the state law was a reasonable time, place, and manner restriction and, was therefore consistent with the First Amendment.

The U.S. Supreme Court granted *certiorari*.

Speaking through Justice John Paul Stevens, the Court voted (6-3) to uphold the law. Stevens wrote:

> Although the statute prohibits speakers from approaching unwilling listeners, it does not require a standing speaker to move away from anyone passing by...nor does it place any restriction on the content of any message that

anyone may wish to communicate to anyone else, either inside or outside the regulated areas. It does, however, make it more difficult to give unwanted advice, particularly in the form of a handbill or leaflet, to persons entering or leaving medical facilities.

The statute's restriction seeks to protect those who enter a health care facility from the harassment, the nuisance, the persistent importuning, the following, the dogging, and the implied threat of physical touching that can accompany an unwelcomed approach within eight feet of a patient by a person wishing to argue vociferously face-to-face and perhaps thrust an undesired handbill upon her.

In a nutshell, the majority in *Hill* held that the law was not unconstitutionally overbroad. To the contrary, it was narrowly tailored to accomplish the state's legitimate interest in protecting a citizen's right to be free from persistent "following and dogging," once an offer to communicate had been rejected. The law was not unconstitutionally vague because its language provided people of normal intelligence to understand the conduct it forbade. It did not impose an unconstitutional prior restraint on speech. Stevens wrote:

Under this statute, absolutely no channel of communication is foreclosed. No speaker is silenced. And no message is prohibited…. Speakers are subject only to narrow place requirement imbedded within the 'approach' restriction. This narrow requirement does not constitute an unlawful prior restraint.

Justices Anthony Kennedy, Antonin Scalia and Clarence Thomas dissented, noting that the ruling was more than a free speech issue. Scalia, in an opinion joined by Thomas, noted the obvious anti-abortion character of the speech involved:

What is before us, after all, is a speech regulation directed against the opponents of abortion, and it therefore enjoys the benefit of the 'ad hoc nullification machine' that the Court has set in motion to push aside whatever doctrines of constitutional law that stand in the way of that highly favored practice. Having deprived abortion opponents of the political right to persuade the electorate that abortion should be restricted by law, the Court today continues and expands its assault upon their individual right to persuade women contemplating abortion that what they are doing is wrong…

As I have suggested throughout this opinion, today's decision is not an isolated distortion of our traditional constitutional principles, but is one of many aggressively pro-abortion novelties announced by the Court in recent years …Today's distortions, however, are particularly blatant. Restrictive views of the First Amendment that have been in dissent since the 1930s suddenly find themselves in the majority. Uninhibited, robust and wide-open debate is replaced by the power of the state to protect an unheard-of 'right to be let alone' on the public streets.

The possibility of limiting abortions by legislative means…has been rendered impossible by our decisions from *Roe v. Wade* to *Stenberg v. Carhart*. For those who share an abiding moral and religious conviction (or for that matter simply a biological appreciation) that abortion is the taking of a human life, there is no option but to persuade women, one by one, not to make that choice.

And as a general matter, the most effective place, if not the only place, where the persuasion can occur is outside the entrances to abortion facilities. By upholding these restrictions on speech in this place, the Court ratifies the state's attempt to make even that an impossible one.

Justice Kennedy wrote:

If, from this time forward, the Court repeats its grave errors of analysis, we shall have no longer the proud decision of free and open discourse in a public forum…The purpose and design of the statute—as everyone ought to know—and as its own defenders urge, in attempted justification—are to restrict speakers on one side of the debate: those who protest abortions…There runs through our First Amendment theory a concept of immediacy, the idea that thoughts and pleas and petitions must not be lost with the passage of time. In a fleeting existence, we have but little time to find truth through discourse. No better illustration of the immediacy of speech, of the urgency of persuasion, of the preciousness of time, is presented than in this case. Here the citizens who claim Fist Amendment protection seek it for speech which, if it is to be effective, must take place at the very time and place a grievous moral wrong, in their view, is about to occur. The Court tears away from the protesters the guarantees of the First Amendment when they most need it. So committed is the Court to its course that it denies these protesters, in the face of what they consider to be one of life's gravest moral crises, even the opportunity to try to offer a fellow citizen a little pamphlet, a hand-held paper seeking to reach a higher law.

Scheidler v. National Organization for Women (NOW), Inc.

Ending a legal dispute which had been in the Federal judicial system since 1986, the Supreme Court resolved *Scheidler v. National Organization for Women, Inc.,* after hearing arguments in the case for the third time.[25]

Ruling unanimously (8-0) on February 28, 2006, the nation's highest tribunal ruled that Federal racketeering and extortion statutes could not be used to ban demonstrators. Justice Samuel Alito did not participate in the case because he was not on the bench when the case was argued. The decision was a major setback to NOW and abortion clinics, which had challenged anti-abortion protesters and their tactics.

Right-to-Life groups brought an appeal after the Seventh Circuit Court of Appeals tried to have a District Court determine whether an injunction could be supported by charges that protesters had made threats of violence. This was done by the lower Federal courts although the U.S. Supreme Court, in 2003, had lifted the nationwide injunction on anti-abortion protesters.

The Supreme Court ruled that the Hobbs Act, a more than 50-year-old Federal extortion statute, could not be used against protesters because they had not illegally "obtained property" from women seeking to enter clinics to procure abortions.

Justice Breyer wrote the 2006 court opinion. He traced the act's meaning and its history before concluding that Congress did not intend to create "a freestanding physical violence offense" in the Hobbs Act. Rather, Breyer said, Congress addressed the problem of violence outside abortion clinics by enacting the 1994 Freedom of Access to Clinic Entrances Act, which set boundaries to such protests.

The legal battle began in 1986, when NOW filed a class action lawsuit in Federal District Court in Chicago, challenging methods used by Joseph Scheidler and the Pro-Life Action Network (PLAN) to block women from entering abortion clinics. Originally, the suit was filed under the Sherman Antitrust Act, but Fay Clayton, a female Chicago lawyer, later conceived a then highly unusual legal strategy. She persuaded NOW to sue Right-to-Life protesters under provisions of the 1970 Racketeer Influenced and Corrupt Organizations Act (RICO), used primarily in criminal cases against the mafia and organized crime. The suit also cited the Hobbs Act. At the time, massive, nationwide anti-abortion demonstrations were being conducted.

In "Round One," the Federal District Court had dismissed the case and was supported by the Seventh Circuit. In its first involvement in the matter, the U.S. Supreme Court reversed the Court of Appeals and remanded the case after holding that no economic motive was necessary to violate RICO laws.[26]

A Federal District Court jury in Chicago found, in 1998, that demonstrators had engaged in a pattern of racketeering by interfering with clinic operations, menacing doctors, assaulting patients and damaging clinic property. The presiding judge then issued a nationwide injunction against the protesters. The Supreme Court, after hearing a second series of arguments in 2003, held that, although demonstrations interfered with and prevented the receiving of abortion services, Pro-Life demonstrations did not constitute acts of extortion.[27]

The nation's highest court then remanded the case to the Seventh Circuit, which kept it alive although the Supreme Court had given instructions to act in accordance with its opinion. Presumably, the 2006 decision ended the matter.

It should be noted that *Scheidler v. National Organization for Women* was more than a typical Pro-Life, Pro-Choice abortion case. True, there were the usual polemics. Abortion protesters were called "mafia thugs," abortion clinics "human slaughterhouses," their doctors "murderers."

But a major issue also was the First Amendment future of all public protests and demonstrations, irrespective of their purpose. For that reason, a large number of *amicus curiae* briefs were filed in support of Scheidler by a wide variety of civil rights groups and labor unions. The AFL-CIO, for example, argued through attorney Jonathan P. Hiatt, that suits based on Federal extortion law could be used to prevent unions from demonstrating for better wages and working conditions.

Whether acts of protest groups should be subject to the draconian provisions of RICO, (20-years-to-life sentences with no parole in criminal actions and treble damages and attorney fees in civil suits) was a disturbing question for any group seeking to right what they perceived to be a social wrong.

As a result of the Court's ruling, the threat of ruinous RICO sanctions under existing Federal and state law has been removed.

WATCHING "DIRTY " MOVIES AT HOME: STANLEY V. GEORGIA

In another privacy landmark, *Stanley v. Georgia,* 394 U.S. 557 (1969), the Court held that Robert E. Stanley, a Georgia resident, had the right to watch pornographic movies in his own home. The case arose when police, armed with a warrant, searched Stanley's home seeking evidence of bookmaking. Police found no evidence of illegal gambling, but did discover three reels of eight-millimeter film and viewed them on a projector in Stanley's living room. He was then arrested for possessing "obscene" material.

Stanley's lawyer argued that this was an unlawful search and seizure and unlawful arrest. The law, he contended, should not "punish mere private possession of obscene material." Stanley, he said, had a right of privacy to view whatever he wished in his own home.

In a unanimous 9-0 decision, the Court held that, if the First Amendment means anything, it means that a State has no business telling a man, sitting alone in his house, what books he may read or films he may watch."

Justice Marshall wrote in part:[28]

Appellant raises several challenges to the validity of his conviction. We find it necessary to consider only one. Appellant argues here, and argued below, that the Georgia obscenity statute, insofar as it punishes mere private possession of obscene matter, cannot constitutionally be made a crime.

It is now well established that the Constitution protects the right to receive information and ideas. This right to receive information and ideas, regardless of their social worth, is fundamental to our free society. Moreover, in the context of this case—a prosecution for mere possession of printed or filmed matter in the privacy of a person's own home—that right takes on an added dimension. For also fundamental is the right to be free, except in very limited circumstances, from unwanted governmental intrusions into one's privacy.

These are the rights that appellant is asserting in the case before us. He is asserting the right to read or observe what he pleases—the right to satisfy his intellectual and emotional needs in the privacy of his own home. He is asserting the right to be free from state inquiry into the contents of his library. Georgia contends that appellant does not have these rights, that there are certain types of materials that the individual may not read or even possess. Georgia justifies this assertion by arguing that the films in the present case are obscene. But we think that mere categorization of these films as 'obscene' is insufficient justification for such a drastic invasion of personal liberties guaranteed by the First and 14th Amendments. Whatever may be the justification for other statutes regulating obscenity, we do not think that they reach into the privacy of one's own home. Our whole constitutional heritage rebels at the thought of giving government the power to control men's minds.

And yet, in the face of these traditional notions of individual liberty, Georgia asserts the right to protect the individual's mind from the effects of obscenity. We are not certain that this argument amounts to anything more than the assertion that the State has the right to control the moral content of a person's thoughts. To some, this may be a noble purpose, but it is wholly inconsistent with the philosophy of the First Amendment. Nor is it relevant that obscene materials in general, or the particular films before the Court, are arguably devoid of any ideological content.

The line between transmission of ideas and mere entertainment is much too elusive for this Court to draw, if indeed such a line can be drawn at all. Whatever the power of the state to control public dissemination of ideas inimical to the public morality, it cannot constitutionally premise legislation on the desirability of controlling a person's private thoughts.

Finally, we are faced with the argument that prohibition of possession of obscene materials is a necessary incident to statutory schemes prohibiting distribution. That argument is based on alleged difficulties of proving an intent to distribute or in producing evidence of actual distribution. We are not convinced that such difficulties exist, but even if they did, we do not think that they would justify infringement of the individual's right to read or observe what he pleases. Because the right is so fundamental to our scheme of individual liberty, its restriction may not be justified by the need to ease the administration of otherwise valid criminal laws.

We hold that the First and 14th Amendments prohibit making mere private possession of obscene material a crime. *Roth* and the cases following that decision are not impaired by today's holding. As we have said, the States retain broad power to regulate obscenity; that power simply does not extend to mere possession by the individual in the privacy of his own home.

In sum, the Court said that an individual has a right to privacy within his or her own home. But the right is not absolute. Justice Thurgood Marshall wrote the majority opinion and it was narrowly drawn to deal with obscenity. It was not a guarantee that an individual could do anything he or she pleased, legal or illegal, as long as it was a private act, done in one's home.

The *Stanley* ruling was modified in 495 U.S. 103 (1990), in *Osborne v. Ohio*. The Court held that states may ban even private, at home, possession of child pornography because the nature of the material fuels a commercial demand for it. This, in turn, results in the exploitation of children involved.

IS SODOMY A CONSTITUTIONAL RIGHT? BOWERS V. HARDWICK

Michael Hardwick tossed away an open beer bottle in front of a gay bar in Atlanta, Georgia. Unfortunately for him, Atlanta Police officer K. R. Torick witnessed the act. Hardwick, who worked at the bar, was given a ticket for drinking in public. When he failed to make his scheduled court appearance in August, 1982, Officer Torick went to his home to arrest him. One of Harwick's housemates admitted Torick to the home, where, in plain view of the officer, Hardwick and another man were engaged in sodomy.

The officer arrested Harwick and his male "companion" for violating a Georgia law that forbids oral and anal sex. Although the Fulton County District Attorney would not prosecute the case and there had been no criminal prosecutions under the law for decades, Hardwick and his ACLU lawyers challenged the statute's constitutionality. They asserted that homosexual activity is private and therefore constitutionally protected. Hardwick also advanced the dubious argument that he was in imminent danger of arrest because he was a practicing homosexual. Georgia argued that American and state legal history and social traditions had condemned this kind of conduct for hundreds of years. In fact, as late as 1961, such conduct was criminal in all 50 states.

The case, brought in U.S. District Court, was dismissed because of a lack of a proper legal claim. However, the 11th Circuit Court of Appeals reversed. It found the Georgia law had violated Hardwick's *Federal* constitutional rights under the Ninth and 14th

Amendments. The U.S. Supreme Court granted a writ of *certiorari* and, in *Bowers v. Hardwick*, 478 U.S. 186 (1986), reversed the Court of Appeals.

Gay activists and their allies, on one hand, and Christian groups and defenders of traditional morality on the other, watched the case unfold with great interest. Disinterested parties viewed the clash as merely another battle in the American cultural war.

Justice White, speaking for the majority, upheld the Georgia law. He wrote:[29]

The issue presented is whether the Federal Constitution confers a fundamental right upon homosexuals to engage in sodomy and hence invalidates the laws of the many States that still make such conduct illegal and have done so for a very long time. The case also calls for some judgment about the limits of the Court's role in carrying out its constitutional mandate.

We first register our disagreement...with respondent that the Court's prior cases have construed the Constitution to confer a right of privacy that extends to homosexual sodomy and for all intents and purposes have decided this case.

Precedent aside, however, respondent would have us announce a fundamental right to engage in sexual sodomy. This we are quite unwilling to do. It is true that despite the language of the Due Process Clauses of the Fifth and 14th Amendments, which appears to focus only on the processes by which life, liberty or property is taken, the cases are legion in which those Clauses have been interpreted to have substantive content, subsuming rights that to a great extent are immune from federal or state regulation or proscription. Among such cases are those recognizing rights that have little or no textual support in the constitutional language.

Striving to assure itself and the public that announcing rights not readily identifiable in the Constitution's text involves much more than the imposition of the justices' own choice of values on the States and the Federal Government, the Court has sought to identify the nature of the rights qualifying for heightened judicial protection. In *Palko v. Connecticut* (1937), it was said that this category includes those fundamental liberties that are 'implicit in the concept of ordered liberty,' such that 'neither liberty nor justice would exist if they were sacrificed.' A different description of fundamental liberties appeared in *Moore v. East Cleveland* (1977), where they are characterized as those liberties that are 'deeply rooted in this Nation's history and tradition.'

It is obvious to us that neither of these formulations would extend a fundamental right to homosexuals to engage in acts of consensual sodomy. Proscriptions against that conduct have ancient roots. Sodomy was a criminal offense at common law and was forbidden by the laws of the original 13 states when they ratified the Bill of Rights. In fact, until 1961, all 50 States outlawed sodomy, and today 24 States and the District of Columbia continue to provide criminal penalties for sodomy performed in private and between consenting adults. Against this background, to claim that a right to engage in such conduct is 'deeply rooted in this Nation's history and tradition' or 'implicit in the concept of ordered liberty' is, at best, facetious.

Respondent....asserts that the result should be different where the homosexual conduct occurs in the privacy of the home. He relies on *Stanley v. Georgia* (1969), where the Court held that the First Amendment prevents conviction for possessing and reading obscene material in the privacy of his home.

Stanley did protect conduct that would not have been protected outside the home, and it partially prevented the enforcement of state obscenity laws; but the decision was firmly grounded in the First Amendment. The right pressed upon us here has no similar support in the text of the Constitution and it does not qualify for recognition under the prevailing principles for construing the 14th Amendment. Its limits are also difficult to discern. Plainly enough, otherwise illegal conduct is not always immunized whenever it occurs in the home. Victimless crimes, such as the possession and use of illegal drugs, do not escape the law where they are committed at home. *Stanley* itself recognized that its holding offered no protection for the possession in the home of drugs, firearms or stolen goods. And if respondent's submission is limited to the voluntary sexual conduct between consenting adults, it would be difficult, except by fiat, to limit the claimed right to homosexual conduct while leaving exposed to prosecution adultery, incest and other sexual crimes even though they are committed in the home. We are unwilling to start down that road.

Chief Justice Burger, in a concurring opinion, quoted Sir William Blackstone who described sodomy as "the infamous crime against nature" and "an offense of deeper malignity than rape, a heinous act, the very mention of which is a disgrace to human nature and a crime not fit to be named." Burger also noted:[30]

Decisions of individuals relating to homosexual conduct have been subject to state intervention throughout the history of Western civilization. Condemnation of these practices is firmly rooted in Judeo-Christian moral and ethical standards. Homosexual sodomy was a capital crime under Roman law.

To hold that the act of homosexual sodomy is somehow protected as a fundamental right would be to cast aside millennia of moral teaching.

This is essentially not a question of personal 'preferences,' but rather the legislative authority of the State. I find nothing in the Constitution depriving a State of the power to enact the statute challenged here.

Although he concurred, Justice Powell expressed concern about the part of Georgia law that provided a prison sentence of up to 20 years for a single, private, consensual act of sodomy. Were such a sentence actually imposed, he suggested, a plaintiff might well have serious cause to bring an action under the Eighth Amendment. A sentence that long, he noted, could be considered dispro-portionate to the crime, a "cruel and unusual punishment."

Four justices, as noted, dissented. Justice Harry Blackmun wrote for the minority:[31]

This case is no more about 'a fundamental right to engage in homosexual sodomy,' as the Court purports to declare, than *Stanley v. Georgia* was about a fundamental right to watch obscene movies, or *Katz v. United States* was about a fundamental right to place interstate bets from a telephone booth. Rather, this case is about 'the most comprehensive rights and the right most valued by civilized men, namely, the right to be let alone.'

A necessary corollary of giving individuals freedom to choose how to conduct their lives in acceptance of the fact that different individuals will make different choices...The court claims that its decision today merely refuses to recognize a fundamental right to engage in homosexual sodomy; what the Court really has refused to recognize is the fundamental interest all individuals have in controlling the nature of their intimate associations with others.

In 1998, the Georgia Supreme Court gutted the nation's most widely publicized sodomy law and overturned the conviction of a man serving a five-year prison sentence. Chief Justice Robert Benham wrote for a 6-1 majority:

> We cannot think of any other activity that reasonable persons would rank as more private and more deserving of protection from governmental interference than consensual, private, adult sexual activity. We conclude that such activity is at the heart of the Georgia Constitution's protection of the right of privacy.

Until the 1990s, homosexuals generally had failed to win substantial legal protection. Many advocates of "gay rights" were disappointed with Bill Clinton, whom they had strongly supported in his campaign against President Bush in 1992. Clinton proposed to permit homosexuals to serve in the military, but backed off when Congress, then controlled by his own Democratic party, strongly opposed the plan. The U.S. Department of Defense (DOD) traditionally has looked at homosexuality as incompatible with military service. The resulting political compromise between Clinton and Congress was the "don't ask, don't tell" policy. Homosexuals in the military cannot be required to admit their sexual preferences, but can be discharged from the services if they engage in verbal or behavioral displays of homosexuality.

Several homosexuals who have been drummed out of the military have protested their discharges by bringing suit against the DOD. Advocates of gay rights and the ACLU have argued that homosexuals are being punished for nothing more than expressing their state of mind. Because of discrepancies in rulings of lower Federal courts, the U.S. Supreme Court probably will deal with the matter in the future.

Significant legal victory was won by homosexuals in *Romer, Governor of Colorado, et al. v. Evans et al.,* 517 U.S. 620 (1996), when the Supreme Court struck down a Colorado constitutional amendment that nullified all existing and any new legal protections for homosexuals. After several Colorado cities, including Aspen, Boulder and Denver, passed ordinances banning discrimination based on sexual orientation in housing, employment, education, public accommodations, health and welfare services, Colorado voters adopted Amendment 2 to the State Constitution. It provided:

> **No Protected Status Based on Homosexual, Lesbian, or Bisexual Orientation:** Neither the States of Colorado, through any of its branches or departments, nor any of its agencies, political subdivisions, municipalities or school districts, shall enact, adopt, or enforce any statute, regulation, ordinance or policy whereby homosexual, lesbian or bisexual orientation, conduct, practices or relationships shall constitute or otherwise be the basis of or entitle any person or class of persons to have or claim any minority status, quota preferences, protected status or claim of discrimination. This Section of the Constitution shall be in all respects self-executing.

Soon after Amendment 2 was adopted, several homosexuals sought a state court injunction, arguing that enforcement of the measure would subject them to immediate and substantial risk of discrimination on the basis of their sexual orientation. Although

Governor Romer was an opponent of Amendment 2, he was named in his capacity as governor as a defendant, together with the Colorado attorney general and the State of Colorado.

The trial court enjoined enforcement of Amendment 2 and the Supreme Court of Colorado affirmed its ruling. The Supreme Court granted *certiorari*.

In a 6-3 ruling, the U.S. Supreme Court held that Colorado's Amendment 2 violated the Equal Protection Clause because it subjects individuals to various forms of discrimination simply because of their sexual preference. The Court concluded that the law had no reasonable purpose but was motivated instead by "animus" or hostility toward homosexuals.

Writing for the majority, Justice Kennedy said:

First, the amendment has the peculiar property of imposing a broad and undifferentiated disability on a single named group, an exceptional and...invalid form of legislation. Second, its sheer breadth is so discontinuous with the reasons offered for it that the amendment seems inexplicable by anything but animus toward the class that it affects; it lacks a rational relationship to legitimate state interests.

Amendment 2...confounds (the) normal process of judicial review. It is at once too narrow and too broad. It identifies persons by a single trait and then denies them protection across the board. The resulting disqualification of a class of persons from the right to seek specific protection from the law is unprecedented in our jurisprudence. The absence of precedent for Amendment 2 is itself instructive. It is not within our constitutional tradition to enact laws of this sort. Central both to the idea of the rule of law and to our own Constitution's guarantee of equal protection is the principle that government and each of its parts remain open on impartial terms to all who seek its assistance. 'Equal protection of the laws is not achieved through indiscriminate imposition of inequalities.'

A related point is that laws of the kind now before us raise the inevitable inference that the disadvantage imposed is born of animosity toward the class of persons affected. If the constitutional conception of equal protection of the laws means anything, it must at the very least mean that a...desire to harm a politically unpopular group cannot constitute a legitimate governmental interest.

Amendment 2 is...a status-based enactment divorced from any factual context from which we could discern a relationship to legitimate state interests; it is a classification of persons undertaken for its own sake, something the Equal Protection Clause does not permit. We must conclude that Amendment 2 classifies homosexuals not to further a proper legislative end but to make them unequal to everyone else. This Colorado cannot do. A State cannot so deem a class of person a stranger to its laws. Amendment 2 violates the Equal Protection Clause, and the judgment of the Supreme Court of Colorado is affirmed.

In *Equality Foundation of Greater Cincinnati v. City of Cincinnati*, 119 S. Ct. 365 (1998), however, the Supreme Court refused to grant *certiorari* or overturn a similar measure barring protective legislation for homosexuals in Cincinnati. Voters there had adopted an amendment to the City Charter in 1993, which the Sixth Circuit Court of Appeals upheld. Although homosexual groups saw little difference between the Charter amendment and the Colorado law, the Court of Appeals did.

That tribunal viewed the Charter amendment as barring only special protection for gay men and lesbians, as opposed to taking the more sweeping step of depriving homosexuals of general anti-discrimination protections available to other groups. Colorado Amendment 2, on the other hand, could be fairly read as depriving homosexuals of "even the protection of general laws," amounting to a "denial of equal protection of the laws in the most literal sense."

Cincinnati voters adopted Issue 3 by a margin of 62% to 38%. The measure provides that "No special class status may be granted based upon sexual orientation, conduct or relationships." It stipulates that the city, including various boards and commissions, "may not enact, adopt, enforce or administer any ordinance, regulation, rule or policy which provides that homosexual, lesbian or bisexual orientation, status, conduct or relationship constitutes, entitles or otherwise provides a person with the basis to have any claim of minority or protected status, quota preference or other preferential treatment."

The Charter amendment, the Appeals Court held, "merely prevented homosexuals, as homosexuals, from obtaining special privileges and preferences," such as affirmative action.

Michael Carvin, attorney for a group called "Equal Rights, Not Special Rights," which campaigned for the amendment, was pleased. He said, "Local citizen initiatives can overturn gay rights laws even if states cannot. The Court will not extend *Romer v. Evans* to the facts of this case."

The ACLU expressed disappointment at the Supreme Court's decision to deny *certiorari*.

Steven R. Shapiro, ACLU national legal director, said:

Nothing in today's order even remotely suggests that the Supreme Court is backing away from its landmark 1996 decision in *Romer v. Evans*. The Sixth Circuit Court of Appeals read the Cincinnati Charter amendment as merely a repeal of what it described as special protections and not as a prohibition of anti-discrimination laws.

In November, 2004, Cincinnati voters went to the polls and overturned the 1993 measure, 65,082 to 55,934. Mayor Charles Luken had urged removal of Article XII from the city charter, saying that the measure created the impression that the city was intolerant and this hurt its ability to compete for global businesses that value diversity.[32]

However, gay rights supporters suffered a major defeat in Ohio when a statewide constitutional amendment forbidding same-sex marriages passed overwhelmingly. Opponents of gay marriages noted that November 2, 2004, was a good day for them because they went 11 for 11. That's the number of states that banned gay marriage on that day.

In addition to Ohio and Michigan, they were Oregon, Arkansas, Georgia, Kentucky, Mississippi, Montana, North Dakota, Oklahoma and Utah.

Encouraged by their successes at the state level, foes of gay marriages pressed for a Federal Marriage Protection Amendment. The U.S. Senate rejected the measure, in 2004 and in 2006, although President Bush supported the measure.

Sen. John McCain, the presumptive Republican presidential nominee in 2008, broke with Bush and voted against it, saying, "The proposed amendment strikes me as antithetical in every way to the core philosophy of Republicans." McCain opposed the amendment because of his views on Federalism, noting, "It usurps from the states a fundamental authority they have always possessed and imposes a Federal remedy for a problem that most states do not believe confronts them."

Homosexuals and First Amendment Rights of Freedom of Association, Speech:

Discrimination by most private clubs is neither forbidden by the U.S. Constitution nor by Federal law. This probably explains the outcome in *Hurley v. Irish American Gay, Lesbian and Bisexual Group* 518 U.S. 557 (1995).

The central issue in *Hurley* was whether sponsors of the St. Patrick's Day parade, held on Boston public streets, could exclude from the parade groups representing views with which the sponsors disagree. The Allied War Veterans Council refused a place in the 1993 parade to the Irish Gay, Lesbian and Bisexual Groups of Boston.

The group filed suit in state court, arguing that the denial violated a state statute forbidding discrimination based on sexual orientation in places of public accommodation. The trial court ordered inclusion of GLIB, finding that the parade had no special expressive purpose. The Supreme Judicial Court of Massachusetts affirmed that decision.

On appeal, a unanimous U.S. Supreme Court reversed. It held that the state of Massachusetts could not apply its public accommodations statute to force a private association of veterans groups—sponsors of the St. Patrick's Day Parade—to include among the marchers a gay rights group whose message the sponsors did not wish their parade to convey. A contrary result would have violated the "fundamental rule" of the First Amendment, that a speaker has the autonomy to choose the content of his own message.

Justice Souter compared the sponsorship of a parade to a person making a public speech. Like a public speech, he wrote, a parade expresses a point of view even though that view is sometimes communicated by symbolic means. Souter also noted that disapproval of a private speaker's statement does not legitimize use of state power to compel the speaker to alter the message by including one more acceptable to others.

Chiding the Massachusetts courts for applying state law in "a peculiar way," Souter wrote:

> Since all speech inherently involves choices of what to say and what to leave unsaid, one important manifestation of the principle of free speech is that one who chooses to speak may also decide what not to say...Petitioners' claim to the benefits of this principle of autonomy to control one's own speech is as sound as the South Boston parade is expressive. Rather like a composer, the Council selects the expressive units of the parade from potential participants, and though the score may not produce a particularized message, each contingent's expression in the Council's eyes comports with what merits celebration on that day...
>
> While the law is free to promote all sorts of conduct in place of harmful behavior, it is not free to interfere with speech for no better reason that promoting an approved message or discouraging a disfavored one, however enlightened either purpose may strike the government...
>
> Disapproval of a private speaker's statement does not legitimize use of the Commonwealth's power to compel the speaker to alter the message by including one more acceptable to others. Accordingly, the judgment of the Supreme Judicial Court is reversed and the case remanded for proceedings not inconsistent with this opinion.

In *Boy Scouts of America v. Dale,* 120 S. Ct. 2446 (2000) the Supreme Court held, 5-4, that a New Jersey public accommodations law could not be applied to keep the Boy Scouts from excluding gays from being Scout leaders. The majority concluded that the Boy Scouts are a private association, and as such have a constitutionally protected right of "expressive association" to exclude people whose beliefs and conduct are inconsistent with the Scouts' views and mission.

James Dale joined the Cub Scouts at the age of eight. He remained a youth member of the Boy Scouts' until his 18th birthday. He had earned 25 merit badges and the highest honor, Eagle Scout, which only 3% of all scouts achieve. Dale later applied for adult membership and was appointed assistant scoutmaster at a troop in Monmouth, N.J.

Some six months later, he left home to attend Rutgers University. He then acknowledged to family and friends that he was gay. He became involved in the school's Lesbian/Gay Alliance.

After seeing a newspaper photo of Dale that identified him as "co-President of the Rutgers University Lesbian/Gay Alliance," Scout officials revoked his membership.

Dale's appeal to Scout leaders to reconsider their decision was rejected. He then sued under a New Jersey law that forbids discrimination in public places because of sexual orientation. The trial court rejected Dale's claim, but he won a reversal in the New Jersey Supreme Court, which found that the Scouts were "a place of public accommodation" subject to the state law.

The Boy Scouts appealed, and the U.S. Supreme Court granted *certiorari.*

Chief Justice Rehnquist, writing for the majority, noted that the Boy Scouts of America are a private organization that believes that homosexuality is inconsistent with the values it seeks to instill in its youth members. New Jersey's public accommodations law could not be interpreted constitutionally to require the Scouts to admit Dale because it violates the organization's First Amendment right of freedom of association. Forced inclusion of an unwanted person in a group infringes on the group's rights if the presence of that person affects the group's ability to advocate its viewpoints, he wrote.

The Chief Justice said:

> We are not, as we must not be, guided by our views of whether the Boy Scouts' teachings with respect to homosexual conduct are right or wrong; public or judicial disapproval of a tenet of an organization's expression does not justify the State's effort to compel the organization to accept members where such acceptance would derogate from the organization's expressive message...
>
> The presence of an avowed homosexual and gay rights activist in an assistant scoutmaster's uniform sends a distinctly different message from the presence of a heterosexual assistant scoutmaster who is on record as disagreeing with Boy Scouts' policy...
>
> The Boy Scouts has a First Amendment right to choose to send one message but not the other. The fact that the organization does not trumpet its views from the housetops or that it tolerates dissent within its ranks does not mean that its views receive no First Amendment protection...
>
> Dale's presence in the Boy Scouts would, at the very least, force the organization to send a message, both to youth members and the world, that the Boy Scouts accepts homosexual conduct as a legitimate form of behavior.

178

Rehnquist was joined in his opinion by Justices Sandra Day O'Connor, Antonin Scalia, Anthony Kennedy, and Clarence Thomas.

In a dissenting opinion, Justice John Paul Stevens said:

> Whatever values BSA seeks to instill in Scouts, the idea that homosexuality is not 'appropriate' appears entirely unconnected to, and is mentioned nowhere in, the myriad of publicly declared values and creeds of the BSA. The idea does not appear to be among any of the principles actually taught to Scouts. Rather, the 1978 policy appears to be no more than a private statement of a few BSA executives that the organization wishes to exclude gays and that wish has nothing to do with any expression BSA actually engages in...

> BSA's broad religious tolerance, combined with its declaration that sexual matters are not its 'proper area,' render its views on the issue equivocal at best and incoherent at worst. We have never held, however, that a group can throw together any mixture of contradictory positions and then invoke the right to associate to defend any one of those views.

Justices Ruth Bader Ginsburg, Stephen Breyer and David Souter joined Stevens in the dissent.

Lawrence v. Texas 539 U.S. 558 (2003)

Houston police responded to a false 911 emergency call that there was a weapons disturbance at the apartment of John G. Lawrence on the night of September 17, 1998. They opened the unlocked door and found Lawrence, a 60-year-old medical technologist, engaged in a homosexual act with Tyron Banner, a 36-year-old street vendor. Both were arrested, tried and convicted under a Texas law forbidding same-sex sodomy. The convictions were appealed, but upheld by Texas courts, which relied on the Supreme Court's *Bowers v. Hardwick* decision.

The question presented to the U.S. Supreme Court was whether the Texas statute violated the "liberty" guaranteed by the due process clause of the 14th Amendment. The state defended the law as essential to protect marriage and child rearing. "Homosexual sodomy," Texas argued, "has nothing to do with marriage, conception or parenthood and it is not on a par with these sacred choices."

The Supreme Court disagreed, striking down the statute and overturning its own verdict in *Bowers*, which supported it. Justice Kennedy wrote for a 6-3 majority. He noted similarities between the Georgia and Texas cases, but held that the Court, in its 1986 ruling, had failed "to appreciate the extent of the liberty at stake." Although laws against homosexual sodomy may reflect popular opinion, "the issue is whether the majority may use the power of the state to enforce the views of the whole society through the operation of the criminal law."[33] Kennedy found that trends throughout the Western world, as well as in the United States, have eroded prohibitions against private homosexual conduct. Laws prohibiting homosexual consensual conduct demean the lives of homosexuals and, in addition to criminal conviction, can result in stigma against them. *Stare decisis* is not, he said, "an inexorable command."

Bowers, Kennedy wrote, "was not correct when it was decided, and it is not correct today. It ought not to remain binding precedent. *Bowers v. Hardwick* should be, and now is, overruled."

The majority opinion stressed that the decision did not involve minors, individuals who might be injured or coerced, public conduct or prostitution. In this case, Kennedy found "no legitimate state interest which can justify its intrusion into the personal and private life of the individual."

Justice O'Connor wrote a concurring opinion, observing that the Texas law "makes homosexuals unequal in the eyes of the law" by specifically outlawing homosexual, but not heterosexual sodomy."[34]

Justice Scalia, joined by Chief Justice Rehnquist and Justice Thomas, dissented, writing that a long history of laws against sodomy demonstrated that it could not be viewed as a fundamental right. He voiced concern that the majority decision could have implications for "criminal laws against fornication, bigamy, adultery, adult incest, bestiality and obscenity."

Scalia said, "This reasoning leaves on pretty shaky grounds state laws limiting marriage to opposite sex couples." Accusing the majority of having "signed on to the so-called homosexual agenda," he concluded that states, through democratic political procedures, should be free to either outlaw or to permit sodomy.[35]

Justice Thomas said that he found the law "uncommonly silly," but could find no constitutional basis on which to invalidate it. If he were a member of the Texas legislature, he added, he would vote to repeal the statute.[36]

Gay rights supporters welcomed the Lawrence decision. Consensual sexual relations in the privacy of one's own home should not be the concern of legislatures, they said. They applauded the ruling as the most important legal advance ever made by American homosexuals.

After *Lawrence*, the Massachusetts Supreme Judicial Court ruled in *Goodridge v. Department of Public Health* that the state constitution required that marriage be available to homosexual, as well as heterosexual, couples. The state legislature followed suit and Massachusetts became the only state in the U.S. to permit homosexual marriage.

The *Lawrence* decision, critics said, could lead to dire consequences, such as other states following Massachusetts' same-sex marriages. The case supplied fuel to fire the gay rights debate, one of the "hot button issues" in America's cultural war.

The California Supreme Court in a mid-May, 2008, ruling, permitted Gay Marriage, although voters of that state were to consider a proposed constitutional amendment in November outlawing it. Florida and Arizona voters also were likely to weigh such proposals.

Four states, Vermont, Connecticut, New Hampshire and New Jersey, have approved "civil unions," under which same-sex "partners" receive many of the benefits available to married couples, including inheritance rights. They are not, however, eligible for Federal spousal benefits, such as Social Security.

In May, 2008, the Michigan Supreme Court upheld a lower court ruling that Michigan's public universities and other government agencies may not extend employee benefits to a worker's same-sex partner. In a 5-2 decision, the state's highest tribunal held that Michigan's constitutional ban on gay marriages also applies to employee benefits.[37]

Issues Ahead: Many legal battles appear to lie ahead in the area of alleged gay and lesbian civil rights. President Clinton, as early as 1996, had signed legislation that permits states to refuse to recognize same-sex marriages, an exception to the "full faith and credit" clause of the constitution which normally requires states to recognize public records of sister states.

Some 26 states, including Michigan, have enacted constitutional amendments or statutory laws providing that marriage could only be between a man and a woman. In June, 2006, the U.S. Senate killed a proposed amendment to ban gay marriage when it refused to end a filibuster and bring the measure to a final floor vote.

American courts also have been hearing cases involving gay parents' demands for child custody. At issue is the question of how much consideration, if any, should be given to a parent's sexual orientation when deciding which of two parents should have custody. The states are divided on the issue. In Florida, a judge awarded custody to a father because the child's mother was a lesbian. The child, the judge ruled, should have the chance to live in a non-lesbian world. In *Ward v. Ward*, Florida appellate courts upheld that decision.

In the past 30 years, there has been a proliferation of homosexual interest groups. There are several thousand of them early in the 21st Century, compared to less than 100 in 1970. Among the most widely known are the Human Rights Campaign Fund and the National Gay and Lesbian Task Force, which focus on state and local gay rights legislation. These and other groups have exerted political pressure on legislatures, the media, schools and churches.

Perhaps the most significant early victory of the homosexual political movement came in 1973. Until then, being "gay" was considered a mental disorder, to be treated by psychiatrists and other mental health professionals. In that year, the American Psychiatric Association voted, 51% to 49%, at its convention in Hawaii, to remove homosexuality from its list of "mental disorders."

THE RIGHT TO DIE: THE CRUZAN CASE

The U.S. Supreme Court found a limited "right to die" in *Cruzan v. Director, Missouri Dept. of Public Health,* 497 U.S. 261 (1990).

Nancy Cruzan's car skidded off an icy road in January, 1983, and flipped into a ditch. When paramedics found her, she was lying face down in the ditch without detectable respiratory or cardiac function. Cruzan was rushed to a hospital where doctors were able to save her life, but not her brain.

She remained bedridden, never regained consciousness and degenerated into a persistent vegetative condition in a Missouri state hospital. In a state similar to a coma, Nancy showed motor reflexes, but no indications of any significant cognitive function.

She was on life support and required feeding and hydration tubes to remain alive. Nancy Cruzan, age 25 at the time of her accident, was not dead and could have lived another 30 years, according to physicians, unless they were authorized to "pull the plug."

Nancy's parents, Joyce and Lester Cruzan, agonized before making a decision to ask physicians to remove the feeding tubes, a step which would end Nancy's life. The hospital objected, as did the state of Missouri, which was paying $130,000 a year to support her. Nancy's parents then sought permission of a state trial court to remove life support.

Their attorney argued that a person in Nancy's condition had a fundamental right to refuse to direct the withdrawal of "death-prolonging procedures." To support their case, the Cruzans presented evidence that their daughter had told a friend that "she would not wish to continue her life unless she live it at least halfway normally."

The trial court authorized discontinuance of life support on grounds that Nancy had a right to refuse treatment, and that her verbal statements before the accident indicated that she would not want to be kept alive under existing circumstances.

The Missouri Supreme Court reversed that judgment, holding in key points that:

- it found no common law "right to die;"
- the state constitution did not contain a broad right to privacy;
- the state had a strong interest in preserving life and, if it wanted to alter this position, then the legislature, not the courts, should do it;
- it was doubtful that the U.S. Supreme Court conferred a "right to die."

State policy, favoring preservation of life, could be overridden only by a formal Living Will or upon a showing of clear and convincing proof that termination of life support was the patient's wish. It held that neither existed in the Cruzan case.

Her parents then sought, and were granted a writ of *certiorari* by the U.S. Supreme Court. It agreed to decide whether the family could require the hospital to withdraw feeding tubes or whether Missouri (and, by implication, other states) could prohibit such an action.

The Cruzan case, complicated enough in itself, became entangled in other controversial issues and pressure group politics.

Pro-life groups said that denying life support to Nancy Cruzan was comparable to abortion. Handicapper groups said her condition was merely a disability, and withholding food and water from her would lead to withholding treatment from other people with disabilities.

In *Cruzan,* the Rehnquist Court, divided 5-4, **established a limited "right to die."** It found that individuals can refuse medical treatment, including food and water, even if this means that they will die. However, **the right does not encompass suicide,** and states may require individuals to make their decisions while mentally competent and alert.   An individual also can prepare a "living will," or designate another person as a proxy to make the decision should he or she be unable to do so. The Court held that Cruzan had not clearly expressed her wishes prior to her accident. Therefore, she would continue in her vegetative state.

Rehnquist's Opinion

Chief Justice Rehnquist delivered the opinion of the Court. He wrote in part:[38]

Before the turn of the century, this court observed that no right is held more sacred, or is more carefully guarded, by the common law, than the right of every individual to the possession and control of his own person, free from all restraint or interference of others, unless by clear and unquestionable authority of law.

The common law doctrine of informed consent is viewed as generally encompassing the right of a competent individual to refuse medical treatment. Beyond that, these decisions demonstrate both similarity and diversity in their approach to what all agree is a perplexing question with unusually strong moral and ethical overtones. State courts have available to them for decision a number of sources—state constitutions, statutes and common law—which are not available to us.

In this Court, the question is simply and starkly whether the United States Constitution grants what is in common parlance referred to as a 'right to die.'

Petitioners insist that under the general holdings of our cases, the forced administration of life-sustaining medical treatment, and even of artificially delivered food and water essential to life, would implicate a competent person's liberty interest...for purposes of this case, we assume that the United States Constitution would grant a competent person a constitutionally protected right to refuse lifesaving hydration and nutrition.

Petitioners go on to assert that an incompetent person should possess the same right in this respect as is possessed by a competent person.

The difficulty with petitioners' claim is that in a sense it begs the question: an incompetent person is not able to make an informed and voluntary choice to exercise a hypothetical right to refuse treatment or any other right. Such a 'right' must be exercised for her, if at all, by some sort of surrogate. Here, Missouri has in effect recognized that under certain circumstances a surrogate may act for the patient in electing to have hydration and nutrition withdrawn in such a way as to cause death, but it has established a procedural safeguard to assure that the action of the surrogate conforms as best it may to wishes expressed by the patient while competent. Missouri requires that evidence of the incompetent's wishes as to the withdrawal of treatment be proved by clear and convincing evidence. The question is whether the United States Constitution forbids the establishment of this procedural requirement by the State. We hold that it does not.

The more stringent the burden of proof a party must bear, the more that party bears the risk of an erroneous decision. We believe that Missouri may permissibly place an increased risk of an erroneous decision on those seeking to terminate an incompetent individual's life-sustaining treatment. An erroneous decision not to terminate results in a maintenance of the status quo, the possibility of subsequent developments such as advancements in medical science, the discovery of new evidence regarding the patient's intent, changes in the law, or simply the unexpected death of the patient despite the administration of life-sustaining treatment, at least create the potential that a wrong decision will eventually be corrected or its impact mitigated. An erroneous decision to withdraw life sustaining treatment, however, is not susceptible of correction.

We conclude that a State may apply a clear and convincing evidence standard in proceedings where a guardian seeks to discontinue nutrition and hydration of a person diagnosed to be in a persistent vegetative state. We note that many courts which have adopted some sort of substituted judgment procedure in situations like this, whether they limit considerations of evidence to the prior expressed wishes of the incompetent individual, or whether they allow more general proof of what the individual's decision would have been, require a clear and convincing standard of proof for such evidence.

The Supreme Court of Missouri held that in this case the testimony adduced at trial did not amount to clear and convincing proof of the patient's desire to have hydration and nutrition withdrawn. In so doing, it reversed a decision of the Missouri trial court which had found that the evidence 'suggested' Nancy Cruzan would not have desired to continue such measures.

The testimony adduced at trial consisted primarily of Nancy Cruzan's statements made to a housemate about a year before her accident that she would not want to live should she face life as a 'vegetable' and other observations to the same effect. The observations did not deal in terms with withdrawal of medical treatment or of hydration and nutrition. We cannot say that the Supreme Court of Missouri committed constitutional error in reaching the conclusion that it did. The judgment of the Supreme Court of Missouri is affirmed.

Brennan, Marshall, Blackmun Dissent

Justice Brennan, joined by Justices Marshall and Blackmun, dissented. Brennan wrote:[39]

Medical technology has effectively created a twilight zone of suspended animation where death commences while life, in some form, continues. Some patients, however, want no part of a life sustained only by medical technology. Instead, they prefer a plan of medical treatment that allows nature to take its course and permits them to die with dignity.

As many as 10,000 patients are being maintained in persistent vegetative states in the United States and the number is expected to increase significantly in the near future. Medical technology, developed over the past 20 or so years, is often capable of resuscitating people after they have stopped breathing or their hearts have stopped beating. Some of those people are brought fully back to life. Two decades ago, those who were not and could not swallow and digest food, died. Intravenous solutions could not provide sufficient calories to maintain people for more than a short time. Today, various forms of artificial feeding have been developed that are able to keep people metabolically alive for years, even decades. In addition, in this century, chronic or degenerative ailments have replaced communicable diseases as the primary causes of death. The 80% of Americans who die in hospitals are 'likely to meet their end in a sedated or comatose state, be tubed nasally, abdominally and intravenously; and far more like manipulated objects than moral subjects.' A fifth of all adults surviving to age 80 will suffer a progressive dementing disorder prior to death.

The new medical technology can reclaim those who would have been irretrievably lost a few decades ago and restore them to active lives. For Nancy Cruzan, it failed, and for others with wasting incurable disease, it may be doomed to failure. In these unfortunate situations, the bodies and preferences and memories of the victims do not escheat to the State; nor does our constitution permit the State or any other government to commandeer them. No singularity of feeling exists upon which such a government might confidently rely as *parens patriae*...Missouri and this Court have displaced Nancy's own assessment of the processes associated with dying. They have discarded evidence of her will, ignored her values, and deprived her of the right to a decision as closely approximating her own choice as humanly possible. They have done so disingenuously in her name, and openly in Missouri's own. That Missouri and this Court may truly be motivated only by concern for incompetent patients makes no matter...I respectfully dissent.

Postscript: In August, 1990, the Cruzans petitioned a local Missouri court for a new hearing. The state withdrew from the case the following month, indicating it had no further role to play once the issue was decided. Three of Nancy's former co-workers testified that she said she would not want to live "like a vegetable." A county judge then ruled that Nancy's feeding tube could be removed. She died on December 26, 1990, some 12 days after the tube was disconnected.

Some constitutional lawyers believe that the Supreme Court ruling in *Cruzan* settled the "right to die" issue. They argue that the Court requires "a living will" in such circumstances. Others contend that new "right to die" cases inevitably will appear on the Court's agenda, as science and medical technology make further technological advances.

Physician Assisted Suicide: A "hot button" political issue at the end of the millennium was physician assisted suicide. Do state laws which ban physicians from "helping" their patients to commit suicide violate the "right to die?" Federal Courts of Appeals for the Ninth and Second Circuits, respectively, declared that such bans by Washington and New York states constituted violations of the 14th Amendment's Equal Protection Clause. Neither court could see much difference between assisting a terminally ill person in ending his or her life and withdrawing life-sustaining treatment from terminally ill patients.

The issue, of course, had to be decided by the U.S. Supreme Court which granted *certiorari* in the two cases, *Vacco, Attorney General of New York, et al. v. Timothy E. Quill, et al.*, 521 U.S. 793 (1997), and *Washington v. Glucksburg*, 521 U.S. 702 (1997).

New York, like all other states except Oregon, makes it a crime to help another to commit or attempt suicide. Patients, however, may refuse even lifesaving medical treatment. Timothy F. Quill, Samuel C. Klagsbrun and Howard Grossman were physicians licensed to practice medicine in New York. The doctors asserted that, although it would be "...consistent with (their) standards of medical practice to prescribe lethal medication for mentally competent, terminally ill patients" who are suffering great pain and desire a doctor's help in taking their own lives, they are deterred from doing so by New York's ban on assisted suicide. The physicians sued the New York Attorney General in the U.S. District Court.

They argued that, because New York permits a competent person to refuse life sustaining medical treatment, and because the result of such treatment is "essentially the same thing" as physician assisted suicide, New York's assisted suicide ban violates the Equal Protection Clause. The District Court disagreed, but the Court of Appeals for the Second Circuit reversed. The Supreme Court granted *certiorari*.

The question presented was whether New York's ban on assisted suicide violated the Equal Protection Clause of the 14th Amendment. The Supreme Court held that it did not. **In short, one does not have a Federal constitutional right to physician-assisted suicide.**

Chief Justice Rehnquist wrote:

> This Court has...recognized, at least implicitly, the distinction between letting a patient die and making that patient die...we disagree with the respondents' claim that the distinction between refusing lifesaving medical treatment and assisted suicide is 'arbitrary' and 'irrational.' By permitting everyone to refuse unwanted medical treatment while prohibiting anyone from

assisting a suicide, New York law follows a long standing and rational distinction.

New York's reasons for recognizing and acting on this distinction—including prohibiting intentional killing and preserving life; preventing suicide; maintaining physicians' role as their patients' healers; protecting vulnerable people from indifference, prejudice, and psychological and financial pressure to end their lives; and avoiding a possible slide toward euthanasia—(are)...valid and important public interests.

In Glucksburg, the court also found no right of physician-assisted suicide to exist.

In November, 1998, Michigan became the center of the nation's political attention when voters went to the polls to consider Ballot Issue B, legalization of physician assisted suicide. The activities of Dr. Jack Kevorkian, who admittedly "helped" more than 100 terminally ill patients to die, focused public attention on the issue. Kevorkian, called "Dr. Death" by the media, and his attorney Geoffrey Fieger, argued that people should be able to "die with dignity." Michigan juries, prior to 1999, had refused to convict Kevorkian on charges related to some of these deaths.

The flamboyant Fieger, a multi-millionaire attorney from Bloomfield Hills, became a major actor in 1998 when he entered the Democratic Party primary and won its gubernatorial nomination. He upset former East Lansing mayor and Michigan State University trustee Larry Owen, and Doug Ross, a former Department of Commerce director. His campaign against incumbent Republican Gov. John Engler, a strong foe of physician assisted suicide, was marked by Fieger's rhetorical extravagance.

He attacked many religious leaders—Orthodox rabbis, Catholic bishops and Conservative Protestants—who disagreed with his stand on the "right to die" and other issues. Many traditional Democrats crossed party lines to vote for Engler.

The two candidates could not have presented a clearer choice to the electorate. Fieger, a University of Michigan graduate, had an undergraduate degree in theater and a master's degree in speech. He went on to earn a law degree at Detroit College of Law. Fieger grew up in Detroit's suburbs in a family of union and civil rights activists.

Engler grew up on a Beal City farm in a Conservative family. He took a degree in agricultural economics from Michigan State. Engler is a practicing Roman Catholic who attended parochial schools as a youth. Fieger is a non-practicing Unitarian with Jewish roots. Both are members of the baby boom generation and both intensely dislike each other.

When the ballots were counted, **Proposal B** was overwhelmingly defeated. The Michigan Secretary of State's office shows that the measure **failed in every one of Michigan's 83 counties.** The final vote was "yes" 859,381 to "no" 2,116,154. Fieger suffered the most one-sided political defeat in the annals of Michigan gubernatorial politics, losing all but one (Wayne) county. The final count was Engler 1,883,005 to Feiger's 1,143,574, a margin of 739,431 in a state noted for close gubernatorial contests.

Exit polls showed that both men (67%) and women (70%) opposed Proposal B. Both Blacks (70%) and whites (68%) voted against it. Those who attended church weekly (87%) were adamantly opposed to the measure, viewing it as a rejection of their core value that "life is sacred."

"We're grateful that Michigan voters realized this would have created a lot of problems and voted no by a margin of better than 2-1," said Dr. Cathy Blight, president of the 14,000 member Michigan State Medical Society and co-chairwoman of the group,

Citizens for Compassionate Care. The coalition consisted of more than 30 groups, led by the medical society, Roman Catholic Church and Right to Life of Michigan. It raised more than $5 million to defeat Proposal B.

Ed Pierce, a retired Ann Arbor physician, led Merian's Friends, a group which raised $1 million and gathered signatures to place the measure before the voters. He said, "This issue won't go away." The group was named for Merian Frederick, a 72-year-old Ann Arbor woman who Kevorkian "helped" to die.

In 1999, CBS aired a "60 Minutes" segment in which Kevorkian ran poison through the veins of Thomas Youk. CBS later turned over unedited tapes of Youk's death to a Michigan prosecutor and Kevorkian was charged with second degree murder. This time, he faced a Michigan jury without Fieger as his lawyer. He was convicted on March 26 and sentenced to 10-25 years in prison.

After serving eight years in prison, Kevorkian was paroled in 2007. He announced early in 2008 that he would be a congressional candidate. Seeking to oust veteran Republican Joe Knollenberg from his Ninth District (suburban Detroit) seat, Kevorkian also faced Democrat Gary Peters, a former Michigan lottery commissioner and state senator. Peters had supported placing physician-assisted suicide before Michigan voters in 1998. The race was expected to be competitive because Knollenberg won only 51.5% of the vote in 2006.

Kevorkian, 79, and appearing frail, was running as an Independent. His candidacy was not expected to make much difference. Some Democrats, however, feared the "Nader effect," a reference to the fact that Ralph Nader took enough Florida Democratic votes away from Al Gore in 2000 to change the outcome of that election.

In his announcement to the *Oakland Tribune*, the man labeled "Dr. Death" by the media, said, "We need some honesty and sincerity instead of corrupt government in Washington."

Gonzales v. Oregon, 546 U.S 243 (2006)

Oregon voters, in 1994, went to the polls and approved Ballot Measure 16, a Death with Dignity Act which allowed physicians to prescribe fatal doses of prescription medicines. In order for a patient to receive the prescription, he or she had to be of sound mind and two doctors had to agree that the patient had six months or less to live.

Efforts to repeal the law in 1997 failed when, in a special election, the measure passed by a margin of more than 200,000 votes. Oregon was the first and, as of mid-2006, the only state to have such a statute.

On November 9, 2001, Attorney General John Ashcroft, reversing the position of his predecessor, Janet Reno, issued a directive intended to halt physician-assisted suicide in Oregon. His "interpretive rule" held that physician-assisted suicide was not a "legitimate medical purpose," as defined in the Controlled Substances Act of 1970. Therefore, he said, any prescriptions written for that purpose would violate the CSA and subject the doctor to civil or even criminal penalties. Alberto Gonzales succeeded Ashcroft as Attorney General after the State of Oregon had challenged the action, and the Supreme Court case bears his name.

In a lawsuit filed in the U.S. District Court for the District of Oregon, the state challenged Ashcroft's directive. The court ruled for Oregon and issued a permanent injunction against enforcement of the "interpretative rule." The decision was upheld by the Ninth Circuit Court of Appeals, which gave the Attorney General a lecture on states' rights, which he appeared to ignore in his directive.

"The principle that state government bears the primary responsibility for evaluating physician-assisted suicide follows from our concept of federalism, which requires that state lawmakers, not the Federal government, are the 'primary regulators of professional conduct'...Contrary to the Attorney General's characterization, physician-assisted suicide is not a form of 'drug abuse' that Congress intended the CSA to cover," Judge Richard Tallman wrote.

On January 17, 2006, the U.S. Supreme Court affirmed the decision of the Ninth Circuit, ruling that the Controlled Substances Act does not give the Attorney General the power to forbid Oregon physicians from prescribing fatal doses of drugs to terminally ill patients who seek to end their lives.

In a majority opinion by Justice Kennedy, joined by Justices Stevens, O'Connor, Souter, Ginsburg and Breyer, the Court held, 6-3, that the Attorney General's directive exceeded the powers that Congress had given him under the Controlled Substances Act. Although the majority conceded that the Federal government had the power to regulate drugs, it held that it could not overrule state laws defining appropriate use of medications that were not themselves prohibited. Kennedy wrote:

> The Government, in the end, maintains that the prescription requirement delegates to a single Executive officer the power to affect a radical shift of authority from the States to the Federal government to define general standards of medical practice in every locality. The text and structure of the CSA show that Congress did not have this far-reaching intent to alter the Federal-State balance and the Congressional role in maintaining it.

Justice Scalia, joined by Chief Justice Roberts and Justice Thomas, dissented, arguing that under Supreme Court precedents, deference should have been given to the Attorney General's interpretation of the statute.

Scalia observed that the court ruling "is perhaps driven by a feeling that the subject of assisted suicide is none of the Federal government's business. It is easy to sympathize with that position...But, at the same time if the term 'legitimate medical purpose' has any meaning, it surely excludes the prescription of drugs to produce death."

Scalia also noted that, if the Federal government could not prohibit assisted suicide, it also could not prohibit recreational use of drugs or discourage drug addiction. "Unless we are to repudiate a long and well-established jurisprudence, using the Federal commerce power to prevent assisted suicide is unquestionably permissible," he concluded.

In a press release lauding the decision, Oregon Gov. Ted Kulongoski said:

> Today the nation's highest court has given the voters of Oregon an important victory in upholding the Oregon Death with Dignity Act. The U.S. Supreme Court recognized the delicate balance between our Federal system and the right of the states to be the crucibles for new ideas and new ways to meet the changing needs of their citizens.
>
> Medical issues traditionally fall within the purview of the states, and today the U.S. Supreme Court strengthened that tradition. Twice the voters of

Oregon gave their approval to the Death with Dignity Act, which clearly responds to the people's wants and needs.

Congress did not intend the Controlled Substances Act to allow a U.S. Attorney General to bring about a radical shift of authority from the states to the Federal government. With this decision, the Supreme Court rejected an attempt of the former Attorney General John Ashcroft to sue the Controlled Substances Act to exert overreaching Federal control over the states.

This was the right decision for Oregon, the right decision for America, and the right decision for the system of constitutional government.

If Governor Kulongoski was pleased, Archbishop John G. Vlazny of Portland, Oregon, definitely was not. He said:

Through the health care ministry of our hospitals and nursing homes, the Catholic Church will continue to support, care for and relieve the pain of those who are sick and dying. Terminally ill patients should have their pain controlled and be supported, not be assisted to commit suicide by their doctors.

Jay Sekulow, chief legal counsel for the American Center for Law and Justice, which had filed an *amicus* brief in support of Gonzales, said:

This is a disappointing decision that is likely to result in a troubling movement by states to pass their own assisted suicide laws. It is unfortunate that a majority of the court stripped the Federal government of an important safeguard to ensure that federally controlled narcotics could not be used by licensed physicians to take the life of a patient who wants to commit suicide. This is a disturbing and dangerous decision that can only lessen the value of protecting life.

Diane Coleman, president and founder of Not Dead Yet, said:

If assisted suicide were really about personal autonomy, it would be available to all suicidal people...But really, assisted suicide statutes are the ultimate societal judgment that the life of a person with a disability is not as worthwhile as that of a non-disabled person.

Clearly, *Gonzales v. Oregon* is a states' rights case. Individual states are free, in view of the Supreme Court's ruling, to adopt physician-assisted suicide laws. But, as noted, the Court ruled unanimously in companion cases, *Washington v. Glucksburg* , 521 U.S. 702 (1997) and *Vacco v. Quill* (521 U.S. 793 (1997) that there is no constitutional right to such a procedure.

Owasso Independent School District v. Falvo, 534 U.S. 426 (2002). The Supreme Court, in 2002, decided *Owasso Independent School District v. Falvo*. The case involved an old elementary school practice, as well as the question of student privacy and educational records.

Philip Pletan, 10, a fifth grade student in the Owasso, Okla., Independent School District, was enrolled in special education classes, but was placed in a "mainstream" class three days a week. The theory behind this was that Philip and other "special education" students would learn to get along with pupils enrolled in "regular classes."

However, Philip's class used "peer grading," a practice where other students corrected his assignments and tests while the teacher read the correct answers aloud. His scores frequently were lower than those of classmates and he often was called "dummy" and "stupid" by his peers, who teased him about his grades.

Philip had two sisters, both straight A students. But they also disliked peer grading because friends pressured them to report higher scores than they had earned.

Philip's mother, Krista Falvo, voiced her concerns to teachers, counselors and the school superintendent, who dismissed her protests. Her letters to the district detailing how its peer grading practices were harming her children's self-esteem were not answered. She finally hired an attorney and filed a lawsuit in the U.S. District Court for the Northern District of Oklahoma.

Falvo's argument was that the school district's grading policy violated the children's 14th Amendment privacy rights and the Family Education Rights and Privacy Act (FERPA), which requires educational institutions to preserve the confidentiality of "education records."

The District Court ruled in Owasso's favor, largely because of a letter from L. S. Rooker, an official in the U.S. Department of Education. Rooker said that, while is not permissible to post student grades, it is permissible to call them out. In short, the Education Department did not see any violation of the Federal statute.

The U.S. Court of Appeals for the 10th Circuit unanimously reversed , holding that the District Court was in error in giving undue deference to the Department of Education's opinion. The District's grading practices violated FERPA, the court ruled. "Grades which students record on one another's homework and test papers and then report to the teacher constitute 'education records' under FERPA."

The ruling meant that in the six states—Colorado, Kansas, New Mexico, Utah, Wyoming and Oklahoma—that comprise the 10th Circuit, it became illegal for students to grade each other's work unless peer grading was done with parental permission, or was done anonymously.

Owasso appealed to the U.S. Supreme Court, which granted *certiorari.*

The High Tribunal, speaking through Justice Anthony Kennedy, issued a unanimous ruling on February 19, 2002. In a nutshell, the Court decided that an act of peer grading by students does not constitute an educational record under FERPA in that it is not recorded yet in the teacher's grade book. Justice Kennedy wrote:

> Even assuming the teacher's grade book is an educational record, the score on a student-graded assignment is not 'contained therein,' until the teacher records it. The teacher does not maintain the grade while students correct their peers' assignments or call their own marks. The student grader only handles assignments for a few moments as the teacher calls out the answers.
>
> ...It is fanciful to say they maintain the papers in the same way the registrar maintains a student's folder in a permanent file. Correcting a classmate's work can be as much a part of the assignment as taking the test itself. It is a way to teach material again in a new context, and it helps show students how to assist and respect fellow pupils.

Kennedy noted that the Court was ruling narrowly:

We limit our holding to peer grading before the teacher has collected the grades and recorded them in his or her grade book, and do not decide the broader question whether the grades on individual student assignments, once they are turned in to teachers, are protected by the Act.

PRIVACY AND THE PRESS

Privacy is also a major area of controversy in communications law. It is quite possible for constitutional values to conflict with one another. Then the Supreme Court is called upon, on a case-by-case basis to choose. Which takes precedence, the First Amendment Freedom of the Press to report the news or the individual's right to be left alone?

The phrase "invasion of privacy" may appear very simple to most students. But it has become a highly complex area of communications law. Over the years, privacy law has evolved into four distinct categories. A personal injury (tort) lawyer can argue that the media has damaged his or her client by invasion of privacy through: (1) intrusion, (2) public disclosure of private, embarrassing facts, (3) "false light" (fictionalization) and (4) appropriation.

Most states, including Michigan, recognize all four categories as actionable torts.[40]

Intrusion

It often is said that the press is, by definition, intrusive. Although editors, publishers, reporters and journalism educators speak at length about "ethics," sometimes getting the story first in a highly pressurized, competitive market becomes more important than "mere ethics."

This depends, to a large extent, upon a number of key variables. **Not all editors, publishers and reporters think in terms of ethics** or restraints upon their freedom to gather the news. Some push the law to the breaking point, if not beyond. Others have exceptional standards of ethics. And in the real world of the early 21st Century, there is always the problem of the tabloid and "**supermarket press**," as well as "**trash TV shows**" which cater to the lowest possible denominator. Repulsive? Perhaps, but people seem to watch those programs and buy those kind of publications.

Celebrities and others often complain that the media has "intruded" into their physical privacy or seclusion and that their private affairs or concerns are not the business of the prying press. In recent years, a "hot topic" in Journalism Ethics courses has been "privacy and the politician: are there any restraints?" When is a political figure's private life a matter of public concern? When should it be?

Intrusion frequently is associated with questionable newsgathering techniques, such as the use of eavesdropping devices, tape recorders or cameras with telephoto lenses. Sometimes it is related to "**checkbook journalism**," which occurs when publications pay photographers, sometimes handsomely, for sensational photos.[41]

Reporters sometimes use fake I.D.s and represent themselves as someone else in order to get a story. They can, at times, make life a "living Hell" for celebrities. Or reporters can be nominated for a Pulitzer Prize for helping to clean up a corrupt government.

The legendary aggressiveness of paparazzo Ron Galella motivated Jacqueline Kennedy Onassis to seek relief from a Federal District Court in New York. Galella, who specializes in celebrity snapshots, harassed not only Mrs. Onassis, but her children, Carolyn and John Kennedy, for several years. The Court granted a restraining order, ruling that the photographer's constant interferences were "intrusion."[42]

Courts do not recognize "intrusion" when the media receives its information, even if illegally obtained, from a third party. If a newspaper or radio-TV station participates in an illegal act, however, a suit for "intrusion" may be successful.

Dietmann: The leading intrusion case is *Dietmann v. Time, Inc.* It involved a plumber who was practicing medicine without a license. Working out of his home, Dietmann was careful to admit only those he knew. In one case, he was not careful enough.

A *Life* magazine editor learned about Dietmann and assigned a female reporter and male photographer to pose as husband and wife and to seek "treatment" from him. The couple worked with the local district attorney, who was anxious to get evidence which could be used to prosecute and convict Dietmann.

The woman concealed a radio transmitter in her handbag and the man wore a tie-clip camera. Another *Life* employee, California Health Department officials and representatives from the district attorney's office were in a parked car outside, listening carefully to every word.

Posing as friends of one of Dietmann's previous clients, they were admitted to his home. The woman reporter complained of a lump in her breast. After examining her, Dietmann had bad news. She had cancer, developed, he said, because she had eaten rancid butter.

As "Dr." Dietmann prescribed clay, herbs and minerals to cure the cancer, his words were recorded. Photos also were taken of the "healer" at work. Dietmann was arrested and charged with practicing medicine without a license. He pleaded no contest. *Life* published the article after Dietmann's arrest, but before he entered his plea.

Dietmann sued for invasion of privacy and was awarded $1000 in damages by a Los Angeles Federal District Court, a verdict later affirmed by the Ninth Circuit Court of Appeals. Appeals Court Judge Hufstedler blasted the reporting methods in strong language:[43]

> Although the issue has not been squarely decided in California, we have little difficulty in concluding that clandestine photography of the plaintiff in his den and the recordation and transmission of his conversation without his consent, resulting in his emotional distress, warrants recovery for invasion of privacy.
>
> Plaintiff's den was a sphere from which he could reasonably expect to exclude eavesdropping newsmen. He invited two of defendant's employees to the den. One who invites another to his home or office takes a risk that the visitor may not be what he seems, and that visitor may repeat all he hears and observes when he leaves. But he does not and should not be required to take the risk that what is heard and seen will be transmitted by photograph or recording, or in our modern world, in full living color and hi-fi to the public at large or to any segment of it that the visitor may select.

Brushing aside Time, Inc., lawyers' argument that cameras and recording devices had indeed become "indispensable tools" in investigative reporting, the court said:[44]

The First Amendment has never been construed to accord newsmen immunity from torts or crimes committed during the course of newsgathering. The First Amendment is not a license to trespass, to steal or to intrude by electronic means into the precincts of another's home or office. It does not become such a license simply because the person subjected to the intrusion is reasonably suspected of committing a crime.

Public Disclosure of Private, Embarrassing Facts

Probably the most familiar, and most troublesome, kind of privacy lawsuits relate to public disclosure of private, embarrassing facts. They inevitably involve editorial decisions that publicity is reasonable and that certain facts are not really private. Individuals, on the other hand, claim a right to be left alone.

Reporters and editors are almost instinctively concerned with newsworthiness: "Is this interesting or important?" When, however, a person's privacy is the issue, the legal questions may be: "Is this story in the public interest? Does public interest surpass the importance of an individual's right to remain out of the news? Even if news is embarrassing to public officials, such as U.S. senators or governors, it is legitimate for reporters to write about matters involving public interest. That is what the First and 14th Amendments are all about.

Publishers, editors and reporters may disagree on many aspects of privacy and the news. They may have heated arguments about "ethical standards." Few, however, questioned the reporting in 1972 of the story that Sen. Thomas Eagleton of Missouri, just chosen by Democratic Party presidential nominee George McGovern as his running mate, had a medical history of mental illness. Senator Eagleton had, on three separate occasions, undergone electroshock therapy for mental depression. Had McGovern simply checked Senator Eagleton's medical history, he would have spared both himself and his running mate considerable embarrassment. The information was readily available. A number of Missouri political writers knew the story, although they chose not to publicize it.

Candor requires one to note that journalists of the pre-Watergate era had somewhat different ethical standards. Journalism in the past was also largely a male preserve. This should help one to understand why male political writers in Washington, D.C., did not report on the "womanizing" of John F. Kennedy or the drinking of Lyndon B. Johnson. Their reputations in these areas was no secret to editors and reporters. But, during the 1960s, political writers covered what the two men did in their public lives as President, not what they did in private. That information was held in reserve as "juicy gossip," to "entertain" visiting editors and publishers.

One well might compare this "kid-gloves" approach to the "iron fist" of today's political writers. In 1987, for example, the leading contender for the Democratic Party's presidential nomination was Gary Hart, former U.S. senator from Colorado. Hart had a reputation for having what one magazine called a "zipper problem."

When *Miami Herald* Editor Heath Meriwether received a news tip that Hart had planned a weekend affair with model Donna Rice, he put a reporter on a Washington flight to look for the young model. *Herald* reporters then spent a night and the next day watching Hart's Georgetown residence.

The *Herald* ran a page-one story in its editions of May 3, telling the "whole world" that, while Gary Hart's wife was back in Colorado, the would-be President had "spent Friday night and most of Saturday" at their home with Rice. Other newspapers and network

TV immediately jumped on the "Rice story" and Hart soon abandoned his quest for the presidential nomination.

Did unethical, trash-peddling reporters sink Gary Hart? Or did he sink himself? Are a candidate's sexual activities a basic indication of a character flaw? Did the American public have a "right to know" the facts?

The sordid story of President Clinton's "affair" with White House intern Monica Lewinsky is too familiar to detail here, but media coverage of it remains controversial today.

Whatever Happened to William Sidis?

One of the leading cases in the "embarrassment" area of privacy law is *Sidis v. F-R Publishing Corp.*, 13 F. 2d 806 (2d Cir. 1940).

New Yorker magazine ran a profile of William J. Sidis, a one-time child mathematical genius who had graduated from Harvard at age 16. Tired of publicity and life in the academic community, Sidis retreated into his own world. He became a recluse, earning a very modest living as a clerk.

Sidis found the article offensive and sued for invasion of privacy. The courts ruled that, even though he preferred obscurity, Sidis had lost most of his claim to privacy because he was newsworthy and his life a matter of public concern. The Court said:[45]

> We express no comment on whether or not the newsworthiness of the matter printed will always constitute a complete defense. Revelations may be so intimate and so unwarranted in the view of the victim's position as to outrage the community's notion of decency. But when focused upon public characters, truthful comments upon dress, speech, habits and the ordinary aspects of personality will usually not transgress this line. Regrettably or not, the misfortunes and frailties of neighbors and 'public figures' are subjects of considerable interest and discussion to the rest of the population. And when such are the mores of the community, it would be unwise for a court to bar their expression in the newspapers, books and magazines of the day.

Typically, four questions are raised in "embarrassment" complaints:

1. Is the information really private? Or has the media obtained it from public records or proceedings?

2. Is it "intimate?" Personal habits and history that one does not ordinarily want known often are at the heart of embarrassment lawsuits. The sterilization of an unwilling teenager was, in the judgment of the courts, an intimate fact. William James Sidis' unfulfilled childhood promise was not considered an intimate fact.

3. Is it "newsworthy?" This question is of basic importance in embarrassment cases. Journalists often quarrel on ethical questions. They also differ in their news judgment. When should names be used? Legally, the critical question is whether identifying a person is in the public interest. Experienced reporters and editors make sure that copy indicates why the story and its subjects are important to the public.

4. Is it "highly offensive?" Courts consider such factors as the facts of the story, its tone and often the motivation ("state of mind") of the writer.

The press has lost privacy cases by publishing stories about a person's private life which offend ordinary sensibilities. Sensational stories about one's health, sex life or other private matters concern private facts. It does not matter how embarrassed a celebrity may be if what he or she has done occurs in public. It may be a highly sensational or lurid story or photograph, but what can be seen in public is not actionable invasion of privacy.

"False Light"

Placing a person in a "false light" is another way to invade his or her privacy. This type of tort resembles libel because it also involves the element of falsity. It most frequently occurs when reporters either carelessly condense a story or attempt to make it more dramatic than the facts warrant. Some senior editors and reporters will recall the old, cynical newsroom saying: "Don't let the facts get in the way of a good story."

"False light" problems have increased for the press in recent years, particularly with the development in broadcasting of the so-called "docudrama." Creation of a fictional character who resembles a living person too much may lead to liability. Courts, however, have found that incidental use of a real person's name in a non-defamatory way is not actionable.

An interesting landmark case involving invasion of privacy and the press is the case of *Time v. Hill*, 385 U.S. 374 (1967). It began late in the summer of 1952 when James Hill, his wife and five children were held hostage in their suburban Philadelphia home for 19 hours by three escaped convicts. The story was page-one news, although none of the Hills were harmed. Hill later tried to stay out of the spotlight. But, despite his wishes, his ordeal attracted widespread publicity.

Novelist Joseph Hayes wrote a book, *The Desperate Hours*. It was a fictionalized version of the real story, portraying the convicts as violent. In the book, Hill and his son were assaulted and his daughter subjected to sexual insults. Later, a play, based on the book, would open. *Life* magazine published an article, "True Crime Inspires Tense Play," which noted similarities between the fictional work and the real event and falsely indicated that the play was based on the Hill's true experiences.

The family sued *Life* and its publisher, Time, Inc., and a jury awarded them $30,000 in damages. The New York Court of Appeals affirmed because of the inaccuracies.

Ultimately, Time, Inc. sought U.S. Supreme Court review of the case. When the Court granted review, Hill had Richard M. Nixon argue his case. The Court ruled against Hill, holding that the press could be held liable only for "calculated falsehood," not for inadvertent errors.

Most significantly, the Court held that plaintiffs had to prove "actual malice," just as public officials and public figures must do in libel actions.

In some cases, individuals have won judgments against the press for "false light" invasion of privacy. After 44 persons died when the Silver Bridge collapsed into the Ohio River at Point Pleasant, W. Va., *Cleveland Plain Dealer* reporter Joseph Eszterhas covered the funeral of one of the victims, Melvin A. Cantrell, 40, who had left a wife and seven children.

Five months later, Eszterhas and a photographer did a follow-up story of the tragedy for the paper's Sunday magazine. Photographer Richard Conway took about 50 pictures of the children, who were home alone, while reporter Eszterhas talked to them for about 90 minutes. He did not talk to Mrs. Cantrell, although his story was written to imply that he had. He wrote:

> Margaret Cantrell will talk neither about what happened nor about how they are doing. She wears the same mask of non-expression she wore at the funeral. She is a proud woman. Her world has changed. She says that after it happened, the people in town offered to help them out with money and they refused to take it.

The Court held Eszterhas responsible for "a calculated falsehood" amounting to "false light."[46]

Eszterhaus later moved to Hollywood, where he did not have to concern himself about accuracy and journalism ethics. He turned to writing "screenplays" and became very rich, making up to $3 million per film. Among his "credits" were Basic Instinct, F.I.S.T., Flashdance, Betrayed and Showgirls.

Reverend Falwell and the Sleaze Magazine

In 1988, the U.S. Supreme Court reviewed an "infliction of mental distress" lawsuit brought by the Rev. Jerry Falwell against Larry Flynt, widely-known pornographer and publisher, among other things, of *Hustler* Magazine.

The facts of the case, as summarized by the Supreme Court itself are as follows:[47]

> The inside front cover of the November, 1983, issue of *Hustler* Magazine featured a 'parody' of an advertisement for Campari Liqueur that contained the name and picture of the respondent and was entitled 'Jerry Falwell talks about his first time.' This parody was modeled after actual Campari ads that included interviews with various celebrities about their 'first times.' Although it was apparent by the end of each interview that this meant the first time they sampled Campari, the ads clearly played on the sexual double entendre of the general subject of 'first times.' Copying the form and layout of these Campari ads, *Hustler's* editor's chose respondent as the featured celebrity and drafted an alleged 'interview' with him in which he states that his 'first time' was during a drunken incestuous rendezvous with his mother in an outhouse. The *Hustler* parody portrays respondent and his mother as drunk and immoral, and suggests that respondent is a hypocrite, who preaches only when he is drunk. In small print at the bottom of the page, the ads contains the disclaimer, 'ad parody—not to be taken seriously.' The magazine's table of contents also lists the ad as 'Fiction: Ad and Personality Parody.'

Falwell's suit charged false light invasion of privacy, libel and **infliction of mental distress.** The trial court directed a verdict for Hustler on the libel charge. It ruled that no one could reasonably have concluded that the ad described true facts about Falwell. But the jury accepted the mental distress claim and awarded Falwell $150,000 in damages.

The U.S. Supreme Court reversed. Although the case involved intentional infliction of mental distress and not libel, Chief Justice Rehnquist said for a unanimous Court that Falwell was a public figure who must meet the "malice" test set out in Hill.

This test requires public figures to prove that a publication contains a false statement of fact and that the authors knew the statement was false or acted with reckless disregard of its truth.

Because Falwell had not asserted that Hustler had printed a "statement of fact," false or not, the test had not been met. As a result of *Flynt*, public figures in both libel and emotional distress suits against the media now have slim chances when seeking damages.

Appropriation

This kind of invasion of privacy deals with the appropriation of a person's name, likeness or personality for one's own benefit. **It is more likely to involve advertising than editorial personnel.** Its roots go back to a New York law that expressly forbids the use of a person's name or likeness for advertising purposes without written consent. In recent years, courts have been calling this "the right of publicity." In effect, celebrities now may prevent others from exploiting their names for commercial gain.

Several states permit newspapers and broadcasters to use a person's name or photo without his or her consent in connection with news of legitimate public interest. They may not, however, exploit entertainers, sports figures and other celebrities, so editors and producers must be careful with feature stories.

One of the leading U.S. Supreme Court cases in this area is *Zacchini v. Scripps Howard Broadcasting*, 433 U.S. 562 (1977).

Hugo Zacchini made his living by being shot out of cannon into a net, placed about 200 yards away. When he appeared at an Ohio county fair, a crew from WEWS-TV in Cleveland recorded his act. It was broadcast as part of a news report on the fair, but Zacchini sued for $25,000, arguing that the station was stealing his act.

The Supreme Court held that the First Amendment protected the station's news broadcast in its entirety. It also observed that there was news value in the "Human Cannonball" segment of the news. But, said the Court, the station had no constitutional right to appropriate Zacchini's entire act. Justice White wrote:[48]

> The broadcast of petitioner's entire performance, unlike the unauthorized use of another's name for purposes of trade or the incidental use of a name or picture by the press, goes to the heart of the petitioner's ability to earn a living as an entertainer. Thus, in this case, Ohio has recognized what may be the strongest case for a 'right of publicity'—involving not the appropriation of an entertainer's reputation to enhance the attractiveness of a commercial product, but the appropriation of the very activity by which the entertainer acquired the reputation in the first place.

MEDIA DEFENSES IN PRIVACY CASES

The right of privacy can be lost in three principal ways: consent, newsworthiness and constitutional privilege:[49]

1. **Consent:** An individual may give up his right to privacy. It is essential to obtain written consent in the case of advertising usage of a person's name,

likeness or personality. But consent is unnecessary when a newspaper, magazine or broadcaster report the activities of those who make the news.

2. **Newsworthiness:** In the case of public officials or public figures, a picture or name may be freely used without consent. Courts have held that public figures, by their actions or achievements, invite public interest and must accept unwelcome publicity as the price of fame.

Even the private life of such celebrities may be publicized without the individual's consent, assuming it relates to matters of public concern. Unlike the law of defamation, however, media may defend themselves whenever they publish a matter of public interest about a private citizen. Unauthorized use of the name or photo of a private citizen who becomes involved in a news event of legitimate public is not an invasion of privacy.

Private citizens, however, may win lawsuits when news stories offend "ordinary sensibilities" and have no legitimate public interest. Generally, a jury determines whether or not such unauthorized news reports are of legitimate public concern.

The U.S. Supreme Court, in *Cox v. Cohn,* 420 U.S. 469 (1975), held that accurate reports of the contents of court records, such as the identify of a rape victim, cannot constitute an invasion of privacy.

3. **Constitutional Privilege:** Newspapers and broadcasters can assert privilege in defending themselves against "false light" invasion of privacy. A person involved in a "false light" case cannot recover damages unless he or she can prove "actual malice." This means that the media made statements knowing that they were false or had serious doubts about them. This defense originated in *New York Times v. Sullivan,* 376 U.S. 254 (1964), a landmark case involving public officials and libel law.

The Court has satisfied neither the press nor strict adherents to the view that privacy should be of paramount importance. It has reached no broad conclusions to satisfy absolutist type "philosophers." It takes a very pragmatic "balancing of competing interests" viewpoint, noted in Chapter I. The press wins some cases. It loses some. Privacy sometimes wins, sometimes loses. It depends on a number of key variables, such as facts of the case, level of government regulating press, purpose of the regulation and, to be candid, the philosophy of the sitting justices.

Not everyone is convinced, as the case of Judge Bork so clearly proved, that there is a constitutional right to privacy.

The Problem of Reporting Names of Rape Victims

In a Georgia case, the U.S. Supreme Court ruled in favor of a television station that reported the name of 17-year-old Cynthia Cox, who had been gang raped and left to die on a neighbor's lawn by six male high school classmates. State law prohibited publication of names of rape victims in order to spare them and their families embarrassment. The victim's father sued the station but the Court held that family privacy had not been invaded because the station had obtained Cynthia's name from public court records.[50]

In *Florida Star v. B.J.F.,* 491 U.S. 524 (1989), the Supreme Court overruled a damage award against a weekly newspaper which printed the name of a rape victim which it had obtained from police records. Although Florida law made it unlawful to "print...in any instrument of mass communication" the name of the victim of a sexual offense, the Court found that, given the facts of this case, prosecuting the newspaper violated the First Amendment.

Conceding that important privacy interests were at stake, the Court also stressed that the newspaper had merely printed truthful information contained in records which the police department had placed in the press room accessible to the public. If fault lay anywhere, it was with the police department, which itself violated the law by including the victim's name in records made available to the public. The police department subsequently admitted its error and settled out of court for $2500.

The state, the Court noted, also could have taken more stringent protective measures to guard against release of this information to the media. The newspaper, the Court held, should not be blamed for printing newsworthy information that was essentially handed to it on a platter, especially in view of the vital free speech interest involved.

In sum, *Florida Star* shows that in a conflict between privacy and First Amendment rights, the latter ordinarily will prevail. The case may well make it as difficult for private plaintiffs to prevail in privacy and infliction of emotional distress lawsuits against the media as Flynt makes it for public figures.

A Gay Hero Sues The San Francisco Chronicle

On September 22, 1975, "Bill" Sipple, a former Marine, was in a San Francisco crowd. He noticed Sara Jane Moore draw a gun as President Ford approached. He grabbed her gun hand, deflected the shot and foiled an assassination attempt.

Reporters wrote stories about Sipple's heroism, including "profile" pieces. Columnist Herb Caen of the *San Francisco Chronicle* revealed that Sipple was a homosexual, a fact he did not want disclosed. Sipple sued, alleging that this "invasion of privacy" caused him embarrassment and many practical problems related to being "out of the closet."

Sipple's parents lived in Detroit, where he had grown up. The *Detroit News* published a story which quoted his mother as saying, "...We were very proud of Oliver, but now I won't be able to walk down the street without somebody saying something."

The *News* story also noted that Sipple had dropped out of high school and was on 100% disability pay after being discharged from the Marines because of mental adjustment problems. These were related to Vietnam combat service, during which time he twice had been wounded.[51]

California courts ruled that Sipple was "newsworthy," whether he wanted to be or not. He had done nothing, the Court held, to conceal his sexual orientation and the publicity was legitimate news. "Newsworthy" persons have a very limited right to privacy.

Sipple clearly was on weak legal ground when he claimed that his sexual orientation was "private information," the Court held. He acknowledged that he had frequented San Francisco's gay neighborhoods, that the had been a member of the Court of the Crowned Emperor of Gay San Francisco, and that he had marched in gay parades in New York, Dallas, Houston, San Diego and Los Angeles long before foiling Moore's attempt to kill Gerald Ford.[52]

Privacy and Tabloid TV

The Supreme Court, on May 25, 1999, ruled unanimously that the police violate "the right of residential privacy," at the core of the Fourth Amendment, when they take journalists and photographers into people's homes to witness searches or arrests. The decision may well curb the widespread practice—questioned by students of journalism ethics—in which reporters and photographers accompany police into private homes to get "dramatic" coverage of law enforcement in action. The activity has supplied much of the film footage for today's "reality (tabloid) television."

The decision came after a major debate on conflicting values: an individual's right to privacy, the police interest in maximizing their effectiveness and the historic "watchdog" role of the press.

Television camera crews and news photographers welcome the opportunity to get videotape or pictures of a dramatic arrest. Media and law enforcement lawyers argue that officers have a legitimate interest in letting the public, through the news media, see how they work. They also contend that courts never have banned the practice and that the public relations value is important because it shows police effectiveness and deters crime. It also helps, they say, to track down fugitives from justice. Finally, media lawyers contend that media presence enables it to monitor abuses of government power at the source.

Opponents of the so-called ride-alongs argue that they constitute a significant invasion of privacy. Since entry into the home is one of the clearest violations of the Fourth Amendment that one could imagine, media presence magnifies that intrusion, lawyers have argued. Finally, they contend that media presence can incite bravado and unnecessary, dangerous behavior by officers.

The ruling has no effect on reporter ride-alongs with police to report on activity in a public place. It is limited to private property. The Court considered only the legal question of the officers' liability in carrying out the raids, not the media's responsibility in being part of the action.

The Court ruled in two cases. One, *Wilson v. Layne*, 526 U.S. 603 (1999), involved a joint Federal-local law enforcement task force which invited the *Washington Post* to send a reporter and photographer along on an operation to arrest fugitives in the Washington area. It is a policy for the U.S. Marshall Service to publicize its hunt for fugitives. The other, *Hanlon v. Berger*, 526 U.S. 808 (1999), involved Federal wildlife agents who brought a CNN camera crew along on a search of a Montana ranch, owned by Paul Berger, who was suspected of poisoning protected eagles.

The two cases went to the Supreme Court after lower Federal courts in Maryland and Montana differed about police liability for ride-alongs. Since the court was ruling for the first time, it decided—by a separate 8-1 vote—that police and Federal law enforcement authorities could not be sued for damages over past ride-alongs.

In both cases, homeowners sued on grounds that media presence violated their Fourth Amendment rights against unreasonable searches, although police had obtained valid arrest and search warrants.

All nine justices were agreed on the underlying Fourth Amendment issue, which led Justice Stevens to conclude that the question is "open and shut."

In the Washington area (Rockville, Md.) case, police went to the wrong address. The home was not that of fugitive Dominic Wilson, but of his parents, Charles and Geraldine Wilson, who were roused from their sleep to find not only police officers, but a photographer taking pictures and a reporter taking notes. The photographer took pictures of the husband in his undershorts, with an officer's knee on his back and a gun to his head. Mrs. Wilson was dressed in a sheer negligee. Their nine-year-old granddaughter also was present when three plainclothes officers, with guns drawn, confronted the Wilsons.

Once the agents realized that they had made a mistake, they left. But the Wilsons, who later convinced their son to surrender to authorities, sued Harry Layne, the team's supervisor and other officers for inviting the media along, arguing that their action violated their Fourth Amendment protection against unreasonable searches and seizures.

The *Washington Post* never published an article about the incident and was not sued by the parents, who were represented by the ACLU. Its representative, Arthur Spitzer, said, "law enforcement agents should now have no doubt that their conduct is governed by the Bill of Rights and not by the demands of infotainment."

In the Montana case, Federal agents, wearing hidden microphones, brought along a Cable News Network (CNN) crew while they spent a full day searching Berger's ranch. Eventually, Berger, 77, was acquitted of killing at least one eagle. He sued U.S. Fish and Wildlife agents for violating his Fourth Amendment rights by allowing media to film the search, expose his conversations and possessions.

The U.S. Court of Appeals for the Ninth Circuit found the search violated Berger's rights.

LEGISLATURES RECOGNIZE PRIVACY RIGHTS

Until relatively recently, as noted, much of the law of privacy has been made by the courts. But Congress has passed a series of laws relating to personal privacy. The **Privacy Act of 1974** was intended to give individuals a degree of control over information maintained about them in government files. It gives people the right to see Federal records containing personal information on them. It also imposes penalties on agencies which improperly release information or records. The idea behind the law now has spread to the states.

The **Fair Credit Reporting Act** (1970) gives citizens the right to see their files, created and maintained by private credit agencies, department stores and banks.

The **Family Education Rights and Privacy Act** (1974) gives parents of students the right to see school records and instructional materials.

As noted, privacy law is a relatively new and emerging area of civil liberties. Many questions remain unanswered as we enter the 21st Century and doubtless many new problems will emerge as technology continues to challenge Americans as they struggle to live together in peace, dignity and mutual respect.

We now turn our attention, last but not least, to the question of the nation's struggle to attain its ideals of equality for all Americans. We will focus primarily, although not exclusively, on problems of achieving racial and sexual equality.

PRIVACY AND THE PATRIOT ACT

On September 11, 2001, the American people were shaken by terrorist attacks on the World Trade Center and the Pentagon. President Bush declared a "War on Terrorism" and Congress quickly responded by passing the "Uniting and Strengthening America by Providing Appropriate Tools, Required to Intercept and Obstruct Terrorism" law, known more commonly as the U.S.A. Patriot Act.

The statute has more than 150 sections and amends more than a dozen Federal laws. It significantly extends the authority of the U.S. government to gather intelligence and investigate anyone suspected of terrorism.

In the aftermath of 9-11, critics charged that Federal officials had failed to coordinate information they had gathered about terrorist groups, such as al Qaeda. The new statute was intended to improve communication between Federal agencies such as the Central Intelligence Agency (CIA) and the Federal Bureau of Investigation (FBI) by improving their ability to investigate and prevent acts of terrorism.

Some Civil Libertarians expressed concern that the Patriot Act threatened individual privacy rights, while others expressed concern about First Amendment issues.[53]

Some persons became concerned that the Federal government could be listening to their cell phone and other conversations, recording their words and checking their financial information and Internet activities.

Groups like the American Civil Liberties Union, the American Library Association and American Booksellers Association objected to the gathering of personal information. The Act authorized government to monitor one's book store purchases and library records. Many ACLU activists pointed out that, for the first time in American history, the Federal government could open a suspect's mail.

To some on the political left, supporters of the Patriot Act were enemies of civil liberties, particularly the right to privacy.

To those on the political right, opponents of the Patriot Act were guilty of giving aid and comfort to Islamic Terrorists.

One of the major problems in the heated debate as Congress voted to renew the Act appeared to be to keep the debate civil.

1. *"The Right To Privacy,"* 4 Harvard Law Review, 193, 15 December (1890)

2. *Annals of Congress,* Vol. I (Washington, D.C.: Gales and Seaton, 1834), p. 456

3. *Ibid.* at p. 452

4. Friendly and Elliott, *The Constitution: That Delicate Balance, op. cit.*, p. 196

5. *Griswold v. Connecticut,* 381 U.S. 479 (1965) at pp. 484-6

6. *Ibid.* at pp. 486-99

7. *Ibid.* at pp. 509-10

8. *Ibid.* at p. 513

9. *Ibid.* at p. 522

10. *Ibid.* at p. 527

11. *Eisenstadt v. Baird,* 405 U.S. 38 (1972). The Brennan dissent may be found on pp. 440-455.

12. *Ibid.* at p. 453

13. *Ibid.* at p. 472

14. For a discussion of the abortion referendum campaign in Michigan, see John Noonan, *A Private Choice: Abortion in America in the Seventies* (New York: The Free Press, 1979).

15. For a detailed, "inside" and naturally biased account of *Roe v. Wade,* see Sarah Weddington, *A Question of Choice* (New York: G. P. Putnam's Sons, 1992). This valuable source details Weddington's personal experience with abortion, legal strategy and post-*Roe* updates.

16. For a detailed account of the internal divisions within the Court over Blackmun's opinion, based largely on "leaks" from Supreme Court law clerks, see Bob Woodward and Scott Armstrong, *The Brethern* (New York: Simon and Schuster, 1979). pp. 165-89 and 229-40.

17. *Roe v. Wade,* 410 U.S. 113 (1973). The text of Blackmun's opinion may be found on pp. 116-67.

18. *Ibid.* at pp. 221-3

19. For a discussion of some of the thinking of competing interest groups in the abortion debate, see Frederick S. Jaffe, Barbara L. Lindheim and Philip R. Lee, *Abortion Politics: Private Morality and Public Policy* (New York: McGraw-Hill, 1981).

20. *Harris v. McRae,* 448 U.S. 297 (1980). Stewart's opinion may be found on pp. 300-27.

21. *Ibid.* at pp. 333-4

22. See *Hodgson v. Minnesota,* 497 U.S. 417 (1990) and *Ohio v. Akron Center for Reproductive Health,* 497 U.S. 502 (1990).

23. See Robert Bork, *The Tempting of America: The Political Seduction of the Law,* (New York: The Free Press, 1990), pp. 111-2.

24. *Ibid.*

25. 547 U.S.— (2006)

26. *National Organization for Women, Inc. v. Scheidler,* 510 U.S. 249 (1994)

27. *National Organization for Women v. Scheidler,* 537 U.S. 393 (2003)

28. *Stanley v. Georgia,* 394 U.S. 557 (1969)

29. *Bowers v. Hardwick,* 478 U.S. 186 (1986). See pp. 187-96 for text of White's opinion.

30. *Ibid.* at pp. 196-7

31. *Ibid.* at p. 199

32. *The Cincinnati Enquirer,* February 2, 2004

33. *Lawrence v. Texas,* 539 U.S. 558 (2003). Justice Kennedy's opinion may be found on pp. 562-579.

34. *Ibid.* at pp. 579-585

35. *Ibid.* at pp. 586-605

36. *Ibid.* at pages 605-6

37. *Detroit Free Press,* May 8, 2008

38. *Cruzan, By Her Parents and Co-Guardians, Cruzan et ux v. Director, Missouri Dept. of Public Health, 497 U.S.261 (1990). Preliminary print.* Rehnquist's opinion is found on pp. 265-287.

39. *Ibid.* at pp. 301-30

40. These four areas were developed by Dean William L. Prosser, University of Southern California Law School, an authority on torts. Prosser concluded that invasion of privacy was not a single tort, but a complex of four. Restatement of Torts, 3rd ed., 1964, Vol. 3, p. 832).

41. For a good discussion of privacy and the press, see Holsinger, *Media Law op. cit.,* pp. 194-245.

42. *Galella v. Onassis,* 353 F. Supp. 196 (S.D., N.Y. 1972). While Mrs. Onassis took the high (judicial) road, actor Marlon Brando took the low road of physical force and broke Galella's jaw when the photographer invaded his privacy.

43. *Dietemann v. Time, Inc.,* 284 F. Supp. 425 (C.D. Calif. 1968), 449 F. 2d 245 (9th Cir. 1971)

44. *Ibid.*

45. *Sidis v. F.R. Publishing Corp.,* 113 F.2d 806 (2d Cir. 1940)

46. *Cantrell v. Forest City Publishing Company,* 419 U.S. 245 (1974)

47. *Hustler Magazine v. Falwell,* 485 U.S. 46 (1988)

48. *Zacchini v. Scripps Howard Broadcasting,* 433 U.S. 562 (1977)

49. See Holsinger, *Supra,* Note 32

50. *Cox Broadcasting Corp. v. Cohn,* 420 U.S. 469 (1975)

51. "Ford's Hero's Mother has Misgivings," *Detroit News,* September 26, 1975

52. H. Eugene Goodwin, *Groping for Ethics in Journalism,* 2nd ed. (Ames: Iowa State University Press, 1987), pp. 246-8

53. See Nat Hentoff, *The War on the Bill of Rights-and the Gathering Resistance.* New York: Seven Stories Press, 2003

CHAPTER IV: TOWARD EQUAL PROTECTION OF THE LAWS

"We hold these truths to be self-evident, that all men are created equal, that they are endowed by their Creator with certain unalienable Rights, that among these are Life, Liberty and the pursuit of Happiness."

—Declaration of Independence, 1776

When Thomas Jefferson composed these beautiful words in the American Declaration of Independence, proclaiming the equality of man, he reflected the Judeao-Christian ethic. Religious philosophers and theologians had embraced the concept that every human being is created in the image of God, has an immortal soul or spirit and is, therefore, equally precious in the eyes of the Creator. Protesting against the abuse of power by King George III and the British Parliament, Jefferson articulated the philosophy of natural rights. John Locke (1632-1704), the great English philosopher, had a profound impact on Jefferson through his classic work, *Two Treatises of Government.* Locke philosophized about a "state of nature" in which individuals lived before governments existed. He developed the theory that men came together and formed a **social contract** and a government which was to be limited, both in its purpose and extent.

Rights were not given by governments, Locke and Jefferson agreed. If governments could confer rights, then logically they could take them away. Rather, rights were God-given. Mere mortals who ran governments could not infringe on people's "natural rights."

Locke developed these arguments in justifying the **Glorious Revolution of 1688** in England. If one wishes to be polite, one might say that Jefferson was intellectually indebted to Locke for the arguments contained in the Declaration of Independence. If one wishes to be blunt, one might say that Jefferson was guilty of blatant plagiarism.

As the late political philosopher William Ebenstein expressed it:[1]

Above all, Locke's defense of the right to rebel seemed to the makers of the American Revolution eminently reasonable. Thomas Jefferson, in many respects a Lockean rationalist and lover of freedom and toleration, expressed the American version of Locke's theory of rebellion in the classical phrase that the '...tree of liberty must be refreshed from time to time with the blood of patriots and tyrants.' The right to rebel remains the great, perhaps the greatest, tradition of British and American politics. Rebelliousness, too, can paradoxically, grow into tradition: the tradition of the dignity of man and of his unbreakable spirit.

But the Lockean-Jeffersonian concept of equality of man did not, in 1776, include slaves, women or Native Americans. Clearly they were not considered equal in the late 18th Century.

EQUALITY IN THEORY AND IN REALITY

The idea of human rights and human equality is one to which many Americans pay lip service. Their actual behavior may be something else entirely. Historically, the rights proclaimed by Jefferson in the Declaration of Independence and those set forth in the U.S. Constitution have not been enjoyed equally by all Americans.

For various minority groups, equality remains only a future hope. In the America of the early 21st Century, for example, the infant mortality rate for Black children is more than double that of white children. The rate of illegitimate births among Black teenagers is skyrocketing. Perhaps most shocking, if anything shocks the media-desensitized American psyche, is that the leading cause of death among young Black males is homicide.[2]

The rate of Black unemployment historically has been about twice that of white America. Medium income of Black families is about two-thirds that of white families. These and other such statistics have been provided by the U.S. Bureau of Labor Statistics and the U.S. Census Bureau.[3]

Therefore, one of the perennial problems facing America (and other societies) is Equality Under Law. Perhaps the gap between what Americans say they believe and how they actually behave is greater here than in any other area.

The value of equality was not a part of the original Constitution. If viewed from a global perspective, "equality" in colonial America was relatively advanced for that era of history. Yet early Americans discriminated in ways which would horrify many of their descendants today. The most obvious denial of equality was found in the institution of slavery.

The Declaration of Independence may have proclaimed the equality of all men, but the enslavement of Africans was to be politically accepted, if not universally supported. In part, this was because of regional differences among delegates to the Constitutional Convention.

Is The Constitution a "Racist" Document?

When the late Supreme Court Justice Thurgood Marshall referred to the original (unamended) Constitution as a "racist document," he had in mind such things as the three-fifths compromise. Delegates agreed, in considering Article I, that a slave would count as three-fifths of a "person" for representation purposes in the U.S. House of Representatives.

Southern states wanted slaves counted just like everyone else, although they certainly did not want to treat them that way. Abolitionists wanted to exclude slaves from the count. Like many other compromises, this one was not particularly logical. But it did make possible the ratification of the new Constitution.

The institution of slavery also won constitutional protection in an Article I provision which prohibited the Federal government from restricting importation of slaves until 1808. Black Americans, like Justice Marshall, do not forget history.

Abraham Lincoln, often called "The Great Emancipator," was hardly an enthusiastic abolitionist. In 1858, long before racial equality became a professed aim of the Union cause in the Civil War, Lincoln elaborated his views:[4]

I will say that I am not, nor ever have been in favor of bringing about in any way the social and political equality of the white and black races—that I am not nor ever have been in favor of making voters or jurors of Negroes, nor of qualifying them to hold office, nor to intermarry with white people, and I will say in addition to this that there is a physical difference between the black and the white races which I believe will forever forbid the two races living together on terms of social and political equality. And inasmuch as they cannot so live, while they do remain together there must be the position of superior and inferior, and I as much as any other man am in favor of having the superior position assigned to the white race.

Post-Civil War Amendments

The Reconstruction Era Amendments (13-14-15), were ratified shortly after the Civil War when Radical Republicans took political control of both the White House and the Congress. They insisted upon three new constitutional amendments which would drastically change the concept of civil rights in the U.S.

The 13th Amendment, ratified on December 18, 1865, specifies: *"Neither slavery nor involuntary servitude, except as punishment for crime whereof the party shall have been duly convicted, shall exist within the United States, or any place subject to their jurisdiction."* There have been few arguments about the 13th Amendment other than those involving the military draft. The Court has ruled that this does not involve "involuntary servitude," as some young men have claimed.

The 14th Amendment, ratified on July 28, 1868, is long, complex and a major source of employment for lawyers who have been arguing about its meaning for more than 140 years. The constitutional foundation of equality, it provides in part that *"no state shall ...deny to any person within its jurisdiction the equal protection of the laws."*

The 14th Amendment effectively overturned the infamous **Dred Scott Decision**. Scott was a slave who had lived in the north for four years. Antislavery forces brought his case to the U.S. Supreme Court, arguing that he had become a free man because he had lived on free soil. But, in order to bring suit, Scott first had to establish that he was a citizen.

This verdict, U.S. historians agree, made the Civil War virtually inevitable. It is also considered by constitutional lawyers to be the worst decision of Chief Justice Roger B. Taney's Court. Taney ruled that the Constitution did not include Blacks as part of the sovereign people of the United States. The Court also declared the Missouri Compromise unconstitutional, the first time since *Marbury v. Madison* (1803) that the Court had nullified an act of Congress.

He wrote:[5]

> Negroes were not intended to be included under the word 'citizen' in the Constitution, and can therefore claim none of the rights and privileges which the instrument provides for and secures to citizens of the United States. On the contrary, they were at that time considered as a subordinate and inferior class of beings, who had been subjugated by the dominant race, and whether emancipated or not, yet remained subject to their authority, and had no rights or privileges but such as those who held the power and the government might choose to grant them.

The primary purpose of the 14th Amendment was to protect the rights of the newly freed slaves. But American history shows that this goal was not to be achieved easily. Although the **Equal Protection Clause** has been the legal pillar for assaults on racial discrimination, it has failed to change the hearts and minds of many individuals.

The 15th Amendment, ratified on March 30, 1870, specifies that *"the rights of citizens of the United States to vote shall not be denied or abridged by the United States or by any State on account of race, color, or previous condition of servitude."*

Although the intent of the Amendment was to enfranchise the Black male, it did so only as long as Union troops occupied the South. When President Rutherford B. Hayes withdrew the Union Army from the states of the Old Confederacy, southerners found many ways to circumvent the amendment. The era gave birth to **poll taxes, literacy and**

understanding tests, white primaries, grandfather clauses, good-character tests and other devices to prevent Black male voting.

One might well consider the impact of these measures by comparing Black voting before and after the Union Army withdrew from the south. In 1896, for example, some 130,334 Blacks were registered to vote in Louisiana. In 1904, the number was 1342![6]

At the end of World War II, the Supreme Court struck down these measures. The "white primary" was the first to die. It was based on the idea that political parties are private organizations, like country clubs. They could, therefore, accept or exclude individuals as they wished. The southern states concluded that political parties, in holding primary elections, were private organizations. This, their logic dictated, was not discriminatory **"state action,"** precluded by the Constitution.

The "white primary" thrived in the era of the **"Solid South."** The only election that mattered then was the Democratic primary. Republicans usually did not bother to seek nomination for public office because they had no chance in the general election. If Blacks could not vote in the Democratic Party primary, they had no effective voice in determining who their public officials would be. In *Smith v. Allwright,* 321 U.S. 649 (1944), the U.S. Supreme Court ruled:[7]

> When primaries become a part of the machinery for choosing officials...the same tests to determine the character of discrimination...would be applied to the primary as are applied to the general election.

The Court also enjoined good-character tests and the understanding clause in *U.S. v. Mississippi*, 380 U.S. 128 (1965) and *Louisiana v. U.S.* 380 U.S. 145 (1965). It was not until the period after enactment of the **Voting Rights Act of 1965** that "Black Power" became a reality in the South.

But what does racial equality mean? What has it meant in the past? Is it true, as the first Justice John Marshall Harlan once said, that the U.S. Constitution is "color-blind?"

19th Century Civil Rights Laws

The Reconstruction Era Congress demanded that the states of the Old Confederacy ratify the 13th, 14th and 15th Amendments before it would seat their ousted representatives. It also enacted a series of Civil Rights Acts between 1865-77, all designed to enforce the amendments.

The first of these measures, vetoed by President Andrew Johnson, was passed in 1866. Anyone born in the U.S. was made a citizen, and Blacks were given full equality under law. The President was authorized to use military force to back the law. Some opponents argued that the law was unconstitutional, but the adoption of the 14th Amendment made that issue a **moot question.**

Congress passed six other measures, one of the most important of which was the **Enforcement Act of 1870.** It provided criminal penalties for interfering with the right to vote as protected by the 15th Amendment or the **Civil Rights Act of 1866.**

The **Anti-Ku Klux Klan Act** of 1872 made it a Federal crime to deprive any person of rights, privileges and immunities secured by the Constitution or Federal law.

The **Second Civil Rights Act,** passed in 1875, prohibited racial segregation in hotels, theaters and public transportation.

But in the **Civil Rights Cases of 1883,** the U.S. Supreme Court declared the statute unconstitutional. It ruled that the 14th Amendment could forbid only discriminatory **state action,** not that of private individuals or business corporations. In essence, the Court ruled that Congress had **no power over individual acts** of racial discrimination.

American law has undergone a major transformation in the "equal protection" area. Shortly after the Civil War, social customs and differences in economic status were enough to maintain a distance between white and colored persons. As Professor C. Vann Woodward points out in his classic book, *The Strange Career of Jim Crow,* "...southern states and communities gradually began to enact laws requiring racial segregation in schools, theatres, public transportation and in places of public accommodations."

MAJOR LANDMARK: THE PLESSY DOCTRINE:

Plessy v. Ferguson came before the U.S. Supreme Court in 1896. Six years earlier, Louisiana had enacted a "Jim Crow" law, requiring racial segregation on passenger trains. Attacks on the law had partially succeeded as the Louisiana Supreme Court invalidated that part of the statute which applied to passengers crossing state lines. Only Congress, under the U.S. Constitution, is empowered to regulate interstate commerce, the Court ruled. But what about travel that is strictly intrastate?

Homer Adolph Plessy, who described himself as "...of seven-eighths Caucasian and one-eighth African blood," purchased a ticket in New Orleans for travel to Covington, La., on the East Louisiana Railroad. He sat in the car reserved for white passengers. When the conductor demanded that Plessy move into the Black car, he refused. Subsequently, he was arrested, jailed, tried and convicted.

His conviction was upheld by all Louisiana appellate courts and was taken to the U.S. Supreme Court, which also upheld the law. The Court opinion, written by Justice Henry B. Brown of Michigan, said:[8]

> This case turns upon the constitutionality of an act of the General Assembly of the State of Louisiana passed in 1890, providing for separate railway carriages for the white and colored races.
>
> By the 14th Amendment, all persons born or naturalized in the United States, and subject to the jurisdiction thereof, are made citizens of the United States and of the State wherein they reside; and the States are forbidden from making or enforcing any law which shall abridge the privileges or immunities of citizens of the United States, or shall deprive any person of life, liberty or property without due process of law, or deny to any person within their jurisdiction the equal protection of the laws.
>
> The object of the amendment was undoubtedly to enforce the absolute equality of the two races before the law, but in the nature of things it could not have been intended to abolish distinctions based upon color, or to enforce social, as distinguished from political, equality or a commingling of the two races on terms unsatisfactory to either. Laws permitting, and even requiring, their separation in places where they are liable to be brought into contact do not necessarily imply the inferiority of either race to the other, and have been generally, if not universally, recognized as within the competency of the state legislatures in the exercise of their police power. The most common instance of this is connected with the

211

establishment of separate schools for white and colored children, which has been held to be a valid exercise of the legislative power even by courts of States where the political rights of the colored race have been longest and most earnestly enforced.

Laws forbidding the intermarriage of the two races may be said in a technical sense to interfere with freedom of contract, and yet have been universally recognized as within the police power of the State.

The distinction between laws interfering with the political equality of the Negro and those requiring the separation of the two races in schools, theatres and railway carriages has been frequently drawn by this court.

Thus, in *Strauder v. West Virginia* (1880), it was held that a law of West Virginia limiting to white male persons, 21 years of age and citizens of the State, the right to sit upon juries, was a discrimination which implied a legal inferiority in civil society, which lessened the security of the right of the colored race, and was a step toward reducing them to a condition of servility. Indeed, the right of a colored man that, in the selection of jurors to pass upon his life, liberty and property, there shall be no exclusion of his race, and no discrimination against them because of color, has been asserted in a number of cases.

So far, then, as a conflict with the 14th Amendment is concerned, the case reduces itself to the question whether the Statute of Louisiana is a reasonable regulation, and with respect to this, there must necessarily be a large discretion on the part of the legislature. In determining the question of reasonableness, it is at liberty to act with reference to the established usages, customs and traditions of the people, and with a view to the promotion of their comfort, and the preservation of the public peace and good order. Gauged by this standard, we cannot say that a law which authorizes or even requires the separation of the two races in public conveyances is unreasonable, or more obnoxious to the 14th Amendment than the acts of Congress requiring separate schools for colored children in the District of Columbia, the constitutionality of which does not seem to have been questioned, or the corresponding acts of state legislatures.

We consider the underlying fallacy of the plaintiff's argument to consist in the assumption that the enforced separation of the two races stamps the colored race with a badge of inferiority. If this be so, it is not by reason of anything found in the act, but solely because the colored race chooses to put that construction upon it. The argument necessarily assumes that if, as has been more than once the case, and is not unlikely to be so again, the colored race should become the dominant power in the state legislature, and should enact a law in precisely similar terms, it would thereby relegate the white race to an inferior position. We imagine that the white race, at least, would not acquiesce in this assumption. The argument also assumes that social prejudices may be overcome by legislation, and that equal rights cannot be secured to the Negro except by an enforced commingling of the two races. We cannot accept this proposition. If the two races are to meet upon terms of social equality, it must be the result of natural affinities, a mutual appreciation of each other's merits and a voluntary consent of individuals. Legislation is powerless to eradicate racial instincts or to abolish distinctions based upon physical differences, and the attempt to do so can only result in accentuating the difficulties of the present situation. If the civil and political rights of both races be equal, one cannot be inferior to the other civilly or politically. If one race be inferior to the other socially, the Constitution of the United States cannot put them upon the same plane.

Justice Harlan Dissents

Only one member of the Court dissented, but it was a historic dissent, penned by Associate Justice John Marshall Harlan, a former slaveholder from Kentucky and grandfather of a later Justice Harlan. Justice Harlan, shocked by the activities of the Ku Klux Klan, became a convert to the cause of civil rights for Blacks. He wrote in part:[9]

> Our Constitution is color-blind, and neither knows nor tolerates classes among citizens. The thin disguise of equal accommodations for passengers in railroad coaches will not mislead anyone, nor atone for the wrong this day done.
> In my opinion, the judgment this day rendered will, in time, prove to be quite as pernicious as the decision made by this tribunal in the Dred Scott case.
> I am of the opinion that the statute of Louisiana is inconsistent with the personal liberty of citizens, white and black, in that State, and hostile to both the spirit and letter of the Constitution of the United States. If laws of like character should be enacted in the several States of the Union, the effect would be in the highest degree mischievous. Slavery, as an institution tolerated by law, would, it is true, have disappeared from our country, but there would remain a power in the States, by sinister legislation, to interfere with the full enjoyment of the blessings of freedom; to regulate civil rights, common to all citizens, upon the basis of race; and to place in a condition of legal inferiority a large body of American citizens, now constituting a part of the political community called the People of the United States, for whom, and by whom, through representatives, our government is administered. Such a system is inconsistent with the guarantee given by the Constitution to each State of a republican form of government, and may be stricken down by Congressional action, or by the courts in the discharge of their solemn duty to maintain the supreme law of the land, anything in the constitution or laws of any State to the contrary notwithstanding.

EROSION OF THE PLESSY DOCTRINE

Out of Homer Plessy's case came the **doctrine of "separate but equal,"** a theory on which the southern states erected an elaborate edifice of segregation and white supremacy. Although the **Plessy Doctrine** was under legal attack for many years, the U.S. Supreme Court did not reverse this dogma overnight. Rather, the doctrine went through a process of erosion and "separate but equal" was not completely overturned until 1954.[10]

This may be illustrated by examining the area of college and university admissions policy in those states which required segregated classrooms.

The U.S. Supreme Court ruled in *Missouri ex. rel. Gaines v. Canada*, 305 U.S. 237 (1938), that the state had violated the 14th Amendment's "Equal Protection" Clause by refusing to admit Lloyd Gaines, a young Black man, to the University of Missouri Law School.

McLaurin was given a separate desk in the library and a separate table in the cafeteria, both with "colored" signs hung on them. A rail surrounded the section of the classroom where McLaurin sat. On it was a sign, "Reserved for Colored."

McLaurin filed a motion with the U.S. District Court to remove these conditions. The court, however, held that such treatment did not violate the 14th Amendment and denied the motion. The case then was appealed to the U.S. Supreme Court, which ruled that Oklahoma's system violated the 14th Amendment's Equal Protection Clause. Speaking for a unanimous Court, Chief Justice Vinson wrote:[12]

> These restrictions were obviously imposed in order to comply, as nearly as could be, with the statutory requirements of Oklahoma. But they signify that the State, in administering the facilities it affords for professional and graduate study, sets McLaurin apart from the other students. The result is that appellant is handicapped in his pursuit of effective graduate instruction. Such restrictions impair and inhibit his ability to study, to engage in discussions and exchange views with other students, and, in general, to learn his profession.

> Our society grows increasingly complex and our need for trained leaders increases correspondingly. Appellant's case represents, perhaps, the epitome of that need, for he is attempting to obtain an advanced degree in education, to become, by definition, a leader and trainer of others. Those who will come under his guidance and influence must be directly affected by the education he receives. Their own education and development will necessarily suffer to the extent that his training is unequal to that of his classmates. State imposed restrictions which produce such inequalities cannot be sustained.

> It may be argued that appellant will be in no better position when these restrictions are removed, for he may still be set apart by his fellow students. This, we think, is irrelevant. There is a vast difference—a Constitutional difference— between restrictions imposed by the state which prohibit the intellectual commingling of students and the refusals of individuals to commingle where the state presents no such bar. The removal of the state restrictions will not necessarily abate individual and group predilections, prejudices and choices. But at the very least, the state will not be depriving appellant of the opportunity to secure acceptance by his fellow students on his own merits.

> We conclude that the conditions under which this appellant is required to receive his education deprive him of his personal and present right to the equal protection of the laws. We hold that, under these circumstances, the 14th Amendment precludes differences in treatment by the state based upon race. Appellant, having been admitted to a state-supported graduate school, must receive the same treatment at the hands of the state as students of other races.

THE WARREN COURT AND THE BROWN DECISION

The end of "separate but equal" came in May, 1954, in *Brown v. Topeka, Kansas, Board of Education*. Linda Brown, an eight-year-old Black child, wanted to be admitted to the city's public schools on an integrated basis. Her father, Oliver Brown, a minister, lived in a predominately white neighborhood only seven blocks from the Sumner Elementary School. Linda's family did not want her to attend the all-Black Monroe Elementary School,

21 blocks from home and involving a daily 7:40 a.m. bus trip, which they regarded as dangerous. The bus arrived at 8:30 a.m., but the school did not open until 9 a.m.

Linda frequently had to wait outside in the cold before the building opened. After classes, on her way home, she had to walk past a dangerous railroad intersection.

Sumner Elementary School was, Oliver Brown believed, a good one, and he wanted his daughter to get an integrated education. With help from the National Association for the Advancement of Colored People (NAACP), the Browns filed suit. They argued that the segregated school system violated their child's rights under the 14th Amendment's Equal Protection Clause. Thurgood Marshall, later to become the first Black ever to serve on the U.S. Supreme Court, represented Linda Brown.

Brown was considered with a number of similar cases from South Carolina, Virginia and Delaware. They were among 17 states and the District of Columbia, all of which legally required segregated schools.

The cases originally were argued before the Vinson Court in December, 1952. In June of that year, the Court ordered that the cases be reargued in December, 1953, with special emphasis to be placed on a series of questions dealing with the history and meaning of the 14th Amendment.

The delay gave new Chief Justice Earl Warren, appointed by recently-elected President Eisenhower, a chance to participate fully in the decision. Warren, history informs us, played a monumental role in this case. He worked hard behind the scenes for Court unity and eventually got a 9-0 vote. He wrote the opinion himself, handed down on May 17, 1954. It was the historic day that segregated public schools in the U.S. met their legal death.[13]

Before the Court was the critical question: Does segregation of children in public schools solely on the basis of race, even though other factors may be equal, deprive children of the minority groups of equal education opportunity? The Warren Court's answer was a resounding yes. Southerners and other segregationists demanded that the Chief Justice be impeached.

Speaking for the Court, Chief Justice Warren wrote:[14]

> In each of these cases, minors of the Negro race, through their legal representatives, seek the aid of the courts in obtaining admission to the public schools of their community on a nonsegregated basis. In each instance, they had been denied admission to schools attended by white children under laws requiring or permitting segregation according to race. This segregation was alleged to deprive the plaintiffs of the equal protection of the laws under the 14th Amendment.

> The plaintiffs contend that segregated public schools are not 'equal' and cannot be made 'equal' and that, hence, they are deprived of the equal protection of the laws. Because of the obvious importance of the question presented, the Court took jurisdiction. Argument was heard in the 1952 term, and reargument was heard this Term on certain questions propounded by the Court.

> Reargument was largely devoted to the circumstances surrounding the adoption of the 14th Amendment in 1868. It covered exhaustive consideration of the Amendment in Congress, ratification by the states, then-existing practices in racial segregation, and the views of proponents and opponents of the Amendment. This discussion and our own investigation convinces us that, although these sources cast some light, it is not enough to resolve the problem with which we are faced. At best, they are inconclusive.

An additional reason for the inconclusive nature of the Amendment's history, with respect to segregated schools, is the status of public education at that time. In the South, the movement toward free common schools, supported by general taxation, had not yet taken hold. Education of white children was largely in the hands of private groups. Education of Negroes was forbidden by law in some states. Today, in contrast, many Negroes have achieved outstanding success in the arts and sciences, as well as in the business and professional world.

It is true that public school education at the time of the Amendment had advanced further in the North, but the effect of the Amendment on Northern States was generally ignored in the congressional debates. Even in the North, the conditions of public education did not approximate those existing today. The curriculum was usually rudimentary; ungraded schools were common in rural areas; the school term was but three months a year in many states; and compulsory school attendance was virtually unknown. As a consequence, it is not surprising that there should be so little in the history of the 14th Amendment relating to its intended effect on public education.

In the first cases in this Court construing the 14th Amendment, decided shortly after its adoption, the Court interpreted it as proscribing all state-imposed discriminations against the Negro race. The doctrine of 'separate but equal' did not make its appearance in this Court until 1896 in the case of *Plessy v. Ferguson*, involving not education but transportation. American courts have since labored with the doctrine for over half a century.

Here, unlike *Sweatt v. Painter*, there are findings below that the Negro and white schools involved have been equalized, or are being equalized, with respect to buildings, curricula, qualifications and salaries of teachers and other 'tangible' factors. Our decision, therefore, cannot turn on merely a comparison of these tangible factors in the Negro and white schools involved in each of the cases. We must look instead to the effect of segregation itself on public education.

In approaching this problem, we cannot turn the clock back to 1868 when the Amendment was adopted, or even to 1896 when *Plessy v. Ferguson* was written. We must consider public education in the light of its full development and its present place in American life throughout the Nation. Only in this way can it be determined if segregation in public schools deprives the plaintiffs of the equal protection of the laws.

Today education is perhaps the most important function of state and local governments. Compulsory school attendance laws and great expenditures for education both demonstrate our recognition of the importance of education to our democratic society. It is required in the performance of our most basic public responsibilities, even service in the armed forces. It is the very foundation of good citizenship. Today it is a principal instrument in awakening the child to cultural values, in helping him to adjust normally to his environment. In these days, it is doubtful that any child may reasonably be expected to succeed in life if he is denied the opportunity of an education. Such an opportunity, where the state has undertaken to provide it, is a right which must be made available to all on equal terms.

We come then to the question presented: does segregation of children in public schools solely on the basis of race, even though the physical facilities and other 'tangible' factors may be equal, deprive the children of the minority group of equal educational opportunities? We believe that it does.

In *Sweatt v. Painter,* in finding that a segregated law school of Negroes could not provide them equal educational opportunities, this Court relied in large part on those qualities which are incapable of objective measurement but which make for greatness in a law school. In *McLaurin v. Oklahoma State Regents,* the Court, in requiring that a Negro admitted to a white graduate school be treated like all other students, again resorted to intangible considerations, saying '...his ability to study, to engage in discussions and exchange views with other students, and, in general, to learn his profession.' Such considerations apply with added force to children in grade and high schools. To separate them from others of similar age and qualifications solely because of their race generates a feeling of inferiority as to their status in the community that may affect their hearts and minds in a way unlikely ever to be undone. Whatever may have been the extent of psychological knowledge at the time of *Plessy v. Ferguson,* this finding is amply supported by modern authority. Any language in *Plessy v. Ferguson* contrary to this finding is rejected.

We conclude that in the field of public education, the doctrine of 'separate but equal' has no place. Separate educational facilities are inherently unequal. Therefore, we hold that the plaintiffs and others similarly situated for whom the actions have been brought are, by reason of the segregation complained of, deprived of the equal protection of the laws guaranteed by the 14th Amendment.

REACTION TO BROWN

It was, of course, one thing to rule that segregated public schools were unconstitutional. It was quite another matter to desegregate them. The Court knew that there would be public resistance to the ruling, particularly in the southern and border states. The justices also knew that they had no formal enforcement powers.

Recognizing the enormity of the problem, the Court, a year later, in what is known as *Brown II,* ordered school districts practicing segregation to desegregate "with all deliberate speed." There was, critics complained, much deliberation and little speed over the next 20 years.

In the South, reaction to *Brown* varied. Probably most citizens, while angered by the decision, were willing to accept it. They were law-abiding citizens. Some others were not and immediately dug up the ghost of John C. Calhoun. Constitutional nonsense filled the air. Some members of Congress even argued that states should be able to "interpose" their own judgment for that of the U.S. Supreme Court or to nullify its verdict. Most constitutional scholars had supposed that the **doctrines of nullification and interposition** were buried at the end of the Civil War.[15]

U.S. Sen. Harry Byrd, (D., Va.,) urged the South to adopt a policy of "interposition" of its authority against alleged violation of the Constitution by the U.S. Supreme Court. **Virginia even tried for a time to abolish public schools rather than to integrate them.**

Six other southern states—Alabama, Georgia, Mississippi, North Carolina, South Carolina and Louisiana—adopted Virginia's interposition plan. Alabama called the Brown decision "null, void and of no effect." Mississippi said that it was "unconstitutional and of no lawful effect," and created a State Sovereignty Committee.[16]

The Southern Manifesto

Some 96 southern congressmen signed a "Southern Manifesto," pledging to take all lawful steps to resist the Court's ruling. Among the signers was Sen. Sam Ervin (D., N.C.), later a hero of Liberals during the Nixon era Watergate hearings. President Eisenhower pledged to enforce the law but refused to use his enormous influence to support the ruling. Privately, he disagreed with the decision. He often said, "You cannot change people's hearts merely by law."

The Herculean task of attempting to desegregate southern and border state public schools was made the responsibility of 58 Federal District and Court of Appeals judges. Many of them, like Eisenhower, personally opposed *Brown*. They knew that *Brown* meant a social revolution.

Desegregation was slow and uneven, particularly in the Confederate states where, as noted, the Virginia legislature closed public schools, and governors fought *Brown*.

Little Rock, 1957

In September, 1957, President Eisenhower was challenged by Gov. Orval E. Faubus (D., Ark.), who, defying Federal court orders, called out the National Guard to prevent nine Black students from entering all-white Little Rock Central High School.

Eisenhower, who had said two months before the crisis that he could not "imagine any set of circumstances that would ever induce me to send Federal troops," ordered 1000 U.S. paratroopers to Little Rock to enforce the law. He also federalized 10,000 Arkansas national guardsmen.[17]

Faubus made political capital of the situation. In 1958-59, he closed down Little Rock's public schools for the academic year. He became a southern hero and was constantly re-elected, serving six terms as chief executive of his state.

Civil Rights in the Eisenhower Era

In 1957, Congress enacted the first civil rights legislation since the Reconstruction Era. Designed primarily to support Black voting rights, its principal provision authorized the Justice Department to seek court injunctions against any denial of voting rights. It also authorized criminal prosecution for violations of an injunction.

The act established a Civil Rights Division within the Justice Department, headed by an assistant attorney general. Finally, it created a bipartisan **Civil Rights Commission** to investigate civil rights violations and to recommend legislation. Among those who chaired the Commission were two widely-known university presidents, the late **John Hannah of Michigan State** and Fr. Theodore Hesburg of Notre Dame.

Dr. Hannah, in a November, 1965, speech, reflected the need for people to deal with civil rights problems at home, rather than in Washington. He said: "If my years of experience have taught me one thing, it is that problems of civil rights will be solved, not by national programs, but by local programs; not by Federal action, but by community action."

Fr. Hesburg considered civil rights essentially a moral issue. Ultimately, he believed, a solution to the problem of civil rights would be found in the minds and hearts of men and women of good will, rather than in acts of Congress or executive orders from the President. But, he conceded, the law did encourage people of good will to work to remove the barriers of discrimination.[18]

The **Civil Rights Act of 1960** was passed during a presidential election year in response to Southern racial turmoil, described above. It authorized Federal courts to appoint referees to help Blacks to register. This would follow a voter-denial conviction under the **1957 Civil Rights Act,** and judicial determination that there was a "pattern or practice" of discrimination against qualified voters.

Ole Miss, 1962

President Kennedy sent U.S. marshals to Oxford, Miss., in September, 1962, to enforce a court order admitting James Meredith to University of Mississippi. Meredith, 29, had served for nine years in the U.S. Air Force. While in service, he took correspondence courses and later attended Black Jackson State College. Meredith, however, wanted to do something more for his people. Had his only concern been for his education or safety, he could have enrolled at any number of northern universities, most of which, in 1962, were more creditable academically than Mississippi.

Gov. Ross Barnett physically blocked Meredith's registration on September 25, and Lt. Gov. Paul Johnson did the same thing the next day. On October 1, U.S. marshals installed Meredith in a dormitory and President Kennedy urged compliance. But on Monday, Oct. 2, Federal officials were assaulted by armed mobs from off-campus who aided students opposed to integration. When dawn came, two men were killed, one of them a French reporter, Paul Guihard, covering the story for Agence France-Presse. Some 29 others were wounded by gunfire and 375 were injured.

An angry President Kennedy ordered Army Secretary Cyrus Vance to send 16,000 troops to the campus area to restore peace and to protect Meredith. Meredith then was registered as a senior transfer student and spent the entire year under constant protection of 300 Federal authorities. In June, 1963, he became the first Black graduate of Mississippi and achieved a major victory for the cause of integration in the South.[19]

Alabama, Summer, 1963

Gov. George C. Wallace stood in the doorway of University of Alabama during the summer of 1963, blocking entry of James Hood and Vivian Malone, two Black students ordered admitted to the university by the courts. Wallace, inaugurated in January, 1963, had said, "I draw the line in the dust and toss the gauntlet before the feet of tyranny and I say segregation now, segregation tomorrow, segregation forever."[20]

Kennedy federalized the Alabama National Guard and ordered it to enforce the court order. Curiously, perhaps, Hood, who dropped out of school a few months later, said on national television early in 1976 that he might support Wallace for President if he were running against Gerald Ford. Hood then was a police official in Detroit.

Miss Malone stuck it out and graduated. She became a U.S. government employee in Georgia and said, in 1976, that she would, under no circumstances, vote for Wallace.

Earlier, in February, 1956, the Supreme Court had ordered Alabama to admit Autherine Lucy for graduate study. She was the first Black student to enroll at "Bama." But mobs threatened her while she was attending classes, and university trustees suspended her for her own safety and "the safety of the students and faculty members." A Federal court then ordered Miss Lucy's reinstatement, but trustees permanently expelled her for making "outrageous" charges against them. The Eisenhower administration refused to intervene and the University of Alabama remained segregated for seven more years.[21]

In 1964, President Johnson urged Congress to pass a major civil rights law as a memorial to the recently assassinated President Kennedy. Kennedy had proposed such legislation in 1963 after southern police used cattle prods, fire hoses and police dogs on Black demonstrators in Birmingham, Ala. This time Congress moved, producing the **Civil Rights Act of 1964 and the Voting Rights Act of 1965.**

CIVIL RIGHTS ACT OF 1964, VOTING RIGHTS ACT OF 1965

The 1964 Civil Rights Act was clearly the most significant civil rights measure enacted since Reconstruction. It finally passed the U.S. Senate after 83 days of debate, the longest filibuster in U.S. history. **Cloture** was imposed to prevent Southern and border state senators from killing the statute. It is a rarely used procedure to terminate debate and force a vote. At the time, it required a 2/3 vote of the Senate. Today, it requires a 3/5 vote.

The act included key political rights provisions. Literacy tests were forbidden in Federal elections, as were unequal applications of registration requirements. Persons with sixth-grade educations were presumed to be literate and special three-judge Federal courts were authorized to hear voting rights suits.

Also of landmark importance are some Title II provisions. They forbid discrimination on grounds of race, color, religion or national origin in most places of **public accommodation** that affect interstate commerce. Restaurants, hotels and motels with more than five rooms, lunch counters, movie theaters, gasoline stations and sports stadiums all are covered by the law.

Title VI permits cutoff of Federal funds to all of the state and local programs practicing discrimination. It has been one of the most effective provisions of the act. The pace of southern school integration suddenly increased when the U.S. threatened to withhold dollars from those school districts which did not comply with desegregation orders.

Title VII makes it illegal to deny anyone **equal employment opportunity—hiring, firing, promotion or pay**—because of race, color, religion, sex or national origin. The **Equal Employment Opportunity Commission** was established to investigate complaints.

The U.S. Supreme Court upheld the public accommodations title in 1965 in *Heart of Atlanta Motel v. U.S.* Lester Maddox, proprietor and owner of the restaurant at the motel, refused to serve Blacks and turned them away with ax handles and a gun. Ordered to comply with the law, Maddox sold his restaurant and went into politics, serving first as governor of Georgia and later as lieutenant governor under Jimmy Carter.[22]

The Voting Rights Act of 1965 extended Federal authority over the election process, traditionally considered within the area of "state's rights," preserved by the 10th Amendment. The U.S. Attorney General was authorized to seek Federal Court findings in voter discrimination and to move against discriminatory poll taxes. The 24th Amendment later banned the poll tax in Federal, but not state, elections. Four southern states retained it, including Virginia. The Supreme Court, in *Harper v. Virginia State Board of Elections,* 383 U.S. 663 (1966), put an end to the poll tax once and for all, ruling that a state violates the Equal Protection Clause "...whenever it makes the affluence of the voter or the payment of any fee an electoral standard."

Under the Voting Rights Act of 1965, specific areas were targeted. Federal examiners were to register voters in states and counties where a discriminatory test or device was in effect in November, 1964, and where less than 40% of the voting age population was registered to vote in the 1964 presidential election.

In 1965, the states covered by the law were Alabama, Alaska, Georgia, Louisiana, Mississippi and Virginia, as well as parts of North Carolina, Arizona, Hawaii and Idaho. A state could be removed from the list by proving that no discrimination had occurred for five years. Literacy tests were suspended, and any changes in state election laws had to be approved by the U.S. Attorney General. The act immediately was challenged as a gross usurpation of states rights. In 1966, South Carolina sued U.S. Attorney General Nicholas Katzenbach, asking that he be restrained from enforcing the law.

Because this dispute involved a state suing a citizen of another state and because of the importance of the issues involved, the U.S. Supreme Court accepted the case under its **original jurisdiction**. It also invited other states to participate and five southern states did so. Some 21 other states submitted legal briefs, urging the Court to support the act. Southern states asserted that the Federal government had invaded the area of "state's rights," guaranteed by the 10th Amendment.

The Court rejected this argument and upheld the law. Speaking through Chief Justice Warren, it said:[23]

> We...reject South Carolina's argument that Congress may appropriately do no more than forbid violations of the 15th Amendment in general terms—that the task of fashioning specific remedies or of applying them to particular localities must necessarily be left entirely to the courts. Congress is not circumscribed by any such artificial rules.

> Congress exercised its authority under the 15th Amendment in an inventive manner when it enacted the Voting Rights Act of 1965. First: The measure prescribes remedies for voting discrimination which go into effect without any need for prior adjudication. This was clearly a legitimate response to the problem, for which there is ample precedent under other constitutional provisions.

> Second: The Act intentionally confines these remedies to a small number of States and political subdivisions which in most instances were familiar to Congress by name. This, too, was a permissible method of dealing with the problem. Congress had learned that substantial voting discrimination presently occurs in certain sections of the country, and it knew no way of accurately forecasting whether the evil might spread elsewhere in the future. In acceptable legislative fashion, Congress chose to limit its attention to the geographic areas where immediate action appeared necessary.

> After enduring nearly a century of widespread resistance to the 15th Amendment, Congress has marshaled an array of potent weapons against the evil, with authority in the Attorney General to employ them effectively. Many of the areas directly affected by this development have indicated their willingness to abide by any restraints legitimately imposed upon them. We here hold that the portions of the Voting Rights Act properly before us are a valid means for carrying out the commands of the 15th Amendment. Hopefully, millions of non-white Americans will now be able to participate for the first time on an equal basis in the government under which they live. 'The right of citizens of the United States to vote shall not be denied or abridged by the United States or by any State on account of race, color or previous condition of servitude.' The bill of complaint is dismissed.

The Voting Rights Act was amended in 1970, 1975 and 1982. It has radically changed southern and presidential politics. Before this landmark statute was enacted, Blacks seldom participated in southern politics. Since 1965, Blacks not only have participated, but also have elected Black mayors, sheriffs and other state and local officials. Blacks also have been chosen as southern members of the U.S. House of Representatives. In the election of 1992, Carol Moseley Braun was elected as the first Black female ever to serve in the U.S. Senate. Some 48 Blacks were chosen to serve in the U.S. House of Representatives.

In the 107th Congress, elected in 2000, there were three racial and ethic minorities in the U.S. Senate and 63 serving in the House of Representatives.

The 110th Congress, elected in 2006, included only one Black in the U.S. Senate (Barack Obama of Illinois) and 40 in the House of Representatives. There were 16 females serving in the U.S. Senate and 71 in the House, including Speaker Nancy Pelosi. In addition, there were 26 Hispanics elected, three of whom were serving in the Senate.

Senator Obama made history in early June, 2008, by becoming the first Black person ever to clinch his party's presidential nomination. This came only after a prolonged and intense battle with Sen. Hillary Clinton of New York.

A Gallup Poll taken in 1958 showed that only 38% of respondents would consider voting for a Black presidential candidate. By 2007, attitudes had undergone a dramatic change. Some 94% of respondents said they would be willing to support a Black candidate.

Some of Clinton's supporters urged Obama to put her on the ticket as his vice presidential running mate. Election of a ticket which shattered years of racial and gender bias was the dream of millions of Democrats in 2008.

In 1968, Congress passed open housing legislation. The law prohibited discrimination in the advertising, financing, sale or rental of most housing. Discrimination based on race, religion and national origin was outlawed. Single-family homes sold without a broker and owner-occupied dwellings with four or less rental units were exempted.

RACIAL INTERMARRIAGE: LOVING V. VIRGINIA

In the aftermath of *Brown*, the Warren Court presumed that racial classifications used to discriminate against Blacks violated the 14th Amendment's Equal Protection Clause. States defending such actions faced a heavy burden of proof. Blacks had the advantages of a **strict scrutiny test.** During the 1960s and 1970s, one after another legal wall between the races came tumbling down.

The greatest fear of segregationists was interracial marriage. By 1967, some 16 southern and border states still had **miscegenation laws** that defined interracial marriages as criminal cohabitation. A number of Western states—California, Arizona, Colorado and Oregon—and one midwestern state, Indiana, had similar laws until the 1960s.

The U.S. Supreme Court considered the case of *Loving v. Virginia*, 388 U.S. 1 (1967). Two residents of Virginia—Richard Loving, a white man, and Mildred Jeter, a Black woman—were wed in Washington, D.C. When they returned to Virginia to live, they were charged with violating the state miscegenation law and faced a possible five-year prison sentence. They pleaded guilty and received one-year sentences. The judge suspended the sentences, provided that the Lovings leave Virginia for 25 years.

The Lovings moved to Washington, D.C., but in 1963 sued to have their sentence set aside, arguing that it infringed their rights under the 14th Amendment's Equal Protection Clause. The Virginia Supreme Court upheld the statute. The U.S. Supreme Court granted review and in 1967 reversed the judgment of Virginia's highest court. Chief Justice Warren wrote in part:[24]

This case presents a constitutional question never addressed by this Court: whether a statutory scheme adopted by the State of Virginia to prevent marriages between persons solely on the basis of racial classifications violates the Equal Protection and Due Process Clauses of the 14th Amendment. For reasons which seem to us to reflect the central meaning of those constitutional commands, we conclude that these statutes cannot stand consistently with the 14th Amendment.

While the state court is no doubt correct in asserting that marriage is a social relation subject to the State's police power, the State does not contend in its arguments before this Court that its powers to regulate marriage are unlimited notwithstanding the commands of the 14th Amendment.

Instead, the State argues that the meaning of the Equal Protection Clause...is only that state penal laws containing an interracial element as part of the definition of the offense must apply equally to whites and Negroes in the sense that members of each race are punished to the same degree. Thus, the State contends that, because its miscegenation statute punishes equally both the white and Negro participants in an interracial marriage, these statutes, despite their reliance on racial classifications, do not constitute an invidious discrimination based upon race. The second argument advanced by the State assumes the validity of its equal application theory. The argument is that, if the Equal Protection Clause does not outlaw miscegenation statutes because of their reliance on racial classifications, the question of constitutionality would thus become whether there was any rational basis for a State to treat interracial marriages differently from other marriages. On this question, the State argues, the scientific evidence is substantially in doubt and, consequently, this Court should defer to the wisdom of the state legislature in adopting its policy of discouraging interracial marriages.

We do not accept the State's contention that these statutes should be upheld if there is any possible basis for concluding that they serve a rational purpose.

There can be no question but that Virginia's miscegenation statutes rest solely upon distinctions drawn according to race. The statutes proscribe generally accepted conduct if engaged in by members of different races. Over the years, this Court has consistently repudiated 'distinctions between citizens solely because of their ancestry' as being 'odious to a free people whose institutions are founded upon the doctrine of equality.'

At the very least, the Equal Protection Clause demands that racial classifications, especially suspect in criminal statutes, be subjected to 'the most rigid scrutiny,'... and, if they are ever to be upheld, they must be shown to be necessary to the accomplishment of some permissible state objective, independent of the racial discrimination which it was the object of the 14th Amendment to eliminate.

There is no legitimate overriding purpose independent of invidious racial discrimination which justifies this classification. The fact that Virginia prohibits only interracial marriages involving white persons demonstrates that the racial classifications must stand on their own justification, as measures designed to maintain White Supremacy.

We have consistently denied the constitutionality of measures which restrict the rights of citizens on account of race. There can be no doubt that restricting the freedom to marry solely because of racial classifications violates the central meaning of the Equal Protection Clause.

These statutes also deprive the Lovings of liberty without due process of law in violation of the Due Process Clause of the 14th Amendment. The freedom to marry has long been recognized as one of the vital personal rights essential to the orderly pursuit of happiness by free men.

Marriage is one of the 'basic civil rights of man,' fundamental to our very existence and survival. To deny this fundamental freedom on so insupportable a basis as the racial classifications embodied in these statutes, classifications so directly subversive of the principle of equality at the heart of the 14th Amendment, is surely to deprive all the State's citizens of liberty without due process of law. The 14th Amendment requires that the freedom of choice to marry not be restricted by invidious racial discriminations. Under our Constitution, the freedom to marry or not marry a person of another race resides with the individual and cannot be infringed by the State.

Postscript: Racial intermarriage was not an issue in the 1990s when Clarence Thomas, a Black man nominated to serve on the Supreme Court, was reported in a press "profile" to reside in Virginia with his white wife.

WHITE BACKLASH

The early and mid-1960s were years of a "Civil Rights Revolution," aided by Warren Court decisions and President Johnson's leadership of the Congress. But the later years of the decade were characterized by "white backlash," brought on partially as a reaction to new, more militant types of Black leaders. Changes in Black strategies, generational conflict between old and new Black leaders and anger over urban riots produced a new mood in America.

Many Americans believe that goodwill is essential to racial understanding and harmony. But the goodwill of the early and mid-1960s was diluted, if not destroyed, by events in the later half of the decade.

MODERATE AND MILITANT BLACK LEADERS

Groups like the **National Association for the Advancement of Colored People (NAACP)** and the **Urban League** had sought the support of whites of good will for the cause of racial justice. They took their cases to the courts and worked within the framework of the "system."[25]

Dr. Martin Luther King Jr.'s **Southern Christian Leadership Conference (SCLC)** stressed religion and the ethical precept of passive, non-violent civil disobedience. If Dr. King and his followers broke the law, they gladly went to jail to demonstrate their convictions. They did not ask for amnesty. Dr. King borrowed this "tactic" from the Indian independence leader, Mahatma Gandhi. Dr. King once said:[26]

We will soon wear you down by our capacity to suffer...and in winning our freedom we will so appeal to your heart and conscience that we will win you in the process.

King, then a 27-year-old Baptist minister, first received widespread national publicity when he lead a year-long **Montgomery Ala., bus boycott** in December, 1955. Rosa Parks, a 43-year-old seamstress, boarded a bus in Montgomery, Ala., as she did every day after work. When white passengers got on, the driver asked Black passengers to move to the rear and give up their seats to whites. Rosa Parks refused, was arrested and fined $10. This lead to a boycott of the bus system by a Black population that had had enough. During the boycott, King went to jail and his home was bombed. But in the long run, he won.

In November, 1956, a Federal court ended segregation of Montgomery, Ala., buses. The boycott, a landmark in the Black civil rights struggle in the South, was followed by **sit-ins** in Greensboro, N.C., **Freedom Rides** in Alabama and **mass demonstrations** against segregation in Birmingham, Ala.

In Birmingham, demonstrators were met by Police Commissioner Eugene "Bull" Connor and his force. They unleashed police dogs and used cattle prods and fire hoses on demonstrators. Network television crews recorded the event for many horrified viewers, who never before had "experienced" such brutality.

Television and news photos, carried in nearly every major northern newspaper, played a major role in searing the American conscience and convincing many religious leaders to get involved in King's crusade, viewed increasingly as a major moral issue of the time.

"I HAVE A DREAM"

In August, 1963, King led a massive, peaceful **"March on Washington for Jobs and Freedom."** An estimated 200,000 Americans, Black and white, jammed the Mall between the Lincoln Memorial and Washington Monument. Television again played a major role in helping to create a better climate for major civil rights legislation. In what is perhaps his most memorable speech, Dr. King stated his vision of what he hoped America might one day become:[27]

I have a dream that one day this nation will rise up and live out the true meaning of its creed.

I have a dream....that my four little children will one day live in a nation where they will not be judged by the color of their skin, but by the content of their character.

So let freedom ring...From every mountainside, let freedom ring...to speed up the day when all of God's children, black and white men, Jews and Gentiles, Protestants and Catholics, will be able to join hands and sing in the words of the old Negro spiritual, 'Free at last! Free at last! Thank God Almighty, we are free at last!'

But new leaders arose in the late 1960s who were impatient and demanded action "now." Shrill voices sought not good will, but fanned the flames of racial hatred and vengeance. These included Stokely Carmichael, who was blamed by many in the media for violent outbreaks on the nation's campuses, and Hubert "Rap" Brown. Brown was a media favorite because of his dramatic quotes. He said, for example, in justifying force, "Violence is as American as cherry pie."

An early proponent of armed self-defense was Malcolm X., an official of the Black Muslims until he was expelled by Elijah Muhammad. His doctrines were clearly contrary to those of traditional Black leaders like Dr. King. Malcolm, in fact, called King "the Reverend Dr. Chickenwing" and described NAACP leader Roy Wilkins as a "Judas" to his people.[28]

"Burn, baby, burn" was another slogan which appealed primarily to militants, but **ghetto riots** took a terrible toll in the late 1960s. They began in August, 1965, in **Watts,** outside Los Angeles. Some 35 persons were killed, more than 1000 injured, and $35 million in property damages was done. Watts was followed by turmoil in **Cleveland and Chicago** in 1966 and even more destructive 1967 riots in **Detroit and Newark, N.J.**

These "disturbances," as they were called, claimed not only lives and property, but also good will. Hatred and racial bitterness erupted in thousands of violent acts. The principal victims of this violence were Blacks themselves, many of whom lost their homes and businesses as flames engulfed their neighborhoods.

Following the assassination of Martin Luther King in April, 1968, outbreaks occurred in Washington, D.C., and more than 100 other cities. More than 13,000 U.S. troops were ordered into the nation's capital where fires were set only a few blocks from the White House. For nearly two weeks, these armed troops occupied the capital.

THE KERNER COMMISSION REPORT

The National Advisory Commission on Civil Disorders, chaired by former Illinois Gov. Otto Kerner and appointed by President Johnson in the aftermath of the Detroit riots, reported in March, 1968:[29]

Our nation is moving toward two societies, one black, one white—separate and unequal. Certain fundamental matters are clear. Of these, the most fundamental is the racial attitude and behavior of white Americans toward Black Americans. Race prejudice has shaped our history decisively; it now threatens to affect our future. White racism is essentially responsible for the explosive mixture which has been accumulating in our cities since the end of World War II.

The Kerner Commission urged a massive national drive to remove racial barriers in education, housing and employment. Although few Americans disputed the gravity of the urban minority problem, many disagreed vehemently with the commission's conclusion. Conservatives and others did not see "white racism" as the cause of the riots.

White and Black leaders who sought the goal of an integrated society of equal opportunity for all, had tried to build bridges of personal communication and understanding between the races. But the civil rights movement and new laws brought no visible change in status to millions of Black Americans who lived in urban ghettoes.

Few outside the discipline of sociology saw Black-white conflicts as anything but racial. However, some sociologists, like Edward C. Banfield, argued that the conflict also involved **social class.** Middle class Blacks saw a very real and fundamental difference between their values, similar to white, middle-class Americans, and those of lower class, ghetto Blacks who account for a disproportionate amount of crime and other social problems.[30]

THE MOYNIHAN REPORT

Harvard sociologist, later U.S. Senator Daniel Patrick Moynihan, (D., N.Y.) authored a famous report, *The Negro Family: The Case for National Action,* in 1965. Written under the auspices of the Office of Policy Planning and Research of the U.S. Labor Department, the Moynihan Report argued that the root cause of the civil rights problems in America was instability in the Black family.

Moynihan cited figures, all of which then were much lower than they are today, of Black divorce rates, illegitimate births, female-headed families and growing welfare dependency.[31]

In Chapter V, Moynihan concluded:[32]

> Three centuries of injustice have brought about deep-seated structural distortions in the life of the Negro American. At this point, the present tangle of pathology is capable of perpetuating itself without assistance from the white world. The cycle can be broken only if these distortions are set right.
>
> In a word, a national effort towards the problems of Negro Americans must be directed toward the question of family structure. The object should be to strengthen the Negro family so as to enable it to raise and support its members as do other families. After that, how this group of Americans chooses to run its affairs, take advantage of its opportunities, or fail to do so, is none of the nation's business.
>
> The President has committed the nation to an all-out effort to eliminate poverty wherever it exists, among whites or Negroes, and a militant, organized and responsible Negro movement exists to join in that effort. Such a national effort could be stated thus:
>
> The policy of the United States is to bring the Negro American to full and equal sharing in the responsibilities and rewards of citizenship. To this end, the programs of the Federal government bearing on this objective shall be designed to have the effect, directly or indirectly, of enhancing the stability and resources of the Negro American family.

Black leaders like the Rev. Jesse Jackson attacked the **subculture of incivility** and the **abdication of personal responsibility.** Jackson argued that Black Americans must develop a **culture of civility,** that Black family life must be improved and discipline firmly administered in ghetto schools where education, rather than merely "keeping the lid on" should be the primary objective.

The mid-1970s were marked by a toning down of violent rhetoric. Some of the more aggressive groups faded away. Moderate Blacks, like civil rights leader Bayard Rustin, said: "Separatism is not a social program. It's a psychological vent. The march now is to the ballot and to union cards."

Black female singer Nancy Wilson said that she believed not in **Black Power,** an ill-defined concept subject to many interpretations, but in **"Green Power,"** economic opportunities for Black people to get good educations, good jobs and responsible positions in American society.

Many psychologists did praise the growth of black pride, reflected in the slogan, "Black is beautiful." Some saw the rise of "**cultural nationalism**," with a renewed interest in the Black's African heritage, Afro haircuts, dress styles and adoption of new African-type names.

During the 1970s, three major problems involving public school education came before the U.S. Supreme Court. It was asked to answer these questions:

1) Is compulsory busing an appropriate way to integrate public schools?

2) Does public school segregation based on neighborhood housing patterns violate the Constitution?

3) Can courts erase traditional school district boundaries to end segregation?

THE BUSING DEBATE

In 1971, the Supreme Court ruled that busing was an appropriate method of correcting public school segregation in the case of *Swann v. Charlotte-Mecklenburg, North Carolina, Board of Education.* By the mid-1970s, the familiar yellow school bus had become a major political symbol and violence often erupted. In **Pontiac, Michigan,** some 10 school buses were firebombed late in the summer of 1971, after a court ordered desegregation by busing there. In Michigan, Mrs. Irene McCabe formed a strong anti-busing coalition; it and a variety of other groups strongly supported the presidential candidacy of Alabama Gov. George C. Wallace in 1972. On the eve of the Michigan Democratic presidential primary in 1972, Wallace wrote an Op-Ed page column at the invitation of the *New York Times.* He said:[33]

The American people are fed up with the interference of government. They want to be left alone. Once the Democratic party reflected true expressions of the rank-and-file citizens. They were its heart, the bulk of its strength and vitality. Long ago, it became the party of the so-called intelligentsia. Where once it was the party of the people, along the way it lost contact with the working man and the businessman. It has been transformed into a party controlled by intellectual snobs.

When Wallace won the primary, much to the dismay of state party leaders and labor union officials, "forced busing" became a major issue. The segregationist governor of Alabama, in a large field, won not a plurality, but an absolute majority of votes.

Among those he defeated were Sen. Ed Muskie of Maine, choice of Michigan labor leaders, former Vice President and Senator Hubert Humphrey, former New York City Mayor John Lindsay, Rep. Shirley Chisholm, a Black congresswoman from New York, Sen. Henry Jackson of Washington and eventual Democratic Party nominee George McGovern.

Shortly after his Michigan victory, however, Governor Wallace was shot by a would-be assassin while campaigning at a Laurel, Md., shopping center, outside Washington, D.C. As a result, he was forced out of the 1972 campaign and left permanently paralyzed. He spent the rest of his life in a wheelchair before dying in 1998.

Violence erupted in South Boston, Mass., in 1974 and efforts to prevent court-ordered busing at South Boston High resulted in bloodshed. When a national public opinion poll was taken that year, some 70% of those interviewed were opposed to busing for better racial balance in the schools.

Segregation De Jure and De Facto

The 14th Amendment clearly forbids state action denying persons the Equal Protection of the Law. It thus applies to *de jure* segregation, that which is imposed by statute. It was *de jure* segregation that the Court declared unconstitutional in *Brown*, and it was *de jure* segregation that existed throughout most of the southern and border states.

School segregation also existed, however, in many northern and western cities, which never used legal segregation. This so-called *de facto* segregation was a result not of law, but of residential patterns, economic status and other non-legal factors that did not appear to fall under the scope of the Equal Protection Clause.

Unlike the southern-type of legally-required, *de jure* segregation of races, northern states have been characterized by *de facto* segregation, the kind resulting from housing patterns.

Justice Lewis Powell believed that *de facto* segregation is just as unconstitutional as *de jure* segregation. A southerner and former president of the American Bar Association, Powell once headed the Richmond, Va., School Board.

In *Keyes v. School District of Denver*, 413 U.S. 189, decided in 1973, Justice Powell said that the Supreme Court should rule that "where segregated public schools exist within a school district to a substantial degree, there is a *prima facie* case that the duly constituted public authorities...are sufficiently responsible...to warrant imposing upon them a nationally applicable burden to demonstrate they nevertheless are operating a genuinely integrated school system."

But in *Dayton, Ohio, Board of Education v. Brinkman*, 443 U.S. 449 (1979), the Court held that a lower Federal court had erred in holding that the simple existence of racial imbalance in a city's schools constituted proof of deliberate segregation. When the Court reviewed *Brinkman* and *Columbus, Ohio, Board of Education v. Penick*, 443 U.S. 449 (1979), it appeared to abandon effort to distinguish between *de jure* and *de facto* segregation.

The Court upheld massive busing for both school systems, upholding lower Federal court verdicts that both systems were illegally segregated, even though Ohio law has not required segregation since 1888. The Court found that school boards are duty-bound to end segregation.

In 1991, the Supreme Court ruled, 5-3, in an Oklahoma City Case, *Board of Education of Oklahoma v. Dowell*, 498 U.S. (1991), that busing need not continue once a school district has made good faith efforts to end racial segregation. Writing for the majority, Chief Justice Rehnquist said: "...court supervised busing was not meant to continue indefinitely, but has been intended as a temporary measure to remedy past discrimination."

The Detroit Case

Another difficult and interesting legal question is school boundaries. If a predominately Black district in the core city is totally surrounded by predominately white suburban districts, is real integration possible?

In a landmark case involving Detroit and surrounding suburban schools, the Supreme Court held in *Milliken v. Bradley*, 418 U.S. 717 (1974), that the Constitution does not require combination of public school districts or cross-district busing where no judicial finding of discrimination in the suburban districts has been made.

In the Court opinion, written by Chief Justice Warren Burger, the tribunal affirmed its belief that racial discrimination should be eliminated, "root and branch," from the nation's schools. The Court also agreed that Detroit schools had been segregated. But the appropriate judicial remedy was not "cross-district busing," as proposed by the NAACP and approved by Judge Roth of the Detroit Federal District Court. Rather, Detroit would have to do its best within the city.

Associate Justice William O. Douglas, speaking for the four dissenters, argued that the Court had staged a dramatic retreat, not only from the *Brown* decision of 1954, but from its 1896 ruling that Blacks should receive equal, although separate treatment. The practical effect of the Michigan case, Douglas said, would be to create city schools which were not only separate but inferior. He wrote:[34]

> When we rule against a metropolitan area remedy, we take a step that will likely put the problem of Blacks and our society back to the period that antedated the separate but equal regime of *Plessy v. Ferguson*. Today's decision, given *Rodriguez*, means that there is no violation of the equal protection clause though the schools are segregated by race and though the Black schools are not only separate but inferior.

Liberal critics of the Burger Court argued that *Milliken v. Bradley* might well legalize *de facto* segregation in American cities. Roy Wilkins, then president of the NAACP, called the verdict, "...the way to apartheid, the South African equivalent of strict racial separation."

Not all Black educators were convinced that quality education depended on busing and desegregation. Wilson Riles, superintendent of education in California, rejected the idea "that a Black child can't learn unless he is sitting next to a white child" and political scientist Charles Hamilton called busing Black children "a subtle way of maintaining Black dependency on whites."

RESTRICTIVE COVENANTS

Restrictive covenants became popular, not only to segregate people by race but also by religion and ethnicity. In parts of Florida, Jews were the target; in parts of New England, Roman Catholics. In the South, it was Blacks and in the Southwest, Hispanics. People from Asia and the Pacific Islands were targets of such agreements on the West Coast.

But were such real estate contracts unconstitutional? This question came before the U.S. Supreme Court in 1948 in *Shelley v. Kraemer,* 334 U.S. 1 (1948).

J.D. and Ethel Lee Shelley, a Black couple, moved from Mississippi to Missouri just before World War II. The couple and their six children wanted to move from their poor, predominately Black neighborhood to what they believed was a more desirable location. In August, 1945, they bought a house in the Grand Prairie neighborhood of St. Louis, a white residential area.

In October, 1945, Louis and Fern Kraemer, along with other neighborhood property holders, filed suit asking the court to divest the Shelleys of their home. Their suit was based on a violation of a **restrictive covenant** signed in 1911. This covenant was a legal contract signed by 30 neighborhood property owners who agreed not to sell their properties for 50 years to any person not of the Caucasian race. The Shelley home was covered by the agreement.

The Missouri Supreme Court ruled that the restrictive covenant should be enforced. The Shelleys, represented by Thurgood Marshall, appealed to the U.S. Supreme Court.

Few lawyers doubted that such covenants constituted invidious discrimination. They were, however, essentially private agreements not regulated by the Equal Protection Clause. Marshall argued that when Missouri courts enforced these agreements, the state itself became a party to the discrimination. Chief Justice Vinson delivered the landmark decision:[35]

Whether the equal protection clause of the 14th Amendment inhibits judicial enforcement by state courts of restrictive covenants based on race or color is a question which this Court has not heretofore been called upon to consider.

Here the particular patterns of discrimination and the areas in which the restrictions are to operate are determined, in the first instance, by the terms of agreements among private individuals. Participation of the State consists in the enforcement of the restrictions so defined. The crucial issue with which we are here confronted is whether this distinction removes these cases from operation of the prohibitory provisions of the 14th Amendment.

Since the decision of this Court in the Civil Rights Cases (1883), the principle has become firmly embedded in our constitutional law that the action inhibited by the first section of the 14th Amendment is only such action as may fairly be said to be that of the States. That Amendment erects no shield against merely private conduct, however discriminatory or wrongful.

We conclude, therefore, that the restrictive agreement standing alone cannot be regarded as violative of any rights guaranteed to petitioners by the 14th Amendment. So long as the purposes of those agreements are effectuated by voluntary adherence to their terms, it would appear clear that there has been no action by the State and the provisions of the Amendment have not been violated.

But here there was more. These are cases in which the purposes of the agreements were secured only by judicial enforcement by state courts of the restrictive terms of the agreements. The respondents urge that judicial enforcement of private agreements does not amount to state action; or, in any event, the participation of the State is so attenuated in character as not to amount to state action within the meaning of the 14th Amendment.

That the action of state courts and judicial officers in their official capacities is to be regarded as actions of the State within the meaning of the 14th Amendment, is a proposition which has long been established by the decisions of this court. That principle was given expression in the earliest cases involving construction of the 14th Amendment.

The short of the matter is that from the time of the adoption of the 14th Amendment until the present, it has been the consistent ruling of this Court that the actions of the States to which the Amendment has reference includes action of state courts and state judicial officials. Although, in construing the terms of the 14th Amendment, differences have from time to time been expressed as to whether particular types of state action may be said to offend the Amendment's prohibitory provisions, it has never been suggested that the state court action is immunized from the operation of those provisions simply because the act is that of the judicial branch of the state government.

Against this background of judicial construction, extending over a period of some three-quarters of a century, we are called upon to consider whether enforcement by state courts of the restrictive agreements in these cases may be deemed to be the acts of those States; and, if so, whether the action has denied these petitioners the equal protection of the laws which the Amendment was intended to insure.

We have no doubt that there has been state action in these cases in the full and complete sense of the phrase. The undisputed facts disclose that petitioners were willing purchasers of properties upon which they desired to establish homes. The owners of the properties were willing sellers and contracts of sale were accordingly consummated. It is clear that but for the active intervention of the state courts, supported by the full panoply of state power, petitioners would have been free to occupy the properties in question without restraint.

These are not cases, as has been suggested, in which the States have merely abstained from action, leaving private individuals free to impose such discriminations as they see fit. Rather, these are cases in which the States have made available to such individuals the full coercive power of government to deny to petitioners, on the grounds of race or color, the enjoyment of property rights in premises which petitioners are willing and financially able to acquire and which grantors are willing to sell. The differences between judicial enforcement and nonenforcement of the restrictive covenants is the difference to petitioners between being denied rights of property available to other members of the community and being accorded full enjoyment of those rights on an equal footing.

State action, as the phrase is understood for the purposes of the 14th Amendment, refers to exertions of state power in all forms. And when the effect of that action is to deny rights subject to the protection of the 14th Amendment, it is the obligation of this Court to enforce the constitutional commands.

We hold that in granting judicial enforcement of the restrictive agreements in these cases, the States have denied petitioners the equal protection of the laws and that, therefore, the action of the state courts cannot stand. We have noted that freedom from discrimination by the States in the enjoyment of property rights was among the basic objectives sought to be effectuated by the framers of the 14th Amendment. That such discrimination has occurred in these cases is clear.

Because of the race or color of these petitioners, they have been denied rights of ownership or occupancy enjoyed as a matter of course by other citizens of different race or color.

The problem of defining the scope of the restrictions which the Federal Constitution imposes upon exertions of power by the States has given rise to many of the most persistent and fundamental issues which this Court has been called upon to consider. That problem was foremost in the minds of the framers of the Constitution and, since that early day, has arisen in a multitude of forms. The task of determining whether the action of a State offends constitutional provisions is one which may not be undertaken lightly. Where, however, it is clear that the action of the State violates the terms of the fundamental charter, it is the obligation of this Court so to declare.

The historical context in which the 14th Amendment became a part of the Constitution should not be forgotten. Whatever else the framers sought to achieve, it is clear that the matter of primary concern was the establishment of equality in the enjoyment of basic civil and political rights and the preservation of those rights from discriminatory action on the part of the States based on considerations of race or color. Seventy-five years ago, this Court announced that the provisions of the Amendment are to be construed with this fundamental purpose in mind. Upon full consideration, we have concluded that in these cases the States have acted to deny petitioners the equal protection of the laws guaranteed by the 14th Amendment.

Public opinion polls show changing attitudes over time on racial questions, even on perhaps the most controversial of all areas, racially-mixed marriages.

When Dr. George Gallup polled the American public on racially-mixed marriages in 1968, he found that some 72% of the American people objected to such unions. This was a year after *Loving v. Virginia*. By 1972, only 60% of the public opposed such marriages.

Many of the nation's racial problems stem from the comparatively rapid migration of Blacks from the rural south into the urban, industrial states of the north. As the 20th Century dawned, more than 90% of the nation's Black population lived in the south. By 1970, more Blacks lived in the north than in the south.

Black migrants often moved into large cities, seeking jobs. Places like New York, Chicago, Detroit and Philadelphia were magnets, attracting those seeking economic opportunities and a better way of life. Because whites often fled to the suburbs, a concentration of Blacks in cities created political opportunities for them. A concentrated Black vote was mobilized as a part of the civil rights movement and it became easier to elect Black candidates.

It should be noted that economic segregation always is present in real estate transactions. One lives where one can afford to live, even if he or she is not the victim of racial, religious or ethnic discrimination. Black ghettoes are the result of Black poverty.

Although progress has been made, much remains to be done. Some conservatives suggest that we will have made real progress in equal opportunity only when employers hire, promote or fire Blacks, on the basis of individual ability rather than merely hire them for purposes of "tokenism." What of **reverse discrimination**" and **quotas?**

THE AFFIRMATIVE ACTION DEBATE

One of the most controversial issues of our times is affirmative action. Praised by its proponents as necessary to achieve real equality, it is damned by its opponents as "reverse discrimination." Affirmative action programs assume that it is not enough simply to end illegal discrimination under the 14th Amendment's Equal Protection Clause.

Rather, it is argued, both government and private institutions must take positive steps to guarantee that the ideal of equality becomes a reality. A long history of racial, sexual and ethnic discrimination have held back minorities for so long that **special preferences** must be given them, at least temporarily, to "level the playing field."

Justice Harlan spoke, in *Plessy v. Ferguson,* of the Constitution as being color-blind. Affirmative action advocates disagree. Because it seeks to aid, rather than penalize specific categories of groups, affirmative action sometimes is called "**benign discrimination**."

Those who dislike affirmative action argue that equality of opportunity should mean literally that. People, they argue, should be judged strictly on their own merits, not their race, sex or ethnicity. Jobs, promotions and admission to professional colleges in universities all are scarce. They should be highly competitive. Whites and males should no more be victims of discrimination than anyone else.

Those negatively effected by affirmative action programs see it as inconsistent with a commitment to genuine equal opportunity. They detest the idea of a guaranteed **equality of result.** The most controversial aspect of affirmative action is the establishment of numerical quotas for hiring or admitting minority applicants. Affirmative action critics attack such programs on two legal grounds.

First is the U.S. Constitution: the Equal Protection Clause of the 14th Amendment and the Due Process Clause of the Fifth. These Amendments, they argue, do not permit government to give special preference to individuals because of race, sex or national origin. Second is Title VII of the 1964 Civil Rights Act. It forbids employers from discriminating against any employee or potential employee because of race, color, religion, sex or national origin.

The Bakke Case: Reverse Discrimination?

In 1978, Alan Bakke's case caught the attention of the American public. It was the first full U.S. Supreme Court review of affirmative action. When it was decided, all three major U.S. weekly news magazines made it their cover story. The case matched affirmative action proponents against those who regarded it as "reverse discrimination."

Bakke had done well as an undergraduate student, graduating from the University of Minnesota with a 3.46 average in Engineering. After combat service with the Marines during the Vietnam War, he earned a Master's degree in biology from Stanford. He had worked as a medic and hospital volunteer before applying for admission to the University of California Medical School at its Davis branch. He had done relatively well (MCAT percentile scores of 96 verbal, 94 quantitative, 97 science, 72 general information). Bakke was rejected.

The University had a two-track admission process, under which non-minority students were competing for 84 slots in the 100 member first-year medical class. Davis, which began operations in 1968, admitted only three minority students, all Asians, in its first three years. To improve minority admissions, 16 slots were "reserved," under an affirmative action program, for disadvantaged and minority students who did not have to meet the same standards for admission. The average of special admits—Blacks, Chicanos, Native Americans and Asians—in the 1974 class was 2.42 in science and 2.62 overall (MCAT percentile scores of 34 verbal, 30 quantitative, 37 science and 18 general information).

Bakke filed suit, arguing that he had been denied equal protection of the laws because he was white. He argued that the state had established a rigid quota system and had failed to treat applicants as individuals. The Supreme Courts of California and the U.S. agreed.

The U.S. Supreme Court sent some mixed signals in its Bakke decision. A majority of justices sided with Bakke. It found that since the Davis medical school had no history of racial discrimination, it could not establish rigid quotas for minority students. It could, however, in the interest of creating a more diverse student body, take minority status into account when reaching an admissions decision. Speaking through Justice Powell, the Court said:[36]

It is evident that the Davis special admissions program involves the use of an explicit racial classification never before countenanced by this Court. It tells applicants who are not Negro, Asian, or Chicano that they are totally excluded from a specific percentage of the seats in an entering class. No matter how strong their qualifications, quantitative and extracurricular, including their own potential for contributions to educational diversity, they are never afforded the chance to compete with applicants from the preferred groups for the special admission seats. At the same time, the preferred applicants have the opportunity to compete for every seat in the class.

The fatal flaw in petitioner's preferential program is its disregard of individual rights as guaranteed by the 14th Amendment. Such rights are not absolute. But when a State's distribution of benefits or imposition of burdens hinges on ancestry or the color of a person's skin, that individual is entitled to a demonstration that the challenged classification is necessary to promote a substantial state interest. Petitioner has failed to carry this burden.

Post-Bakke: Based on the Bakke precedent, the U.S. Justice Department filed suit against the University of California, Berkeley, in the fall of 1992, for giving preferential treatment to minority applicants. Yet in *Fullilove v. Klutznick,* 448 U.S. 448 (1980), a law under which Congress had set aside 10% of public works funds for minorities was upheld. Professor Alexander Bickel of Yale, a leading scholar in the field of constitutional law, seriously questioned quota systems and preferential treatment on the basis of race. In his book, *The Morality of Consent,* Bickel wrote:[37]

Those for whom racial equality was demanded are to be more equal than others. Having found support in the Constitution for equality, they now claim support for inequality under the same Constitution.

The Weber Case: Private Affirmative Action

At issue in Weber was a "voluntary" affirmative action plan negotiated by the United Steelworkers Union and the Kaiser Aluminum and Chemical Corporation for its Gramercy, La., plant. Under the plan, half of the available positions in a voluntary on-the-job training program were reserved for Blacks.

Brian Weber was excluded solely because of race—he was white. Weber sued in U.S. District Court, claiming violation of Title VII of the 1964 Civil Rights Act. This section of the law categorically bans any racial discrimination in employment and specifically states that its provisions are not to be interpreted.

The U.S. Supreme Court reversed lower Federal courts in a 5-2 ruling, with Justices Powell and Stevens abstaining. Justice Brennan, writing for the majority, concluded that lower Federal courts had followed the letter of the law, but not its "spirit."

Chief Justice Burger and Justice Rehnquist dissented vehemently, charging the majority with the crassest kind of judicial activism by legislating—"totally rewriting a crucial part of" – the law. The Chief Justice wrote, "Congress expressly prohibited the discrimination against Brian Weber."

Rehnquist concluded that the majority was acting like Harry Houdini, the escape artist. Congress sought to require racial equality in government, Rehnquist contended, and

"...there is perhaps no device more destructive to the notion of equality than the quota. Whether described as affirmative action or reverse discrimination, the racial quota is the creator of castes, a two-edged sword that must demean one in order to prefer the other."[38]

Other Affirmative Action Cases

In *Firefighters Local Union No. 1784 v. Stotts*, 467 U.S. 561 (1984), the Supreme Court ruled that layoffs of Memphis firefighters had to be done by seniority unless there were Black employees who could prove that they were victims of racial bias.

But in *Wygant v. Jackson Board of Education*, 476 U.S. 267 (1986), the Court held that affirmative action could apply to hiring, but not to layoffs. Wygant involved a group of white teachers in **Jackson, Michigan,** challenging a labor contract that called for laying off three white teachers for every one minority group teacher in order to preserve the school system's racial and ethnic ratios. Deeply divided, 5-4, the Court majority said that the Jackson plan violated the 14th Amendment's Equal Protection clause.

Johnson v. Transportation Agency of Santa Clara County, California, 480 U.S. 616 (1987): In the first affirmative action case involving women, the Court upheld a plan of preferential treatment for women. The agency had designed a program for employee promotions. The Court ruled that sex, like race, could legally be a factor in hiring and promotion even if the employer had no prior history of discrimination.

We have seen that the Reconstruction Era Amendments were designed to protect the individual. The power and authority of government, be it federal, state or local, has been a constant source of concern. When government has a monopoly on lawfully granted **coercive power and authority**, restraints must be imposed on it to preserve freedom. We have been concerned with judicial enforcement of constitutional rights.

It should now be abundantly clear to the serious student that history is filled with horror stories involving abuse of human liberty. Indeed **the whole concept of liberty is foreign to some cultures.** But laws enacted by governments—federal, state and local—can and do have limited Equal Protection of the Law.

Executive acts of city managers, mayors, governors and even Presidents can abuse human rights. The courts, in recent years, have been the bulwark of human liberty. But, as has been demonstrated, even the U.S. Supreme Court has tended to reflect the "wisdom of the times," sometimes nothing more than the superstition of the era.

In 1991, Congress enacted a civil rights bill, characterized by its Liberal supporters as a **Civil Rights Restoration Act** and by President Bush as a quota bill. The act overturned several U.S. Supreme Court decisions of the Reagan-Bush Era. The Justice Department, until 1993, argued that affirmative action programs were unconstitutional.

In 1989, the Court retreated from its past support for affirmative action in *Wards Cove Packing Co. v. Atonio.* In *Wards Cove,* the Rehnquist Court ruled that employees filing discrimination suits had to prove that hiring practices and standards that adversely affected women and minorities were not job-related.

Employers previously had to prove that employment practices that affected women and minorities were related to job performance. The 1991 Civil Rights Act overturned *Wards Cove* and limited management's ability to reopen previously agreed-upon affirmative action plans.

Recent Developments in Affirmative Action

In *City of Richmond v. J.A. Croson Co.*, 488 U.S. 469 (1989), the Supreme Court upheld a decision of the Fourth Circuit Court of Appeals, declaring unconstitutional a program requiring that 30% of all money appropriated for municipal public works be set aside for minority-owned construction firms. The Supreme Court ruled, 6-3, that the law violated the rights of white businessmen and women to equal protection of the laws.

The city's plan violated strict scrutiny in that it was: (1) not justified by a compelling government interest, since the record revealed no prior discrimination by the city itself in awarding contracts and (2) the 30% set-aside was not narrowly tailored to accomplish a remedial purpose. Justice O'Connor, writing for the majority, said:

> A generalized assertion that there has been past discrimination in the entire construction industry cannot justify the use of an unyielding racial quota, since it provides no guidance for the city's legislative body to determine the precise scope of the injury it seeks to remedy and would allow race-based decision-making essentially limitless in scope and duration.
>
> None of the 'facts' cited by the city...provide a basis for a...case of a constitutional or statutory violation by anyone in the city's construction industry. The fact that the Plan declares itself to be 'remedial' is insufficient since the mere recitation of a 'benign' or legitimate purpose for a racial classification is entitled to little or no weight.
>
> Since there is absolutely no evidence of past discrimination against Spanish-speaking, Oriental, Indian, Eskimo or Aleut persons in any aspect of the city's construction industry, the Plan's random inclusion of these groups strongly impugns the city's claim of remedial motivation. The Plan is not narrowly tailored to remedy the effects of prior discrimination, since it entitles a black, Hispanic or Oriental entrepreneur from anywhere in the country to an absolute preference over other citizens based solely on their race. Moreover, the Plan's rigid 30% quota rests upon the completely unrealistic assumption that minorities will choose to enter construction in lockstep proportion to their representation in the local population.

Following the *Croson* decision, some communities modified their affirmative action plans, and many lawsuits have been filed challenging the legality of state and local "set-aside" programs.

In *Adarand Construction Co. v. Pena*, 115 S. Ct. 2097 (1995), the Court overturned one of its own precedents. It sharply curtailed Federal affirmative action authority when it invalidated a congressional program that required "not less than 10%" of funds appropriated to the Department of Transportation be spent on contracts awarded to small businesses "owned and controlled by socially and economically disadvantaged individuals." The law defined such individuals as having been "subject to racial or ethnic prejudice or cultural bias."

The case arose when Adarand, a Colorado-based highway construction firm, submitted the low bid for a project, but a Hispanic-owned firm was chosen to do the work. Adarand sued, alleging that the program violated the Due Process Clause of the Fifth Amendment. The Court agreed, holding that any government affirmative action plan that uses racial or ethnic classifications as the basis for making decisions is subject to "strict scrutiny" by the courts.

Under a **"strict-scrutiny" test,** a discriminatory law, to be constitutional, must be **narrowly tailored** to meet a **compelling** government interest.

A minority preference program, the Court explained, must be a response to specific past acts of discrimination, not just discrimination in a historic sense. Washington, the Court said, cannot set aside contracts for minority applicants unless it can demonstrate past discrimination particular to a situation. Even then, it must devise a program "narrowly tailored" to the problem that is being remedied. In short, government cannot issue general requirements, such as 10% set-asides, to remedy past discrimination.

Adarand has provided a basis for challenging many minority preference programs that have been established by departments and agencies of the Federal government.

In *Hopwood v. State of Texas*, 84 F ed. 720 (5th Cir. 1996), two white law school applicants sued University of Texas, alleging that the Law School's admissions policy—which sought to increase the number of Blacks and Hispanics admitted to the school—discriminated against them. The Court of Appeals for the Fifth Circuit held that the school could not use race as a basis for admitting students. It found that the UT program violated the 14th Amendment's Equal Protection Clause because it discriminated in favor of minority applicants.

The Appeals Court, in fact, went a step further, directly challenging the Supreme Court's *Bakke* decision. It held that the use of race, even as a means of achieving diversity on college campuses, "undercuts the 14th Amendment."

The Supreme Court decided not to consider the appeal, raising serious questions about whether *Bakke* was still valid. Many university administrators were left wondering whether their schools' admissions policies were constitutional.

The immediate result of *Hopwood* was that the Austin, Texas, campus became distinctively whiter. As the 1997-98 academic year began, there were only 150 Black students on campus, half the number of the preceding year. The Law School had only four Blacks and 26 Hispanics in its first year class of 488. This is in sharp contrast to experience of decades where typically the first year law class would include about 40 Blacks and 60 Hispanics. UT Law School alumni include 650 Blacks and 1300 Hispanics.

Michael Sharlot, dean of the Law School, said:

> We are deeply concerned. We're a school that over the past decades has produced more African American and Hispanic lawyers than any other law school in the United States. We've played a major role in diversifying the legal profession. It's tragic because we're not going to be able to continue.
>
> This is the school that produced Secretary of Energy Federico Pena...this is the school that produced Mayor Ron Kirk of Dallas (a Black). We're not talking about East Muleshoe University."[39]

Voters Reject Affirmative Action: In November, 1996, California voters went to the polls, after a heated debate, to decide the fate of the highly charged Civil Rights Initiative (Proposition 209). The measure provided:

Section 31 is added to Article I of the California Constitution as follows:

- The state shall not discriminate against, or grant preferential treatment to, any individual or group on the basis of race, sex, color, ethnicity or national origin in the operation of public employment, public education or public contracting.

- This section shall apply only to action taken after the section's effective date.

- Nothing in this section shall be interpreted as prohibiting bona fide qualifications based on sex, which are reasonably necessary to the normal operation of public employment, public education or public contracting.

- Nothing in this section shall be interpreted as invalidating any court order or consent decree which is in force as of the effective date of this section.

- Nothing in this section shall be interpreted as prohibiting action which must be taken to establish or maintain eligibility for any federal program, where ineligibility would result in a loss of federal funds to the state.

- For the purposes of this section, "state" shall include, but not necessarily be limited to, the state itself, any city, county, city and county, public university system (including the University of California), community college district, school district, special district or any other political subdivision or governmental instrumentality of or within the state.

- The remedies available for violations of this section shall be the same, regardless of the injured party's race, sex, color, ethnicity or national origin, as are otherwise available for violations of then-existing California anti-discrimination law.

- This section shall be self-executing. If any part or parts of this section are found to be in conflict with federal law or the United States Constitution, the section shall be implemented to the maximum extent that federal law and the United States Constitution permit. Any provision held invalid shall be severable from the remaining portions of this section.

Arguments in Favor of Proposition 209: Supporters of the measure argued that they favored fairness, not favoritism. They argued that a generation ago, civil rights laws were passed to prohibit discrimination, but that special interests highjacked the civil rights movement. Instead of equality, these interest groups were able to pressure governments into imposed quotas, preferences and set-asides.

Governor Pete Wilson, Ward Connerly and Pamela A. Lewis, sponsors of the Civil Rights Initiative, maintained that students were being rejected from public universities because of their race. Connerly, a Sacramento businessman and University of California regent, considers affirmative action to be a form of reverse discrimination, which taints his accomplishments as an African American. Job applicants were being turned away because their race did not meet a "goal" or "timetable," and contracts were being awarded to high bidders because they were of the preferred race.

This, proponents argued, is wrong and unjust. Government should not discriminate. It must not give a job, a university admission or a contract based on race or sex. Government must judge all people equally, without discrimination.

Supporters of Proposition 209 concluded that the only honest and effective way to address inequality of opportunity is by making sure that *all* California children are provided with the tools to compete in our society. In an election eve statement, they said:

> Let them succeed on a fair, color-blind, race-blind, gender-blind basis. Let's not perpetuate the myth that minorities and women cannot compete without special preferences. Let's instead move forward by returning to the fundamentals of our democracy: individual achievement, equal opportunity and *zero tolerance for discrimination against— or for— any individual*.

Arguments Against Proposition 209: Opponents of the measure argued that it harmed women and minorities, that the proposal's language was so broad and misleading that it eliminated equal opportunity programs including tutoring for minority and women students; affirmation action that encourages hiring and promotion of qualified women and minorities; outreach and recruitment programs to encourage applicants for government jobs and contracts; and programs designed to encourage girls to study and pursue careers in math and science.

Prominent opponents included Los Angeles Mayor Richard Riordan, Fran Packard, President of the California League of Women Voters, civil rights leader Rosa Parks and Maxine Blackwell, vice president, Congress of California Senior Citizens. They enlisted retired General Colin Powell, hero of the Persian Gulf War and a prominent Republican, to counteract the endorsement of Proposition 209 by GOP presidential nominee Bob Dole. General Powell said:

> Efforts such as the California Civil Rights Initiative which poses as an equal opportunities initiative, but which puts at risk every outreach program, sets back the gains made by women and puts the brakes on expanding opportunities for people in need.

The Vote: Proposition 209 was passed by a margin of 54.6% to 45.4%. Some 5.27 million voters supported the measure, while 4.39 million opposed it.

In November, 1998, voters in Washington state went to the polls and considered Initiative 200. It banned "preferential treatment" in hiring, contracting and college admissions. Patterned after California's Proposition 209, the measure was approved by the electorate, making Washington the second state to reject affirmative action as public policy. The vote in favor of the amendment was 58.5% to 41.5% against, despite the fact that it was a Democratic year in Washington state and opponents of the amendment outspent proponents by a ratio of about 4-1.

Postscript: Stories in California and Washington newspapers detailed the impact of the two referenda on university enrollments in those states. As a direct result of Proposition 209, campuses of California's most prestigious public universities became dramatically less diverse. At the University of California, Berkeley, of 8000 students offered admission for fall term, 1998, only 191 were Black, compared to 562 the preceding year. Admission of Hispanic students fell from 1045 to 434. The trend was the same at UCLA and at most other colleges and universities in the California system. Berkeley officials said that they turned away more than 800 Black, Hispanic and other minority applicants who had SAT scores of at least 1200 because the school had applicants with even better credentials.

Critics of affirmative action said the new admissions figures from Berkeley and UCLA have exposed how much both campuses rely on a double standard in their process of choosing students—one for whites and Asians, another for Blacks, Hispanics and other minority groups. They also said the figures show how badly many minority students are being prepared by the state's public schools to compete for admission at academically selective colleges.

In mid-June, 1999, the *Seattle Times* reported that University of Washington Law School would have its least diverse class in three years, including only two Blacks among its 178 students. Only 41 minority students were admitted to the school, compared to 55 the preceding year, before Initiative 200 was passed. That number includes three Filipinos, seven Native Americans, five Hispanics and 24 Asians, in addition to the two Blacks. The only minority group showing an increase in Law School enrollment was Native Americans, none of whom enrolled last year.

University of Washington President Richard McCormick said that the Law School did energetically recruit and that he personally contacted all minority students who met UW standards, encouraging them to attend.

The affirmative action debate appears to be a permanent fixture of American politics because Americans are so deeply divided in their views about equality. Issues of racial equality which split the nation today probably will continue to challenge it in the years ahead. The U.S. racial problem may well have been best described by Swedish social scientist Gunnar Myrdal, who long ago called it "The American Dilemma." The nation may face no greater challenge in this new century than trying to achieve "equal protection of the law."

The Fifth Circuit disallowed the use of race as an admissions factor at University of Texas Law School and the Supreme Court refused to hear an appeal from that case in 2001. It also rejected a case from the Ninth Circuit that upheld the use of race in admissions at University of Washington Law School. The 11th Circuit struck down the use of race in admissions in a University of Georgia case. Rather than take the case to a higher court, UG officials changed their admissions policies.

University of Texas minority enrollment dropped steeply after the ruling, but Texas has since implemented a "10% solution," that automatically guarantees admission to any student finishing in the top 10% of his or her high school class. After California voters abolished affirmative action in 1996, most schools in the University of California systems made substantial gains in minority enrollment because of aggressive outreach policies. The liberal Ninth Circuit (which is overruled more by the U.S. Supreme Court than any other U.S. appellate court) embraced racial preferences in 2001, although Washington voters, in 1998, had forbidden them in admissions.

UNIVERSITY OF MICHIGAN AFFIRMATIVE ACTION CASES

Many students of the American Constitution considered it probable that the Supreme Court would revisit affirmative action issues raised in Bakke. Conflicting rulings by lower courts resulted in confusion about what universities could and could not do to promote diversity on their campuses. The Court granted *certiorari* in two cases growing out of admissions policies at University of Michigan, Ann Arbor.

Gratz v. Bollinger involved undergraduate admissions and *Grutter v. Bollinger*, involved admissions to the UM Law School.

Jennifer Gratz and Patrick Hamacher sued UM President Lee Bollinger and others after being denied admission to the undergraduate program. At the time, UM used a "selection index" system that rated prospective students on a 150-point scale.

A student needed 100 or more points to be guaranteed admission. Applicants with scores of 90-99 were admitted or postponed. Those with scores between 75-89 were delayed, and those below 75 were generally rejected.

High school grade point average and standardized test scores were worth 100 points. Other factors in the admission decision included the academic quality of the student's high school and its curriculum, family-alumni relationship, personal essay and personal achievement or leadership.

An automatic "bonus" of 20 points was given to an applicant who was a member of an underrepresented racial or ethnic minority group. UM asked its Admissions Review Committee in 1999 to "flag" for additional attention any underrepresented racial or ethnic minority group member who had been given 20 points, provided that he or she proved to be academically able to succeed, had achieved a minimum selection index and had shown characteristics considered important to the composition of the freshman class.

Jennifer Gratz grew up in Southgate, Michigan, where she graduated from Anderson High School in 1995. She had a GPA of 3.8 and an ACT score of 25, which placed her in the 82nd percentile of average national scores. She applied to the UM College of Literature, Science and Arts in the fall of 1995. Gratz had been vice president of student council, a member of the national honor society, member of the science club, a varsity cheerleader for four years, her class historian, a math tutor and had performed community service as a volunteer at a local senior center.

UM notified Gratz in January, 1996, that, although she was "well qualified," a final decision on her application would be delayed until April. At that time, she was denied admission because she was "less competitive" than students who had been accepted on first review.

Gratz was convinced that she was rejected because she was white. "If I was a minority, I probably would have gotten in," she said. She said that she had friends who were minorities who were accepted by Michigan, individuals with lower grades and test scores than she had.

With legal support from the Center for Individual Rights, Gratz filed suit in Federal District Court in Detroit, claiming that the university had violated her 14th Amendment rights, as well as Title VI of the Civil Rights Act. Judge Patrick Duggan ruled for Gratz, finding that the University of Michigan had no justification "in using race as a factor in admissions to remedy the present effects of past discrimination."

The UM appealed the Gratz decision to the Sixth Circuit Court of Appeals, which never ruled on the matter. The U.S. Supreme Court consolidated Gratz with *Grutter v. Bollinger* and decided the two cases on June 23, 2003.

Jennifer Gratz was to score a historic victory in the U.S. Supreme Court, which ruled, 6-3, that a public university system that awards an automatic 20 points out of a required 100 points needed for admission to underrepresented minorities violates the equal protection clause of the 14th Amendment.

Chief Justice Rehnquist wrote the opinion and reasoned that all racial classifications are subject to strict scrutiny under the equal protection clause. Programs using such classifications must be "narrowly tailored" to "further compelling governmental interests." Citing Bakke, Rehnquist concluded that such narrow tailoring required "individualized consideration" of applicants. The Michigan undergraduate admissions program was, he found, excessively mechanical, and did not provide such individualized consideration.

Justices Stevens, Souter and Ginsburg dissented.

After her historic victory, Gratz said:[40]

I cried because it is overwhelming, after almost six years. The whole thing is very overwhelming. I was also very pleased. I am happy the Court recognized the inherent unfairness in the undergraduate system...I believe this decision will make it harder for schools to use race-based preferences.

After her rejection by Ann Arbor, Gratz enrolled at University of Michigan, Dearborn, from which she graduated in 1999.

Patrick Hamacher, the second plaintiff in the undergraduate case, said:

I'm delighted, but I'm baffled the court didn't see the same in law school cases. After his rejection by Michigan, Hamacher enrolled at Michigan State University, from which he graduated with a degree in public administration and public policy.

Grutter v. Bollinger, 539 U.S. 306 (2003)

Barbara Grutter, a white Michigan resident, applied to the University of Michigan Law School, but was rejected. She had an undergraduate GPA of 3.8 at Michigan State University and a score of 161 out of a possible 180 on the LSAT.

After investigating her rejection, she found that Blacks and other minority applicants who had overall lower admission scores had been accepted by the Law School in the same year. White students accepted that year had a median GPA of 3.67, while minorities had a median 3.35.

Michigan made it clear that it looked beyond undergraduate transcripts and high LSAT scores to admit students to its Law School. Other criteria included letters of recommendation, quality of undergraduate institution attended, applicant's essay, courses taken as an undergraduate and "applicant's likely contributions to the intellectual and social life of the institution."

In short, UM argued, diversity was the key to its admission policy. Barbara Grutter disagreed with Michigan's stated commitment to "racial and ethnic diversity with special preference to the inclusion of students from groups which have been historically discriminated against, like African Americans, Hispanics and Native Americans, who without this commitment might not be represented in our student body in meaningful numbers." This policy, she contended, discriminated against her on the basis of race and violated the 14th Amendment and Title VI of the Civil Rights Act.

Federal District Judge Bernard A. Friedman agreed. In March, 2001, he struck down the school's use of race, finding that "the practical effect of the Law School's policy is indistinguishable from a straight quota system." He rejected Michigan's argument that its Law School admissions policy was constitutionally justified as a means to attain a diverse student body.

But UM took its case to the Sixth Circuit Court of Appeals, which overruled Judge Friedman and held that the school's consideration of race was narrowly tailored toward the permissible goal of increasing diversity.

In *Grutter v. Bollinger*, the full Sixth Circuit heard the case, bypassing the usual three-judge panel. It ruled, 5-4, that UM could use race as one factor in deciding whom to admit to its law school. The majority opinion, written by Judge Boyce Martin, Jr., stressed the educational benefits of "diversity." It said, in part:

> Justice Lewis Powell recognized that a diverse student body promotes an atmosphere of 'speculation and creation' that is essential to the quality of higher education. Moreover, he noted that, by enriching students' education with a variety of perspectives, experiences and ideas, a university with a diverse student body helps equip its students to be productive members of society. Accordingly, Powell concluded, 'the interest of diversity is compelling in the contexts of a university's admission program.'
>
> Because Justice Powell's opinion is binding on this court and because Bakke remains the law of the land until the Supreme Court instructs us otherwise, we reject the district court's conclusion and find that the Law School has a compelling interest in achieving a diverse student body...We find that the Law School's consideration of race and ethnicity is virtually indistinguishable from the Harvard plan Justice Powell approved in Bakke.

The minority opinion by Judge Danny Boggs disagreed vehemently:

> This case involves a straightforward instance of racial discrimination by a state institution. Other than in the highly charged context of discrimination in education decisions in favor of 'underrepresented minorities,' the constitutional justification offered for this practice would not pass even the slightest scrutiny.
>
> ...In our case, the intent of the framers of the policy, the statistics as to its impact and the effect, and the history of its inception all point unmistakably to a denial of equal protection of the laws...
>
> Michigan's plan does not seek diversity for education's sake. It seeks racial number for the sake of the comfort that those abstract numbers may bring. It does so at the expense of the real rights of the real people to fair consideration. It is a long road from Herman Sweatt to Barbara Grutter. But they both ended up outside a door that a government's use of racial considerations denied them a fair chance to enter. I therefore respectfully dissent from the court's legitimation of this unconstitutional policy.

In an appendix to his dissent, Judge Boggs ruffled the feathers of the majority by contending that the court didn't follow correct procedures in deciding the case. Initially, a three-judge panel was assigned to hear the case, but it delayed asking the other judges whether it should be heard by the full court until two conservative judges retired from the bench.

While some of his Sixth Circuit colleagues criticized Judge Boggs for severely undermining public confidence in the court, others praised him for his courage in reminding us that the judiciary is very much a part of the political system.

Grutter appealed to the Supreme Court, which granted *certiorari* and consolidated the case with Gratz, giving it the opportunity to clarify issues raised in Bakke.

A deeply divided Supreme Court ruled, 5-4, in favor of UM Law School. It had, the Court held, made special efforts "to achieve racial and ethnic diversity." Unlike the undergraduate program, it used no point system based in part on race.

Writing for the majority, Justice O'Connor held that the law school's admission policy was based on a "highly individualized, holistic review of each applicants file" and did not use race as a factor in a "mechanical way." That policy, she found, was compatible with Bakke's holding that race may be used as a "plus factor" in achieving a diverse student body. She wrote:[41]

> In order to cultivate a set of leaders with legitimacy in the eyes of the citizenry, it is necessary that the path to leadership be visibly open to talented and qualified individuals of every race and ethnicity. All members of our heterogeneous society must have confidence in the openness and integrity of the educational institutions that provide this training. As we have recognized, law schools 'cannot be effective in isolation from the individuals and institutions with which the law interacts.' Access to legal education (and thus to the legal profession) must be inclusive of talented and qualified individuals of every race and ethnicity, so that all members of our heterogeneous society may participate in the educational institutions that provide the training and education necessary to succeed in America."

O'Connor also noted, "We expect 25 years from now, the use of racial preferences will no longer be necessary."

Chief Justice Rehnquist and Associate Justices Scalia, Thomas and Kennedy dissented. They argued that race may never be used as a consideration in college admissions. Justice Thomas, the only Black member of the Court, wrote a strong criticism of affirmative action, which he believes is a well-motivated, but patronizing attempt by whites to help Blacks. He said:

> It is uncontested that each year, the Law School admits a handful of Blacks who would be admitted in the absence of racial discrimination...Who can differentiate between those who belong and those who do not? The majority of Blacks are admitted to the Law School because of discrimination, and because of this policy all are tarred as undeserving. The problem of stigma does not depend on determinancy as to whether those stigmatized are actually the 'beneficiaries' of racial discrimination. When Blacks take positions in the highest places of government, industry or academia, it is an open question today whether their skin color played a part in their advancement. The question itself is the stigma— because either racial discrimination did play a role, in which case the person may

be deemed 'otherwise unqualified,' or it did not, in which case asking the question itself unfairly marks those Blacks who would succeed without discrimination...

The Court's civics lesson presents yet another example of judicial selection of a theory of political representation based on skin color—an endeavor I have previously rejected...The majority appears to believe that broader utopian goals justify the Law School's use of race, but the Equal Protection Clause commands the elimination of racial barriers, not their creation, in order to satisfy our theory as to how society ought to be organized."

Despite her disappointment at being the loser in a historic case, Barbara Grutter was convinced that putting up a six-year battle against University of Michigan was the right thing to do. She said:[42]

I'm certainly very happy to have had the opportunity to be involved in the case...Six years ago when we started this, the universities practiced in the shadows. Now it's been brought into light. The issues are exposed.

Lee Bollinger, who left Michigan to become President of Columbia University in New York, said that he felt relieved when he heard the news. He committed UM to spend whatever was necessary to defend itself when the suits were filed. Ultimately, it cost Michigan more than $9 million. Bollinger said:[43]

I feel privileged to have played a role in this...It also has taught me how, when the world looks bleak from the standpoint of values you believe in...that sustained devoted effort to your principles can really bring about a change of attitude and opinion.

SEATTLE AND LOUISVILLE: STUDENT PLACEMENT AND RACIAL DIVERSITY

In 2007, the U.S. Supreme Court reviewed two cases involving voluntary integration plans in school districts in Seattle, Washington, and Louisville, Ky. Both school systems established guidelines which permitted race to be a deciding factor if two persons sought admission to a school which had room for only one of them.

School administrators sought to achieve "racial diversity" by limiting transfers on the basis of race or using race as a "tiebreaker" for admissions to specific public schools.

Parents, most of them white, challenged these policies because they had been denied admission to their preferred school on racial grounds. Divided, 5-4, the U.S. Supreme Court held that the Louisville and Seattle K-12 policies violated the Equal Protection Clause of the 14th Amendment.

Chief Justice Roberts wrote the majority opinion. He said:[44]

...Both cases present the same underling legal question—whether a public school that had not operated legally segregated schools...may choose to classify students by race and rely upon that classification in making school assignments...

It is well established that when government distributes burdens or benefits on the basis of individual racial classifications, that action is reviewed under strict scrutiny...Racial classifications are simply too pernicious to permit any but the most exact connection between justification and classification...

Accepting racial balancing as a compelling state interest would justify the imposition of racial proportionality throughout American society, contrary to our repeated recognition that 'at the heart of the Constitution's guarantee of equal protection lies the simple command that the government must treat citizens as individuals, not as simply components of a racial, religious or national class...'

...Allowing racial balancing as a compelling end in itself would 'effectively assure that race will always be relevant in American life,' and that the 'ultimate goal' of eliminating entirely from governmental decision-making such irrelevant factors as a human being's race will never be achieved...racial balancing has no logical stopping point...

...Racial balancing is not transformed from 'patently unconstitutional' to a compelling state interest simply by relabeling it 'racial diversity.'

...For schools that never segregated on the basis of race, such as Seattle, or that have removed the vestiges of past segregation, such as Jefferson County, the way to achieve a system of determining admission to the public schools on a non-racial basis is to stop assigning students on a racial basis. The way to stop discrimination on the basis of race is to stop discriminating on the basis of race...

In a nutshell, the Chief Justice said that public schools seeking to achieve integration through measures that take explicit account of a student's race violate the basic law of the land.

Roberts was joined in his opinion by Justices Scalia, Thomas and Alito. Although he agreed that the Seattle and Louisville programs were unconstitutional, Justice Kennedy wrote a concurring opinion in which he said that certain "race-conscious" measures could be used to achieve diversity without violating the Constitution.

Justice Breyer wrote the main dissenting opinion, observing that the Court was taking a sharp and seriously mistaken turn. He said:[45]

...The last half-century has witnessed great strides toward racial equality, but we have not yet realized the promises of Brown. To invalidate the plans under review is to threaten the promise of Brown. The plurality position, I fear, would break that promise. This is a decision that the Court and the Nation will come to regret.

The Michigan Civil Rights Initiative

In March, 2006, the Michigan Supreme Court ended a bitter state legal debate over putting a proposal to ban affirmative action before voters on November 7. The move to ban affirmative action was sparked by *Grutter v. Bollinger*, the decision which cleared the way for minority preferences in admission to University of Michigan's Law School.

The Michigan Civil Rights Initiative, (MCRI) was led by California businessman Ward Connerly and Jennifer Gratz, who won her case, challenging University of Michigan's undergraduate admissions policies. Connerly led a successful petition drive

(Proposition 209) to outlaw affirmative action in the Golden State. Although MCRI submitted sufficient signatures to place the measure before Michigan voters, the State Board of Canvassers failed to clear the proposal until ordered to do so by the Michigan Court of Appeals.

Opponents of the measure, led by a group called One United Michigan, launched a last-ditch effort to prevent voters from considering the proposal. They argued with allowing the phrase "preferential treatment" on the ballot, and also said that some signatures to get the issue on the ballot were obtained through misrepresentation, a charge denied by MCRI. The state Supreme Court denied review.

In January, 2006, the Board of Canvassers voted, 3-0, to approve language for the controversial initiative which would ban some affirmative action programs. The ballot language read as follows:

> A proposal to amend the state constitution to ban affirmative action programs that give preferential treatment to groups or individuals based on their race, gender, color, ethnicity, or national origin for public employment, education or contracting purposes. The proposed constitutional amendment would:
>
> - Ban public institutions from using affirmative action programs that give preferential treatment to a group or individuals based on their race, gender, color, ethnicity or national origin for public employment, education or contracting purposes. Public institutions affected by the proposal include state government, local governments, public colleges and universities, community colleges and school districts.
>
> - Prohibit public institutions from discriminating against groups or individuals due to their gender, color, ethnicity, race, color or national origin (A separate provision of the state constitution already prohibits discrimination on the basis of race, color or national origin.)
>
> - Should the proposal be adopted? Yes /No.

Both major party candidates for governor, incumbent Democrat Jennifer Granholm and Republican Dick DeVos, opposed the Civil Rights Initiative. Interest groups fighting to defeat the measure included the Michigan Catholic Conference, the Michigan Jewish Conference, the Arab-American Chamber of Commerce and several unions, including the United Auto Workers. Large corporations and major universities also opposed the measure. CRI supporters complained that they were being outspent by a margin of 10-1.[46]

Battle lines appeared to be clearly drawn, pitting, as often happens, Detroit against its suburbs and outstate areas of Michigan.

After the votes were counted, CRI supporters were jubilant. The amendment passed with about 59% of the vote. Some 1.8 million voters had effectively overturned a decision of the U.S. Supreme Court.

SEXUAL EQUALITY

Although sexual discrimination is deeply rooted in Western history, it has become an important legal issue only in recent times. Sexual discrimination lawsuits have increased dramatically in the past 20 years. Until the 1970s, women seldom achieved landmark victories in the U.S. Supreme Court. Ironically, the "Liberal" Warren Court did little to advance the cause of sexual equality. The "Conservative" Burger Court began that "revolution." Early American women had very few rights. They could not vote. They were legally subservient to their husbands. A married woman could not own property, incur debt or even keep her wages if she had a job. On entering into the marriage contract, the two lovers became one. But which one? In return for yielding her independence, the law guaranteed the new bride that her husband would provide for all her needs, **as he defined them**.

Women first became involved in political causes through the abolitionist movement. Male abolitionists, however, denied women a leadership role and separate male and female anti-slavery societies were formed. Female delegates were excluded from active roles in London's 1840 World Antislavery Convention. Elizabeth Cady Stanton and Lucretia Mott, two pioneer feminists, returned home with their own agenda to advance women's rights.

Stanton and Mott organized the first Women's Rights Conference, held at Seneca Falls, N.Y., in 1840. There about 300 delegates who approved a declaration that: "We hold these truths to be self-evident: that all men and women are created equal." But with the coming of the Civil War, most early feminists suspended their activities. They spent all of their energies on the Union war effort.

For a time, the women's suffrage movement split female leaders. Some "militant" feminists wanted to add sex to "race, color or previous condition of servitude" in the text of the 15th Amendment. Others, whose main priority was ratification of the Amendment, opposed this idea. The racial equality and women's suffrage movements were separated.

In 1869, Stanton and Anthony formed the National Suffrage Association. They believed that, if women got the vote, their lives would be much better. Their economic, political and social futures would be bright. Lucy Stone, who believed that the vote was the *only* issue, founded the American Women's Suffrage Association. It joined forces in 1890 with the Stanton-Anthony group.

Early in the 20th Century, splinter groups formed, such as Alice Paul's Congressional Union. Willing to use "radical" means, they had only one cause, women's suffrage. Paul's group took to the streets, picketed the White House and went on "hunger strikes." Some were arrested and jailed. In 1920, some 72 years after the **Senaca Falls Convention,** the 19th Amendment was passed. It provides that, *"The rights of citizens of the United States to vote shall not be denied or abridged by the United States or by any State on account of sex."*

With the exception of the suffrage movement, the issue of women's legal rights was generally ignored. The fact that most lawyers were males may have had something to do with that. Laws limiting women did not aim at segregating them from men, but were intended to protect them. These statutes dealt with such "bread and butter" union issues as wages and hours, working conditions and physical challenges to female endurance. Enacted during the first half of the 20th Century, these laws generally were viewed as "progressive," protecting the growing number of women working outside the home. Women and children were then considered particularly vulnerable to exploitation by the labor market. Many women today regard such laws as paternalistic, based on an assumption of female inferiority.

As long ago as *Mueller v. Oregon,* 208 U.S. 412 (1908), the Supreme Court upheld an Oregon law which limited female laundry workers to a 10-hour workday. The Supreme Court held that men and women differed in strength, functions and self-reliance, and so women required special protection. This traditional doctrine, sometimes called "**protective paternalism**" held until recent times. Some feminists complain that such laws, however well-intentioned they may have been at the time, have the net result of "protecting" women from higher-paying jobs.

College students of today may be surprised to learn that in 1948 the U.S. Supreme Court, in *Goesaert v. Cleary,* 335 U.S. 464 (1948), upheld a **Michigan** statute which forbade women from working as bartenders unless they were the wife or daughter of the owner. They could, however, work as waitresses. The Court was persuaded by the argument that the law protected women from the "unwholesome elements" encountered by bartenders. The exception for wives and daughters was reasonable, the Court held, because "Michigan evidently believes that the oversight assured through ownership of a bar by the barmaid's husband or father minimizes hazards that may confront a barmaid without such protecting oversight. This Court is certainly not in a position to gainsay such a belief by the Michigan legislature."[47]

THE MODERN WOMEN'S MOVEMENT

The modern feminist movement began in the late 1950s and early 1960s. Contemporary feminists often call it the "**second wave**." The "Bible" of the movement was a book by Betty Friedan called *The Feminine Mystique.* It attacked "**sexism**," or "the disease which has no name."[48]

Friedan tried to make the nation more aware of legal discrimination against females. She founded the National Organization for Women (NOW) primarily because she was unhappy with existing female organizations. She also fought against "**stereotypes**" of women.

One issue which NOW took up with great passion was sexually segregated job ads in American newspapers. Traditionally, these ads read "Help Wanted: Male" or "Help Wanted: Female." NOW, which began with about 300 members, today claims about 250,000 members.

Yet American culture changes slowly. It is very difficult to alter long-held attitudes which picture women as the "weaker sex." Even in the early years of the 21st century, some unrepentant male chauvinists believe that women ought to follow the old axiom that "a woman's place is in the home." But many other people have different attitudes, reflected in the bumper sticker slogan: "a woman's place is in the House...or the Senate."

Women, however, are **different** from men. The principle of equal protection of the laws, when applied to women, does not mean that all legal discrimination is invalid. Men have been drafted into the military services. Women have not. Although the issue of women in the military has been a topic of heated debate recently, the controlling law still is *Rostker v. Goldberg.*

Rostker v. Goldberg

Under the Selective Service Act, the President, as Commander-in-Chief, can require every male citizen and resident alien between the ages of 18-26 to register for the draft. In

1971, several draft-age men, including Robert Goldberg, sued in a Federal District Court, challenging constitutionality of the registration law. Because the draft was suspended in 1975, the suit became dormant. But in 1980, President Jimmy Carter reactivated draft registration. The President also urged Congress to change the law to require females, as well as males, to register. Congress rejected Carter's idea.

The Goldberg case then was reactivated and a U.S. District Court declared the draft registration law unconstitutional because of its single-sex provisions. "Men only" draft registration, the court held, violated the Due Process Clause of the Fifth Amendment. Bernard Rostker, director of Selective Service, appealed to the U.S. Supreme Court. As it traditionally has done in the past, the Court deferred to the Congress on military policy. It ruled, 6-3, that Congress may choose to draft men, but not women, if it considers this the best public policy. The majority opinion, written by Justice Rehnquist, said in part:[49]

> This is not...merely a case involving the customary deference accorded congressional decisions. The case arises in the context of Congress' authority over national defense and military affairs, and perhaps in no other area has the Court accorded Congress greater deference. This Court has consistently recognized Congress' 'broad constitutional power' to raise and regulate armies and navies. As the Court noted in considering a challenge to the selective service laws: 'The constitutional powers of Congress to raise and support armies and to make all laws necessary and proper to that end is broad and sweeping.'

> Not only is the scope of Congress' constitutional power in this area broad, but the lack of competence on the part of the courts is marked. None of this is to say that Congress is free to disregard the Constitution when it acts in the area of military affairs. In that area, as any other, Congress remains subject to the limitations of the Due Process Clause, but the tests and limitations to be applied may differ because of the military context. We, of course, do not abdicate our ultimate responsibility to decide the constitutional question, but simply recognize that the Constitution itself requires such deference to congressional choice. In deciding the question before us, we must be particularly careful not to substitute our judgment of what is desirable for that of Congress, or our own evaluation of evidence for a reasonable evaluation by the Legislative Branch.

> In this case, the courts are called upon to decide whether Congress, acting under an explicit constitutional grant of authority, has by that action transgressed an explicit guarantee of individual rights which limits the authority so conferred. Simply labeling the legislative decision 'military' on the one hand or 'gender-based' on the other does not automatically guide a court to the correct constitutional result.

> No one could deny that...the Government's interest in raising and supporting armies is an 'important governmental interest.' Congress and its Committees carefully considered and debated two alternative means of furthering that interest: the first was to register only males for potential conscription, and the other was to register both sexes. Congress chose the former alternative.

> When that decision is challenged on equal protection grounds, the question a court must decide is not which alternative it would have chosen, had it been the primary decision-maker, but whether that chosen by Congress denies equal protection of the laws. This case is quite different from several of the gender-based discrimination cases we have considered in that, despite appellees' assertions, Congress did not act 'unthinkingly' or 'reflexively and not for any considered

reason.' The question of registering women for the draft not only received considerable national attention and was the subject of wide-ranging public debate, but also was extensively considered by Congress in hearings, floor debate and in committee. Hearings held by both Houses of Congress in response to the President's request for authorization to register women adduced extensive testimony and evidence concerning the issue. The hearings built on other hearings held the previous year addressed to the same question.

While proposals to register women were being rejected in the course of transferring funds to register males, Committees in both Houses which had conducted hearings on the issue were also rejecting the registration of women.

The decision to exempt women from registration was not the 'accidental by-product of a traditional way of thinking about females.'

The issue was considered at great length, and Congress clearly expressed its purpose and intent.

Women as a group...unlike men as a group, are not eligible for combat. The restrictions on the participation of women in combat in the Navy and Air Force are statutory. The Army and Marine Corps preclude the use of women in combat as a matter of established policy. Congress specifically recognized and endorsed the exclusion of women from combat in exempting women from registration.

This is not a case of Congress arbitrarily choosing to burden one of two similarly situated groups, such as would be the case with an all-black or all-white, or an all-Catholic or all-Lutheran, or an all-Republican or all-Democratic registration. Men and women, because of the combat restrictions on women, are simply not similarly situated for purposes of a draft or registration for a draft.

Congress' decision to authorize the registration of only men, therefore, does not violate the Due Process Clause.

The gender classification is not invidious, but rather realistically reflects the fact that the sexes are not similarly situated in this case. The Constitution requires that Congress treat similarly situated persons similarly, not that it engage in gestures of superficial equality.

We conclude that Congress acted well within its constitutional authority when it authorized the registration of men, and not women, under the Military Selective Service Act.

Congress and the country are deeply divided on the question of women in combat. When the Persian Gulf War began in 1991, women were officially barred from combat. They were, however, exposed to the risks of battle. Women died and were taken prisoner during that conflict. At war's end, Congress voted to permit females to fly on Navy and Air Force combat missions. Some women, both in and out of the armed forces, felt that this did not go far enough and pressed President Clinton to lift the ban entirely. This plunged the Congress and nation into a rhetorical war.

In the past, women were considered "too pure" for the man's world. Certainly something as "dirty" as politics or as "cutthroat" as business were not their "proper" domain. Women were romantic and charming, if perhaps illogical in their thinking. Cultural norms of the time dictated that females should marry and be properly protected and supported by a man.

From an economic standpoint, people pitied the poor father who had an "old maid" daughter whom nobody would marry. He would be obliged to support her for the rest of his

254

life. Comparatively few fathers, certainly not those in the lower-middle classes, would consider sending their daughters to college. Why bother? They would only get married anyway.

An economics professor once told his introductory course in "Principles of Economics" in the early 1950s that only ugly "coeds" remain on campus by the junior-senior year because all of the attractive ones have married and dropped out of school. Although social attitudes change slowly, consider how that statement would be taken today. One should remember that two generations ago, the professor who made that comment did so in a class with fewer than a handful of "coeds" in it. Female students likely would be a majority of the class today.

Reed v. Reed

In 1971, the U.S. Supreme Court, in *Reed v. Reed,* considered a challenge to an Idaho law that gave men preference over women in the appointment of administrators of the estates of deceased children. Sally Reed challenged the law, arguing that it violated the 14th Amendment's Equal Protection Clause. Idaho argued that it was inefficient to hold full court hearings on the relative merits of competing candidates to administer estates, especially small estates. Cecil Reed, Sally's separated spouse, had been designated to administer an estate worth less than $1000. Imposing arbitrary criteria, Idaho said, saved court time and helped to avoid family squabbles. The Supreme Court rejected this line of argument, holding that administrative convenience is hardly a reason to violate the Constitution.

Idaho also contended that favoring males over females made sense because the man usually will have more education and experience in financial matters than a competing woman. The Court rejected this view, holding that laws containing overbroad, sex-based assumptions violate the Equal Protection Clause. The Court, speaking through Chief Justice Burger, struck down the law. Burger wrote:[50]

> To be constitutionally permissible, any law that classifies people on the basis of sex must be reasonable, not arbitrary, and must rest on some ground of difference having a fair and substantial relation to the object of the legislation so that all persons similarly circumstanced shall be treated alike.

Under this **"reasonableness standard,"** courts have permitted some distinctions based on sex and have overturned others. For example, courts have permitted the following differences based on sex:

- A California statutory rape law that punishes males, but not females, is constitutional because male and female are not "similarly situated" with respect to sexual relations. Only females can become pregnant. The statute addressed a substantial inequality between males and females based on "harmful and inescapably identifiable consequences of teenage pregnancy" (*Michael M. v. Superior Court of Sonoma County,* 450 U.S. 464, 1981).

- Florida may give widows a $500 property tax exemption not given to widowers. Because economic inequality long had existed between men and women, the Court held, the state may compensate females for past discrimination (*Kahn v. Shevin,* 416 U.S. 351, 1974).

Courts, however, also have ruled against some differences based on sex. For example:

- A state cannot set different ages at which males and females become legal adults. A law requiring child support for males until they reach age 21, but support for females only until they reach the age of 18 violates the Equal Protection Clause (*Stanton v. Stanton*, 421 U.S. 7, 1975).

- Oklahoma cannot set different ages at which males (21) and females (18) are allowed to buy beer. Oklahoma argued that young men between 18-21 were more likely to drive while drunk than young women. While conceding that traffic safety was an important state objective, the Court held that it could not approve a stereotype: that all young women were cautious drivers because they were females and that all men were reckless because they were males (*Craig v. Boren*, 429 U.S. 191, 1976).

- The Cleveland School Board cannot require female teachers to take mandatory, unpaid pregnancy leaves five months before a child is due without considering their physical ability to continue working (*Cleveland Board of Education v. LaFleur*, 414 U.S. 632, 1974).

- The Court held invalid a company retirement plan that provided smaller benefits to females by using sex-based actuarial tables which reflected the fact that females live longer than males. Employers must pay women monthly retirement benefits equal to those received by men (*Arizona Governing Committee for Tax Deferred Annuity and Deferred Compensation Plans v. Norris*, 463 U.S. 1073, 1983).

WHAT IS "SEXISM?"

When graduate students in political science studied the "isms" a generation ago, they focused on capitalism, socialism and communism. Today, although the traditional isms are still taught, they may be "less important" to political activists than other isms: racism and sexism.

One area in which there are important generational differences is on the question of woman's role in society, sex and gender. Students might well ask their grandmothers what was expected of them when they were growing up. Clearly, feminism and "women's liberation" have profoundly changed the nature of many aspects of contemporary American life.

The ERA Debate

Women of all ages supported the Equal Rights Amendment, although not in the same proportions. Originally introduced in 1923, ERA finally passed Congress in 1972. The Senate supported the measure, 84-8, and the House backed it 354-24, far more than the constitutionally required two-thirds vote in each chamber. Public opinion polls reflected strong support and prospects for ratification appeared excellent as Congress sent the measure to the states. The proposed amendment read as follows:

> *Equality of rights under the law shall not be denied or abridged by the United States or any State on account of sex.*

Congress, in proposing ERA, had specified, not at all unusual in U.S. constitutional history, a time limit of eight years. Within the first year, 22 states ratified the measure. But by 1974-75, ERA was in deep trouble. It barely passed in the Montana and North Dakota legislatures. Two states, Tennessee and Nebraska, voted to **rescind** their earlier ratifications. By 1978, some 35 states had ratified, but ERA supporters, still three states short, faced an uphill fight.

As March 22, 1979, neared, Congress extended the deadline to June 30, 1982. This infuriated some legislators, including Sam Ervin (D., N.C.), chairman of the Senate Judiciary Committee. Ervin argued that such action was unconstitutional and the process must start anew. No state which refused to ratify ERA changed its position. Why did ERA, which started out so strongly, wind up being so controversial?[51]

One issue that troubled both men and women was Selective Service. A large number of people who otherwise favored ERA were bothered by the thought that women might be drafted into the military and sent into combat. Groups like the National Organization for Women (NOW), which, more than any other women's group, championed ERA, had trouble defusing that issue. Another problem centered on the impact of ERA on existing "protective" legislation. Religious groups, particularly the National Council of Catholic Women and the Mormon Church, stressed this issue. Some conservative women, such as Phyllis Schlafly of Illinois, energetically campaigned against the amendment. Schlafly, a Republican activist who became a lawyer after raising five children, stressed the positive contributions of traditional women to American society. Through organizations called Stop-ERA and the Eagle Forum, Schlafly emphasized the issues of abortion on demand and homosexuality, linking ERA with several highly divisive social issues.

Schlafly and her followers were very effective. They suggested that women could lose custody of their children or be **forced** to work outside the home if ERA were ratified. Some ERA opponents even argued that, if ratified, it would mean "unisex" public toilets. When ERA lost, Schlafly said that its defeat was "the greatest victory for women's rights since the women's suffrage amendment in 1920."

In the final analysis, the political problem may well have been one of strategy. Some feminists, perhaps unwittingly, "clouded" the issue by bringing in "fringe issues." This diluted support for ERA and stressed the "culture war" going on in America. It was difficult, for example, for many middle-class suburban housewives, not all that unhappy with their lifestyles, to concern themselves with the "rights" of lesbians and the desire for some militant feminists to open up military combat service to women. When the Republican Party abandoned its historic support for the measure in its 1980 platform and presidential nominee Ronald Reagan actively opposed it, ERA was dead, at least for the foreseeable future.

Was ERA Necessary?

Some legal scholars, both men and women, argue that ERA, while symbolically important, gives women no new rights. They already have, it is argued, all the rights they seek under the 14th Amendment's Equal Protection Clause. If one examines the decisions of both Federal and state courts in recent years, a strong argument can be made that women are winning many of their legal battles with the 14th Amendment. They also are winning many legislative battles.

Fundamentals reviewed: In studying the process by which constitutional amendments are proposed and ratified, students should remember that:

- Even if two-thirds of both houses of Congress agree to submit a proposal to the states, it is very difficult to win a three-fourths ratification vote on a deeply divisive issue.

- A minority of 13 states can prevent any amendment from becoming law. When geographic regions oppose a measure (the Mormon influence was strong in the Rocky Mountain states and social conservatism powerful in the South), ratification may be impossible.

SEX AND GENDER

Sex roles relate to biology. It is who and what we are because we are male or female. Gender is a term used by sociologists and others to refer to "normal" behavior expected of males and females in a particular society. It should be noted that behaviors considered quite "normal" in one society may be considered quite "strange" in another. "Social deviance" also is a changing concept. Many of today's accepted behaviors hardly would have been acceptable years ago. Again, students might ask their grandparents what they could and could not do without risking severe disapproval.

Sexism may be viewed as those arrangements in which societies express preferences for males over females. Historically, most societies have been—and still are—**patriarchal,** or male-dominated. Although feminists find much discrimination against American women, such discrimination pales into relative insignificance when compared to what women suffer elsewhere in the world, particularly in traditional societies.

Such societies generally prefer traditional male and female roles. This division of labor, they believe, benefits the nation as well as individual males and females. In "traditional" social systems, what is expected of men and women is very clearly defined. The result is both family and social stability.

Not All Feminists Are Alike

American feminists argue as much among themselves as they do with "outsiders." Indeed, what is feminism? Few, particularly males, would dare to pontificate on that question. Some feminists, however, focus on **power.** Sex roles are not equal in power and women lack the power, prestige and resources enjoyed by men, they conclude. Males, they argue, try to control females through power arrangements, particular those relating to economic power.

One widely known feminist is Kate Millett, whose book, *Sexual Politics,* reflects one view of American society. Ms. Millett wrote:[52]

What goes largely unexamined, often even unacknowledged...in our social order, is the birthright priority whereby males rule females. Through this system, a most ingenious form of 'interior colonization' has been achieved. It is one which tends moreover to be sturdier than any form of segregation, and more rigorous than class stratification, more uniform, certainly more enduring. However muted its present appearance may be, sexual domination obtains nevertheless as perhaps the most pervasive ideology of our culture and provides its most fundamental concept of power. This is so because our society, like all other historical civilizations, is a patriarchy. The fact is evident at once if one recalls that the military, industry, technology, universities, science, political office and finance—in short, every avenue of power within the society, including the coercive force of the police—is entirely in male hands. As the essence of politics is power, such realization cannot fail to carry impact.

ECONOMICS

One of the more dramatic changes in American life in the past half-century has been the move of women from the home to the job market. In 1940, a year before the U.S. entered World War II, less than 20% of U.S. females age 16 and older were in the labor force. This doubled to more than 40% by 1970. In 2002, according to the U.S. Department of Labor, nearly two-thirds were in the labor force.

Equal Pay Act

In 1963, Congress passed the **Equal Pay Act.** Essentially, the law forbids sex-based discrimination in wages paid for equal work on jobs when their performance requires efforts, skills and responsibility under comparable conditions. But what kinds of jobs do American women have?

Evidence is convincing that there is a **"pink-collar ghetto"** in the American job market. These "female jobs" involve a relatively small number of occupations: secretary (99% female), telephone operator (88% female) and nurse (94% female). Other examples include clerical workers, waitresses, salespersons, domestics and elementary and secondary school teachers.

Whatever the reasons, women tend to be more likely to work in the **"secondary" job sector** of the economy. Such jobs are characterized by their relatively low wages and poor fringe benefits, lack of promotional opportunity, poor working conditions and little or no job security.

Even women who "make it" into the professions often have problems winning acceptance from some of their male peers.

Journalism, two generations ago, was largely a male preserve, with a few exceptions. There were the "society" and "women's" news sections and an occasional female reporter who tended to be "one of the guys." But male city editors generally would not send female reporters on "dangerous" assignments, such as the police beat. Edna Buchanan of *The Miami Herald*, one of many women police reporters today, has won the coveted Pulitzer Prize for her work.

Females working on copy desks, in sports departments, as photographers and especially as editors were rare until recently. Today they are commonplace. Some newspaper readers may well conclude that American women have made remarkable progress.

The Comparable Worth Debate

The recognition that "pink collar ghetto" and other traditional female jobs are undervalued has called for a new approach to setting wages, called "**comparable worth**." Proponents of comparable worth argue that women should receive equal pay for work requiring comparable skill, education and effort. The state of Washington, which lost a $500 million "comparable worth" lawsuit, and several local communities have introduced such plans, although resistance to the idea is strong. The late Clarence Pendleton, chairman of the Civil Rights Commission during the Reagan presidency, once referred to comparable worth as "the looniest idea since Looney Tunes."

Early in the 21st Century, Mr. Pendleton's view notwithstanding, comparable worth is a concept that probably will be presented by feminist lawyers in the courts.

Title VII of the Civil Rights Act of 1964 forbids discrimination in employment on the basis of sex, as well as race, color, religion and national origin. But, initially, government was slow to use the act to combat cases of sex discrimination. Federal courts often tolerated discrimination based on "sex-plus" distinction to justify corporate policies that provided for compensation for all non-job related disabilities except pregnancy. Such policies, the Court ruled, do not constitute sex discrimination because they are not based simply on sex but on sex plus the characteristics of pregnancy.[53] In 1978, Congress overturned the decision by enacting the **Pregnancy Discrimination Act.**

The Sexual Harassment Debate

Title VII is now used to attack sexual harassment in the workplace, but judicial acceptance of harassment as discrimination was slow to develop. Initially, courts simply refused to view sexual harassment as discrimination, ruling that such matters were private disputes not covered by Title VII.

The U.S. Supreme Court did not rule on the matter until it considered *Meritor Savings Bank v. Vinson,* 477 U.S. 57 (1986). It held that sexual harassment need not result in promotion or job loss to be forbidden. Sex discrimination could also be the result of a **hostile environment.**

The creation of an offensive or hostile working environment is, the majority held through Justice Rehnquist, enough to satisfy the definition of sex discrimination. Not every case of offensive behavior constitutes harassment, but the Court concluded that a pattern of behavior that includes such things as requests for sexual favors, sexual innuendoes or sexual insults creates an employment disparity prohibited by Title VII.

The issue of sexual harassment received enormous national publicity in 1991. Anita Hill, a University of Oklahoma Law School professor, charged that Clarence Thomas had sexually harassed her while she was one of his subordinates at the Equal Employment Opportunity Commission. Hill's charges came in testimony before the Senate Judiciary Committee, reviewing Thomas' qualifications to become a U.S. Supreme Court justice. The nominee, undergoing examination before the spotlight of national TV cameras, denied the charges and eventually won Senate confirmation.

The Hill-Thomas controversy was but a prelude to a major national debate on sexual harassment during the 1990s. The Supreme Court's docket clearly reflected this.

In *Harris v. Forklift Systems, Inc.*, 510 U.S. 17 (1993), Teresa Harris sued her former employer, Forklift Systems, Inc., claiming that the conduct of Forklift President Charles Hardy toward her constituted "abusive work environment" harassment because of her gender, in violation of Title VII of the Civil Rights Act of 1964.

Declaring this to be "a close case," the District Court found that Forklift's president often insulted Harris because of her gender and often made her the target of unwanted sexual innuendos. Hardy told Harris on several occasions, "You're a woman, what do you know?" He also said, "You are a dumb ass woman." He suggested, in front of witnesses, that the two of them "go to the Holiday Inn to negotiate."

In August, 1987, Harris complained to Hardy about his conduct. He said that he was surprised that she was offended, claimed that he was only joking and apologized. Based on his assurances that he would stop the offensive behavior, Harris stayed on the job. But within a month, Hardy resumed his harassment. Harris quit and sued in U.S. District Court.

The court concluded, however, that the comments in question did not create an abusive environment because they were not "so severe as to...seriously affect Harris' psychological well-being or lead her to suffer injury." The decision was affirmed by the Sixth-Circuit Court of Appeals. The U.S. Supreme Court granted *certiorari* and reversed that decision.

Justice O'Connor found that a victim of sexual harassment need not prove psychological harm to win damages and that the law protects victims of sexual harassment "before the harassing conduct leads to a nervous breakdown." She wrote:[54]

> A discriminatorily abusive work environment, even one that does not seriously affect employees' psychological well-being, can and often will detract from employees' job performance, discourage employees from remaining on the job or keep them from advancing in their careers. Moreover, even without regard to these tangible effects, the very fact that the discriminatory conduct was so severe or pervasive that it created a work environment abusive to employees because of their race, gender, religion or national origin offends title VII's broad rule of workplace equality.

> We therefore believe that the District Court erred in relying on whether the conduct 'seriously affected plaintiff's psychological well-being' or led her to 'suffer injury.' Such an inquiry may needlessly focus the fact-finder's attention on concrete psychological harm, an element Title VII does not require.

> We therefore reverse judgment of the Court of Appeals and remand the case for further proceedings consistent with this opinion.

The 1997-98 term of the Supreme Court was noteworthy for the fact that the justices decided four cases involving sexual harassment. In so doing, it clarified the rules for determining the liability of employers and, in the instance of sexual harassment committed by teachers, the liability of school districts. It also, for the first time, considered the question of same-sex harassment.

In the 1998-99 term, it decided a case which raised the question of whether a school district can be found liable under Federal law for one student's harassment of another.

Employer Liability for Sexual Harassment: On June 26, 1998, the Supreme Court issued rulings in two cases involving employer responsibility for sexual misconduct of supervisors. *Faragher v. City of Boca Raton, Fla.*, 524 U.S. 775 (1998), and *Burlington Industries v. Ellerth*, 524 U.S. 742 (1998), raised the question: Can employers be held responsible for harassment, even if they know nothing about the behavior?

By 7-2 votes in both cases, the Court made it clear that workers need no longer prove that an employer knew or should have known about the sexual harassment and failed to stop it. Victims do not necessarily have to show that they lost out on a promotion or were fired because they spurned a boss's sexual advances. If the boss's threats and other abuses were severe or pervasive, that's sufficient grounds for a lawsuit.

The decision sent a clear message to American businesses. Sexual misconduct must be taken seriously and any firm that doesn't can expect to pay a price.

The Boca Raton case involved Mary Beth Faragher, a college student who worked part-time and during summers as an ocean lifeguard for the Marine Safety section of the Parks and Recreation Department between 1985 and 1990. In June, 1990, she resigned and said that two of her supervisors, Bill Terry and David Silverman, had harassed her. Faragher alleged that her bosses slapped her on the rear, patted her thigh, tackled her to the ground and made vulgar comments about her breasts. Terry, she said, called women "bitches" and Silverman performed a pantomime in front of female lifeguards depicting a sex act and told Faragher, "Date me or clean the toilets for a year!"

She never complained to recreation department management about the conduct, but sued for harassment, asserting that Terry and Silverman were agents of the city and their conduct amounted to discrimination in the "terms, conditions and privileges" of her employment. She sought a judgment against the city for damages, costs and attorney's fees.

Although the City of Boca Raton had adopted a sexual harassment policy in 1986 and revised it in 1990, it failed to circulate memos and statements of its policy among employees of the Marine Safety section, with the result that Terry, Silverman and other lifeguards were unaware of it.

The Federal District Court ruled that the harassment was sufficiently serious and met the test for discrimination under Title VII of the 1964 Civil Rights Act. But the U.S. Court of Appeals for the 11th Circuit reversed the ruling, holding that employers were liable only if they had given supervisors authority to harass. Other appeals courts had ruled that employers would be liable if they were **negligent** in permitting the supervisor's conduct to occur. The U.S. Department of Justice entered the case on Faragher's side, arguing that the appeals court interpreted the law too narrowly. The Supreme Court granted *certiorari*.

The justices set a new national standard, lowering the bar for workers and said that an employer is responsible for supervisors' misconduct in situations such as Faragher's that constitute what is known as a **"hostile work environment"** or for misconduct carried on by co-workers and supervisors that is severe or pervasive.

Lower Federal courts have been in agreement that employers are responsible for **"quid pro quo"** sexual harassment, in which a boss typically links requests for sexual favors with some job consequence. In *Faragher*, the Court ruled that employer liability should be the same for the two kinds of cases, partly because employers should anticipate such misconduct and try to prevent it. Justice David Souter, writing for a 7-2 majority, said:[55]

When a person with supervisory authority discriminates in the terms and conditions of subordinates' employment, his actions necessarily draw upon his superior position over the people who report to him, or those under them, whereas an employee generally cannot check a supervisor's abusive conduct the same way that she might deal with abuse from a co-worker. When a fellow employee harasses, the victim can walk away or tell the offender where to go, but it may be difficult to offer such responses to a supervisor, whose 'power to supervise, to hire and fire, to set work schedules and pay rates does not disappear when he chooses to harass through insults and offensive gestures rather than directly with threats of firing or promises of promotion.' Recognition of employer liability when discriminatory misuse of supervisory authority alters the terms and conditions of a victim's employment is underscored by the fact that the employer has a greater opportunity to guard against misconduct by supervisors than by common workers; employers have greater opportunity and incentive to screen them, train them and monitor their performance.

The judgment of the Court of Appeals of the 11th Circuit is reversed and the case is remanded for reinstatement of the judgment of the district court.

A companion case involved Kimberly Ellerth, a marketing representative for Burlington Industries in Chicago from March, 1993, until May, 1994. Her supervisor, Ted Slowik, a Burlington vice president, allegedly told her, "I could make your job very hard or very easy," asked her to wear shorter skirts and touched her inappropriately. Ellerth did not submit and did not lose her job or a promotion. But after she quit her job, she sued in Federal District Court in Chicago. The trial court granted summary judgment to Burlington. Although it found Slowik's behavior created a hostile work environment, it also found that Burlington neither knew nor should it have known about the conduct. The Court noted that Ellerth had not used Burlington's internal complaint procedures.

The U.S. Court of Appeals for the Seventh Circuit reversed, Burlington appealed, and the Supreme Court granted *certiorari*.

Justice Kennedy, writing for the majority in *Burlington Industries v. Ellerth*, held that harassment victims need not show an obvious job consequence. But the Court also held that if there is no clear job loss, the employer can overcome liability by showing that it took reasonable care to prevent and correct harassment and that the employee herself failed to take reasonable stops to either prevent or stop the harassment. Kennedy wrote:[56]

> An employer is subject to vicarious liability to a victimized employee for an actionable hostile environment created by a supervisor with immediate…authority over the employee. When no tangible employment action is taken, a defending employer may raise an affirmative defense to liability or damages, subject to proof by preponderance of the evidence.

> The defense comprises two necessary elements (a) that the employer exercised reasonable care to prevent and correct promptly any sexually harassing behavior and (b) that the plaintiff employee unreasonably failed to take advantage of any preventive or corrective opportunities provided by the employer or to avoid harm otherwise.

> While proof that an employer had promulgated an anti-harassment policy with complaint procedure is not necessary in every instance, as a matter of law, the need for a stated policy suitable to the employment circumstances may

appropriately be addressed in any case when litigating the first element of defense. And while proof that an employee failed to fulfill the corresponding obligation of reasonable care to avoid harm is not limited to showing any unreasonable failure to use any complaint procedure provided by the employer, a demonstration of such failure will normally suffice to satisfy the employer's burden under the second element of the defense. No affirmative defense is available, however, when the supervisor's harassment culminates in a tangible employment action, such as discharge, demotion or undesirable reassignment.

Although Ellerth has not alleged she suffered a tangible employment action at the hands of Slowik, which would deprive Burlington of the availability of the affirmative defense, this is not dispositive. In light of our decision, Burlington is still subject to...liability for Slowik's activity, but Burlington should have the opportunity to assert and prove the affirmative defense to liability.

For these reasons, we will affirm the judgment of the court of appeals, reversing the grant of summary judgment against Ellerth. On remand, the district court will have the opportunity to decide whether it would be appropriate to allow Ellerth to amend her pleading or supplement her discovery.

Same-Sex Sexual Harassment: *Oncale v. Sundowner Offshore Service*, 523 U.S. 75 (1998). Joseph Oncale was working as a roustabout on a Chevron U.S.A., Inc., oil platform in the Gulf of Mexico in 1991. His supervisor, John Lyons, the crane operator, and two co-workers, drillers Danny Pippen and Brandon Johnson, allegedly sexually taunted, abused and humiliated him.

Oncale's case involved far more than aggressive horseplay or typical hazing in an all-male environment. He complained to an official of Sundowner Offshore Services about abuse that included threats of rape, but the company did nothing about it. At one point, two men grabbed him in the shower and forced a bar of soap between his buttocks. After that incident, Oncale, then 21, quit his job and sued under Title VII of the 1964 Civil Rights Act, which forbids sexual harassment on the job.

The U.S. District Court for the Eastern District of Louisiana threw out the case, saying that a man who claims that he was victimized by other men cannot rely on a law that was written to protect women from men. On appeal, a panel of the Fifth Circuit affirmed.

The Supreme Court granted *certiorari* to clarify the law. Some lower Federal courts had held that "harassment is harassment regardless of whether it is caused by a member of the same or opposite sex." Some have held that same-sex sexual harassment claims are never cognizable under Title VII. Other decisions say that such claims are actionable only if the plaintiff can prove that the harasser is homosexual.

On March 5, 1998, the Supreme Court held that Title VII covers misconduct even when the victim and harasser are the same sex. The justices said that the law covers homosexual situations, as well as harassment between two people of the same sex, when neither person is gay. In Oncale, all four men involved in the dispute were heterosexual.

Justice Scalia, writing for the majority, said:[57]

Male-on-male sexual harassment in the workplace was assuredly not the principal evil Congress was concerned with when it enacted Title VII. But statutory prohibitions often go beyond the principal evil to cover reasonably comparable evils, and it is ultimately the provisions of our laws rather than the principal concerns of our legislators by which we are governed. Title VII prohibits discrimination because of sex in the terms or conditions of employment. Our holding that this includes sexual harassment must extend to sexual harassment of any kind that meets the statutory requirements.

Responding to concerns of the business community about frivolous lawsuits, Justice Scalia stressed that "common sense" should prevail in harassment cases. Courts, he said, should not "mistake ordinary socializing in the workplace—such as male-on-male horseplay"—for sexual discrimination. He wrote:

> The prohibition of harassment on the basis of sex requires neither asexuality nor androgyny in the workplace; it forbids only behavior so objectively offensive as to alter the conditions of the victim's employment. Conduct that is not severe or pervasive enough to create an objectively hostile or abusive work environment—an environment that a reasonable person would find hostile or abusive—is beyond Title VII's purview. We have always regarded that requirement as crucial, and as sufficient to ensure that courts and juries do not mistake ordinary socializing in the workplace—such as male-on-male horseplay or intersexual flirtation—for discriminatory 'conditions of employment.'

Justice Scalia concluded:[58]

> In same-sex harassment cases…inquiry requires careful consideration of the social context in which particular behavior occurs and is experienced by its target. A professional football player's working environment is not severely or pervasively abusive, for example, if the coach smacks him on the buttocks as he heads onto the field—even if the same behavior would reasonably be experienced as abusive by the coach's secretary (male or female) back at the office. The real social impact of workplace behavior often depends on a constellation of surrounding circumstances, expectations and relationships which are not fully captured by a simple recitation of the words used or the physical acts performed. Common sense and an appropriate sensitivity to social context will enable courts and juries to distinguish between simple teasing or roughhousing among members of the same sex, and conduct which a reasonable person in the plaintiff's position would find severely hostile or abusive.
>
> Judgment of the Court of Appeals for the Fifth Circuit is reversed, and the case is remanded for further proceedings consistent with this opinion.

Thus, the effect of the Oncale ruling was that plaintiffs must show that they were targeted because of their sex. It left open the question about how easy it would be for someone working in an all-male environment to prove that men picked on him because he was a man. The ruling sent the case back to Federal District Court to determine whether Joseph Oncale was singled out because of his sex and whether the harassment was severe and pervasive.

The U.S. Equal Opportunity Commission reports that sexual harassment claims have more than doubled since 1991, to about 16,000 complaints a year. About 12% of those are filed by men.

Sexual Harassment of Students by Teachers: On Monday, June 22, 1998, the Court held, 5-4, in *Gebser v. Lago Vista Independent School District*, 524 U.S. 274 (1998), that **a school district could not be held liable for harassment unless it knew of the abuse and was deliberately indifferent to it.** The case involved a school district near Austin, Texas, where Frank Waldrop, 52, a high school teacher, had seduced a ninth grader in 1992 and engaged in sexual relations with her over the course of a year. The girl, Alida Star Gebser, was in a program for gifted and talented students. She later testified that she was both flattered and flustered by Waldrop's attention and did not know who to tell about it. She never told school officials about the relationship, which ended in January, 1993, when a police officer discovered the two engaging in sexual intercourse in a car. Waldrop was arrested, fired by the Lago Vista School District, lost his Texas teaching license and was criminally prosecuted.

Gebser and her mother filed suit in Federal District Court in Austin against the Lago Vista Independent School District. They sought damages under Title IX of the Education Amendments of 1972, which forbids sex discrimination by educational institutions that receive Federal money, a definition that applies to all public school districts. The district court dismissed the suit, holding that the school district could be liable only if a supervisory employee "actually knew of the abuse, had the power to end the abuse and failed to do so." The Fifth Circuit Court of Appeals affirmed the ruling. Because of inconsistencies with other Federal court rulings in similar cases, the Supreme Court granted *certiorari*.

Justice O'Connor, writing for the majority, said:[59]

It does not appear that Congress contemplated unlimited recovery in damages against a funding recipient where the recipient is unaware of discrimination in its programs. When Title IX was enacted in 1972, the principal civil rights statutes containing an express right of action did not provide for recovery of monetary damages at all, instead allowing only injunctive and equitable relief. It was not until 1991 that Congress made damages available under Title VII, and even then, Congress carefully limited the amount recoverable in any individual case. Adopting petitioners' position would amount then, to allowing unlimited recovery of damages under Title IX where Congress has not spoken on the subject of either the right or the remedy, and in the face of evidence that when Congress expressly considered both in Title VII, it restricted the amount of damages available.

The number of reported cases involving sexual harassment of students in schools confirms that harassment unfortunately is an all too common aspect of the educational experience. No one questions that a student suffers extraordinary harm when subjected to sexual harassment and abuse by a teacher, and that the teacher's conduct is reprehensible and undermines the basic purposes of the educational system. The issue in this case, however, is whether the independent misconduct of a teacher is attributable to the school district that employs him under a specific federal statute designed primarily to prevent recipients of federal financial assistance from using the funds in a discriminatory manner.

Our decision does not affect any right of recovery that an individual may have against a school district as a matter of state law or against the teacher in his individual capacity under state law. Until Congress speaks directly on the subject, however, we will not hold a school district liable in damages under Title IX for a teacher's sexual harassment of a student absent actual notice and deliberate indifference. We therefore affirm the judgment of the Court of Appeals.

Dissents: In a dissenting opinion, Justice Stevens said that the Court had given school districts an incentive not to take steps to protect vulnerable students. He wrote, "As long as school boards can insulate themselves from knowledge about this sort of conduct, they can claim immunity from damages liability." The majority's logic, he concluded, suggests that: "No damages should ever be awarded in a Title IX case."

In a separate dissent, Justice Ginsburg wrote that, if a school district had an effective policy in place for reporting and redressing sexual harassment, such a policy could be an "affirmative defense" against a lawsuit by a plaintiff who had not taken proper advantage of the policy.

Sexual Harassment of Students by Students: During its 1998-99 term, the Supreme Court considered the question of whether students who are sexually harassed by other students may sue their schools for money damages under Federal law.

The case, *Davis v. Monroe County Board of Education*, 526 U.S. 629 (1999), is an appeal by the mother of a 10-year-old girl, LaShonda Davis, who was harassed repeatedly by a boy in her Hubbard School fifth-grade classroom in Macon, Ga. The boy, identified as G.F. in the case, repeatedly attempted to touch the child's breasts and genitals and said, "I want to get in bed with you." He rubbed up against her in the hallways of the elementary school. The child reported each of these incidents to her mother and to her classroom teacher, Diane Fort. The teacher took no action, refusing for three months to let the girl change her assigned seat. The principal also took no action and the school made no attempts to separate LaShona and G.F.

As the situation worsened, the girl's previously high grades dropped and she threatened suicide. When it became obvious that the school, which had no sexual harassment or grievance procedure, was not going to act to protect LaShonda, her mother filed a criminal complaint against G .F. The boy pleaded guilty to sexual battery in Juvenile Court and was ordered to attend counseling sessions.

Seeking to hold the school accountable, the girl's mother then filed a lawsuit against the district, alleging that Title IX had been violated. The suit initially was dismissed by U.S. District Court Judge Wilbur Owens of Macon, Ga. The U.S. Court of Appeals in Atlanta ruled in 1998 that institutions have no obligation to address complaints of student-on-student sexual harassing.

Relying on Title IX's plain language, and its own 1998 decision in *Gebser v. Lago Vista Independent School District*, a Supreme Court (5-4) majority reversed that decision, concluding that, when schools are indifferent, they can be held liable for monetary damages.

Writing for the majority, Justice O'Connor emphasized that "damages are not available for simple acts of teasing and name-calling among school children" but rather for behavior "so severe, pervasive, and objectively offensive that it denies its victims the equal access to education" guaranteed under Title IX of the Education Amendments of 1972. School officials must have known of the harassment and, acting with "deliberate indifference," failed to take reasonable steps to stop it.

O'Connor wrote:[60]

The statute makes clear that, whatever else it prohibits, students must not be denied access to educational benefits and opportunities on the basis of gender.

We thus conclude that funding recipients are properly held liable in damages only where they are deliberately indifferent to sexual harassment, of which they have actual knowledge, that is so severe, pervasive, and objectively offensive that it can be said to deprive the victims of access to the educational opportunities or benefits provided by the school.

The most obvious example of student-on-student sexual harassment capable of triggering a damages claim would thus involve the overt, physical deprivation of access to school resources.

Consider, for example, a case in which male students physically threaten their female peers every day, successfully preventing the female students from using a particular school resource—an athletic field or a computer lab, for instance. District administrators are well aware of the daily ritual, yet they deliberately ignore requests for aid from the female students wishing to use the resource. The district's knowing refusal to take any action in response to such behavior would fly in the face of Title IX's core principles and such deliberate indifference may appropriately be subject to claim for monetary damages.

A plaintiff must establish sexual harassment of students that is so severe, pervasive and objectively offensive, and that so undermines and detracts from the victims' educational experience, that the victim-students are effectively denied equal access to an institution's resources and opportunities.

Whether gender-oriented conduct rises to the level of actionable 'harassment' thus 'depends on a constellation of surrounding circumstances, expectations and relations' including, but not limited to, the ages of the harasser and the victim and the number of individuals involved.

Courts, moreover, must bear in mind that schools are unlike the adult workplace and that children may regularly interact in a manner that would be unacceptable among adults. Indeed, at least early on, students are still learning how to interact appropriately with their peers. It is thus understandable that, in the school setting, students often engage in insults, banter, teasing, shoving, pushing and gender-specific conduct that is upsetting to the students subjected to it. Damages are not available for simple acts of teasing and name-calling among school children, however, even where these comments target differences in gender. Rather, in the context of student-on-student harassment, damages are available only where the behavior is so severe, pervasive and objectively offensive that it denies its victims the equal access to education Title IX is designed to protect.

Dissent: Justice Kennedy, writing for the dissenters, said that nothing in Title IX suggests that Congress intended or contemplated the result the court reaches. Kennedy said:[61]

The majority seems oblivious to the fact that almost every child, at some point, has trouble in school because he or she is being teased by his or her peers. After today, Johnny will find that the routine problems of adolescence are to be resolved by invoking a federal right to demand assignment to a desk two rows away. We can be assured that suits will follow suits, which in cost and number will impose serious financial burdens on local school districts, the taxpayers who support them and the children they serve.

The norms of the adult workplace that have defined hostile environment sexual harassment are not easily translated to peer relationships in schools where teen-age romantic relationships and dating are a part of everyday life...a teen-ager's romantic overtures to a classmate (even when persistent and unwelcome) are an inescapable part of adolescence.

The Supreme Court decision permitted LaShonda Davis and her mother to go ahead with their $500,000 civil rights lawsuit against the Monroe County (Forsyth, Ga.) Board of Education. For her case to prevail, Davis must show that the school board knew her daughter was being sexually harassed and did nothing about it, and that the harassment was so severe it hampered LaShonda's ability to learn.

POLITICS AND GOVERNMENT

Males clearly dominate American politics. No woman ever has been nominated for President by a major political party. None was nominated for Vice President until Democrat Walter Mondale chose Geraldine Ferraro as his running mate in 1984. Until 1981, when President Ronald Reagan appointed Sandra Day O'Connor, no woman ever served on the U.S. Supreme Court. President Clinton appointed Ruth Bader Ginsburg, a noted feminist lawyer and law school professor at Columbia University as the second female member of the Court. Justice Ginsburg, who was sworn in on August 10, 1993, said at her oath-taking, "Times are changing...a system of justice will be the richer for diversity of background and experience." Few women, until the past generation, were elected to Congress on their own merits. There once was the **"widow's mandate,"** under which a woman sometimes was appointed by a governor to succeed her husband, who had died while serving in the U.S. Senate. Some women succeeded their husbands as governor where state constitutions prohibited them from serving consecutive terms. Examples would be "Ma and Pa" Ferguson of Texas in the 1930s and Lurleen Wallace, who succeeded her spouse, George, as governor of Alabama.

Women like Rep. Clare Booth Luce (R., Mass.), were exceptional in the 1950s. Not until the 1970s, when Ella Grasso (Ct., 1974) and Dixy Lee Ray (Wa., 1976) were elected in their own right, did women begin to win gubernatorial elections. In 2008, there are eight female governors. They are Democrats Ruth Minner of Delaware, Jennifer Granholm of Michigan, Janet Napolitano of Arizona, Kathleen Sebelius of Kansas, Christine Gregoire of Washington, and Republicans Linda Lingle of Hawaii, Jodi Rell of Connecticut, and Sarah Palin of Alaska.

The number of female office holders has grown greatly, but still is hardly equitable. Although Blacks contend that they are under-represented in Congress, the numbers indicate quite clearly that women—a majority of the U.S. population—have only token representation in the 110th Congress. In 2008, only 16 of 100 U.S. senators and 70 of 435 House members are women.

That figure, however, represented a gain of seven female senators, all but one Democrats, and 21 women representatives over the 106th Congress. Former First Lady

Hillary Clinton was elected to the Senate from New York, replacing retiring Democrat Daniel Patrick Moynihan.

In a race between two MSU alumni, Debbie Stabenow became the first female ever elected to the U.S. Senate from Michigan, defeating incumbent Republican Spence Abraham. Abraham later was appointed as Secretary of Transportation in the Bush Administration.

In one of the strangest elections on record, voters in Missouri elected a dead man, Gov. Mel Carnahan, over Republican incumbent John Ashcroft. The lieutenant governor of Missouri, who became Chief Executive when Carnahan was killed in a plane crash, promised that he would appoint the governor's widow to her husband's seat, if he were elected posthumously. Jean Carnahan was sworn in on January 3, 2001, becoming the first woman in Missouri history ever to serve in the U.S. Senate. President Bush subsequently appointed Ashcroft as U.S. Attorney General

Senator Carnaham had a brief legislative career, losing a special election for the remainder of the six-year term in November, 2002, to U.S. Rep. James Talent, a Republican. Talent lost in 2006 to a woman, Claire McCaskill.

The Carnaham and Stabenow victories helped Democrats to gain a 50-50 tie with Republicans. They later took control of that body when Vermont Republican James Jeffords, convinced that his party was becoming "too conservative," announced that he was becoming an Independent. This temporarily gave Democrats a 50-49-1 edge and control of the Senate. Republicans regained control after the mid-term election of 2002 and increased their margin from 51-48-1 to 55-44-1 after the presidential contest of 2004.

The fourth woman added to the ranks of senators elected in 2000 was Maria Cantwell of Washington, a native of Indiana and a graduate of Miami, Ohio, University.

A familiar name again in the Senate is Dole. This time, it's Elizabeth Dole, wife of former GOP leader and 1996 presidential nominee Bob Dole, who represents North Carolina.

WHAT ARE LITTLE GIRLS MADE OF?

In learning to become female in America, older women were taught as children that little girls were made of *"sugar and spice and everything nice,"* but little boys were made of *"snakes and snails and puppy dog tails."*

Sociology texts commonly stress the fact that parents treat boys and girls differently. American schools have reinforced sex role stereotypes by their curriculum, in textbooks, in teacher-student relations and in guidance counseling given female students. Women themselves have often limited little girls by suggesting that they should consider, for example, nursing careers rather than become physicians. Seldom in the past did counseling centers suggest that females go into law, architecture or engineering. Times, however, have changed.

Unwanted in Illinois: Female Lawyers

In *Bradwell v. Illinois* (1873), the U.S. Supreme Court heard a challenge to an action by the Illinois Supreme Court denying Myra Bradwell a license to practice law solely because of her sex. Bradwell, who was editor of the *Chicago Legal News,* had been certified as educationally qualified to practice law. But her application to become an attorney was rejected by the Illinois Bar. She then advanced a new argument, that this denial violated the Equal Protection Clause of the 14th Amendment. The Court upheld the Illinois Bar and reflected a common, 19th Century male attitude, as Justice Joseph Bradley observed:[62]

> The civil law, as well as nature herself, has recognized a wide difference in the respective spheres and destinies of man and woman. Man is, or should be, women's protector and defender. The natural and proper timidity and delicacy which belongs to the female sex evidently unfits it for many of the occupations of civil life.

One can only wonder what Justice Bradley would think of modern feminism, women (Hillary Clinton) running for President, women serving in the military, particularly under combat conditions. Two females, Sandra Day O'Connor and Ruth Bader Ginsburg, have been Supreme Court justices and a Black female, Carol Moseley Braun, formerly represented Illinois in the U.S. Senate. Lest Justice Bradley be unduly pilloried, one should note that only Chief Justice Salmon P. Chase dissented in *Bradwell*.

Actually, feminists insist, all social institutions in America are sexist. Some want a more "democratic" marriage system. Other, more radical feminists, denounce marriage as an institution. Wives, they say, are legal prostitutes.

Some feminists supported the 1970s move toward easier, no-fault divorce. They convinced several state governors and legislatures to enact such laws, along with liberalization of alimony and child custody statutes. Indeed, the entire area of family law has changed drastically in the past generation. We have gone from no divorce to "no-fault" divorce. Today some women may be having second thoughts about no-fault divorces which, research indicates, have contributed significantly to the **"feminization of poverty."**

DISCRIMINATION AND THE DISABLED

Only in the past 30 years have people with disabilities become an active force in American politics. In 1973, Congress began to react to the idea that discrimination against the disabled was unacceptable. It passed the Rehabilitation Act, forbidding discrimination against persons with disabilities in programs receiving Federal aid.

In 1978, Congress amended the statute, establishing the Architectural and Transportation Barriers Compliance Board. Regulations for ramps and elevators in all Federal buildings were implemented. Congress also passed the Education for all Handicapped Children Act, guaranteeing that youngsters with disabilities will receive an "appropriate" education.

The most important piece of legislation, however, came in 1990, when Congress passed the **Americans with Disabilities Act (ADA)**. The law requires that all public buildings and public services be accessible to disabled persons. It also requires employers to provide reasonable accommodations to the needs of workers with disabilities.

As a practical matter, this means better doorways, ramps, handrails, wheelchair accessible bathrooms, counters and drinking fountains, as well as more accessible mass transit.

The law requires employers to "reasonably accommodate" the needs of the disabled unless to do so would cause the employer to suffer an "undue hardship."

Who is disabled? The statute defines persons with disabilities as persons who have physical or mental impairments that "substantially limit" their everyday activities. Although the law does not require employers to hire or retain employees who are unqualified, job applicants and employees with disabilities must be provided "reasonable accommodations."

The U.S. Supreme Court has issued a number of rulings in recent years involving the interpretation of the ADA.

A highly-publicized case, decided in 2001, involved professional golfer Casey Martin.

Martin suffers from a rare, degenerative circulatory disorder, Klippel-Trenaunay-Webber syndrome. It obstructs the flow of blood from his right leg back to his heart. There is the risk of hemorrhaging, blood clots and fracturing a tibia so badly that eventual amputation of his withered right leg could be necessary. He knows that every painful step he takes could be his last.

Despite his handicap, diagnosed at his birth, Martin became an accomplished golfer, winning 17 junior titles in Oregon. He won the state championship as a high school senior and was awarded a scholarship to play at Stanford University. There he teamed with Tiger Woods and Notah Beggay to capture the 1994 NCAA championship.

During his college years, Martin's conditioned deteriorated, his right leg atrophied, and he became unable to walk an entire 18-hole golf course. Stanford asked the Pacific 10 Conference and the NCAA to permit Martin to use a golf cart. Permission was granted.

After receiving his degree in economics from Stanford, Martin joined the Professional Golfers Association tour, but was told he could not use a cart. The position of the PGA, stated by Commissioner Tim Finchem, was that everyone had to walk. Finchem said:

> Professional golf is an athletic competition and the ability to walk five miles each day for four consecutive competitive rounds, week after week, often under adverse conditions and over challenging terrain, is part of the challenge of playing professional golf at its highest level. The average golfer on the PGA Tour competes in 20 events, and walks about 400 miles per season.
>
> As a result, fatigue, and loss of concentration caused by fatigue, can negatively affect a player's ability to execute golf shots. Unquestionably, being allowed to use motorized transportation gives an individual an advantage over the rest of the field. The ability to maintain concentration while spending five or more hours on your feet in difficult conditions is one of the fundamental skills a professional golfer must bring to the PGA Tour.

Martin filed suit in an Oregon Federal District Court in 1998, arguing that the PGA Tour was violating the Americans with Disabilities Act, which requires organizations to provide disabled men and women with full enjoyment of facilities or any place of public accommodation. The trial court ruled in Martin's favor, rejecting the Tour's position that the fatigue factor was significant in golf, and noted that Martin still was walking about 25% of the course, much of it inaccessible by cart.

The PGA Tour appealed to the Ninth Circuit, which affirmed the ruling, then to the U.S. Supreme Court, which granted *certiorari.*

On May 29, 2001, the nation's highest tribunal sided with Martin (7-2). It found that Title III of the ADA clearly forbade the PGA from denying Martin equal access to its tours on the basis of his disability. The Court rejected the Tour's arguments that allowing Martin to use a cart is a modification in its walking requirement that would either fundamentally alter the nature of the tours or give a disabled player an advantage over others and therefore fundamentally change the character of the competition.

Justice John Paul Stevens wrote the majority opinion. He was joined by Chief Justice William Rehnquist and Associate Justices Sandra Day O'Connor, Anthony Kennedy, David Souter, Ruth Bader Ginsburg and Stephen Breyer.

Stevens , referring to the first recorded rules of golf, contained in a Scottish publication in 1744, said:

> From early on, the essence of the game has been shot-making using clubs to cause a ball to progress from the teeing ground to a hole some distance away with as few strokes as possible.

> ...The walking rule is not an indispensable feature of tournament golf...Petitioner permits golf carts to be used on the Senior PGA Tour...

Justices Antonin Scalia and Clarence Thomas dissented. Scalia wrote:

> It had been rendered the solemn duty of the Supreme Court of the United States to decide What Is Golf. I am sure that the Framers of the Constitution, aware of the 1457 edict of King James II of Scotland prohibiting golf because it interfered with the practice of archery, fully expected that sooner or later the paths of golf and government, the law and the links, would once again cross...

> Is someone riding around a golf course from shot to shot really a golfer? The answer, we learn, is yes. The Court ultimately concludes, and it will henceforth be the Law of the Land, that walking is not a fundamental aspect of golf...Either out of humility or out of self-respect (one or the other) the Court should decline to answer this incredibly difficult and incredibly silly question.

Although Martin won his case, the Supreme Court has narrowed the meaning of the Americans with Disabilities Act. It ruled in *University of Alabama, Birmingham, Board of Trustees v. Garrett*, 99-1240 (2001), that state workers cannot use the ADA to win damages for on the job discrimination. The Court held that the disability rights law does not override states' 11th Amendment constitutional immunity against being sued for damages in Federal courts.

The Supreme Court recently ruled that the Americans with Disabilities Act does not entitle people to jobs which could threaten their health. In *Chevron v. Echazabal* (No. 00-1406), decided June 10, 2002, the Court rejected the arguments of Mario Echazabal that he should be permitted to decide for himself whether to assume the risk of working in an oil refinery, where chemicals could aggravate his liver ailment.

Writing for a unanimous Court, Justice David Souter held that the Equal Employment Opportunity Commission "was certainly acting within the reasonable zone when it saw a difference between rejecting workplace paternalism and ignoring specific and documented risks to the employee himself, even if the employee would take his chances for the sake of getting a job."

Ezchazabal was rejected for a job with Chevron when tests showed that he suffered from chronic, active hepatitis C, a progressive condition that may lead to cirrhosis, liver failure and death. Chevron argued that Echazabal risked further liver damage by working around chemicals and toxins at the plant and that his medical condition puts him outside the protection of the ADA.

At oral argument, the Court clearly was bothered by the notion that a firm's hands would be tied if a worker insisted on doing a job that might lead to serious illness or death. Justice Anthony Kennedy showed little sympathy for the position taken by Echazabal's attorney, commenting:

> We want employers to care about their employees. You want employers to take a position that's completely barbarous.

Besides Echazabal, the Court also recently ruled against:

(1) an assembly line worker with carpel tunnel syndrome, *Toyota Motor Mfg., Ky., Inc. v. Williams,* 534 U.S. 184 (2002),

(2) an airline baggage handler with a back injury, *U.S. Airways Inc., v. Barnett,* 535 U.S. 391 (2002) and

(3) a disabled prisoner who sought punitive damages for injuries suffered when being taken to jail in Kansas City Mo., *Barnes v. Gorman,* 536 U.S. 181 (2002).

EQUAL PROTECTION AND INDIANA'S PHOTO ID VOTING LAW

The U.S. Constitution contains no specific provision that confers a right to vote. However, the Supreme Court has considered several cases and ruled that the 14th Amendment grants equal access to the franchise.[63]

During its 2007-08 term, the Court considered a challenge to an Indiana law requiring that citizens voting in person produce photo identification in order to cast their ballots. The photo must be issued by either the state or Federal government, in a form such as a driver's license or a passport. If one does not have such an ID, one can get an alternative, but that usually requires a birth certificate.

The Indiana Democratic Party and civil rights groups tested the statute, stressing that some voters had difficulty in getting the required documents. The argument was that this amounted to a denial of equal protection of the law under the 14th Amendment.

It should be noted that Democrats generally are hostile to photo ID voting laws. They impose a burden, they contend, on minorities, the elderly, the poor, the disabled, and urban residents without automobiles. These are the kind of people who usually support Democratic candidates.

Republicans generally support such laws because, they say, they are necessary to prevent fraudulent voting.

Indiana's law is by no means unique. Some 25 states require some form of ID. Seven, including Michigan, require some form of photo ID. Michigan's law, however, is more flexible than Indiana's. The state accepts any of the following: 1) a Michigan driver's license or personal ID card issued by another state, 2) Federal or state government-issued photo identification, 3) a U.S. passport, 4) a military ID card with photo, 5) high school or college ID with photo and the student's name, 6) Tribal ID card with photo.

After plaintiffs lost their cases in both the Federal District Court in Indianapolis and the U.S. Court of Appeals for the Seventh Circuit, the U.S. Supreme Court granted *certiorari.* The Supreme Court ruled on April 28, 2008, that evidence was insufficient to support a claim that citizens were deterred from casting votes or otherwise harmed by the Indiana law. Justice Stevens, writing for the 6-3 majority, said:[64]

> The State has a valid interest in participating in a nationwide effort to improve and modernize elective procedures that have been criticized as antiquated and inefficient. The State also argues that it has a particular interest in preventing voter fraud in response to what is in part the product of its own maladministration—namely that Indiana's voter registration rolls include a large number of names of persons who are either deceased or no longer live in Indiana...
>
> ...Indiana's own experience with fraudulent voting in the 2003 Democratic mayoral primary for East Chicago demonstrates that not only is the risk of voter fraud real, but that it could affect the outcome of a close election.
>
> ...There is no question about the legitimacy or importance of the State's interest in counting only the votes of eligible voters...

Chief Justice Roberts and Justice Kennedy joined Stevens' opinion. Justice Scalia wrote a concurring opinion, joined by Justices Thomas and Alito. Scalia wrote:[65]

> ...I prefer to decide the cases on the grounds that the petitioner's premise is irrelevant and that the burden is minimal and justified.
>
> The universally applicable requirements of Indiana's voter-identification law are eminently reasonable. The burden of acquiring, possessing, and showing a free photo identification is simply not severe...
>
> ...That the State accommodates some voters by permitting...the casting of absentee or provisional ballots is an indulgence—not a constitutional imperative that falls short of what is required.

Justices Souter, Ginsburg and Breyer dissented. Souter wrote:[66]

Indiana's Voter ID law threatens to impose nontrivial burdens on the voting rights of tens of thousands of the state's citizens and a significant percentage of those individuals are likely to be deterred from voting.

1. William Ebenstein and Alan O. Ebenstein, *Great Political Thinkers: Plato To The Present*, 5th ed., (Ft. Worth, Texas: Holt, Rinehart and Winston, Inc., 1991)

2. Darnell F. Hawkins, editor, *Homicide Among Black Americans* (Lanham, Md.: University Press of America, 1986)

3. Bureau of the Census, "Poverty in the United States: 1987," Washington, D.C. Government Printing Office, 1989

4. Quoted in C. Vann Woodward, *The Strange Career of Jim Crow*, 2nd rev. ed. (New York: Oxford University Press, 1966), p. 21.

5. *Dred Scott v. Sanford,* 19 Howard 393 (1857)

6. C. Vann Woodward, *op. cit.,* p. 85

7. *Smith v. Allwright,* 321 U.S. 64 (1944)

8. *Plessy v. Ferguson,* 163 U.S. 537 (1896)

9. *Ibid,* at pp. 552-564

10. See Joseph Tussman, *The Supreme Court on Racial Discrimination* (New York: Oxford University Press, 1963).

11. *Sweatt v. Painter,* 339 U.S. 629 (1950)

12. *McLaurin v. Oklahoma State Regents For Higher Education,* 339 U.S. 637 (1950)

13. Eisenhower invited Chief Justice Warren to dinner at the White House when *Brown* reached the Supreme Court. He indicated his support for the segregationists. See Earl Warren, *The Memoirs of Earl Warren* (Garden City, N.Y.: Doubleday, 1977) p. 291.

14. *Brown v. Topeka, Kansas, Board of Education,* 347 U.S. 483 (1954)

15. For an excellent account of resistance to the Brown ruling in Virginia, see Benjamin Muse, *Virginia's Massive Resistance* (Bloomington: Indiana University Press, 1961).

16. C. Vann Woodward, *op. cit.,* pp.156-7

17. For President Eisenhower's view of the Faubus episode, see Dwight D. Eisenhower, *The White House Years: A Personal Account, 1956-1961* (Garden City, N.Y.: Doubleday & Company, 1965), pp. 162-75.

18. Foster Rhea Dulles, *The Civil Rights Commission, 1957-1965* (East Lansing, Mi.: Michigan State University Press, 1968), p. 260

19. Hugh Sidey, *John F. Kennedy, President* (New York: Atheneum, 1963) pp. 262-67

20. Quoted in C. Vann Woodward, *op. cit.,* pp. 175-6

21. *Ibid.* p. 163

22. *Heart of Atlanta Motel v. U.S.,* 379 U.S. 241 (1965)

23. *South Carolina v. Katzenbach,* 383 U.S. 301 (1966)

24. *Loving v. Virginia,* 388 U.S. 1 (1967)

25. For a good "nutshell" summary of the NCAA's birth and development, see Ira Glasser, *Visions of Liberty, op. cit.,* pp. 204-7.

26. Quoted in C. Vann Woodward, *op. cit.,* p. 170

27. Taylor Branch, *Parting the Waters* (New York: Simon and Schuster, 1988)

28. Herbert H. Haines, *Black Radicals and the Civil Rights Mainstream*, 1954-1970 (Knoxville: University of Tennessee Press, 1988) pp. 55-61

29. *Report of the National Advisory Commission on Civil Disorders,* Kerner Commission (New York: Bantam, 1968)

30. Edward C. Banfield, *The Unheavenly City* (Boston: Little, Brown and Company, 1970)

31. Daniel P. Moynihan, *The Negro Family: The Case for National Action* (1965), Washington, D.C.: Office of Policy Planning and Research, U.S. Labor Department

32. *Ibid.*

33. Quoted in Theodore White, *The Making of President, 1972 (*New York: Atheneum), p. 97

34. *Milliken v. Bradley,* 418 U.S. 717 (1974)

35. *Shelley v. Kraemer,* 334 U.S. 1 (1948)

36. *Regents of University of California v. Bakke,* 438 U.S. 265 (1978)

37. Alexander Bickel, *The Morality of Consent* (New Haven, Ct.: Yale University Press, 1975), p. 133

38. *United Steelworkers of America v. Weber,* 444 U.S. 193 (1979)

39. *Washington Post*, Aug. 28, 1997, p. 1, "Texas Campus Attracts Fewer Minorities"

40. "Lead plaintiff celebrates," *Detroit News*, June 24, 2003, page 8-A

41. *Grutter v. Bollinger,* 539 U.S. 306 (2003)

42. "Law applicant proud of fight, despite loss," *Detroit News*, June 24, 2003, page 8-A

43. Ex-president: Ruling rational, *Detroit News*, June 24, 2003, page 8-A

44. *Parents v. Seattle School District,* consolidated with *Jefferson County Board of Education,* 551 U.S. – (2007)

45. *Ibid.*

46. Barbara A. Perry, *The Michigan Affirmative Action Cases*: University Press of Kansas, 2007, pp. 166-170

47. *Goesaert v. Cleary,* 335 U.S. 464 (1948)

48. Betty Friedan, *The Feminine Mystique* (New York: W.W. Norton, 1963)

49. *Rostker v. Goldberg,* 453 U.S. 57 (1981)

50. *Reed v. Reed,* 404 U.S.71 (1971)

51. See Jane J. Mansbridge, *Why We Lost the ERA* (Chicago: University of Chicago Press, 1986). See also Gilbert Y. Steiner, *Constitutional Inequality: The Political Fortunes of the Equal Rights Amendment* (Washington, D.C.: Brookings Institute, 1985).

52. Kate Millett, *Sexual Politics* (Garden City, N.Y.: Doubleday, 1970)

53. *General Electric v. Gilbert,* 429 U.S. 125 (1976)

54. *Harris v. Forklift Systems, Inc.*, 510 U.S. 17 (1993)

55. *Faragher v. City of Boca Raton, Fla.*, 524 U.S. 775 (1998)

56. *Burlington Industries v. Ellerth,* 524 U.S. 742 (1998)

57. *Oncale v. Sundowner Offshore Services,* 523 U.S. 75 (1998)

58. *Ibid.*

59. *Gebser v. Lago Vista Independent School District,* 524 U.S. 274 (1998)

60. *Davis v. Monroe County Board of Education,* 526 U.S. 629 (1999)

61. *Ibid.*

62. *Bradwell v. Illinois,* 16 Wall 130 (1873)

63. The most famous case involving the 14th Amendment and voting was, of course, *Bush v. Gore*, 531 U.S. 98 (2000) which virtually decided the outcome of the 2000 presidential election. The majority halted the Florida recount primarily on 14th Amendment grounds.

64. *Crawford v. Marion County Election Board,* consolidated with *Indiana Democratic Party v. Rokita*, 553 U.S. — (2008)

65. *Ibid.*

66. *Ibid.*

SELECTED REFERENCES

GENERAL:

Abraham, Henry. *Freedom and the Court: Civil Rights and Liberties in the United States.* Fifth edition. New York: Oxford University Press, 1988.

Alderman, Ellen and Caroline Kennedy. *In Our Defense: The Bill of Rights in Action.* New York: William Morrow and Company, 1991.

Arsenault, Raymond, editor. *Crucible of Liberty: 200 Years of the Bill of Rights.* New York: The Free Press, 1991.

Barth, Alan. *The Rights of Free Men.* New York: Alfred A. Knopf, 1984.

Blasi, Vincent, editor. *The Burger Court: The Counterrevolution That Wasn't.* New Haven, Conn.: Yale University Press, 1983.

Bogus, Carl T. *The Second Amendment in Law and History.* New York: New Press, 2000.

Brigham, John. *Civil Liberties and American Democracy.* Washington, D.C.: Congressional Quarterly Press, 1984.

Casper, Jonathan D. *The Politics of Civil Liberties.* New York: Harper & Row, 1973.

Congressional Quarterly. *The Supreme Court and Individual Rights.* Washington, D.C.: Congressional Quarterly Inc., 1979.

Cox, Archibald. *The Warren Court: Constitutional Decision as an Instrument of Reform.* Cambridge, Mass.: Harvard University Press, 1968.

Cushman, Robert F. *Cases in Civil Liberties.* Fifth edition. Englewood Cliffs, N.J.: Prentice-Hall, 1989.

Ducat, Craig R. and Harold W. Chase. *Constitutional Interpretation: Rights of The Individual.* Fifth edition. St. Paul, Minn.: West Publishing Company, 1992.

Dye, Thomas R., Harmon Zeigler and S. Robert Lichter. *American Politics in the Media Age.* Fourth edition. Pacific Grove, Calif.: Brooks/Cole Publishing Company, 1992.

Emerson, Thomas, David Haber and Norman Dorsen. *Political and Civil Rights in the United States.* Student's edition. Boston: Little, Brown and Company, 1967.

Friendly, Fred and Martha J.H. Elliott. *The Constitution: That Delicate Balance.* New York: Random House, 1984.

Glasser, Ira. *Visions of Liberty: The Bill of Rights for All Americans.* New York: Arcade Publishing, 1991.

281

Glick, Henry R. *Courts, Politics and Justice*. Third edition. New York: McGraw-Hill, 1993.

Goldman, Sheldon. *Constitutional Law: Cases and Essays*. Second edition. New York: Harper Collins, 1991.

Grimes, Alan P. *Equality in America*. New York: Oxford University Press, 1964.

Hickok, Eugene W. Jr. *The Bill of Rights: Original Meaning and Current Understanding*. Charlottesville, Va.: University Press of Virginia, 1991.

Irons, Peter. *The Courage of Their Convictions*. New York: The Free Press, 1988.

Kukla, Jon, editor. *The Bill of Rights: A Lively Heritage*. Richmond: Virginia State Library and Archives, 1987.

Kauper, Paul G. *Civil Liberties and the Constitution*. Ann Arbor: University of Michigan Press, 1962.

Kelly, Alfred, Winfred Harbison and Herman Beltz. *The American Constitution: Its Origins and Development*. Seventh edition. New York: W. W. Norton, 1991.

Leeson, Susan M. and James C. Foster. *Constitutional Law: Cases in Context*. New York: St. Martin's, 1992.

Levine, Herbert and Jean E. Smith. *Civil Liberties and Civil Rights Debated*. Englewood Cliffs, N.J.: Prentice-Hall, 1988.

Lieberman, Jethro K. *The Evolving Constitution*. New York: Random House, 1992.

Morgan, Richard E. *The Law and Politics of Civil Rights and Liberties*. New York: Knopf, 1985.

O'Brien, David M. *Constitutional Law and Politics: Civil Rights and Civil Liberties*, 6th ed., New York: Norton, 2005.

Peck, Robert S. *The Bill of Rights and the Politics of Interpretation*. St. Paul, Minn.: West Publishing Company, 1992.

Peltason, J.W. *Understanding the Constitution*. 11th edition. New York: Holt, Rinehart and Winston, 1988.

Perry, Richard L., editor. *Sources of Our Liberties*. New York: McGraw-Hill, 1959.

Rehnquist, William H. *The Supreme Court*. New York: Morrow, 1989.

Sandoz, Ellis. *Conceived in Liberty: American Individual Rights Today*. North Scituate, Mass.: Duxbury Press, 1978.

Spaeth, Harold J. and Edward C. Smith. *The Constitution of the United States.* 13th edition. New York: Harper Collins, 1987.

Thomas, William R. *The Burger Court and Civil Liberties.* Brunswick, Ohio: King's Court Communications, Inc., 1976.

Vile, John R. *A Companion To The United States Constitution and Its Amendments.* Westport, Conn.: Prager, 1993.

Walker, Thomas G. and Lee Epstein. *The Supreme Court of the United States: An Introduction.* New York: St. Martin's Press, 1993.

Way, H. Frank. *Liberty in the Balance.* Fifth edition. New York: McGraw-Hill, 1981.

Wellington, Harry H. *Interpreting the Constitution: The Supreme Court and the Process of Adjudication.* New Haven, Conn.: Yale University Press, 1991.

White, Theodore H. *America in Search of Itself.* New York: Harper and Row, 1982.

White, Theodore H. *The Making of the President, 1972.* New York: Atheneum, 1973.

White, G. Edward. *Earl Warren: A Public Life.* New York: Oxford University Press, 1987.

Woodward, Bob and Scott Armstrong. *The Brethren.* New York: Simon and Schuster, 1979.

CHAPTER I: THE FIRST FREEDOMS

Abrams, Floyd. *Speaking Freely.* New York: Viking/Penguin, 2005.

Berns, Walter. *The First Amendment and the Future of American Democracy.* New York: Basic Books, 1976.

Biegel, Stuart. *Beyond Our Control? Confronting the Limits of Our Legal System in the Age of Cyberspace.* Cambridge, Mass., MIT Press, 2001.

Blum, Virgil C., S.J. *Quest for Religious Freedom.* Milwaukee, Wisc.: The Catholic League for Religious and Civil Rights, 1984.

Bollinger, Lee C. *Images of a Free Press.* Chicago: University of Chicago Press, 1991.

Cullen, Maurice R. *Mass Media & the First Amendment.* Dubuque, Iowa: Wm. C. Brown Company, 1981.

Demac, Donna A. *Liberty Denied: The Current Rise of Censorship in America.* Revised edition. New Brunswick, N.J.: Rutgers University Press, 1990.

Dill, Barbara. *The Journalist's Handbook on Libel and Privacy.* New York: The Free Press, 1986.

Dunn, Charles W. *Religion in American Politics.* Washington, D.C.: Congressional Quarterly Inc., 1989.

Emerson, Thomas I. *Toward a General Theory of the First Amendment.* New York: Random House, 1966.

Friendly, Fred W. *Minnesota Rag: The Dramatic Story of the Landmark Supreme Court Case That Gave New Meaning to Freedom of the Press.* New York: Vintage, 1982.

Gillmor, Donald M. *Free Press and Fair Trial.* Washington, D.C.: Public Affairs Press, 1966.

Goodwin, H. Eugene. *Groping for Ethics in Journalism.* Second edition, Ames, Iowa: Iowa State University Press, 1987.

Goodwin, Mike. *Cyber Rights: Defending Free Speech in the Digital Age.* Cambridge, Mass.: MIT Press, 2003.

Graber, Doris. *Media Power in Politics.* 4th edition. Washington, D.C.: Congressional Quarterly Press, 2000.

Haiman, Franklyn C. *Speech and Law in a Free Society.* Chicago: University of Chicago Press, 1981.

Hamlin, David. *The Nazi/Skokie Conflict.* Boston: Beacon Press, 1980.

Hentoff, Nat. *The First Freedom: The Tumultuous History of Free Speech in America.* New York: Delacorte Press, 1980.

--------*Free Speech for Me—But Not for Thee.* New York: Harper Collins, 1992.

--------*Living the Bill of Rights.* New York: Harper Collins, 1998.

Holmes, Paul. *Retrial: Murder and Dr. Sam Sheppard.* New York: Bantam Books, Inc., 1966.

Holsinger, Ralph L. and John Paul Dilts. *Media Law.* Third edition. New York: McGraw-Hill, 1994.

Howe, Mark DeWolfe. *The Garden and the Wilderness: Religion and Government in American Constitutional History.* Chicago: University of Chicago Press, 1965.

Krinsky, Fred. *The Politics of Religion in America.* Beverly Hills, Calif.: The Glencoe Press, 1968.

284

Levy, Leonard W. *Legacy of Suppression: Freedom of Speech and Press in Early American History*. Revised edition. New York: Oxford University Press, 1985.

--------*The Establishment Clause: Religion and the First Amendment*. New York: Macmillan, 1986.

--------*Make No Law: The Sullivan Case and the First Amendment*. New York: Random House, 1991.

Lewis, Anthony. *Freedom for the Thought We Hate: Tales of the First Amendment*. New York: Basic Books, 2008.

Lichter, S. Robert, Stanley Rothman and Linda S. Lichter. *The Media Elite*. New York: Hastings House, 1990.

MacKinnon, Catherine. *Only Words*. Cambridge: Harvard University Press, 1993.

Mill, John Stuart. *On Liberty*. Indianapolis: The Bobbs-Merrill Company, Inc., 1956. Mill's work was published originally in 1859.

Noonan, John T. *The Lustre of Our Country: The American Experience of Religious Freedom*. Berkeley, Calif.: University of California Press, 1998.

Paletz, David L. *The Media in American Politics*. Second edition. New York: Longman, 2002.

Pfeffer, Leo. *God, Caesar and the Constitution: The Court as Referee of Church-State Confrontation*. Boston: Beacon Press, 1975.

Press, Charles and Kenneth Verburg. *American Politicians and Journalists*. Glenview, Ill.: Scott, Foresman and Company, 1988.

Pritchett, C. Herman. *Constitutional Civil Liberties*. Englewood Cliffs, N.J.: Prentice-Hall, 1984.

Reardon, Paul C. and Clifton Daniel. *Fair Trial and Free Press*. Washington, D.C.: American Enterprise Institute, 1968.

Rehnquist, William H. *All the Laws but One: Civil Liberties in Wartime*. New York: Knopf, 1998.

Reston, James. *The Artillery of the Press*. New York: Harper & Row, 1967.

Rosini, Neil J. *The Practical Guide to Libel Law*. New York: Praeger, 1991.

Schmuhl, Robert, editor. *The Responsibilities of Journalism*. Notre Dame, Ind.: University of Notre Dame Press, 1984.

Sheehan, Neil. *The Pentagon Papers*. New York: Bantam, 1971.

Siebert, Fred S., Theodore Peterson and Wilbur Schramm. *Four Theories of the Press*. Urbana: University of Illinois Press, 1963.

Smolla, Rodney A. *Suing The Press: Libel, The Media, & Power*. New York: Oxford University Press, 1986.

Sorauf, Frank J. *The Wall of Separation: The Constitutional Politics of Church and State*. Princeton, N.J.: Princeton University Press, 1976.

Strossen, Nadine. *Defending Pornography*. New York: Scribner's, 1995.

Stedman. Murray S., Jr. *Religion and Politics in America*. New York: Harcourt, Brace & World, 1964.

Tedford, Thomas and Dale Herbeck. *Freedom of Speech in the United States*. Fourth edition. State College, Pa.: Strata Publishing, Inc., 2001.

Tussman, Joseph. *The Supreme Court on Church and State*. New York: Oxford University Press, 1962.

Wald, Kenneth. *Religion and Politics in the United States*. New York: St. Martin's Press, 1987.

Wilson, John F. *Church and State in American History*. Boston: D.C. Heath, 1965.

CHAPTER II: RIGHTS OF THE ACCUSED

Ackerman, Bruce. *Before the Next Attack: Preserving Civil Liberties in an Age of Terrorism*. New Haven, CT: Yale University Press, 2006.

Baker, Liva. *Miranda: Crime, Law and Politics*. New York: Atheneum, 1983.

Banner, Stuart. *The Death Penalty: An American History*. Cambridge, Mass.: Harvard University Press, 2002.

Bedau, H., editor. *The Death Penalty in America*. Third edition. New York: Oxford University Press, 1982.

Berns, W. *For Capital Punishment: Crime and the Morality of the Death Penalty*. New York, Basic Books, 1979.

Blumberg, Abraham. *Criminal Justice*. New York: New Viewpoints, 1974.

Carter, Dan T. *Scottsboro: A Tragedy of the American South*. Revised edition. Baton Rouge: Louisiana State University Press, 1979.

Casper, Jonathan D. *American Criminal Justice: the Defendant's Perspective.* Englewood Cliffs, N.J., Prentice-Hall, 1972.

Cole, David. *Enemy Aliens: Double Standards and Constitutional Freedoms in the War on Terrorism.* New York: The New Press, 2003.

Donner, Frank J. *The Age of Surveillance.* New York: Vintage, 1980.

Fuller, Lon. *The Morality of Law.* New Haven: Yale University Press, 1964.

Hart, H.L.A. *Law, Liberty and Morality.* Palo Alto: Stanford University Press, 1963.

Hentoff, Nat. *The War on the Bill of Rights and the Gathering Resistance.* New York: Seven Stories Press, 2003.

Leiser, Burton. *Liberty, Justice and Morals.* Third edition. New York: Macmillan, 1986.

Lewis, Anthony. *Gideon's Trumpet.* New York: Vintage, 1964.

Meltsner, Michael. *Cruel and Unusual: The Supreme Court and Capital Punishment.* New York: Morrow, 1973.

Silberman, Charles. *Criminal Violence, Criminal Justice.* New York: Random House, 1978.

Wilson, James Q. *Thinking About Crime.* New York: Basic Books, 1975.

Zalman, Marvin and Larry Siegel. *Criminal Procedure: Constitution and Society.* St. Paul, Minn.: West Publishing Company, 1991.

CHAPTER III: PRIVACY

Albanese, Jay S. Justice. *Privacy and Crime Control.* Lanham, Mass.: University Press of America, 1984.

Barnett, Randy E., editor. *The Rights Reserved by the People; The History and Meaning of the Ninth Amendment.* Fairfax, Va.: George Mason University Press, 1989.

Barnett, Walter. *Sexual Freedom and the Constitution.* Albuquerque: University of New Mexico Press, 1973.

Batchelor, Edward Jr. *Abortion: The Moral Issues.* New York: Pilgrim Press, 1982.

Bork, Robert H. *The Tempting of America: The Political Seduction of the Law.* New York: The Free Press, 1990.

Cushman, Clare, editor. *Supreme Court Decisions and Women's Rights.* Washington, D.C.: Congressional Quarterly Press, 2000.

Goldberg-Hiller, Jonathan. *The Limits to Union: Same Sex Marriages and the Politics of Civil Rights*. Ann Arbor: University of Michigan Press, 2002.

Hentoff, Nat. *The War on the Bill of Rights and the Gathering Resistance*. New York: Seven Stories Press, 2003.

McWhirter, Darien A. and Jon D. Bible. *Privacy as a Constitutional Right: Sex, Drugs, and the Right to Life*. New York: Quorum Books, 1992.

Noonan, John T., Jr. *The Morality of Abortion: Legal and Historical Perspectives*. Cambridge: Harvard University Press, 1970.

--------*A Private Choice: Abortion in America in the Seventies*. New York: The Free Press, 1979.

Rubin, Michael R. *Private Rights, Public Wrongs: The Computer and Personal Privacy*. Norwood, N.J.: Ablex Publishing Corporation, 1988.

Tribe, Laurence H. *Abortion: The Clash of Absolutes*. New York: Norton, 1990.

Weddington, Sarah R. *A Question of Choice*. New York: Putnam's, 1992.

Wessel, Milton R. *Freedom's Edge: The Computer Threat to Society*. Reading, Mass.: Addison-Wesley, 1974.

Westin, Alan F. *Privacy and Freedom*. New York: Atheneum, 1967.

Wenz, Peter S. *Abortion Rights as Religious Freedom*. Philadelphia: Temple University Press, 1992.

Zelermyer, William. *Invasion of Privacy*. Syracuse, N.Y.: Syracuse University Press, 1959.

CHAPTER IV: TOWARD EQUAL PROTECTION OF THE LAWS

Baer, Judith A. *Equality Under the Constitution: Reclaiming the Fourteenth Amendment*. Ithaca, N.Y.: Cornell University Press, 1983.

Banfield, Edward C. *The Unheavenly City*. Boston: Little, Brown, 1974.

Barzun, Jacques. *Race: A Study in Superstition*. New York: Harper & Row, 1965.

Bergman, Barbara. *In Defense of Affirmative Action*. New York: Basic Books, 1996.

Branch, Taylor. *Parting the Waters: America in the King Years, 1954-63*. New York: Simon and Schuster, 1988.

Browning, Rufus P., Dale Rogers Marshall, and David H. Taab. *Racial Politics in American Cities*. New York: Longman, 1990.

288

Carmichael, Stokely and Charles Hamilton. *Black Power.* New York: Random House, 1967.

Carter, Stephen L. *Reflections of an Affirmative Action Baby.* New York: Basic Books, 1991.

Cashman, Sean Dennis. *African-Americans and the Quest for Civil Rights, 1900-1990.* New York: New York University Press, 1991.

Deloria, Vine, Jr., and Clifford M. Lytle. *The Nations Within.* New York: Pantheon, 1984.

Dent, David J. *In Search of Black America.* New York: Simon & Schuster, 2000.

D'Souza, Dinesh. *Illiberal Education: The Politics of Race and Sex on Campus.* New York: The Free Press, 1991.

--------*The End of Racism.* New York: Free Press, 1995.

Dulles, Foster Rhea. *The Civil Rights Commission: 1957-1965.* East Lansing: Michigan State University Press, 1968.

Ezorsky, Gertrude. *Racism and Justice: The Case for Affirmative Action.* Ithaca, N.Y.: Cornell University Press, 1991.

Franklin, John H. *From Slavery to Freedom.* Sixth edition. New York: Knopf, 1988.

Friedan, Betty. *The Feminine Mystique.* New York: Norton, 1963.

Garrow, David J. *Bearing the Cross: Martin Luther King and the Southern Christian Leadership Conference: A Personal Portrait.* New York: William Morrow, 1986.

Gelb, Joyce and Marian L. Palley. *Women and Public Policies.* Revised and expanded edition. Princeton, N.J.: Princeton University Press, 1987.

Glazer, Nathan. *Affirmative Discrimination: Ethnic Inequality and Public Policy.* New York: Basic Books, 1975.

Hacker, Andrew. *Two Nations, Black and White, Separate, Hostile, Unequal.* New York: Scribner, 1992.

Haines, Herbert H. *Black Radicals and the Civil Rights Mainstream, 1954-1970.* Knoxville: University of Tennessee Press, 1988.

Hawkins, Darnell F. *Homicide Among Black Americans.* Lanham, Md.: University Press of America, 1986.

Huff, Joan. *Law, Gender, and Injustice: A Legal History of U.S. Women.* New York: New York University Press, 1991.

Humphrey, Hubert H, editor. *School Desegregation: Documents and Commentaries.* New York: Thomas Y. Crowell Company, 1964.

King, Martin Luther. *Strength To Love.* New York: Harper & Row, 1963.

Kluger, Richard. *Simple Justice: The History of Brown v. Board of Education and Black America's Struggle for Equality.* New York: Knopf, 1976.

Loury, Glenn C. *The Anatomy of Racial Inequality.* Cambridge, MA: Harvard University Press, 2002.

MacKinnon, Catherine A. *Only Words.* Cambridge, Mass.: Harvard University Press, 1993.

--------*Women's Lives, Men's Laws.* Cambridge, Mass.: Belknap Press of Harvard University Press, 2005.

Mansbridge, Jane J. *Why We Lost the ERA.* Chicago: University of Chicago Press, 1986.

Mikulski, Barbara, et al. *Nine and Counting: the Women of the Senate.* New York: William Morrow, 2000.

Murray, Charles. *Losing Ground: American Social Policy, 1950-1980.* New York: Basic Books, 1984.

Muse, Benjamin. *Virginia's Massive Resistance.* Bloomington: Indiana University Press, 1961.

Perry, Barbara. *The Michigan Affirmative Action Cases.* University Press of Kansas, 2007.

Schlesinger, Arthur M. *The Disuniting of America: Reflections on a Multicultural Society.* New York: Norton, 1992.

Sindler, Allan P. *Bakke, DeFunis and Minority Admissions.* New York: Longman, 1979.

Tussman, Joseph, editor. *The Supreme Court on Racial Discrimination.* New York: Oxford University Press, 1963.

Urofsky, Melvin I. *A Conflict of Rights: The Supreme Court and Affirmative Action.* New York: Scribner's, 1991.

Whitehurst, Carol A. *Women in America: The Oppressed Majority.* New York: Random House, 1977.

Wilkinson, J. Harvie III. *From Brown to Bakke: The Supreme Court and School Integration: 1954-1978.* New York: Oxford University Press, 1979.

Williams, Juan. *Eyes on the Prize: America's Civil Rights Years, 1954-1965.* New York: Viking, 1987.

Wilson, William J. *The Declining Significance of Race.* Chicago: University of Chicago Press, 1978.

Woodward, C. Vann. *The Strange Career of Jim Crow.* Third revised edition. New York: Oxford University Press, 1974.

Zelnick, Bob. *Backfire: A Reporter's Look at Affirmative Action.* Lanham, Md.: Regnery, 1996.

The Constitution of the United States

Preamble

We the People of the United States, in Order to form a more perfect Union, establish Justice, insure domestic Tranquility, provide for the common defence, promote the general Welfare, and secure the Blessings of Liberty to ourselves and our Posterity, do ordain and establish this Constitution for the United States of America.

Article I

Section 1. All legislative Powers herein granted shall be vested in a Congress of the United States, which shall consist of a Senate and House of Representatives.

Section 2. [1] The House of Representatives shall be composed of Members chosen every second Year by the People of the several States, and the Electors in each State shall have the Qualifications requisite for Electors of the most numerous Branch of the State Legislature.

[2] No Person shall be a Representative who shall not have attained to the Age of twenty five Years, and been seven Years a Citizen of the United States, and who shall not, when elected, be an Inhabitant of that State in which he shall be chosen.

[3] Representatives and direct Taxes shall be apportioned among the several States which may be included within this Union, according to their respective Numbers, which shall be determined by adding to the whole Number of free Persons, including those bound to Service for a Term of Years, and excluding Indians not first Meeting of the Congress of the United States, and within every subsequent Term of ten Years, in such taxed, three fifths of all other Persons. The actual Enumeration shall be made within three Years after the Manner as they shall by Law direct. The Number of Representatives shall not exceed one for every thirty Thousand, but each State shall have at Least one Representative; and until such enumeration shall be made, the State of New Hampshire shall be entitled to chuse three, Massachusetts eight, Rhode Island and Providence Plantations one, Connecticut five, New York six, New Jersey four, Pennsylvania eight, Delaware one, Maryland six, Virginia ten, North Carolina five, South Carolina five, and Georgia three.

[4] When vacancies happen in the Representation from any State, the Executive Authority thereof shall issue Writs of Election to fill such Vacancies.

[5] The House of Representatives shall chuse their Speaker and other Officers; and shall have the sole Power of Impeachment.

Section 3. [1] The Senate of the United States shall be composed of two Senators from each State, chosen by the Legislature thereof, for six Years; and each Senator shall have one Vote.

[2] Immediately after they shall be assembled in Consequence of the first Election, they shall be divided as equally as may be into three Classes. The Seats of the Senators of the first Class shall be vacated at the Expiration of the Second Year, of the second Class at the Expiration of the fourth Year, and of the third Class at the Expiration of the sixth Year, so that one third may be chosen every second Year; and if Vacancies happen by Resignation, or otherwise, during the Recess of the Legislature of any State, the Executive thereof may make temporary Appointments until the next Meeting of the Legislature, which shall then fill such Vacancies.

[3] No Person shall be a Senator who shall not have attained to the Age of thirty Years, and been nine Years a Citizen of the United States, and who shall not, when elected, be an Inhabitant of that State for which he shall be chosen.

[4] The Vice President of the United States shall be President of the Senate, but shall have no Vote, unless they be equally divided.

[5] The Senate shall chuse their other Officers, and also a President pro tempore, in the Absence of the Vice President, or when he shall exercise the Office of President of the United States.

[6] The Senate shall have the sole Power to try all Impeachments. When sitting for that Purpose, they shall be on Oath or Affirmation. When the President of the United States is tried, the Chief Justice shall preside: And no Person shall be convicted without the Concurrence of two thirds of the Members present.

[7] Judgment in Cases of Impeachment shall not extend further than to removal from Office, and disqualification to hold and enjoy any Office of honor, Trust, or Profit under the United States: but the Party convicted shall nevertheless be liable and subject to Indictment, Trial, Judgment, and Punishment, according to Law.

Section 4. [1] The Times, Places and Manner of holding Elections for Senators and Representatives, shall be prescribed in each State by the Legislature thereof; but the Congress may at any time by Law make or alter such Regulations, except as to the Places of chusing Senators.

[2] The Congress shall assemble at least once in every Year, and such Meeting shall be on the first Monday in December, unless they shall by Law appoint a different Day.

Section 5. [1] Each House shall be the Judge of the Elections, Returns, and Qualifications of its own Members, and a Majority of each shall constitute a Quorum to do Business; but a smaller Number may adjourn from day to day, and may be authorized to compel the Attendance of absent Members, in such Manner, and under such Penalties as each House may provide.

[2] Each House may determine the Rules of its Proceedings, punish its Members for disorderly Behavior, and, with the Concurrence of two thirds, expel a Member.

[3] Each House shall keep a Journal of its Proceedings, and from time to time publish the same, excepting such Parts as may in their Judgment require Secrecy; and the Yeas and Nays of the Members of either House on any question shall, at the Desire of one fifth of those Present, be entered on the Journal.

[4] Neither House, during the Session of Congress, shall, without the Consent of the other, adjourn for more than three days, nor to any other Place than that in which the two Houses shall be sitting.

Section 6. [1] The Senators and Representatives shall receive a Compensation for their Services, to be ascertained by Law, and paid out of the Treasury of the United States. They shall in all Cases, except Treason, Felony and Breach of the Peace, be privileged from Arrest during their Attendance at the Session of their respective Houses, and in going to and returning from the same; and for any Speech or Debate in either House, they shall not be questioned in any other Place.

[2] No Senator or Representative shall, during the Time for which he was elected, be appointed to any civil Office under the Authority of the United States, which shall have been created, or the Emoluments whereof shall have been increased during such time; and no Person holding any Office under the United States, shall be a Member of either House during his Continuance in Office.

Section 7. [1] All Bills for raising Revenue shall originate in the House of Representatives; but the Senate may propose or concur with Amendments as on other Bills.

[2] Every Bill which shall have passed the House of Representatives and the Senate, shall, before it becomes a Law, be presented to the President of the United States; If he approve he shall sign it, but if not he shall return it, with his Objections to the House in which it shall have originated, who shall enter the Objections at large on their Journal,

and proceed to reconsider it. If after such Reconsideration two thirds of that House shall agree to pass the Bill, it shall be sent together with the Objections, to the other House, by which it shall likewise be reconsidered, and if approved by two thirds of that House, it shall become a Law. But in all such Cases the Votes of both Houses shall be determined by yeas and Nays, and the Names of the Persons voting for and against the Bill shall be entered on the Journal of each House respectively. If any Bill shall not be returned by the President within ten Days (Sundays excepted) after it shall have been presented to him, the Same shall be a Law, in like Manner as if he had signed it, unless the Congress by their Adjournment prevent its Return in which Case it shall not be a Law.

[3] Every Order, Resolution, or Vote, to Which the Concurrence of the Senate and House of Representatives may be necessary (except on a question of Adjournment) shall be presented to the President of the United States; and before the Same shall take Effect, shall be approved by him, or being disapproved by him, shall be repassed by two thirds of the Senate and House of Representatives, according to the Rules and Limitations prescribed in the Case of a Bill.

Section 8. [1] The Congress shall have Power To lay and collect Taxes, Duties, Imposts and Excises, to pay the Debts and provide for the common Defence and general Welfare of the United States; but all Duties, Imposts and Excises shall be uniform throughout the United States;

[2] To borrow money on the credit of the United States;

[3] To regulate Commerce with foreign Nations, and among the several States, and with the Indian Tribes;

[4] To establish an uniform Rule of Naturalization, and uniform Laws on the subject of Bankruptcies throughout the United States;

[5] To coin Money, regulate the Value thereof, and of foreign Coin, and fix the Standard of Weights and Measures;

[6] To provide for the Punishment of counterfeiting the Securities and current Coin of the United States;

[7] To Establish Post Offices and Post Roads;

[8] To promote the Progress of Science and useful Arts, by securing for limited Times to Authors and Inventors the exclusive Right to their respective Writings and Discoveries;

[9] To constitute Tribunals inferior to the supreme Court;

[10] To define and punish Piracies and Felonies committed on the high Seas, and Offenses against the Law of Nations:

[11] To declare War, grant Letters of Marque and Reprisal, and make Rules concerning Captures on Land and Water;

[12] To raise and support Armies, but no Appropriation of Money to that Use shall be for a longer Term than two Years;

[13] To provide and maintain a Navy;

[14] To make Rules for the Government and Regulation of the land and naval Forces;

[15] To provide for calling forth the Militia to execute the Laws of the Union, suppress Insurrections and repel Invasions;

[16] To provide for organizing, arming, and disciplining, the Militia, and for governing such Part of them as may be employed in the Service of the United States, reserving to the States respectively, the Appointment of the Officers, and the Authority of training the Militia according to the discipline prescribed by Congress;

[17] To exercise exclusive Legislation in all Cases whatsoever, over such District (not exceeding ten Miles square) as may, by Cession of particular States, and the Acceptance of Congress, become the Seat of the Government of the United States, and to exercise like Authority over all Places purchased by the Consent of the Legislature of the

State in which the Same shall be, for the Erection of Forts, Magazines, Arsenals, dock-Yards, and other needful Buildings;-And

[18] To make all Laws which shall be necessary and proper for carrying into Execution the foregoing Powers, and all other Powers vested by this Constitution in the Government of the United States, or in any Department or Officer thereof.

Section 9. [1] The Migration or Importation of Such Persons as any of the States now existing shall think proper to admit, shall not be prohibited by the Congress prior to the Year one thousand eight hundred and eight, but a Tax or duty may be imposed on such Importation, not exceeding ten dollars for each Person.

[2] The privilege of the Writ of Habeas Corpus shall not be suspended, unless when in Cases of Rebellion or Invasion the public Safety may require it.

[3] No Bill of Attainder or ex post facto Law shall be passed.

[4] No Capitation, or other direct, Tax shall be laid, unless in Proportion to the Census or Enumeration herein before directed to be taken.

[5] No Tax or Duty shall be laid on Articles exported from any State.

[6] No Preference shall be given by any Regulation of Commerce or Revenue to the Ports of one State over those of another: nor shall Vessels bound to, or from, one State be obliged to enter, clear, or pay Duties in another.

[7] No money shall be drawn from the Treasury, but in Consequence of Appropriations made by Law; and a regular Statement and Account of the Receipts and Expenditures of all public Money shall be published from time to time.

[8] No Title of Nobility shall be granted by the United States: And no Person holding any Office of Profit or Trust under them, shall, without the Consent of the Congress, accept of any present, Emolument, Office, or Title, of any kind whatever, from any King, Prince, or foreign State.

Section 10. [1] No State shall enter into any Treaty, Alliance, or Confederation; grant Letters of Marque and Reprisal; coin Money; emit Bills of Credit; make any Thing but gold and silver Coin a Tender in Payment of Debts; pass any Bill of Attainder, ex post facto Law, or Law impairing the Obligation of Contracts, or grant any Title of Nobility.

[2] No State shall, without the Consent of the Congress, lay any Imposts or Duties on Imports or Exports, except what may be absolutely necessary for executing it's inspection Laws: and the net Produce of all Duties and Imposts, laid by any State on Imports or Exports, shall be for the Use of the Treasury of the United States; and all such Laws shall be subject to the Revision and Controul of the Congress.

[3] No State shall, without the Consent of Congress, lay any Duty of Tonnage, keep Troops, or Ships of War in time of Peace, enter into any Agreement or Compact with another State, or with a foreign Power, or engage in War, unless actually invaded, or in such imminent Danger as will not admit of delay.

Article II

Section 1. [1] The executive Power shall be vested in a President of the United States of America. He shall hold his Office during the Term of four Years, and, together with the Vice President, chosen for the same Term, be elected, as follows:

[2] Each State shall appoint, in such Manner as the Legislature thereof may direct, a Number of Electors, equal to the whole Number of Senators and Representatives to which the State may be entitled in the Congress; but no Senator or Representative, or Person holding an Office of Trust or Profit under the United States, shall be appointed an Elector.

[3] The Electors shall meet in their respective States, and vote by Ballot for two Persons, of whom one at least shall not be an Inhabitant of the same State with

themselves. And they shall make a List of all the Persons voted for, and of the Number of Votes for each; which List they shall sign and certify, and transmit sealed to the Seat of the Government of the United States, directed to the President of the Senate. The President of the Senate shall, in the Presence of the Senate and House of Representatives, open all the Certificates, and the Votes shall then be counted. The Person having the greatest Number of Votes shall be the President, if such Number be a Majority of the whole Number of Electors appointed; and if there be more than one who have such Majority, and have an equal Number of Votes, then the House of Representatives shall immediately chuse by Ballot one of them for President; and if no Person have a Majority, then from the five highest on the List the said House shall in like Manner chuse the President. But in chusing the President, the Votes shall be taken by States the Representation from each State having one Vote; A quorum for this Purpose shall consist of a Member or Members from two thirds of the States, and a Majority of all the States shall be necessary to a Choice. In every Case, after the Choice of the President, the Person having the greater Number of Votes of the Electors shall be the Vice President. But if there should remain two or more who have equal Votes, the Senate shall chuse from them by Ballot the Vice President.

[4] The Congress may determine the Time of chusing the Electors, and the Day on which they shall give their Votes; which Day shall be the same throughout the United States.

[5] No person except a natural born Citizen, or a Citizen of the United States, at the time of the Adoption of this Constitution, shall be eligible to the Office of President; neither shall any Person be eligible to that Office who shall not have attained to the Age of thirty-five Years, and been fourteen Years a Resident within the United States.

[6] In case of the removal of the President from Office, or of his Death, Resignation or Inability to discharge the Powers and Duties of the said Office, the Same shall devolve on the Vice President, and the Congress may by Law provide for the Case of Removal, Death, Resignation or Inability, both of the President and Vice President, declaring what Officer shall then act as President, and such Officer shall act accordingly, until the Disability be removed, or a President shall be elected.

[7] The President shall, at stated Times, receive for his Services, a Compensation, which shall neither be increased nor diminished during the Period for which he shall have been elected, and he shall not receive within that Period any other Emolument from the United States, or any of them.

[8] Before he enter on the Execution of his Office, he shall take the following Oath or Affirmation: "I do solemnly swear (or affirm) that I will faithfully execute the Office of President of the United States, and will to the best of my Ability, preserve, protect and defend the Constitution of the United States."

Section 2. [1] The President shall be Commander in Chief of the Army and Navy of the United States, and of the militia of the several States, when called into the actual Service of the United States; he may require the Opinion, in writing, of the principal Officer in each of the Executive Departments, upon any Subject relating to the Duties of their respective Offices, and he shall have Power to grant Reprieves and Pardons for Offenses against the United States, except in Cases of Impeachment.

[2] He shall have Power, by and with the Advice and Consent of the Senate to make Treaties, provided two thirds of the Senators present concur; and he shall nominate, and by and with the Advice and Consent of the Senate, shall appoint Ambassadors, other public Ministers and Consuls, Judges of the supreme Court, and all other Officers of the United States, whose Appointments are not herein otherwise provided for, and which shall be established by Law; but the Congress may by Law vest the Appointment of such

inferior Officers, as they think proper, in the President alone, in the Courts of Law, or in the Heads of Departments.

[3] The President shall have Power to fill up all Vacancies that may happen during the Recess of the Senate, by granting Commissions which shall expire at the End of their next Session.

Section 3. He shall from time to time give to the Congress Information of the State of the Union, and recommend to their Consideration such Measures as he shall judge necessary and expedient; he may, on extraordinary Occasions, convene both Houses, or either of them, and in Case of Disagreement between them, with Respect to the Time of Adjournment, he may adjourn them to such Time as he shall think proper; he shall receive Ambassadors and other public Ministers; he shall take Care that the Laws be faithfully executed, and shall Commission all the Officers of the United States.

Section 4. The President, Vice President and all civil Officers of the United States, shall be removed from Office on Impeachment for, and Conviction of, Treason, Bribery, or other high Crimes and Misdemeanors.

Article III

Section 1. The judicial Power of the United States, shall be vested in one supreme Court, and in such inferior Courts as the Congress may from time to time ordain and establish. The Judges, both of the supreme and inferior Courts, shall hold their Offices during good Behaviour, and shall, at stated Times, receive for their Services a Compensation, which shall not be diminished during their Continuance in Office.

Section 2. [1] The judicial Power shall extend to all Cases, in Law and Equity, arising under this Constitution, the Laws of the United States, and Treaties made, or which shall be made, under their Authority; to all Cases affecting Ambassadors, other public Ministers and Consuls; to all Cases of admiralty and maritime Jurisdiction; to Controversies to which the United States shall be a Party; to Controversies between two or more States; between a State and Citizens of another State; between Citizens of different States; between Citizens of the same State claiming Lands under the Grants of different States, and between a State, or the Citizens thereof, and foreign States, Citizens or Subjects.

[2] In all Cases affecting Ambassadors, other public Ministers and Consuls, and those in which a State shall be a Party, the supreme Court shall have original Jurisdiction. In all the other Cases before mentioned, the supreme Court shall have appellate Jurisdiction, both as to Law and Fact, with such Exceptions, and under such Regulations as the Congress shall make.

[3] The trial of all Crimes, except in Cases of Impeachment, shall be by Jury; and such Trial shall be held in the State where the said Crimes shall have been committed; but when not committed within any State, the Trial shall be at such Place or Places as the Congress may by Law have directed.

Section 3. [1] Treason against the United States, shall consist only in levying War against them, or, in adhering to their Enemies, giving them Aid and Comfort. No Person shall be convicted of Treason unless on the Testimony of two Witnesses to the same overt Act, or on Confession in open Court.

[2] The Congress shall have Power to declare the Punishment of Treason, but no Attainder of Treason shall work Corruption of Blood, or Forfeiture except during the Life of the Person attainted.

Article IV

Section 1. Full Faith and Credit shall be given in each State to the public Acts, Records, and judicial Proceedings of every other State. And the Congress may by general Laws prescribe the Manner in which such Acts, Records and Proceedings shall be proved, and the Effect thereof.

Section 2. [1] The Citizens of each State shall be entitled to all Privileges and Immunities of Citizens in the several States.

[2] A Person charged in any State with Treason, Felony, or other Crime, who shall flee from Justice, and be found in another State, shall on demand of the executive Authority of the State from which he fled, be delivered up, to be removed to the State having Jurisdiction of the Crime.

[3] No Person held to Service or Labour in one State, under the Laws thereof, escaping into another, shall, in Consequence of any Law or Regulation therein, be discharged from such Service or Labour, but shall be delivered up on Claim of the Party to whom such Service or Labour may be due.

Section 3. [1] New States may be admitted by the Congress into this Union; but no new State shall be formed or erected within the Jurisdiction of any other State; nor any State be formed by the Junction of two or more States, or Parts of States, without the Consent of the Legislatures of the States concerned as well as of the Congress.

[2] The Congress shall have Power to dispose of and make all needful Rules and Regulations respecting the Territory or other Property belonging to the United States; and nothing in this Constitution shall be so construed as to Prejudice any Claims of the United States, or of any particular State.

Section 4. The United States shall guarantee to every State in this Union a Republican Form of Government, and shall protect each of them against Invasion; and on Application of the Legislature, or of the Executive (when the Legislature cannot be convened) against domestic Violence.

Article V

The Congress, whenever two thirds of both Houses shall deem it necessary, shall propose Amendments to this Constitution, or, on the Application of the Legislatures of two thirds of the several States, shall call a Convention for proposing Amendments, which, in either Case, shall be valid to all Intents and Purposes, as part of this Constitution, when ratified by the Legislatures of three fourths of the several States, or by Conventions in three fourths thereof, as the one or the other Mode of Ratification may be proposed by the Congress; Provided that no Amendment which may be made prior to the Year One thousand eight hundred and eight shall in any Manner affect the first and fourth Clauses in the Ninth Section of the first Article; and that no State, without its Consent, shall be deprived of its equal Suffrage in the Senate.

Article VI

[1] All Debts contracted and Engagements entered into, before the Adoption of this Constitution shall be as valid against the United States under this Constitution, as under the Confederation.

[2] This Constitution, and the Laws of the United States which shall be made in Pursuance thereof; and all Treaties made, or which shall be made, under the Authority

of the United States, shall be the supreme Law of the Land; and the Judges in every State shall be bound thereby, any Thing in the Constitution or Laws of any State to the Contrary notwithstanding.

[3] The Senators and Representatives before mentioned, and the Members of the several State Legislatures, and all executive and judicial Officers, both of the United States and of the several States, shall be bound by Oath or Affirmation, to support this Constitution; but no religious Test shall ever be required as a Qualification to any Office or public Trust under the United States.

Article VII

The Ratification of the Conventions of nine States shall be sufficient for the Establishment of this Constitution between the States so ratifying the Same.

ARTICLES IN ADDITION TO, AND AMENDMENT OF, THE CONSTITUTION OF THE UNITED STATES OF AMERICA, PROPOSED BY CONGRESS, AND RATIFIED BY THE LEGISLATURES OF THE SEVERAL STATES PURSUANT TO THE FIFTH ARTICLE OF THE ORIGINAL CONSTITUTION.

Amendment I [1791]   Congress shall make no law respecting an establishment of religion, or prohibiting the free exercise thereof; or abridging the freedom of speech, or of the press; or the right of the people peaceably to assemble, and to petition the Government for a redress of grievances.

Amendment II [1791]   A well regulated Militia, being necessary to the security of a free State, the right of the people to keep and bear Arms, shall not be infringed.

Amendment III [1791]   No Soldier shall, in time of peace be quartered in any house, without the consent of the Owner, nor in time of war, but in a manner to be prescribed by law.

Amendment IV [1791]   The right of the people to be secure in their persons, houses, papers, and effects, against unreasonable searches and seizures, shall not be violated, and no Warrants shall issue, but upon probable cause, supported by Oath or affirmation, and particularly describing the place to be searched, and the persons or things to be seized.

Amendment V [1791]   No person shall be held to answer for a capital, or otherwise infamous crime, unless on a presentment or indictment of a Grand Jury, except in cases arising in the land or naval forces, or in the Militia, when in actual service in time of War or public danger; nor shall any person be subject for the same offence to be twice put in jeopardy of life or limb; nor shall be compelled in any criminal case to be a witness against himself, nor be deprived of life, liberty, or property, without due process of law; nor shall private property be taken for public use, without just compensation.

Amendment VI [1791]   In all criminal prosecutions, the accused shall enjoy the right to a speedy and public trial, by an impartial jury of the State and district wherein the crime shall have been committed, which district shall have been previously ascertained by law, and to be informed of the nature and cause of the accusation; to be confronted with the witnesses against him; to have compulsory process for obtaining witnesses in his favor, and to have the Assistance of Counsel for his defence.

Amendment VII [1791] In Suits at common law, where the value in controversy shall exceed twenty dollars, the right of trial by jury shall be preserved, and no fact tried by jury, shall be otherwise re-examined in any Court of the United States, than according to the rules of the common law.

Amendment VIII [1791] Excessive bail shall not be required, nor excessive fines imposed, nor cruel and unusual punishments inflicted.

Amendment IX [1791] The enumeration in the Constitution, of certain rights, shall not be construed to deny or disparage others retained by the people.

Amendment X [1791] The powers not delegated to the United States by the Constitution, nor prohibited by it to the States, are reserved to the States respectively, or to the people.

Amendment XI [1798] The Judicial power of the United States shall not be construed to extend to any suit in law or equity, commenced or prosecuted against one of the United States by Citizens of another State, or by Citizens or Subjects of any Foreign State.

Amendment XII [1804] The Electors shall meet in their respective states and vote by ballot for President and Vice President, one of whom, at least, shall not be an inhabitant of the same state with themselves; they shall name in their ballots the person voted for as President, and in distinct ballots the person voted for as Vice President, and they shall make distinct lists of all persons voted for as President, and of all persons voted for as Vice President, and of the number of votes for each, which lists they shall sign and certify, and transmit sealed to the seat of the government of the United States, directed to the President of the Senate; the President of the Senate shall, in the presence of the Senate and House of Representatives, open all the certificates and the votes shall then be counted; the person having the greatest number of votes for President, shall be the President, if such number be a majority of the whole number of Electors appointed; and if no person have such majority, then from the persons having the highest numbers not exceeding three on the list of those voted for as President, the House of Representatives shall choose immediately, by ballot, the President. But in choosing the President, the votes shall be taken by states, the representation from each state having one vote; a quorum for this purpose shall consist of a member or members from two-thirds of the states, and a majority of all the states shall be necessary to a choice. And if the House of Representatives shall not choose a President whenever the right of choice shall devolve upon them before the fourth day of March next following, then the Vice President shall act as President, as in the case of the death or other constitutional disability of the President. The person having the greatest number of votes as Vice President, shall be the Vice President, if such number be a majority of the whole number of Electors appointed, and if no person have a majority, then from the two highest numbers on the list, the Senate shall choose the Vice President; a quorum for the purpose shall consist of two-thirds of the. whole number of Senators, and a majority of the whole number shall be necessary to a choice. But no person constitutionally ineligible to the office of President shall be eligible to that of Vice President of the United States.

Amendment XIII [1865]

Section 1. Neither slavery nor involuntary servitude, except as a punishment for crime whereof the party shall have been duly convicted, shall exist within the United States, or any place subject to their jurisdiction.

Section 2. Congress shall have power to enforce this article by appropriate legislation.

Amendment XIV [1868]

Section 1. All persons born or naturalized in the United States, and subject to the jurisdiction thereof, are citizens of the United States and of the State wherein they reside. No state shall make or enforce any law which shall abridge the privileges or immunities of citizens of the United States; nor shall any state drprive any person of life, liberty, or property, without due process of law; nor deny to any person within its jurisdiction the equal protection of the laws.

Section 2. Representatives shall be apportioned among the several States according to their respective numbers, counting the whole number of persons in each State, excluding Indians not taxed. But when the right to vote at any election for the choice of electors for President and Vice President of the United States, Representatives in Congress, the Executive and Judicial officers of a State, or the members of the Legislature thereof, is denied to any of the male inhabitants of such State, being twenty-one years of age, and citizens of the United States, or in any way abridged, except for participation in rebellion, or other crime, the basis of representation therein shall be reduced in the proportion which the number of such male citizens shall bear to the whole number of male citizens twenty-one years of age in such State.

Section 3. No person shall be a Senator or Representative in Congress, or elector of President and Vice President, or hold any office, civil or military, under the United States, or under any State, who having previously taken an oath, as a member of Congress, or as an officer of the United States, or as a member of any State legislature, or as an Executive or Judicial officer of any State, to support the Constitution of the United States, shall have engaged in insurrection or rebellion against the same, or given aid or comfort to the enemies thereof. But Congress may by a vote of two-thirds of each House, remove such disability.

Section 4. The validity of the public debt of the United states, authorized by law, including debts incurred for payment of pensions and bounties for services in suppressing insurrection or rebellion, shall not be questioned. But neither the United States nor any State shall assume or pay any debt or obligation incurred in aid of insurrection or rebellion against the United States, or any claim for the loss or emancipation of any slave; but all such debts, obligations and claims shall be held illegal and void.

Section 5. The Congress shall have power to enforce, by appropriate legislation, the provisions of this article.

Amendment XV [1870]

Section 1. The right of citizens of the United states to vote shall not be denied or abridged by the United States or by any State on account of race, color, or previous condition of servitude.

Section 2. The Congress shall have power to enforce this article by appropriate legislation.

Amendment XVI [1913]

The Congress shall have power to lay and collect taxes on incomes, from whatever source derived, without apportionment among the several States, and without regard to any census or enumeration.

Amendment XVII [1913]

[1] The Senate of the United States shall be composed of two Senators from each State, elected by the people thereof, for six years; and each Senator shall have one vote. The electors in each State shall have the qualifications requisite for electors of the most numerous branch of the State legislatures.

[2] When vacancies happen in the representation of any State in the Senate, the executive authority of such State shall issue writs of election to fill such vacancies: *Provided,* That the legislature of any State may empower the executive thereof to make temporary appointments until the people fill the vacancies by election as the legislature may direct.

[3] This amendment shall not be so construed as to affect the election or term of any Senator chosen before it becomes valid as part of the Constitution.

Amendment XVIII [1919]

Section 1. After one year from the ratification of this article the manufacture, sale, or transportation of intoxicating liquors within, the importation thereof into, or the exportation thereof from the United States and all territory subject to the jurisdiction thereof for beverage purposes is hereby prohibited.

Section 2. The Congress and the several States shall have concurrent power to enforce this article by appropriate legislation.

Section 3. This article shall be inoperative unless it shall have been ratified as an amendment to the Constitution by the legislatures of the several States, as provided in the Constitution, within seven years from the date of the submission hereof to the States by the Congress.

Amendment XIX [1920]

[1] The right of citizens of the United States to vote shall not be denied or abridged by the United States or by any State on account of sex.

[2] Congress shall have power to enforce this article by appropriate legislation.

Amendment XX [1933]

Section 1. The terms of the President and Vice President shall end at noon on the 20th day of January, and the terms of Senators and Representatives at noon on the 3d day of January, of the years in which such terms would have ended if this article had not been ratified; and the terms of their successors shall then begin.

Section 2. The Congress shall assemble at least once in every year, and such meeting shall begin at noon on the 3d day of January, unless they shall by law appoint a different day.

Section 3. If, at the time fixed for the beginning of the term of the President, the President elect shall have died, the Vice President elect shall become President. If the President shall not have been chosen before the time fixed for the beginning of his term, or if the President elect shall have failed to qualify, then the Vice President elect shall act as President until a President shall have qualified; and the Congress may by law provide for the case wherein neither a President elect nor a Vice President elect shall have qualified, declaring who shall then act as President, or the manner in which one who is to act shall be selected, and such person shall act accordingly until a President or Vice President shall have qualified.

Section 4. The Congress may by law provide for the case of the death of any of the persons from whom the House of Representatives may choose a President whenever the right of choice shall have devolved upon them, and for the case of the death of any of the persons from whom the Senate may choose a Vice President whenever the right of choice shall have devolved upon them.

Section 5. Sections 1 and 2 shall take effect on the 15th day of October following the ratification of this article.

Section 6. This article shall be inoperative unless it shall have been ratified as an amendment to the Constitution by the legislatures of three-fourths of the several States within seven years from the date of its submission.

Amendment XXI [1933]
Section 1. The eighteenth article of amendment to the Constitution of the United States is hereby repealed.

Section 2. The transportation or importation into any State, Territory, or possession of the United States for delivery or use therein of intoxicating liquors, in violation of the laws thereof, is hereby prohibited.

Section 3. This article shall be inoperative unless it shall have been ratified as an amendment to the Constitution by conventions in the several States, as provided in the Constitution, within seven years from the date of the submission hereof to the States by the Congress.

Amendment XXII [1951]
Section 1. No person shall be elected to the office of the President more than twice, and no person who has held the office of President, or acted as President, for more than two years of a term to which some other person was elected President shall be elected to the office of President more than once. But this Article shall not apply to any person holding the office of President when this Article was proposed by the Congress, and shall not prevent any person who may be holding the office of President, or acting as President, during the term within which this Article becomes operative from holding the office of President or acting as President during the remainder of such term.

Section 2. This article shall be inoperative unless it shall have been ratified as an amendment to the Constitution by the legislatures of three-fourths of the several States within seven years from the date of its submission to the States by the Congress.

Amendment XXIII [1961]
Section 1. The District constituting the seat of Government of the United States shall appoint in such manner as the Congress may direct: A number of electors of President and Vice President equal to the whole number of Senators and Representatives in Congress to which the District would be entitled if it were a State, but in no event more than the least populous state; they shall be in addition to those appointed by the states, but they shall be considered, for the purposes of the election of President and Vice President, to be electors appointed by a state; and they shall meet in the District and perform such duties as provided by the twelfth article of amendment.

Section 2. The Congress shall have power to enforce this article by appropriate legislation.

Amendment XXIV [1964]

Section 1. The right of citizens of the United States to vote in any primary or other election for President or Vice President, for electors for President or Vice President, or for Senator or Representative in Congress, shall not be denied or abridged by the United States, or any State by reason of failure to pay any poll tax or other tax.

Section 2. The Congress shall have power to enforce this article by appropriate legislation.

Amendment XXV [1967]

Section 1. In case of the removal of the President from office or of his death or resignation, the Vice President shall become President.

Section 2. Whenever there is a vacancy in the office of the Vice President, the President shall nominate a Vice President who shall take office upon confirmation by a majority vote of both Houses of Congress. **Section 3.** Whenever the President transmits to the President pro tempore of the Senate and the Speaker of the House of Representatives his written declaration that he is unable to discharge the powers and duties of his office, and until he transmits to them a written declaration to the contrary, such powers and duties shall be discharged by the Vice President as Acting President.

Section 4. Whenever the Vice President and a majority of either the principal officers of the executive departments or of such other body as Congress may by law provide, transmit to the President pro tempore of the Senate and the Speaker of the House of Representatives their written declaration that the President is unable to discharge the powers and duties of his office, the Vice President shall immediately assume the powers and duties of the office as Acting President. Thereafter, when the President transmits to the President pro tempore of the Senate and the Speaker of the House of Representatives his written declaration that no inability exists, he shall resume the powers and duties of his office unless the Vice President and a majority of either the principal officers of the executive department or of such other body as Congress may by law provide, transmit within four days to the President pro tempore of the Senate and the Speaker of the House of Representatives their written declaration and the President is unable to discharge the powers and duties of his office. Thereupon Congress shall decide the issue, assembling within forty-eight hours for that purpose if not in session. If the Congress, within twenty-one days after receipt of the latter written declaration, or, if Congress is not in session, within twenty-one days after Congress is required to assemble, determines by two-thirds vote of both Houses that the President is unable to discharge the powers and duties of his office, the Vice President shall continue to discharge the same as Acting President; otherwise, the President shall resume the powers and duties of his office.

Amendment XXVI [1971]

Section 1. The right of citizens of the United States, who are eighteen years of age or older, to vote shall not be denied or abridged by the United States or by any State on account of age.

Section 2. The Congress shall have power to enforce this article by appropriate legislation.

Amendment XXVII [1992]

No law, varying the compensation for the services of the Senators and Representatives, shall take effect, until an election of representatives shall have intervened.